Praise for Lawrence Wright's

Thirteen Days in September

"Fascinating personal and historic detail."
—The Christian Science Monitor

"Brilliant, penetrating scholarship. . . . Elucidates the issues that continue to plague the Middle East. . . . Wright expertly captures every move of the three-way realpolitik chess match." *—Entertainment Weekly*

"Exceedingly balanced, highly readable, and appropriately sober." *—Los Angeles Times*

"A splendid and suspenseful account of the negotiations that led to the Camp David accord." *—Minneapolis Star Tribune*

"A chronicle of diplomatic success. . . . The heart of the book is the daily, sometimes hourly shifts in tactics and postures, stands and counter-stands, that unfolded over thirteen days in 1978." *—The Plain Dealer*

"A unique moment in history superbly captured. . . . A day-by-day account of the tense negotiations that shaped these historic talks. . . . Yet another triumph for Wright."

—*Kirkus Reviews* (starred)

"Meticulously researched. . . . Almost nail-bitingly tense. . . . An authoritative, fascinating, and relatively unbiased exploration of a pivotal period and a complicated subject."

—*Publishers Weekly* (starred)

LAWRENCE WRIGHT
Thirteen Days in September

Lawrence Wright is a staff writer for *The New Yorker* and the author of six previous books of nonfiction, including *In the New World*, *Remembering Satan*, *The Looming Tower*, *Going Clear*, and one novel, *God's Favorite*. His books have received many prizes and honors, including a Pulitzer Prize for *The Looming Tower*. He is also a playwright and screenwriter. He and his wife are longtime residents of Austin, Texas.

www.lawrencewright.com

Thirteen Days
in September

Thirteen Days in September

The Dramatic Story of the
Struggle for Peace

LAWRENCE WRIGHT

VINTAGE BOOKS

A DIVISION OF PENGUIN RANDOM HOUSE LLC

NEW YORK

For Ann Close

•

FIRST VINTAGE BOOKS EDITION, APRIL 2015

Copyright © 2014 by Lawrence Wright

All rights reserved. Published in the United States by
Vintage Books, a division of Penguin Random House LLC,
New York, and distributed in Canada by Random House of
Canada, a division of Penguin Random House Ltd., Toronto.
Originally published in hardcover in the United States by
Alfred A. Knopf, a division of Penguin Random House LLC,
New York, in 2014.

Vintage and colophon are registered trademarks
of Penguin Random House LLC.

Maps on pages vi and vii by Mapping Specialists.

The Library of Congress has cataloged the
Knopf edition as follows:
Wright, Lawrence.
Thirteen days in September : Carter, Begin, and Sadat
at Camp David / Lawrence Wright.—First edition.
pages cm
Includes bibliographical references and index.
1. Begin, Menachem, 1913–1992. 2. Carter, Jimmy, 1924–
3. Sadat, Anwar, 1918–1981. 4. Camp David Agreements (1978).
5. Israel-Arab War, 1973—Peace. 6. United States—Foreign
relations—1977–1981. I. Title.
DS128.183.W75 2014   956.04   2013497329

Vintage Books Trade Paperback ISBN: 978-0-8041-7002-4
eBook ISBN: 978-0-385-35204-8

Author photograph © Kenny Braun
Book design by Cassandra J. Pappas

www.vintagebooks.com

Printed in the United States
10   9   8   7   6   5   4   3   2   1

Contents

Israel after the 1947 UN Partition and after the 1949 Armistice Agreement

LEBANON

SYRIA

Golan Heights

Sea of Galilee

Haifa

Nazareth

MEDITERRANEAN SEA

WEST BANK

Nablus

Tel Aviv
Jaffa

Ramallah

Jordan River

Jerusalem

Gaza City

GAZA

Dead Sea

Beersheba

ISRAEL

JORDAN

N E G E V   D E S E R T

EGYPT

S I N A I

P E N I N S U L A

	Israel
	Proposed Arab state, 1947
	Area under Egyptian control, 1949
	Area under Jordanian control, 1949
	Demilitarized areas
	International Zone, 1947

| 0 | 20 | 40 miles |
| 0 | 30 | 60 kilometers |

Aqaba

Gulf of Aqaba

SAUDI ARABIA

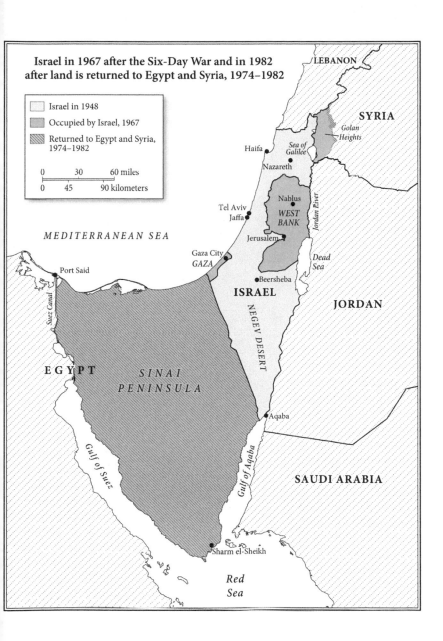

Israel in 1967 after the Six-Day War and in 1982
after land is returned to Egypt and Syria, 1974–1982

Israel in 1948

Occupied by Israel, 1967

Returned to Egypt and Syria,
1974–1982

0   30   60 miles
0   45   90 kilometers

LEBANON

SYRIA

Golan
Heights

Haifa

Sea of
Galilee

Nazareth

MEDITERRANEAN SEA

Nablus

WEST
BANK

Jordan River

Tel Aviv
Jaffa

Jerusalem

Dead
Sea

Gaza City
GAZA

ISRAEL

Beersheba

JORDAN

Port Said

Suez Canal

NEGEV DESERT

EGYPT

SINAI
PENINSULA

Aqaba

Gulf of Suez

Gulf of Aqaba

SAUDI ARABIA

Sharm el-Sheikh

Red
Sea

Author's Note

Three men, representing three religions, met for thirteen days at the presidential retreat of Camp David in the autumn of 1978 in order to solve a dispute that religion itself had largely caused. Beliefs built on ancient texts and legends conspired to create one of the most obdurate conflicts of modern times, one that has drowned the Middle East in a timeless blood feud, brought the superpowers of the time to the brink of nuclear war, flooded the region with refugees, and spawned terrorist movements that have created mayhem and heartbreak all over the world. This book is an account of how these three flawed men, strengthened but also encumbered by their faiths, managed to forge a partial and incomplete peace, an achievement that nonetheless stands as one of the great diplomatic triumphs of the twentieth century and one that has yet to be repeated.

When the leaders of Egypt and Israel met at Camp David, their two countries had engaged in four wars in the previous thirty years—five, if one counts the so-called War of Attrition, which occupied the two countries between 1969 and 1970. The conflict began as part of a larger struggle for Israel's existence, but it evolved into a tug-of-war over territory—mainly, the

Sinai Peninsula—and the right of the Palestinians to return to their former homeland. Although clashes continue between Israel and its other neighbors, the Camp David agreement removed the only Arab adversary that posed a genuine military threat to the future of Israel. And yet the peace envisioned between Israel and the Palestinians was never fully implemented, which is why the turmoil in the region continues.

The reader will observe that there are three chronologies at work in this book. The thirteen days of the Camp David summit form the architecture of this account. Beneath that is a history of the modern Middle East as seen through the eyes of the remarkable men who were present at the negotiation and in many respects made that history. At bottom are the tectonic plates of the three religions as revealed in the stories of the Torah, the Bible, and the Quran. The struggle for peace at Camp David is a testament to the enduring force of religion in modern life, as seen in its ability to mold history and in the difficulty of shedding the mythologies that continue to lure societies into conflict.

War seldom achieves what was expected or hoped for by its participants; even victory often breeds a future defeat. The Middle East from distant times till now is a cautionary story of the failure of war to impose a lasting and just peace. There is never a perfect time or ideal people to bring an end to bloody conflicts, and unlike the talent for war, the ability to make peace has always been rare. The goal of this book is to provide some insight into how that arduous process is accomplished, even by violent men who are prejudiced by their backgrounds, hampered by domestic politics, and blinded by their beliefs. Camp David tells us of the compromises that peace demands, and of the courage and sacrifice required of leaders whose greatest challenge is to overcome their own limitations.

Thirteen Days
in September

Prologue

LATE ONE NIGHT in a rustic lodge on the edge of Jackson Lake, in the Grand Teton National Park, Jimmy Carter took a break from his vacation to open a thick briefing book compiled for him by the Central Intelligence Agency. He had spent one last glorious day, August 29, 1978, fly-fishing on the Snake River, horseback riding through the park, and picking huckleberries with his daughter, Amy, which went into an after-dinner pie. It was a brief escape from the tumult of Washington and his weakened and unpopular presidency. The briefing book contained psychological profiles of two leaders, Anwar Sadat, the president of Egypt, and Menachem Begin, the prime minister of Israel, who would be coming to America in a few days with the unlikely goal of making peace in the Middle East. The ways in which Carter would relate to these leaders—and they to each other—would determine the success or failure of this historic gamble.

The man reading the book had entered the presidency with little experience in foreign policy. He had grown up in the rural South and served a single term as the governor of Georgia. He had never met an Arab until he sat next to one at a stock car race in Daytona. The only Jew he had known as a child was Louis Braunstein, an insurance salesman in Chattanooga, who married Carter's aunt. Uncle Louie loved professional wrestling and could chin himself with one arm—a feat that had thrilled the young Carter. There were a few Jewish merchants in Americus, Georgia, near Carter's hometown of Plains, and Carter always thought of them as "exalted" people, in part because of his Bible studies, which informed him that God had chosen them above all others. It wasn't until he became governor and moved to Atlanta that Carter became familiar with the genteel but ingrained anti-Semitism of the urban South that kept Jews out of country clubs and off government boards.

In 1973, while he was governor, Carter and his wife, Rosalynn, made a pilgrimage to the Holy Land. Prime Minister Golda Meir lent them an old Mercedes station wagon with a driver, and they rode through the tiny country—less than one-eighth the size of the state of Georgia. Rosalynn wept at the commercialization of the holy sites, but Jimmy told her it was just like that when Jesus overturned the tables of the money changers in the temple. They crossed into the occupied West Bank, where they got special permission to wash themselves in the River Jordan, where Jesus was baptized. The river was not much bigger than a creek in south Georgia, but it echoed in Carter's imagination. He had studied the Bible since he was a child, and the geography of ancient Palestine was more familiar to him than that of most of the United States. He could mentally trace the journey of Abraham from the Mesopotamian city of Ur to Canaan's sere and rocky landscape two thousand years before Christ was born. To walk the same streets where Jesus walked, to stand in the hallowed shrines, and to wade into the Jordan filled Carter with awe and a dawning sense of purpose.

Few people knew he was secretly planning to run for president—indeed, scarcely anyone outside of Georgia had ever heard of him—but becoming familiar with Israel and its problems was essential for any aspiring national politician. Carter visited several Jewish settlements in the territories that had been occupied by Israel since the Six-Day War in 1967. Israel was still dizzy with euphoria following its lightning victory over four Arab armies, which left it in control of the Golan Heights of Syria, the entire Sinai Peninsula of Egypt, the Gaza Strip, the West Bank of Jordan, and the great prize—the Old City of Jerusalem. United Nations Resolution 242, adopted after the war ended, provided guidelines for ending the conflict, including the termination of all claims of belligerency, acknowledgment of the sovereignty of the states in the area, and respect for the residents' right to live with secure and recognized borders free from the threat of force. It also obliged Israel to withdraw from land it had seized during the war, but the country's leaders were in no hurry to abandon the 28,000 square miles of occupied territories, which had tripled the size of the country. The question of what to do with a million and a half Arabs living in those territories was rarely addressed, although they posed a potentially fatal demographic threat to the Jewish state, which contained 2,385,000 Jews at the time, along with 100,000 Christians and the 290,000 Arab Muslims who had not fled.

Menachem Begin, then head of a new minority coalition called Likud, was among the most strident of those arguing for the need to hold on to the gains of the war, especially the West Bank, which he called by its biblical names, Judea and

Samaria. Begin's ideology envisioned a vastly expanded Israel; he did not even acknowledge the existence of the Kingdom of Jordan, which he believed should be conquered and folded into an exclusively Jewish nation—a dream he never entirely surrendered. Many Israelis considered him a crank, a fascist, or just an embarrassing reminder of the terrorist underground that stained the legend of the country's glorious struggle for independence. "Begin is a distinctly Hitleristic type," David Ben-Gurion, Israel's revered founder and first prime minister, wrote of his lifelong political antagonist. "He is a racist who is willing to kill all the Arabs in order to gain control of the entire land of Israel." Prominent American Jews, including Hannah Arendt and Albert Einstein, denounced Begin's career as a terrorist chieftain. "Teachers were beaten up for speaking against them, adults were shot for not letting their children join them," they wrote to *The New York Times* in 1948, when Begin made his first trip to the U.S. "By gangster methods, beatings, window-smashing, and widespread robberies, the terrorists intimidated the population and exacted a heavy tribute."

Few could have imagined, when Governor Carter was visiting the Holy Land and Begin was still on the fringe of Israeli politics, that only four years later these two outsiders would be leading their respective countries.

Israel, as Carter experienced it then, was hopeful, prosperous, and surprisingly complacent. The only men in uniform were traffic police. Arabs from the West Bank traveled freely into Israel proper, and a crush of Jewish tourism, along with liberal investment, had raised the standard of living for Palestinians well above what they had endured under Jordanian rule. There were some troubling signs, however. Carter estimated that there were about 1,500 Jewish settlers on the West Bank and in Gaza then, but he could already see that they posed a formidable threat to peace. He and Rosalynn attended a service at a synagogue on the Sea of Galilee and were shocked that there were only two other people present. When they returned the station wagon to Golda Meir, she asked if Carter had any concerns. He knew that Meir, like all her predecessors in that office, was a secular Jew, so he hesitated before mentioning his experience in the synagogue and the general lack of interest in religion that he found in the country. He pointed out that in the Bible whenever Jews turned away from God they suffered political and military losses. Meir laughed in his face. The governor of Georgia! But that very fall, Anwar Sadat sent the Egyptian Army across the Suez Canal, catching the Israelis by surprise and waking the country from a dream of invulnerability. Meir was forced to resign the following spring. Meantime, the Carters returned to Georgia committed to helping Israel in any way they could. The governor began speaking of Meir as "an old friend," although they had met only that one time.

Soon after he arrived in the White House, Carter began to focus on the Middle East. Walter Mondale, his vice president, was struck by the fact that on Carter's first day in office he announced that peace in the Middle East was a top priority. That seemed wildly naive. One after another, American presidents had waded into the fray, at great political expense and with little to show for their efforts. Former Secretary of State Henry Kissinger, who had spent years under Presidents Richard Nixon and Gerald Ford trying to disarm the explosive temperaments in the Middle East, warned Carter that no American president should ever become involved in a negotiation where the outcome was in doubt. Carter's closest advisers told him that he should wait until his second term to risk any of his fragile political capital. His approval rating with the American public had reached 75 percent in his first months in office, but it had been plummeting ever since. For Carter, however, this was not entirely a political decision. He had come to believe that God wanted him to bring peace, and that somehow he would find a way to do so.

The dangerous political calculus of this venture was baldly laid out for him in a memo written by his former campaign manager, Hamilton Jordan, which was so sensitive that he typed it himself and kept the only copy in his office safe in the White House. Jews were an outsized presence in American political life, Jordan explained. "Heavy support for the Democratic Party and its candidates was founded in the immigrant tradition of the second and third generation of American Jews and reinforced by the policies of Wilson and Roosevelt," he wrote. "Harry Truman's role in the establishment of Israel cemented this party identification." Although Jews were only 3 percent of the American population, they cast nearly 5 percent of the vote, with turnout close to 90 percent in most elections. In New York State, for instance, Jews and blacks made up about the same percentage of the population, but in the election that brought Carter into the White House, only 35 percent of the black community in New York cast ballots, compared with 85 percent of the Jews. "You received 94% of the black vote and 75% of the Jewish vote," Jordan wrote. "This means that for every black vote you received in the election, you received almost two Jewish votes." More than 60 percent of the large donors to the Democratic Party were Jewish, Jordan pointed out. Jews maintained a "strong but paranoid lobby"—the American Israel Public Affairs Committee (AIPAC)—which reflected the attitudes and goals of the government of Israel and controlled a reliable majority of votes in the U.S. Senate. Carter was a southerner with an unknown history, at least to Jewish leaders. He had made statements in public—about secure and recognized borders for Israel, the need for a Palestinian homeland—that were usually conveyed behind closed doors, which caused Jordan to worry that Jews were already lining up to take a stand against Carter: "I am sure you are familiar with Kissinger's experience in the Spring of 1975, when the Jewish lobby circulated a letter which had the names of 76 senators which reaffirmed U.S. support for Israel in a way that completely undermined the Ford-Kissinger hope for a new and comprehensive U.S. peace initiative." The tenor of the memo was that Carter stood to make a formidable enemy of the Jewish community if he brought pressure to bear on Israel, which he would have to do if he hoped to achieve a peace agreement. Jordan, his chief political adviser, was telling him this was a no-win situation. It was a paradox: nothing could be a greater gift to Israel than peace, and nothing was more politically dangerous for an American politician than trying to achieve it.

Carter's immediate goal was to restart talks at the Geneva Conference on the Middle East. The Geneva Conference had met once in 1973, under the auspices of the United Nations, the United States, and the Soviet Union; it then went into recess and disappeared into the wasteland of good intentions. In his first year in office Carter set about meeting the most prominent Arab leaders—a discouraging ritual, beset with overheated rhetoric and impractical demands. And then Anwar Sadat came to the White House. Carter was immediately taken by him. By comparison with the other Arab heads of state, Sadat was a "shining light" who was "extraordinarily inclined toward boldness." At last, Carter believed, he had found a partner for peace. The president had a penchant for exaggerating personal connections, perhaps trying to disguise the fact that he was a highly controlled and remote personality who let few people get close to him; still, Carter's aides saw that he and Sadat were genuinely smitten with each other. Soon after that first meeting, Carter began speaking of the pious Egyptian autocrat as his "dearest friend," words rarely used by heads of state.

Carter also met with the Israeli prime minister, Yitzhak Rabin, whom he found quarrelsome and pessimistic about the prospects for peace. "It was like talking to a dead fish," he recalled. Soon after that, Rabin was driven from office by a financial scandal, and Menachem Begin was elected in the most surprising upset in Israeli history.

Carter knew little about the new Israeli leader; nor did the CIA have much to offer. With rising alarm, Carter had watched Begin's appearance on an American news show, during which he renounced the basis of all peace negotiations for the last decade, United Nations Resolution 242. Whenever a questioner referred to territories that Israel had occupied in the Six-Day War, Begin adamantly corrected him by saying that the territories weren't "occupied," they were "liberated." On the West Bank, he said, he intended to establish a Jewish majority. When asked if his position did not place him in direct conflict with Carter's well-known views on a peaceful resolution to the Israeli-Palestinian dispute, Begin responded, "President Carter knows the Bible by heart, so he knows to whom this land by right belongs."

THE PROFILES Carter was studying in Wyoming came from a meeting he had at the CIA a few weeks earlier. He had directed the analysts to answer a number of questions about Begin and Sadat:

What made them leaders? What was the original root of their ambition?
What were their goals?
What previous events had shaped their characters?
What were their religious beliefs? Were they sincere?
Who was important to them? What were their family relations?
How was their health?
What promises and obligations had they made?
How did they react under pressure?
What were their strengths and weaknesses?
What were their attitudes toward the U.S. and Carter personally?
What did they think of each other?
Whom did they trust, especially within their delegations?

The resulting profiles of Begin and Sadat drew sharply opposing portraits. Sadat was a visionary—bold, reckless, and willing to be flexible as long as he believed his overall goals were being achieved. He saw himself as a grand strategic thinker blazing like a comet through the skies of history. The CIA noted his penchant for publicity, terming it his "Barbara Walters Syndrome," after the famous television personality, but by the time the profile was prepared for Carter that category had been upgraded to Sadat's "Nobel Prize Complex." Begin, on the other hand, was secretive, legalistic, and leery of radical change. History, for Begin, was a box full of tragedy; one shouldn't expect to open it without remorse. When put under stress, Sadat drifted into generalities and Begin clung to minutiae. Clashes and misunderstandings were bound to occur. There was some doubt among the analysts preparing the dossiers whether two such opposing personalities should ever be put into the same room together. The two leaders seemed alike only in unpromising ways. Both men had blood on their hands. They had each spent long stretches in prison and in hiding and were deeply schooled in conspiracy. They were not the kind of men Carter had ever known before.

Carter believed he instinctively understood Sadat, however, even though they came from distant cultures. Part of their bond was the fact that they had both been farmers. As a boy, Carter had plowed the red clay of southwest Georgia behind a mule, feeling the damp cool of the freshly turned earth between his toes. He was struck by the observation that Jesus and Moses would have felt at home on a farm in the Deep South during the first part of the twentieth century. Around the globe but on the same meridian as Plains, Georgia, there is a village of mud huts in Egypt called Mit Abul Kum, where Sadat spent his early years. Farmers in the black alluvial soil of the Nile Delta irrigated their fields using an Archimedes screw, which the Greek sage reputedly invented when he visited Egypt in the third century BCE. One could see painted in the tombs of the pharaohs scenes of village life that were still being lived three thousand years later.

Changelessness is the essential feature of such rural

childhoods—a feeling of being cocooned, at once protected and entrapped. And yet, even as a child, a dark-skinned peasant from a small village in the Nile Delta, Sadat sensed his unique role in Egyptian society. Once, when he was playing with some other children near an irrigation canal, they jumped into the water and Anwar leaped in after them. Only then did he remember that he couldn't swim. He thought, "If I drown, Egypt will have lost Anwar Sadat!"

Although he rarely talked about his race, Sadat was only two generations away from slavery—his maternal grandfather, an African man called Kheirallah, had been brought as a slave to Egypt and was emancipated only after the British occupiers demanded the practice be abolished. Kheirallah's daughter, Sitt el-Barrein (woman of two banks), was also a black African. She was chosen as a wife for Mohamed el-Sadaty, an interpreter for a British medical group.* She covered herself in traditional black clothing, with long sleeves and a skirt that reached the floor. She was Mohamed's sixth wife; the first five bore him no children, so he divorced them one after another. Sitt el-Barrein would bear him three sons and a daughter. Anwar was her second child.

The racial dynamics in the Sadaty family were highly charged, as they were in Egyptian society as a whole. Mohamed el-Sadaty's mother, called by custom Umm Mohamed (mother of Mohamed), was an overbearing figure who had arranged the match with Sitt el-Barrein. It's a bit of a mystery why she made such a choice, since Umm Mohamed was of Turkish lineage, with fair features, and she despised her dark-skinned daughter-in-law. Mohamed inherited his mother's Turkish features; he

---

* Anwar Sadat dropped the final "y" of his family name after the 1952 revolution.

had blue eyes and blond hair. In Islam, a man is permitted four wives at a time, and Mohamed would eventually marry twice more when the family moved to Cairo. In addition to his three wives and his formidable mother, Mohamed's vast household grew to thirteen children. Sitt el-Barrein occupied the lowliest place because of her race. She was little more than a maid, occasionally beaten by her husband in front of her children. Sadat rarely spoke of her.

It was his grandmother, Umm Mohamed, the strongest figure in the family, who made the biggest impression on Sadat. "How I loved that woman!" he recalls in his autobiography. She was illiterate, but she insisted that her children and grandchildren become educated. Anwar often spent summers in Umm Mohamed's mud-walled hut in Mit Abul Kum, where her influence was unequivocal. From an early age he began to imagine himself as a figure of destiny, his imagination fired by the stories his grandmother would tell.

His favorite was the legend of Zahran. It is a tale of martyrdom. In June 1906, several years before Anwar was born, a party of British soldiers was pigeon hunting in a nearby village called Denshawi. They shot some domesticated fowl, infuriating the villagers. Total chaos followed. One of the soldiers accidentally shot and wounded the wife of the local imam. The villagers responded with a hail of stones. The soldiers fired into the mob, injuring five people. A local silo caught on fire, perhaps because of a stray bullet. Two soldiers raced back to camp to get help, but the other members of the hunting party surrendered to the villagers. One soldier who escaped died of sunstroke in the intense heat, although he may also have suffered a concussion from the stoning. British soldiers who came to the rescue killed an elderly peasant who was trying to assist the dying man, wrongly assuming that he had murdered their comrade. The British occupiers decided to make an example of Denshawi. Fifty-two villagers were rounded up and quickly brought before a tribunal. Most of the villagers were flogged or sentenced to long prison sentences. Four were hanged.

This confused and tragic incident marked a turning point in the British occupation, inflaming nationalist sentiments in Egypt and stirring outrage even in Great Britain. Denshawi became a byword for the inevitable clumsy by-products of imperialism. No one embodied the face of Denshawi more than the young man named Zahran, the first of the condemned to be hanged. According to the oral ballad that Sadat's grandmother told to him, Zahran was the son of a dark mother and a father of mixed blood—just like Anwar. "The ballad dwells on Zahran's courage and doggedness in the battle, how he walked with his head high to the scaffold, feeling proud that he had stood up to the aggressors and killed one of them," Sadat writes. He heard this legend night after night, and it worked its way deep into his imagination. "I often saw Zahran," he writes, "and lived his heroism in dream and reverie—I wished I were Zahran."

It was in Cairo that Anwar first actually encountered the hated occupiers. He recalls "the odious sight of the typical British constable on his motorcycle, tearing through the city streets day and night like a madman—with a tomato-colored complexion, bulging eyes, and an open mouth—looking like an idiot, with his huge head covered in a long crimson fez reaching down to his ears. Everybody feared him. I simply hated the sight of him."

In 1931, when Anwar was twelve, Mahatma Gandhi passed through the Suez Canal on his way to London to negotiate the fate of India. The ship stopped in Port Said, whereupon Egyptian journalists besieged the ascetic leader. The correspondent for *Al-Ahram* marveled that Gandhi was wearing "nothing but a scrap of cloth worth five piasters, wire rim glasses worth three piasters and the simplest thong sandals worth a mere two piasters. These ten piasters of clothing tell Great Britain volumes." The example of this poor, dark-skinned man who turned the empire upside-down made a deep impression on the young Sadat. "I began to imitate him," he writes. "I took off all my clothes, covered myself from the waist down with an apron, made myself a spindle, and withdrew to a solitary nook on the roof of our house in Cairo. I stayed there for a few days until my father persuaded me to give it up. What I was doing would not, he argued, benefit me or Egypt; on the contrary, it would certainly have given me pneumonia." Sadat's obsession with great men must have seemed comical, especially when he imitated Gandhi by sitting under a tree, pretending he didn't want to eat, or dressing in an apron and leading a goat. He was consciously shopping for the qualities of greatness, trying on attributes and opinions. It wasn't just Gandhi's asceticism that appealed to him; he was drawn to the autocratic side of Gandhi's nature, which favored action over deliberation and cared nothing for consensus.

Despite Sadat's hatred of the British, it was through an English doctor who knew Sadat's father that he was able to enter the Royal Military Academy. Sadat was rescued from the menial destiny he had been born to. The academy had been the exclusive province of the Egyptian aristocracy until 1936, when the British allowed the Egyptian Army to expand. During this period, Sadat read books on the Turkish Revolution and became increasingly devoted to Kemal Atatürk, the creator of modern Turkey. Sadat was already beginning to see himself as a transformational figure whose iron will would rearrange his society into a new paradigm. In that way, he and Begin were much alike.

Paradoxically, those were the same qualities that drew him to Hitler. "I was in our village for the summer vacation when Hitler marched forth from Munich to Berlin, to wipe out the consequences of Germany's defeat in World War I and rebuild his country," Sadat recounts. "I gathered my friends and told them we ought to follow Hitler's example by marching forth from Mit Abul Kum to Cairo. I was twelve. They laughed and ran away." Two decades later, after Germany was in ruins and sixty million people were dead, Sadat and other prominent Egyptians were asked by a Cairo magazine to write a letter to Hitler as if he were still alive. "My Dear Hitler," Sadat wrote,

> I admire you from the bottom of my heart. Even if you appear to have been defeated, in reality you are the victor. You have succeeded in creating dissension between the old man Churchill and his allies, the sons of Satan. . . . Germany will be reborn in spite of the Western and Eastern powers. . . . You did some mistakes . . . but our faith in your nation has more than compensated for them. You must be proud to have become an immortal leader of Germany. We will not be surprised if you showed up anew in Germany or if a new Hitler should rise to replace you.

THE FACT THAT Sadat was black may have awakened protective and fraternal feelings in Carter. When Jimmy was

Anwar Sadat in military
uniform in Egypt, 1954

four years old, his family had moved to the little hamlet of
Archery, two miles west of Plains. They were the only whites in
a community of fifty-five black families. Jimmy's main play-
mates were the sons of these black tenant farmers; in fact, his
dialect at the time was indistinguishable from theirs. Jimmy
and his best friend, Alonzo Davis, would occasionally be given
the chance to ride the train to the nearby town of Americus to
watch a movie together, although they had to separate into the
"white" and "colored" sections both on the train and in the
theater. At the time, Carter simply accepted such practices as
natural features of a society in which whites were the owners
and blacks the renters.

From the age of five Jimmy began selling peanuts that he
picked, boiled, and bagged himself, then carried in a wagon to

Jimmy Carter with his
dog, Bozo, 1937

downtown Plains, where he sold them to the disabled veterans
and loafers who played checkers in front of the livery stable. In
1932, at the peak of the Great Depression, the price of cotton
plummeted to five cents a pound. By then, Jimmy, age eight,
had accumulated enough savings from peanut sales to buy
five bales for twenty-five dollars each; then, when cotton went
back up to eighteen cents several years later, he sold the cotton
and bought five tenant houses, which he rented by the month,
joining the landlord class while still a child. It was about this
time that two of his black friends opened a gate and then stood
back and let Jimmy pass through. He thought it must be a trick
they were playing, but this symbolic action signaled a powerful social change. "The constant struggle for leadership among
our small group was resolved, but a precious sense of equality

had gone out of our personal relationship," Carter writes, "and things were never again the same between them and me."

Religion was the elixir that both Carter and Sadat drank in excess. Sadat had gone to the Islamic school in his village, where he memorized the Quran as a young child. Later, he sported the dark callus on his forehead that is the imprint of endless hours of prayerful prostration. This was well before such outward displays of religious zeal were fashionable in cosmopolitan Cairo. He called himself the "Believer President." Although Carter didn't advertise it, that's how people thought of him as well. He had begun memorizing Bible verses at the age of three and publicly declared his faith at a revival meeting when he was eleven. He was baptized into the Plains Baptist Church, where the pastor, Royall Callaway, preached that the Jews would soon return to Palestine and bring on the return of Christ and the rapture of true Christians into Heaven—a doctrine known as premillennialism.

As with Sadat, the military had also provided a means of escape for Jimmy Carter. He had an uncle in the Navy whom he idolized, and he spent his entire childhood obsessed with the goal of entering the U.S. Naval Academy in Annapolis, Maryland. That would require a congressional appointment. Carter's father continually lobbied their local congressman, but it wasn't until two years after Jimmy graduated from high school that the precious appointment came through. Carter started teaching Sunday school as an eighteen-year-old midshipman at Annapolis, a practice he would continue for the rest of his life. Even on submarines, he held services in the cramped spaces between torpedoes.

Because of his southern background, Carter's classmates at Annapolis made assumptions about his racial attitudes. And yet when the academy admitted black cadet Wesley Brown, Carter shielded him from the harassment and bigotry that was the fate of so many civil rights pioneers. Carter was called a "nigger lover" and treated, as another classmate recalled, "as if he was a traitor."

In 1949, Carter studied nuclear physics and reactor technology at Union College in Schenectady, New York. Admiral Hyman Rickover, known as the "Father of the Nuclear Navy," had chosen him to be the chief officer of the USS *Seawolf,* one of two nuclear submarine prototypes under development. Rickover was—like Menachem Begin—a Polish Jew, as renowned for his impatience as he was for his intelligence. At their first meeting, Rickover offered Carter the opportunity to talk about any subject he chose. Carter was a relentless autodidact, but with each topic he brought up—current events, literature, electronics, gunnery, tactics, seamanship—Rickover would ask a series of questions of increasing difficulty, showing his own superior knowledge of the subject. When Carter discussed classical music, for instance, Rickover dissected nuances of particular pieces that Carter said he admired, such as "Liebestod" from Wagner's *Tristan und Isolde.* Throughout the interview, an unsmiling Rickover stared directly into Carter's eyes. His goal was to see how an applicant behaved under pressure. By the end, Carter was soaking in sweat and humiliation.

Finally, Rickover asked how Carter ranked in his class at the Naval Academy. "Sir, I stood 59th in a class of 820!" Carter said proudly.

"Did you do your best?" Rickover asked.

Carter started to answer in the affirmative, but then he gulped and admitted that he had not always done his best.

Rickover just stared at him, and then turned his chair away, ending the interview. "Why not?" he asked in parting.

Carter was unable to answer. He sat quietly for a moment, shaken by the frankness of the question and the cool dismissal, then he stood and left the room. "He would ask me questions until he proved that I didn't know anything about anything," Carter complained to Rosalynn afterward. She would note that, years later, when Carter was governor, he would still break into a cold sweat if he was told that Admiral Rickover was on the line.

As one of Rickover's protégés, Carter was on track toward a significant military career. But in 1953, Carter's father was diagnosed with cancer and Jimmy went home to say good-bye. He had been away for eleven years. He was deeply moved by the procession of hundreds of people who came to pay tribute to Mr. Earl as he lay on his deathbed, so many of whom had been aided by his quiet charity over the years. Even though Carter had a secure job with an important future, it seemed to him that his own life would never be so meaningful as the one his father had lived in this small community. There was the additional fact that no one else in the family could take over the farm and the peanut warehouse business that his father had built. Jimmy's younger brother, Billy, was still in high school, and harvest season would soon begin. As he mulled his decision, Carter concluded, "God did not intend for me to spend my life working on instruments of destruction to kill people." He resigned his commission and returned to Plains.

Southwest Georgia was Ku Klux Klan country, and Carter became a target because of his progressive views. He was not an activist, but he was the only white man in Sumter County who refused to join the White Citizens' Council, a segregationist organization that held Dixie in its thrall. His business was boycotted. When he ran for governor the first time, in 1966, he hoped that Georgia was ready to step away from its racist past. He lost to Lester Maddox, who made his reputation by chasing black customers out of his Atlanta restaurant with a pistol and an ax handle. Carter was despondent. "I could not believe that God, or the Georgia voters, would let this person beat me and become the governor of our state," he lamented. His loss to Maddox prompted a crisis in his lifelong faith. His sister, Ruth Carter Stapleton, an author and evangelist, had a talk with him. She quoted some scripture from the Epistle of James that advised believers to take joy in their failures because they can lead to wisdom. Carter wasn't ready to hear her advice at the time, but he would later say it was a turning point—what was referred to as his "born again" experience. He announced for governor once more, this time determined to do whatever it took to win.

Race was still the most dangerous subject to navigate in Georgia. Carter defined himself in the 1970 campaign as a populist and a friend of the workingman, appealing to the same constituency that Maddox and other demagogues in Georgia had cultivated. At times he signaled that he was close to Alabama governor George Wallace and other prominent segregationists, even borrowing Wallace's slogan, "our kind of man," to wink at the racists in the crowd. He went so far as to endorse Lester Maddox, who could not succeed himself and was running for lieutenant governor, calling him "the embodiment of the Democratic Party." There was a photograph of Carter's chief opponent in the Democratic primary, Carl Sanders, standing next to black members of the Atlanta Hawks basketball team (which he partly owned), who were pouring champagne over his head. Atlanta reporters said that staffers in the Carter campaign mailed leaflets with the photograph to white barbershops and churches around the state and even passed them out at Klan rallies. Although Carter himself was not linked to these activities, because he was a south Georgia peanut farmer, it was already assumed that he must be a racist and a plantation owner. "I am not a land baron," Carter was finally forced to declare. "I do not have slaves on my farm in Plains."

One of Carter's main supporters was a wealthy Iranian Jew from Savannah named David Rabhan. He had a shaky business empire that ranged from catfish farms to nursing homes. Tall and muscular, with a shaved head, and typically attired in a blue jumpsuit and sneakers, Rabhan was an author, sculptor, and gourmet cook. He was also a pilot, and during the campaign he flew Carter back and forth across the state in his twin-engine Cessna. They spent so much time together in the air that Carter learned to fly the plane while Rabhan napped.

Rabhan was a liberal, especially on race. He had been marked as a child by seeing the body of a black man who had been murdered by whites; as an adult, he cultivated friendships with some of the most important figures in Atlanta's influential black community. He quietly introduced Carter to this crowd, along with black preachers and funeral directors throughout the state. Those meetings were kept secret so they would not destroy Carter's chances. Black voters in the know were able to imagine that Carter was a closet progressive, in the same way that white racists assumed that he was one of them.

On one of the final days of the campaign, as the two men were flying from the Georgia coast across the state, Carter took the controls as Rabhan closed his eyes. They were flying at eight thousand feet when both engines sputtered and died. Carter panicked. He punched Rabhan, who didn't stir. Then he hit him hard. "What's the matter?" Rabhan asked.

"We're out of gas!"

In that case, Rabhan said, they were going to crash.

Rabhan let that sink in, then he turned a valve and opened up the spare gas tank. The engines coughed back to life.

Very few people get away with teasing Jimmy Carter.

After Carter cooled off, he observed that Rabhan had done so much for him. "This is the end of the campaign," he said. "I think I've got a good chance to win. Is there anything I can do for you?"

"No, I don't need your help as governor," Rabhan replied. "What I'd like you to do is tell the Georgia people what you think about the millstone of racism that has oppressed our state."

Carter picked up an old flight map. On the back he wrote, "I know this state as well as anyone. I say to you quite frankly that the time for racial discrimination is over." He handed it to Rabhan. "If I'm elected, in my inaugural speech I will make this statement."

"Sign it," Rabhan demanded.

That declaration from the Georgia governor's mansion on January 12, 1971, put Carter on the cover of *Time* magazine and planted the seed of his presidential candidacy.

THE AMERICAN INTELLIGENCE COMMUNITY had scarcely noticed Anwar Sadat in his early political career. Then, he was obscured by the giant shadow of Gamal Abdel Nasser, the charismatic architect of the Egyptian revolution. When Nasser died of a heart attack in 1970, Vice President Sadat was universally seen as a placeholder until the next strongman pushed him aside. Instead, he proved to be a master of the unexpected. First, he stunned Egypt by rounding up Nasser's corrupt cronies, who controlled the main positions of government power, and throwing them in jail. In 1972, he expelled fifteen thousand Soviet troops and military advisers from Egypt. Until that point, Egypt had been essentially a Soviet military base, Russia's main foothold in the Middle East. There was as much puzzlement as joy in Washington, which had been caught by complete surprise. The Israelis were convinced that without the Russians the Egyptians were incapable of waging war. The very next year, on Yom Kippur, Sadat sent his army across the Suez Canal, catching the Israelis off guard and bringing the superpowers to the point of a nuclear showdown. By then, the mercurial Egyptian leader had become an object of obsession among American policy makers and intelligence analysts.

With all the surprises that Sadat had pulled out of his hat, none equaled the moment, on November 9, 1977, when he set aside the prepared text of a long-winded speech he was making to the Egyptian People's Assembly and announced, "I am ready to travel to the ends of the earth if this will in any way protect an Egyptian boy, soldier, or officer from being killed or wounded. . . . Israel will be surprised to hear me say that I am willing to go to their parliament, the Knesset itself, and debate with them." Few believed it. The Egyptian parliamentarians routinely cheered; even Yasser Arafat, the head of the Palestinian Liberation Organization, who was present as a guest, dutifully applauded. Cairo newspapers omitted the statement the next morning. Everyone thought it was an empty gesture.

Ten days later Sadat's plane took off for Ben Gurion Airport. He now held the world spellbound. Israel was in a state of confused delirium because of the visit, the first in Israel's history by any Arab leader. Ten thousand soldiers, police, and security personnel were waiting to guard the Egyptian president, in addition to the 2,500 foreign journalists who had rushed to cover the historic event. At eight thirty p.m., two hours after the end of Shabbat, searchlights picked up the white plane against the black sky, flying low and circling over Tel Aviv. Egyptian flags of red, white, and black intermingled with the blue and white of Israel, even though the two countries were still in a state of war. Without sheet music for the Egyptian national anthem, the Israeli military orchestra had learned how to play it by listening to Cairo radio. Sharpshoot-

Anwar Sadat being greeted by Menachem Begin upon arrival in Jerusalem, 1977

ers were stationed on the rooftops of the terminal buildings in case terrorists suddenly emerged from the presidential plane rather than Sadat himself. But then there he was.

Sadat's enemies were waiting on the tarmac, and he walked among them, joking with the generals and the cabinet officers, greeting Menachem Begin and former Israeli leaders.

"Madame, I've waited a long time to meet you," Sadat said as he kissed Golda Meir.

"We've been expecting you," she said.

"And now I'm here."

He joked with Ariel Sharon, perhaps the greatest field commander in Israel's history, saying that the next time he crossed the canal he would have him arrested. "Oh, no, sir," Sharon replied. "Now I'm just the minister of agriculture."

By presenting himself to Israel, Sadat was introducing two cultures that were almost entirely unknown to one another. Few Israelis had ever met an Egyptian, except for the Jews who had emigrated from there, so the shock of having Sadat himself in their midst was compounded by curiosity and wonder. The same was true for the Egyptians watching the event on television. To see Sadat staring into the faces of the enemy—until now, figures of legend—suddenly and unsettlingly humanized the Israelis in the Egyptian mind. Sadat was convinced that 70 percent of the conflict between Israel and the Arabs was psychological; if he could make peace seem real and available, not only to the Israelis but also to the Arabs, most of the work would be done. Then, perhaps, there would be a chance for the prosperity that Egyptians desperately needed but which wars had chronically destroyed.

Sadat's decision to go to Israel shattered the taboo against speaking to Israelis or even acknowledging the existence of a Jewish homeland. Both the foreign minister and the man Sadat had appointed to succeed him had resigned, protesting that Egypt would now be isolated in the Arab world. Sadat compounded the insult by timing his arrival for the eve of Eid al-Adha, one of the main holy days in Islam. On that day, the king of Saudi Arabia goes to unlock the door of the Kaaba, the cubical stone building in Mecca where all Muslims direct their prayers. "I have always before gone to the Kaaba to pray for somebody, never to pray against anyone," King Khalid said. "But on this occasion I found myself saying, 'Oh God, grant that the airplane taking Sadat to Jerusalem may crash before it gets there, so that he may not become a scandal for all of us.'"

As the presidential motorcade climbed through the rocky hillsides toward Jerusalem, crowds along the highway sang "Hevenu Shalom Aleikhem" ("We've Brought Peace upon You"). The Israelis had no armored limousine for Sadat, so they had borrowed one from the American ambassador. All along the way people were openly weeping. Some wore T-shirts saying "All You Need Is Love." The Egyptian entourage gaped at the scene; it was like being on another planet. The motorcade came to a halt at Jerusalem's King David Hotel, which Begin's irregulars had blown up during the British Mandate three decades before. A crowd of 250 people waited in the lobby crying out to Sadat. Across the street, the carillon at the YMCA played "Getting to Know You."

JERUSALEM—the most contested piece of property in history—was the object of longing and worship for the three great Abrahamic religions and the source of centuries of bloodshed. Israel had seized East Jerusalem ten years before in the 1967 war, thrilling Christians and Jews all over the world and throwing Muslims into despair. Now, from their rooms at the King David, the Egyptian delegation had a magnificent view of the honeyed limestone walls of the Old City and the building cranes that rose like a giant forest around it. "All that construction!" one of the delegates said. "I fear that Jerusalem is lost to the Arabs." Although Sadat himself seemed serenely untouched, the intermixed feelings of anxiety, hope, and dread among the Egyptians led to great stress and confusion. One of Sadat's bodyguards actually died of a heart attack in the hotel. His corpse was smuggled into a cargo plane to keep rumors of assassination from taking root.

At the heart of the Old City stands the Temple Mount. According to Jewish tradition, it is where Adam was made from its dust, where Cain killed Abel, and where God's spirit dwells. King Solomon was said to have built the First Temple on this spot a thousand years before the birth of Jesus in order to house the Ark of the Covenant, which contained the stone tablets with the Ten Commandments that God gave to Moses on Mount Sinai. The First Temple stood until 586 BCE, when the Babylonian ruler Nebuchadnezzar tore it down and herded the Jews into Babylon. Seventy years later the Jews were freed by the Persian ruler Cyrus the Great, and the Second Temple was established on the same spot. King Herod expanded it into one of the largest structures in the ancient world. It was here that Jesus drove out the money changers and the sellers of animals for sacrifice, saying, "Take these out of here, and stop making my Father's house a marketplace." The temple was sacked once again in 70 CE, by the Romans, following the Jewish revolt against the empire.

In 1099, the Crusaders arrived in Jerusalem and killed everybody in town. Jews were rounded up and slaughtered in their synagogues. One witness describes Christian knights riding through a lake of blood after slaying ten thousand Muslims who had taken refuge on the Temple Mount. Control of the city passed back and forth between Christians and Muslims until the twelfth century, when Saladin peacefully recaptured the city and allowed each religion the right to worship in its holy places—an example that would prove difficult for his successors to follow. The Ottomans seized Jerusalem in 1517, and maintained control for four hundred years, until the British expelled the Turks and their German advisers at the end of the First World War. By that time, Jerusalem had been reduced to a pestilential town of 55,000 starving souls, overrun with prostitutes and venereal diseases. Conscious of the precedent, the victorious general, Sir Edmund Allenby, entered the city on foot, rather than in a martial display. As he received the keys to the city, Allenby declared, "The Crusades have now ended." But even then, the British and the French were carving up the Ottoman Empire among themselves. At this imperial feast, the Zionist campaign in Europe succeeded in getting the support of the British to gain a homeland for the Jews in Palestine. A bloody new era was born.

Muslims call the Temple Mount the Noble Sanctuary—Haram al-Sharif. Two mosques now stand atop the mount where the Jewish temples once had been. According to the Bible, this is where Abraham demonstrated his faithfulness to God by offering up his son Isaac. (Muslims believe that Abraham's son Ishmael, father of the Arabs, was the intended victim.)

The day after Sadat arrived in Jerusalem was the feast of Eid al-Adha, which commemorates God's mercy in sparing Ishmael. Stalked by television cameras and helicopters, Sadat entered the silver-domed Al-Aqsa Mosque for dawn prayers. His presence in this sacred space sent electrifying currents throughout the Muslim world, alternately of hope and betrayal. On the one hand, the loss of Jerusalem was symbolically greater than that of Sinai and the entire West Bank, and the fact that the city's future was once again on the bargaining table was almost unbearably thrilling; on the other hand, the mere fact that Sadat was dealing with the occupiers stoked fear and paranoia. This was the same mosque where, in 1951, a Palestinian tailor assassinated King Abdullah I of Jordan because he had dared to negotiate with the Israelis. The bullet holes were still visible in the alabaster columns. As Sadat worshipped, Palestinian protesters outside the mosque loudly denounced him for the same crime.

Sadat moved on to the seventh-century Dome of the Rock, the oldest building in Islam, a magnificent eight-sided structure with ornate porcelain mosaics and a golden cupola that dominates the Old City. It is a resonant icon of Islamic spirituality as well as the ubiquitous political emblem of the Palestinians' yearning for restitution. The shrine encloses the rocky outcropping that is the summit of the Temple Mount. According to Jewish tradition, the stone is the perch that God made for himself when he created the universe. Muslims believe that the Prophet Muhammad made his night journey to heaven atop his steed, al-Buraq, from this rock. At the End of Days, according to Islamic tradition, the Final Judgment will take place in this sanctuary, with the blessed and the damned going their separate ways for eternity.

Sadat made his way into the Old City at the base of the Temple Mount, stopping at the Church of the Holy Sepulchre.

A monk showed him the stone where the body of the crucified Jesus was said to have been washed and the tomb where he was buried. Outside, demonstrators were beginning to break through the ranks of security. "Sadat, what do you want from us?" Palestinians cried as he left. "We are against you. We don't want you here."

Afterward, Sadat laid a wreath at a memorial for Israeli soldiers killed in all the wars since the founding of the state. Then he joined Begin at the Yad Vashem Holocaust Memorial. Sadat was handed a skullcap. "It's a *kippah*," Begin explained. "It's our custom to cover our heads during prayers or when entering a house of prayer."

Sadat silently moved through the somber memorial, with the tools of genocide starkly displayed. There was the gate to Auschwitz, with its grotesquely ironic motto, *Arbeit macht frei* (Work makes you free), through which more than a million Jews passed on their way to death. The Hall of Names contained brief biographies of two million of the six million Jews who perished in the Holocaust. In the middle of the room there was a great cone lined with images of the victims; it rose skyward like the smokestacks of the death camps. "All this befell us because we had no state of our own," Begin told Sadat.

Begin's own parents, Ze'ev Dov and Chasia, as well as his older brother, Herzl, were among the names in this grim repository. In June 1941, the Nazis captured his hometown of Brisk* and began their systematic annihilation of all Polish Jews. Ze'ev Dov had been attempting to emigrate to Palestine when the Nazis arrived, but Chasia was in the hospital

---

* Brisk was the name Jews gave to the town otherwise known as Brest-Litovsk, between Russia and Poland, each of which claimed it at various times. In the sixteenth century, it briefly became the capital of Lithuania. It is now Brest, Belarus.

with pneumonia. The Germans murdered her in her bed, along with the other patients. Five thousand Jews from Brisk, including Ze'ev Dov and Herzl, were rounded up. Some were shot and thrown into a pit; Ze'ev Dov was weighted down with rocks and drowned in the River Bug. Menachem learned that his father's final words were to curse his executioners: "A day of retribution will come upon you too!"

"May God guide our steps toward peace," Sadat wrote in the guest book. "Let us put an end to all the suffering for mankind."

SADAT, master of the bold gesture, was indifferent to trifling details, but his confounded Israeli hosts were obsessed with the fine print. What did Sadat want in exchange for this stunning overture? Did he expect Sinai? Some concession on the West Bank or Gaza? They kept trying to pin Sadat down, but he was maddeningly evasive. "We have to concentrate on the heart of the issue, not on technicalities and formalities," he declared. He wanted to arrive at an "agreed program"— a statement of principles in which Israel would pledge to withdraw from the occupied territories and come to a solution on the Palestinian question. But exactly what did that mean? *All* the occupied territories, or was that negotiable? What "solution" was there to the plight of the Palestinians? "Every side wants to deal with details," Begin insisted, "not only general declarations." The Israelis were so busy trying to read the nuances of Sadat's language that they were blind to the fact that Sadat's presence in Jerusalem was the message itself.

Part of the Israeli dilemma was that they had never really

confronted what they themselves wanted. Perpetual conflict had pushed the issue of permanent borders into some distant future, but the rude prospect of actual peace demanded immediate choices. What was peace worth to them? Swollen with territories seized in 1948 and 1967, Israel now stretched all the way from the hills of southern Lebanon to the Red Sea, and from the River Jordan to the Mediterranean. All this space provided strategic depth, something Israel had never had before. Sinai had been a historic concourse for attacking armies; the Golan Heights had been the dominating redoubt for Syrian artillery; the West Bank was a hideout for terrorists. Why surrender any of it? Would peace replace the security that Israel gained from having these territories under military control?

There was also something deeply appealing about the largeness of the space the occupation afforded; aesthetically, Israel looked properly filled out. Before the occupation of the West Bank, the country had appeared almost bitten in half. The little fishing village of Sharm el-Sheikh, strategically located at the southernmost tip of the peninsula at the juncture of the Red Sea and the Gulf of Aqaba, had been turned into an Israeli resort town, with classy hotels and dive shops. Radio stations in Tel Aviv regularly gave weather reports for the Red Sea beaches. Israelis had settled into a comfortable feeling of ownership over all this real estate, even if the threat of war never quite disappeared. Moreover, Sinai had oil, which resource-poor Israel was helping itself to. And finally, there was the issue of Jerusalem, the object and focus of Jewish prayers for millennia. Was peace really worth surrendering any of these precious properties?

After lunch, Sadat journeyed to the Knesset to make his speech. The eerie and unprecedented moment of his entrance was heralded by bugle calls. For the first time in the institution's history, members of the Knesset were permitted to applaud—although not everyone did so. A psychological wall still stood between them, which Sadat meant to obliterate. Even his bitterest foes recognized that Sadat had placed his life dangerously on the line. He had made it harder for the two peoples to hate each other, and the loss of that luxurious emotion on both sides stirred up feelings of murderous rage against him.

"Ladies and gentlemen, there are moments in the life of nations and peoples when it is incumbent on those known for their wisdom and clarity of vision to overlook the past, with all its complexities and weighing memories, in a bold drive towards new horizons," Sadat began. He spoke words that no Arab leader had ever said before—words many in the audience never imagined they would hear. "You want to live with us in this part of the world. In all sincerity, I tell you, we welcome you among us, with full security and safety," Sadat declared. "We used to reject you," he admitted. "We had our reasons and our claims, yes. We used to brand you as 'so-called' Israel, yes. We were together in international conferences and organizations and our representatives did not, and still do not, exchange greetings, yes. This has happened and is still happening."

Then his tone sharpened. "Frankness makes it incumbent upon me to tell you the following," he said. "I have not come here for a separate agreement between Egypt and Israel." Many in the room, including Begin, hoped to set the Palestinian issue aside; in fact, Sadat himself had occasionally seemed ambivalent on the subject, but now he was adamant. "Let me tell you without the slightest hesitation that I have not come to you under this dome to make a request that your troops evacuate the occupied territories. Complete withdrawal from the Arab territories occupied after 1967 is a logical and undisputed necessity. Nobody should plead for that." He went on: "Peace cannot be worth its name unless it is based on justice, and not on the occupation of the land of others. It would not be appropriate for you to demand for yourselves what you deny others. . . . You have to give up, once and for all, the dreams of conquests, and give up the belief that force is the best method for dealing with the Arabs."

Sadat promised that Israel could live safely and securely among her Arab neighbors, under certain conditions. "Any talk about permanent peace based on justice, and any move to ensure our coexistence in peace and security in this part of the world, would become meaningless, while you occupy Arab territories by force of arms," he said, adding, "We insist on complete withdrawal from these territories, including Arab Jerusalem."

The mood in the Knesset, which had been so buoyant, quickly deflated. The parliamentarians settled in for what now seemed very familiar Arab demands, although no other leader had ever offered real peace in the bargain. "It is no use to refrain from recognizing the Palestinian people and their rights to statehood and rights of return," Sadat continued, mopping his gleaming forehead in the stiflingly hot room. "If you have found the legal and moral justification to set up a national home on a land that did not all belong to you, it is incumbent upon you to show understanding of the insistence of the people of Palestine on establishing, once again, a state on their land." Ezer Weizman, the minister of defense, scribbled a note: "We have to prepare for war." Begin took it and nodded.

It was a strange performance. When has it ever happened

that the defeated party—defeated in four wars, in fact—has entered the enemy capital to lay down the terms of peace? When Sadat finished, Begin did not applaud.

Although Begin was well known for his oratory in this chamber, his response was improvised and full of rebuke. The sense of grievance was never far from his lips under any circumstances, and in the curious role reversal that was being played out in this encounter, Begin did not offer his own terms of peace; instead, he defended Israel's right to exist at all. "No, sir, we took no foreign land," he exclaimed. "We returned to our homeland. The bond between our people and this land is eternal. It was created at the dawn of human history. . . . Here we became a nation. And when we were exiled from our land because of the force that was applied against us, and when we were thrust far from our land, we never forgot this land, even for one day. We prayed for her. We longed for her." He mentioned Sadat's trip to the Holocaust museum earlier in the day. "With your own eyes you saw what the fate of our people was when this homeland was taken from it," he said. "No one came to our rescue, not from the East and not from the West. And therefore we, this entire generation, the generation of Holocaust and resurrection, swore an oath of allegiance: never again shall we endanger our people."

Peace had seemed so close at hand when Sadat's plane had landed in Israel, but when he left it was still very far away.

CARTER HAD MET Begin when he came to Washington in July 1977, only a month after the Israeli had taken office. Carter immediately recognized the man's formidable intellect— "His IQ is probably as high as anybody I've ever met," he noted—as well as his biblical knowledge, which Carter hoped would help them find common ground. On the other hand, he was shocked by Begin's arrogance and evident indifference to the effort that the president of the United States was putting into making peace in the Middle East. In Carter's opinion, Begin made it clear from the beginning that "he wasn't going to do a damn thing."

Begin was slightly built, with a large balding head and a long chin, which gave his head something of the shape of a light bulb. Behind glasses with heavy frames, his eyes were blue-gray; the thinning strands of hair that remained were reddish brown. When he smiled, he exposed a prominent gap in his front teeth. His disinterest in fashion had become a trademark, but on the other hand he was elaborately formal by nature and addicted to ceremonies. Dignity was an obsession with him. His stiff-necked code of honor and rococo manners encouraged caricature and ridicule among his opponents. "Begin is absolutely convinced that he holds the truth in his back pocket," Ezer Weizman observed. "Consequently, in addressing others—including the heads of great nations—he adopts the manner of a teacher talking to his pupils. There is something overbearing in his manner." Views that did not correspond to his ironclad philosophy of life were rejected as naive or subversive. "Begin simply drives anyone who disagrees with him up the wall," noted Samuel Lewis, the American ambassador to Israel. Lewis considered it merely one of Begin's many tactics. "He exhibited a rich arsenal of tools: anger, sarcasm, bombast; exaggeration, wearying repetition of arguments, historical lessons from dark chapters of Jewish history; and stubbornness."

The prime minister carried an emotional burden that was

particularly acute for Holocaust survivors. "Against the eyes of every son of the nation appear and reappear the carriages of death," he said in one of his despairing proclamations from the underground. "The Black Nights when the sound of an infernal screeching of wheels and the sighs of the condemned press in from afar and interrupt one's slumber; to remind one of what happened to mother, father, brothers, to a son, a daughter, a People. *In these inescapable moments every Jew in the country feels unwell because he is well.* He asks himself: Is there not something treasonous in his own existence. He asks: Can he sit by and allow the terrible contradiction between the march to death *there* and the flow of life here." He concluded: "And there is no way to run from these questions."

In private, Begin was guarded and suffered frequent mood swings that would prompt him to retreat into his office and cancel meetings. The prime minister surrounded himself with aides who were little more than acolytes, most of them drawn from the underground, who humored him and dared not question his authority. He was by no means a skilled administrator. He had little understanding of the economy or international affairs beyond his region. In his entire career, he had one main political idea, which was to expand Israel's borders. His attitude toward the Arabs who lived inside those borders was ambivalent. He devoutly believed that the State of Israel itself belonged entirely to the Jewish people; on the other hand, he suggested that if Israel annexed the territories it acquired through war, the country should award citizenship to every Arab who desired it.

He was not intensely religious. He went to temple mainly on the holidays. Still, he was totally absorbed by the tragic conundrum of Jewish history. Other countries could be multireligious, and other religions could be multinational, he believed, but with Jews there was only one nationality and a single religion, and neither could be separated from the other. His adviser and speechwriter, Yehuda Avner, recalled an evening of Bible study in Begin's home, the night before he was flying to Washington. Begin proposed to discuss the text from Numbers 22–24. In the story, forty years had passed since the Jews fled Egypt, and their wandering in the wilderness was nearly at an end. The fearful Moabite King Balak attempted to bribe the prophet Balaam to curse the Israelites before they could enter the Promised Land, where the Moabites resided. Balaam refused. "How shall I curse, whom God has not cursed?" he tells the king, and then he adds, referring to the Israelites, "Lo, the people shall dwell alone, and shall not be reckoned among nations."

"Is this not a startlingly accurate prophecy of our Jewish people's experience in all history?" Begin asked the assembled guests. Why did Israel endure such solitude in the world? There were many Christian states, and Muslim states, and Buddhist states; there were many countries that spoke English, French, Arabic, and so on; but there was only one Jewish country in the world, and only one that spoke Hebrew. Israel stood alone. "Why have we no sovereign kith and kin anywhere in the world?" he asked. "No other country in the world shares our unique narrative." The only bond Israel enjoyed with any other people was with fellow Jews in the Diaspora, "and everywhere they are a minority and nowhere do they enjoy any form of national or cultural autonomy."

Begin started his first meeting with Carter in the White House with an overview of the modern history of Israel, recounting the attacks by Arabs on Jews in the 1948 War of

Independence. "There were only 650,000 Jews [in Palestine] in those days, and we had to fight three armies, plus the Iraqis," he said. "I am not exaggerating when I say that sometimes we had to fight with our bare hands and sometimes with home-made arms that didn't always work. We lost one percent of our population in that war, 6,000 people." Begin grew emotional as he spoke about the terror attacks on the part of the Palestinians. "The bloodshed has gone on permanently. My grandchild was bombed in Jerusalem.*

"In May of 1967, I remember being at the Independence Day parade when we got news of Egypt's mobilization in Sinai," Begin continued. "For two weeks we were surrounded by a ring of steel. There were more tanks facing us than those that Germany had sent against the Soviet Union in 1941. All of the Arab capitals were calling for our death, and wanting to throw us into the sea." Faced with such a threat, he said, "we decided to take the initiative. The Six-Day War was an act of legitimate self-defense to save ourselves from total destruction."

Begin had brought along Dr. Shmuel Katz, a trenchant ideologue and a colleague from their days in the Jewish underground. The meeting took a turn into the dark forest of anxiety that enshrouded Begin and his intimates. Katz unrolled a map of the region, showing the small state of Israel in blue surrounded by twenty-one Arab countries in red—roughly like New Jersey compared to the rest of the United States. Katz asserted that it was a pure myth that there were Palestinians living on the land before Israel was established, and to prove

---

* Begin was apparently referring to an incident in October 1966 in the Jerusalem suburb of Romema Elite, when two buildings were bombed by infiltrators associated with the Palestinian terror group el-Fatah. Four people were injured, none seriously. Begin's son, Benny, and his family were living in one of the buildings, but they were not listed among the injured.

it, he referenced Mark Twain's dyspeptic account of his travels in the Holy Land in *Innocents Abroad,* in which he described Upper Galilee in 1867. ("There is not a solitary village throughout its whole extent—not for thirty miles in either direction. There are two or three clusters of Bedouin tents, but not a single permanent habitation.") Katz went on to say that the Arabs who fled after 1948 had no real roots in the country. "Peasants after all do not flee, even in the midst of war," he said airily.

Yehuda Avner observed Carter's clenched jaw and pinched expression as the indefatigable Katz continued his obtuse attempt to undermine any claims that Palestine was ever home to anyone but the Jews. Finally Begin put a restraining arm on his old comrade. "I want to discuss the question you raised about settlements," he said to Carter. "I want to speak with candor. No settlements will be allowed to become obstacles to negotiations." However, his policy was that Jews should be allowed to live anywhere they pleased. The West Bank was dotted with towns of historical importance to Jews. "There are many towns named Hebron in the United States, and many named Bethel and Shiloh," he pointed out. In Genesis, Bethel is the place where Jacob fell asleep and dreamed of a ladder into Heaven. When he climbed to the top, God was waiting and promised him the land of Canaan. Shiloh was a capital of the ancient Israelites before Jerusalem.

"Just twenty miles from my hometown there is a Bethel and a Shiloh, each of which has a Baptist church!" Carter pointed out.

"Imagine the governor of such a state declaring that all American citizens except Jews could go to live in those towns," Begin exclaimed. "Can we be expected, as the government of Israel, to prevent a Jew from establishing his home in the original Bethel? In the original Shiloh? These will not be an obstacle to negotiation. The word 'non-negotiable' is not in our vocabulary. But this is a great moral issue. We cannot tell Jews in their own land that they cannot settle in Shiloh."

THE CIA PROFILERS HAD scrambled to prepare the dossier on Begin. The analysts read his two memoirs: *White Nights,* about his imprisonment in Soviet labor camps; and *The Revolt,* which chronicled his experience as the head of Irgun Zvai Leumi (the "National Military Organization," known in Israel as Etzel, but abroad as Irgun), an underground group that carried out terror strikes on British forces before independence and then against Palestinian villagers afterward. In his autobiographies, Begin comes off as intransigent, supremely sure of his great intelligence, passionate, riven with guilt, and full of rage. He presents himself as a "new specimen of human being" born out of the ashes of the Holocaust: "the Fighting Jew." His eloquence teetered on the edge of sophistry and bombast, but he had a genius for picking away at a single word until he had turned its meaning inside out. For instance: "It is axiomatic that those who fight have to hate—something or somebody," he wrote.

> We had to hate first and foremost, the horrifying, age-old inexcusable utter *defenselessness* of our Jewish people, wandering through millennia, through a cruel world, to the majority of whose inhabitants the defenselessness of the Jews was a standing invitation to massacre them. . . . We had to hate . . . foreign rule in the land of our ancestors. . . .

Who will condemn the hatred of evil that springs from the love of what is good and just? Such hatred has been the driving force of progress in the world's history—"not peace but a sword"—in the cause of mankind's advancement. And in our case, such hate has been nothing more and nothing less than a manifestation of that highest human feeling: love. For if you love Freedom, you must hate Slavery; if you love your people, you cannot but hate the enemies that compass their destruction; if you love your country, you cannot but hate those who seek to annex it.

The author of this statement was deaf to the same argument made by Palestinians about their own struggle to overcome weakness and achieve justice. His life had hardened him to the suffering of others. He told Carter that his earliest memory was of Polish soldiers flogging a Jew in a public park. His father, Ze'ev Dov, a wood merchant, inculcated Zionist doctrines into his three children, but insisted on sending them to the Polish high school rather than the private Jewish one. The state school was free, and the Begins had little money to spare; also, in Ze'ev Dov's opinion, the Polish school would give his children a better chance of getting into a profession. He wanted his youngest, Menachem, to be a lawyer. (Eventually, Menachem would graduate with a law degree from Warsaw University.)

One day, Ze'ev Dov was walking with a rabbi in the street when a Polish policeman tried to cut off the rabbi's beard. "It was a popular sport among anti-Semitic bullies in those days," Begin explained, when he told the story to Carter in their first meeting. "My father did not hesitate. He hit the sergeant's hand with his cane, which, in those times, was tantamount to inviting a pogrom." The rabbi and Ze'ev Dov got off with a beating. "My father came home that day in terrible shape, but he was happy. He was happy because he had defended the honor of the Jewish people and the honor of the rabbi." Begin went on: "Mr. President, from that day forth I have forever remembered those two things about my youth: the persecution of our helpless Jews, and the courage of my father in defending their honor." Later, Begin told his private secretary that he had related the story to Carter because he wanted him to know "what kind of a Jew he was dealing with."

Menachem was a small, pale child; with his thick, round spectacles, and his full, sensual lips, he was a natural target for bullies. Instead of fleeing, he learned to fight back against the anti-Semites in school—"to beat those who beat us, and to insult our insulters." He was too frail to inspire caution in his

Menachem Begin
in his Betar uniform,
Warsaw, 1938

tormenters. "We returned home bleeding and beaten, but with the knowledge we had not been humiliated," he recalled. What he lacked in physical strength he made up for in his gift for public speaking. Even as a precocious young child, he would recite poetry at the Zionist rallies his father organized, and by the time he was a teenager he was speaking to crowds of hundreds who marveled at his ability to stir powerful and unsettling emotions.

In 1929 Begin experienced a political transformation. Vladimir Jabotinsky, a Russian journalist who advocated an expansive form of Zionism called Revisionism, was speaking at a theater in Brisk. The Revisionists opposed the gradualism that mainstream Zionists endorsed; they insisted on gaining the entire land of Israel rather than compromising with the Arabs already living there. The event was sold out, but Begin sneaked into the orchestra pit. Jabotinsky believed that the Diaspora had left the Jewish people so weakened that they no longer knew how to act in their own interest. Only a state could provide the sanctuary Jews needed to become a people once again. One of his responses was to found Betar, a paramilitary Jewish youth group. The mission of Betar was to create a new species of Jew, one that could quickly build—and ably defend—a Jewish state. He wrote songs for the movement to reach the young minds he hoped to form:

> From the pit of decay and dust
> Through blood and sweat
> A generation will arise to us
> Proud, generous, and fierce.

Crowded into the orchestra pit, fifteen-year-old Menachem Begin may have imagined that Jabotinsky was describing him.

He felt a spiritual connection with the Betar leader that he later compared to holy matrimony. "Jabotinsky became God for him," one of Menachem's friends later remarked.

At the time Jabotinsky was speaking, Jews were outnumbered in Palestine by about eight to one.* "Emotionally, my attitude to the Arabs is the same as to all other nations—polite indifference," Jabotinsky wrote in 1923. "Politically, my attitude is determined by two principles. First of all, I consider it utterly impossible to eject the Arabs from Palestine. There will always be two nations in Palestine—which is good enough for me, provided the Jews become the majority." He recognized that it was "utterly impossible" to persuade the Palestinian Arabs to surrender their sovereignty. "Every native population, civilized or not, regards its lands as its national home, of which it is the sole master, and it wants to retain that mastery always," he observed. There is not "one solitary instance of any colonization being carried out with the consent of the native population." Because a voluntary agreement with the Arabs is an illusion, he wrote, there had to be an "iron wall" erected between the Jews and the Arabs—in other words, a powerful military force, which most Zionists believed would have to be their British protectors. Jabotinsky maintained instead that it could only be the Jews themselves. An agreement would not be possible until the Arabs understood that there was no longer any hope of getting rid of the Jews; only then would the leadership pass to more moderate Arab voices, who would ask for mutual concessions. "Then we may expect them to discuss honestly practical questions, such as a guarantee against Arab displacement, or equal rights for Arab citizens, or Arab national integrity.

---

* The British census of Palestine in 1922 recorded 84,000 Jews and 670,000 Arabs, of whom 71,000 were Christian, most of the remainder being Muslim.

"*And when that happens,*" he emphasized, "*I am convinced that we Jews will be found ready to give them satisfactory guarantees, so that both peoples can live together in peace, like good neighbors.*"

Half a century after Jabotinsky wrote these words, his most famous acolyte was being forced to decide whether that day had finally arrived. Sadat's gesture had left Begin confused and distrustful, groping in the air. It was far easier to deal with violence than it was with peace. Begin later admitted to Carter that Sadat's bold move had reminded him of Jabotinsky—as if the Egyptian were the actual heir to his idol's legacy and not Begin himself.

AFTER THIRTY-SIX HOURS Sadat departed Jerusalem convinced that he had scored a great triumph. "All you journalists are going to find yourselves with nothing to do," he teased reporters in Cairo. "Everything has been solved. It's all over." What about the West Bank, Gaza, Jerusalem? "In my pocket!"

Sadat was being hailed in the international media as a modern prophet or even a savior. "It was as if a messenger from Allah had descended to the Promised Land," *Time* magazine gushed. Sadat believed every word. "The Middle East after my initiative to Jerusalem will never be the Middle East that was before," he exulted on ABC. But the transformation he had wrought came at a cost. The Arab world turned its back on Egypt. There were demonstrations against his visit in several Arab cities, and Egypt Air offices were bombed in Beirut and Damascus. Palestinians in Athens attacked the Egyptian embassy there, killing one person; another was killed in a rocket attack on the embassy in Beirut.

There was an obvious key player excluded from talk of peace: the Palestinians. Sadat was not authorized to represent their interests, and Carter was constrained by a secret U.S. pledge to Israel, made during the Ford administration, not to talk to the Palestinian Liberation Organization—the only authorized representative of the Palestinian people—as long as it failed to recognize Israel's existence and accept UN Resolution 242. Yasser Arafat, the chairman of the PLO, refused to accept 242 unless the U.S. would guarantee that a Palestinian state would be established and the PLO would lead it. That was too much for Carter, who lost interest in engaging with Arafat.

Meanwhile, the world awaited Israel's response to Sadat's historic overture.

Begin came up with a proposal he called the autonomy plan. He presented it to Carter in another White House meeting the month after Sadat's visit to Jerusalem. Under this plan, the Palestinians would continue to live on the West Bank and choose whether to be citizens of Israel or Jordan. A handicapped local administrative authority would be able to locate sewer pipes and issue building permits but could not print money or raise an army—anything that might resemble a functioning state. The Israeli settlements on the West Bank and in Gaza would remain, along with the Israeli military presence. Egypt would have sovereignty over the entire Sinai, but the Israeli settlements there would also remain, as well as two Israeli airfields in a buffer area controlled by the United Nations. "It's a very interesting plan," Carter conceded. Begin returned to Israel, exhilarated. "I haven't met such an intellect since Jabotinsky," he said of Carter. As for his autonomy scheme, "All who beheld it praised it," Begin reported.

But any goodwill he might have accumulated with the

Americans he promptly exploded when he endorsed a scheme by General Ariel Sharon to place a number of dummy settlements in Sinai—specifically, in places that the Israelis had previously pledged to restore to Egypt under a prospective peace agreement. The idea was to swiftly create "facts on the ground" in order to enhance Israel's claim on the peninsula. The "settlements" were nothing more than phony water derricks and rusted old buses. If nothing else, Sharon argued, these props could be used as bargaining chips to preserve the actual settlements that Israel hoped to keep. It was a stunning misstep. International scorn was heaped on Begin, even in Israel, where he was accused of trying to destroy the peace process. Sadat's predictable reaction was to issue an ultimatum: "Not a single Israeli settlement shall remain in the Sinai!" If the Israelis insisted on leaving the settlements in place, he said, he would personally set them afire.

Carter was also enraged. He made it clear that the settlements in Sinai and the West Bank were illegal; moreover, he publicly rejected Begin's autonomy proposal except as a basis for negotiation. Even as this was happening, Begin authorized Sharon to send bulldozers to the West Bank to build an entirely new settlement. Only a rebellion in the Israeli cabinet brought the plan to a halt.

While everything was falling apart, the PLO shouldered its way into the discussion.

On February 18, 1978, two Palestinian terrorists entered the lobby of the Hilton Hotel in Nicosia, Cyprus, and murdered Youssef el-Sebai, a popular writer who was the editor of Egypt's main daily newspaper, *Al-Ahram*. He was also a close friend of Sadat's and had traveled with him to Jerusalem. The killers then hijacked a plane, but it was forced to return to

Cyprus when several Arab governments refused to give them asylum. "Everyone who went to Israel with Sadat will die," the hijackers told their hostages, "including Sadat."

Sadat responded by sending Egyptian commandos to capture the terrorists and take them to Egypt for trial. Evidently, he did not inform the Cypriots of his intentions. As soon as the Egyptian plane landed, the commandos raced toward the hijacked aircraft and immediately came under fire from Cypriot forces, who thought they were being invaded. Fifteen Egyptian soldiers were killed. It happened that the hijackers had already agreed to surrender just before the surprise attack. Egyptians largely blamed the Palestinians for the fiasco, accusing them of ingratitude for the hundred thousand casualties Egypt had suffered in the wars against Israel.

One month later, on March 11, eleven Palestinian militants landed a Zodiac boat on a beach forty miles north of their intended destination, Tel Aviv. They were carrying Kalashnikov rifles, rocket-propelled grenades, mortars, and explosives. The first person they encountered was Gail Rubin, an American photographer and the niece of Senator Abraham Ribicoff. She was taking pictures at a nature preserve. The terrorists asked her where they were, and after she told them, they murdered her. Then they ran to the highway, shooting at cars and throwing grenades. They hijacked a taxi and then two buses, taking the passengers hostage. Most of them were shot in cold blood, even children who were clinging to their parents. The episode ended in a wild shootout with police. Thirty-eight Israelis were killed, including thirteen children; more than seventy were wounded. It was the worst terrorist attack in Israel's history.

The assassination of Sadat's friend and the massacre of

Israelis on the Coastal Highway were clear messages that the PLO sought to capsize the negotiations. By themselves, however, the attacks were not enough. The terrorists were counting on a violent reprisal from Begin that would inflame the Arab world and subvert Sadat's initiative. They understood as well as anyone the spell of enchantment that had taken over the Middle East, in which violence could only be answered by greater violence. The actors by now were playing out their roles in a trance. The terrorists calculated that Begin would be incapable of a measured response. "Those who killed Jews in our times cannot enjoy impunity," Begin said in a trembling voice, his eyes rimmed in red. Three days later, Israeli forces invaded Lebanon with the declared mission of punishing Palestinian forces there, but in the process killing more than a thousand civilians, leaving a hundred thousand homeless, and raising Arab fears that Israel would annex the southern part of the country.

Carter was appalled by what he saw as a terrible overreaction and upset by the use of American weapons that were specifically forbidden for such conflicts, including highly indiscriminate cluster bombs intended for a large-scale war against military targets. When Begin visited the White House again, ten days after the attack, with Israeli troops still in Lebanon, he sought to enlist Carter's understanding. He said he was "wounded in the heart" when Carter backed away from his autonomy plan. Begin claimed that Sadat's visit to Jerusalem was merely a grand gesture, and that what Sadat really wanted was a Palestinian state and Israel's total withdrawal from its captured territories.

Carter enumerated the prime minister's main positions: Begin was "not willing to withdraw politically or militarily from any part of the West Bank; not willing to stop the construction of new settlements or the expansion of existing settlements; not willing to withdraw the Israeli settlers from the Sinai, or even leave them there under UN or Egyptian protection; not willing to acknowledge that UN Resolution 242 applies to the West Bank-Gaza area; not willing to grant the Palestinian Arabs any real authority, or a voice in the determination of their own future." Carter's accurate summation of the Israeli position came to be known as "the six noes." The next day, he told a delegation of top U.S. senators that Begin's intransigence had destroyed the prospects for negotiations. Begin was shaken by the exchange. He told his aides it was the worst moment of his life. But as soon as he returned to Jerusalem, he became defiant. There would be no Israeli response to Sadat's peace overture. He would get "nothing for nothing."

This was the situation Carter faced at the end of the summer of 1978, less than a year after Sadat had visited Jerusalem and the whole world had believed that peace was within easy reach. Now it seemed a foolish dream. The remorseless legions of war were awake again and on the march. Terror was rampant. Bombs were falling. Populations were being uprooted and scattered. Ancient ethnic hatreds, always boiling under the surface, erupted once more, prompted by the twentieth-century struggle to create modern nation-states and fueled by savage memories and losses so profound it seemed that history could never bury the bodies.

THE THREE MEN WHO now placed themselves at the center of this endless tragedy had arrived in their offices largely by accident or luck. Sadat's radical reforms had shaken his country and alienated Arab oil sheikhs, whose economic support was badly needed. His overture to Israel had stirred Islamic extremists into frenzy. Several Arab leaders were actually scheming to have Sadat assassinated. He seemed to court their hatred, calling his rivals "pygmies." Despite the forces rising against him, Sadat had become alarmingly grandiose. There was a sharp increase in his use of the first-person singular; he spoke about "my economy" or "my army." The CIA profilers noted that his circle of advisers had shrunk to a handful of sycophants, allowing him to wander further away from political reality. He had delusions about Carter's ability to impose a solution on Israel. "If the Middle East is a deck of cards, America holds ninety-nine percent of them," he said again and again, as if Carter could wave a wand and persuade Menachem Begin to willingly abandon his lifetime project.

Begin had spent his political career in the opposition, where he was expected to remain, until Sadat launched the 1973 war and a shocked Israel turned to the man who embodied the most wounded and aggressive qualities in the Israeli psyche. Obstruction, not leadership, was his nature. Rather than becoming more accommodating and flexible in order to gain political consensus, Begin stayed rooted in his ideology. The CIA profilers noted an increase in his provocative remarks and antagonistic behavior. The worst traits in both men were seizing control of their personalities, wrecking any chance that they could work together, or even understand each other.

Of the three, Carter was in the weakest position. His presidency was sliding toward failure. He had come into office by defeating an unelected president, Gerald Ford, who had pardoned Richard Nixon, the most reviled figure in modern American politics. The very qualities that had persuaded people to vote for Carter—his earnestness, his outsider status, his pledge to "never lie"—now read as the grating naïveté of a political amateur. He was intelligent but impersonal, with a kind of mechanical affect that made it difficult for people to like him. He frequently displayed a huge, toothy smile—the subject of countless caricatures—but rather than warmth or humor the effect was often goofy, or insincere, or even menacing to people who saw the wrath behind it. Carter was by nature cool and reticent, but when he was angry he turned icy. His voice would go quiet, his eyes hardened into bullets, and he would smile inappropriately in what looked like a rictus. People who encountered him in this state rarely forgot it.

He was personally virtuous, but there were other important qualities that he lacked. "If I had to choose one politician to sit at the Pearly Gates and pass judgment on my soul, Jimmy Carter would be the one," James Fallows, his disaffected former speechwriter, observed. Fallows portrayed Carter as unsophisticated, passionless, trapped in a maze of details, and unable to prioritize or even articulate his goals. "I came to believe that Carter believes fifty things, but no one thing," Fallows wrote after his resignation. Carter made lists of to-dos without any priorities, discussing everything from abortion to zero-based budgeting in alphabetical order. He would take the time to correct the spelling of memos he received, and he left his staff with the feeling that they could never do enough to please him. Fallows described him as being as smart as any president ever elected but not a real intellectual. Carter's exceptional self-discipline expressed itself in typed lists of the classical music he would listen to during the day; he would quote Reinhold Niebuhr or Bob Dylan to show off the range of his influences; and yet, these references tended to be shallow and unexplored, a way of countering the insecurity that constantly shadowed him, despite the know-it-all manner that he affected. His attempt at Camp David to solve a conflict that no one had ever been able to bring to a conclusion displayed his impressive tenacity but also a stunning degree of hubris. His major task would be to overcome his own limitations.

All three men saw themselves as living exemplars of prophetic tradition. The words of the prophets echoed in their minds. Begin devoutly believed that God had given the Promised Land to his forefathers, and that Israel was the last refuge of the Jewish people, who were constantly stalked by the specter of extinction. It was his historic burden to make them safe. Sadat represented himself as the savior of his own humiliated and downtrodden people. "God Almighty has made it my fate to assume the responsibility on behalf of the Egyptian People and to share in the fate-determining responsibility of the Arab Nation and the Palestinian People," he had said in the Knesset. Carter was well acquainted with the gory history of the Old Testament; nonetheless, he said, "I felt that God wanted peace in the Holy Land, and I might be useful." The faith of these men in their traditions empowered them to believe in the rightness of their cause, but at the same time, religious thinking posed the main barrier to peace. The presence of divine commandments that brooked no compromise still guided the thinking of men who lived partly in the modern secular world, filled with diverse perspectives and competing demands, and partly in the world of prophecy and revelation. The task of making peace in the Middle East would require reconciling these distant perspectives, something that much stronger and more popular figures were unable to do or unwilling to even attempt.

In July 1978 the Carters went to Camp David for a quiet family weekend. The president's efforts to bring the antagonists to the peace table had gone nowhere; in fact, events seemed to be drifting in the opposite direction, toward war and wider conflict. Jimmy spoke to Rosalynn about his frustration with the stalled peace process, and she suggested that he make one last effort. Perhaps he could bring them here, to Camp David. Carter immediately kindled to the idea. "It's so beautiful here," he agreed. "I don't believe anyone could stay in this place, close to nature, peaceful and isolated from the world, and still carry a grudge." He would come to appreciate the naïveté of that statement.

Rosalynn pointed out that it would be impossible for the two men to retreat from their strident positions without a third party who was willing to take the blame. "Are you willing to be the scapegoat?" she asked.

"What else is new?" Carter replied. He was already being pilloried and ridiculed in the press, but that was nothing compared to what would happen if the "most powerful man in the world" staged a peace summit and it turned into the fiasco everyone predicted.

"You've never been afraid of failure before," Rosalynn reminded him.

A couple of weeks later, Carter sent his secretary of state, Cyrus Vance, to Egypt and Israel with handwritten invitations to the two leaders to come to Camp David in early September.

His horrified advisers tried to lower his expectations. His vice president, Walter Mondale, his national security advisor, Zbigniew Brzezinski, and his defense secretary, Harold Brown, all warned him that the plan had little chance of success. The administration had already devoted an extraordinary amount of time to the Middle East with nothing to show for it, while many other important issues were allowed to slide off the table. The differences between the two parties were too wide to be resolved, the advisers argued. For Carter to invest any more of his political capital in a project that was so clearly headed to the morgue could sabotage his fragile administration. "If you fail, we're done," Mondale had warned him. "We will sap our stature as national leaders. We've got to find some less risky way of trying to find peace there."

There was little Carter could say to refute their doubts. Even on his vacation in Wyoming, he read their cautions in his briefing books. "Our main objective at Camp David is to break the present impasse at the highest political level so that ministerial-level negotiations can proceed toward detailed agreements," Vance advised. "Our object is not to produce a detailed agreement."

It was too late now. Against the counsel of his closest aides and his own political interest, Carter had decided to risk everything. Camp David would not be about breaking a political impasse so that more talks could take place; it would be about creating a lasting peace agreement in the Middle East, with the signatures of all three leaders on the line. On a scratch pad, Carter listed all the reasons that the two countries had to make peace, and then confidently wrote, "First Egyptian-Jewish peace since the time of Joseph." He then scratched out "Joseph" and wrote "Jeremiah"—the despairing prophet of the seventh century BCE, who foretold the destruction of both the Israelites and the Egyptians because of their faithlessness and stubbornness:

> We wait for peace to no avail;
>   For a time of healing, but terror comes
>   instead.

Day One

Menachem Begin, Jimmy Carter, and Anwar Sadat in front of the Aspen Lodge at Camp David

THE 140-ACRE PRESIDENTIAL RETREAT of Camp David lies inside Maryland's heavily wooded Catoctin Mountain Park sixty miles north of the White House. Franklin Roosevelt, the first president to make use of it, had named it "Shangri-La." In 1942, in the midst of the Second World War, he had sought a secret refuge, where he could sleep late, work on his stamp collection, and occasionally entertain world leaders whom he wouldn't mind having as houseguests. Winston

Churchill was one of the first in that category, arriving in the spring of 1943 to plan the Normandy invasion. The two men took time away from their somber duties to drive through the countryside and fish in a nearby mountain stream. When word of Shangri-La's existence leaked out, there was concern that the hideaway would be vulnerable to enemy bombs, and the president was urged to transfer his retreat to the U.S. Naval Base at Guantánamo, Cuba. Roosevelt refused. "Cuba is absolutely lousy with anarchists, murderers, etcetera and a lot of prevaricators," he observed.

It was Dwight Eisenhower who renamed the retreat Camp David, after his grandson. He invited the Soviet leader Nikita Khrushchev there in September 1959 to try to reduce tensions between the superpowers. Khrushchev later wrote, "I couldn't for the life of me find out what this Camp David was." He worried that it might be a place "where people who were mistrusted would be kept in quarantine." Little was accomplished at the meeting, but the press began speaking of the "spirit of Camp David." "I don't know what it means," Eisenhower admitted. "It must simply mean that it looks like we can talk together without being mutually abusive."

Carter, a tight-fisted populist, came into office with the intention of selling off the property as a budget-saving move and as an attempt to democratize the imperial image of the presidency. In his first year in office, he had already sold the presidential yacht and banned the playing of "Hail to the Chief." He was looking for other symbolic cuts. He loathed any outward display of pomp and privilege; even as a presidential candidate, he continued to carry his own suit bag. Camp David, one of the world's most exclusive retreats, beckoned to him as a perfect sacrificial victim, and he ordered it sold.

The director of the White House Military Office asked him if he knew what was at Camp David.

"Cabins," Carter responded.

Yes, there are cabins—on the surface—the aide said. But deep underground there is a presidential bunker to be inhabited in the case of nuclear apocalypse. It's called Orange One. Around the property several hidden elevators lead down into the subterranean facility; one of them is inside a closet in the president's bedroom in Aspen Lodge. Eisenhower had the shelter constructed at the height of the Cold War. In 1959 he took the British prime minister Harold Macmillan on a tour of the bunker. "A sort of Presidential Command Post in the event of atomic war," Macmillan reported in his diary. "It holds fifty of the President's staff in one place and one hundred and fifty Defense staff in another. The fortress is underneath the innocent looking huts in which we lived, hewn out of the rock. It cost 10 million dollars." Six miles from Camp David is a much larger underground facility—265,000 square feet—blasted out of a mountain called Raven Rock, which was meant to serve as an alternative Pentagon in case of a catastrophic attack. At the time Carter took office, the most likely cause of such an event was the conflict in the Middle East, which was always threatening to escalate out of control.

Once Carter visited Camp David, all talk about selling it came to a halt. The retreat was only thirty-five minutes by helicopter from the South Lawn of the White House, but it was a world away from Washington. It seemed to stand outside of time, peaceful and silent, except for the croaks and chirps of nature. The staff would sometimes observe the president and the first lady taking moonlit walks and holding hands. Instead of state dinners, they could enjoy casual dining with their ten-

year-old daughter, Amy. Both of the Carters liked to fish—
Carter had become an expert at tying his own flies—and they
would try their luck at the little trout stream where Roosevelt
and Churchill had come up empty. Such respites were rare and
priceless.

In the weeks leading up to the summit, the staff had been
frantically preparing to get the accommodations ready for
the three delegations and preparing recipes to accommodate
halal and kosher diets. In addition to the leaders and their top
advisers, each delegation included secretarial staff, physicians,
personal chefs, communications specialists, and "bullshit artists," as Carter termed the hangers-on—more than a hundred
people in total, who strained the capacity of this rustic mountain retreat. They were crammed into the dozen lodges spread
around the camp, which were named after native American
trees. Sadat was in Dogwood and Begin in Birch, on either side
of the Carters in Aspen. The frustrated press was kept well
beyond the gates. The delegates assumed that their telephone
calls would be monitored, which inhibited the temptation to
leak details of the talks while they were still going on.* The
setting provided for total concentration on a singular goal,
without the partisan commentary that might have subverted
any attempts at compromise. As far as the world outside was
concerned, Camp David was a black hole.

The summit happened at an inconvenient time, politically speaking, for all of them. Egypt was still shaking from
Sadat's shift away from socialism. Under Nasser, the govern-

---

* Carter says that, in fact, there were no taps on the phones or in the rooms.
Despite this, most of the important discussions within the delegations took place
outdoors. According to William Quandt, the Egyptian team brought scramblers
anyway.

ment provided price supports for many consumer goods and guaranteed employment to all qualified graduates of the country's technical and professional schools—tens of thousands of them every year. These measures fed inflation, widened the budget deficit, and created a monstrous bureaucratic apparatus filled with people who had practically nothing to do except obstruct change. Sadat had reduced the subsidy on many consumer goods, setting off mass riots across the country over the price of bread. A number of policemen were killed, and Vice President Hosni Mubarak's summer home in Alexandria was sacked and burned. Sadat then suspended the price rises and imposed a curfew, but the country was still smoldering with discontent and barely contained rage. The CIA warned Carter that, in the absence of economic improvement or tangible progress at Camp David, there was a possibility of renewed civil chaos, which could prompt a military coup. In Israel, steep inflation—exceeding 35 percent—was pushing the economy toward anarchy, growth was frozen, and defense spending was 40 percent of the GNP. A thousand Israelis per month were deserting the country, and few new Jewish immigrants arrived to replace them. "What can I do?" Begin would ask his ministers plaintively. He was losing control of his cabinet and there was rebellion in his party.

Americans already believed Carter was wasting too much time on the Middle East when there were more pressing problems at home. The country was experiencing double-digit inflation coupled with high unemployment and anemic growth—a confounding phenomenon tagged "stagflation." As for the president's job performance, the two dreaded lines on the graph finally crossed in the spring of 1978, with more Americans disapproving than approving of Carter's efforts in office. It was certainly time for him to mend his image, but not by wasting his time on a fruitless quest to bring peace to people who seemed not to want it as much as he did. Carter had budgeted three days for the summit, although he was willing to stay as long as a week if he felt that success was within reach. It would be out of the question for an American president—or, indeed, for the other leaders—to be away from the responsibilities of office for longer, given their daunting domestic problems.

Carter brought one great asset to Camp David: a unified and experienced foreign policy team. Vance and Brzezinski, who were at odds on so many aspects of American foreign policy, were uncharacteristically in tune on matters relating to the Middle East, and their teams reflected that cohesion. William Quandt, who was on the National Security Council, was a veteran of Mideast diplomacy since the Nixon administration, as were Assistant Secretaries of State Alfred "Roy" Atherton and Harold Saunders. Hermann Eilts, the U.S. ambass-ador to Egypt, and Samuel Lewis, the ambassador to Israel, were esteemed professionals who had ready access to the thinking of the leaders of those countries. Without the team Carter brought to Camp David, he could not have achieved any of his goals, and without the commitment of the chief executive, the peace process would have come to a dead end.

When the opening day of the summit finally arrived, on September 5, 1978, Carter felt like a soldier on the eve of a battle. "There was a curious fatalism about the process," he later recalled.

ANWAR SADAT EMERGED from the helicopter with his arms wide open. He embraced Carter, then kissed Rosalynn on each cheek. Sadat and his wife, Jehan, had visited Camp David seven months earlier, a freezing weekend when the snow was knee-deep. Sadat had arrived then in a rebellious frame of mind, indicating that he was going to break off all efforts to reach a settlement with Begin. Carter had worked strenuously to keep him from taking such a drastic step. The casual setting allowed the Carters and the Sadats to get to know each other better. They even went for a snowmobile race on the helicopter lawn. Afterward, Anwar and Jehan argued over whether snowmobiles would work in the sand. By the end of the weekend, Sadat had softened his views on the peace process and agreed to let Carter continue to press for a way to resolve the impasse. Carter had been counting on the wives to provide a social bridge between the opposing personalities of Sadat and Begin. This time, however, Sadat arrived without Jehan; she was in Paris with their grandson, who was in the hospital.

The team traveling with Sadat was almost wholly opposed to the Camp David summit. Mohamed Ibrahim Kamel, his foreign minister and ostensibly his most important adviser, had only recently been placed in the job. The two men who preceded him in that position resigned in protest over Sadat's trip to Jerusalem. An otherwise pleasant and easygoing diplomat, Kamel was dogmatic on the subject of Arab unity, although he had never actually visited another Arab country. Even talking to Israelis was an act of treason, in his opinion. Kamel's intransigence influenced other members of the Egyptian delegation, and yet they worried about his judgment and his ability to keep his emotions in check. Boutros Boutros-Ghali, whose title was minister of state for foreign affairs, observed of Kamel, his superior, "His knowledge of the Arab world and the Palestinian issue had little relationship to reality."

Sadat brought along his deputy prime minister, Hassan el-Tohamy, a former intelligence agent who also functioned as Sadat's astrologer, court jester, and spiritual guru. Physically powerful—an accomplished boxer in the army—with a neatly trimmed beard, Tohamy was a Sufi mystic. "He has something godly in him and he can see the unknown," Sadat marveled. Tohamy was constantly reporting prophetic dreams or conversations he had just had with angels. He carried stores of ambergris and royal jelly to fortify the resolve of the other Egyptians, and would lecture to anyone within earshot about how God intended to slaughter the Jews. "We all thought he was mad," Boutros-Ghali recalled.

Sadat had assured his delegation that the summit was a simple affair. He would present the Egyptian proposal; the Israelis would spurn it; then Carter would step in to pressure Begin to accept the Egyptian offer. Either the Israelis would cave in, in which case Egypt would have achieved a great victory, or the summit would fail, in which case nothing was lost, but Egypt would still benefit from the closer relationship to the U.S. "What we are after is to win over world opinion," he told his advisers. "President Carter is on our side. This will end in Begin's downfall!"

That afternoon, Carter and Sadat spoke privately on the terrace of Aspen Lodge. Sadat told him that he was ready to conclude a comprehensive peace—"comprehensive" being a favorite term of both men—and in fact he had a plan "here in my pocket" that he intended to present. The agreement would have to provide a solution for the Palestinians and the removal of all Israelis from Sinai when it was returned to Egypt. Sadat did not want to be seen as making a separate peace with the Israelis and essentially withdrawing from the Palestinian cause. Such an action would remove Egypt from its accustomed role as the leader of the Arab world. Despite the terrible cost that continual war had imposed on his country, a peace that appeared dishonorable in the eyes of other Arabs and his own countrymen would be impossible to defend. "Israel has to withdraw from my land," Sadat said. "Anything else, my good friend, you can do what you want to, and I'll agree to it." Carter was a little alarmed at what seemed to be a carte blanche to negotiate on Sadat's behalf. He wondered if the Egyptian leader fully understood what would be asked of him, but Sadat seemed buoyant. "We can do it, Mr. President!" he exclaimed. "We can do it!"

Two hours later, Begin and his team arrived. Begin followed exactly the same ritual greeting as Sadat—an awkward embrace of Carter, then kissing Rosalynn on each cheek. The Carters were relieved that Begin's wife, Aliza, would be arriving soon. Carter noticed that Begin was wearing a suit and tie, as if he were meeting in the Oval Office. At Camp David, Carter said, there was a spirit of informality; for instance, he preferred to wear jeans and western shirts, or even running shorts and T-shirts. He encouraged Begin to follow his example. "It will be like a resort," he suggested. Begin was aghast. He was not a head of state, he reminded Carter; he was merely the prime minister—a rather meaningless distinction—and he intended to follow strict rules of protocol when dealing with the two presidents, no matter how they were attired.

With the help of several interfaith groups in Washington, Rosalynn had prepared a prayer for the success of the summit.

Sadat had immediately agreed to the idea, but Begin insisted on reading the text and making minor modifications. "After four wars, despite vast human efforts," the prayer finally read, "the Holy Land does not yet enjoy the blessings of peace. Conscious of the grave issues which face us, we place our trust in the God of our fathers, from whom we seek wisdom and guidance. As we meet here at Camp David, we ask people of all faiths to pray with us that peace and justice may result from these deliberations." It was the first joint communiqué issued from the talks, and would be the last, until the summit concluded thirteen days later.

MEMBERS OF THE ISRAELI DELEGATION descended from the helicopter and walked toward the camp, elbowing their way into view of the cameras trained on Begin and Carter, "like a bunch of boy scouts on an outing," one of them later recalled, "with everyone trying to huddle up as close as possible to the instructor in an attempt to get into the snapshot." The team that Begin brought with him was contentious and sharply divided against each other. To the Americans, the Israeli team seemed to be composed of "prima donnas," but the members of the delegation were also reflective of the intimate and contentious style of Israeli politics, in which the American concept of team players had little relevance. The Israelis arrived believing that the summit would last no more than a couple of days, and that no agreement would come out of it.

Aside from Begin, the most significant member of the Israeli delegation was Moshe Dayan, the legendary one-eyed Israeli warrior. As minister of defense, he received much of the credit for the lightning Israeli victory in 1967. But in 1973, Egyptian troops poured across the canal, catching the Israelis unprepared, and Dayan's legend, along with Israel's image of itself, shattered. He was in disgrace, blamed and reviled for the cruel shock Israel had endured. Although he told no one, he was ill, going blind, and desperately hoping for a last chance at redemption. Peace might be that chance.

In the late afternoon, the two delegations wandered around the camp in clumps, mostly avoiding each other. Everyone had been given a map of the premises and a blue Camp David windbreaker. There was a tennis court, a swimming pool, a bowling alley, a billiard room, a driving range, and a theater showing movies continually. It was early fall, and the leaves were beginning to turn red and gold. The lush forest was strange to both groups. Dayan felt threatened by the trees, which he couldn't see that well; he longed for the bright desert.

Ezer Weizman jumped on one of the many bicycles available to the guests and rode over to Begin's cabin. On the way, he encountered Sadat, who was on his brisk daily walk, accompanied by Foreign Minister Kamel, who was struggling to keep up. Weizman and Sadat embraced. "I'm glad to see you again!" Weizman said.

Brash, irrepressible, and gregarious by nature, Weizman was part of the "Mayflower generation" of Israel. His uncle Chaim Weizmann was Israel's first president.* Young Ezer grew up in Haifa, a mixed city. His mother spoke fluent Arabic and endeavored to teach it to her children—with imperfect success in his case. His father was a German agronomist who became a forestry officer in the northern part of Pales-

---

* Ezer Weizman later modified the English spelling of his name.

tine. "We were seasoned travelers in a world of open borders, not yet sealed by Arab-Jewish hatred," Weizman later recalled. His ideal of living in harmony with his Arab neighbors was abruptly shattered in May 1948, when Egypt and other neighboring Arab armies attacked as soon as the State of Israel was declared. "As for the Egyptians, I simply couldn't grasp what had gotten into them," he would later write. "What interest could they have in the conflict in Palestine?"

Weizman eventually came to think of the Arabs as patient realists, who counted on their vastly greater numbers and fabulous oil wealth to give them the advantage in the long run. In the meantime, they burned with hatred and envy of Israeli success. "Imagine that you're Arabs," Weizman would tell his subordinates. "What do you see? The State of Israel doing a strip-tease, that's what you see. A strip-tease! Green, flourishing, prosperous, twinkling at night with a mass of lights. And whatever the Arab eye doesn't see, his imagination invents. Now, you know what happens to a healthy man when he watches a rousing strip-tease act . . ."

The formidable Israeli air force was Weizman's creation, designed to knock the lust for conquest out of the Arab heart. "I've never hated the Arabs," Weizman maintained. "But instead of building and developing and living in peace, the Jew is forced to learn to kill more Arabs in less time." In 1967, Weizman's planes wiped out the Egyptian Air Force in three hours, determining the outcome of that conflict from its very start. Weizman believed that the war should not end until the Israelis had taken Cairo, Amman, and Damascus. He proudly advertised himself as a "raging hawk" who advocated the immediate annexation of all the territories it had acquired in that war.

Like most of his countrymen, Weizman reveled in the total rout of the Arab armies. There were photographs in the Israeli press of Egyptian boots in the Sinai sand, left behind so the soldiers could run away faster. The Israelis laughed at their pathetic adversaries, and even pitied them—emotions that made the Arabs' loss all the more mortifying. "It was only after my first meetings with the Egyptians that I began to grasp the mistake we had made," Weizman later admitted. "Whenever the Egyptians referred to their humiliation in the Six-Day War, their eyes grew moist. I suddenly realized how painful the blow had been and how it had spurred them on to redoubled efforts of revenge."

Alone among the Israelis, Weizman had forged a personal relationship with Sadat, wrought through many hours of negotiations. He always thought of the Egyptian leader as the personification of masculine elegance, perfectly groomed and exquisitely dressed, trailing a whiff of Aramis cologne. Now, at Camp David, encountering the Egyptian president in a sweaty tracksuit made him appear rather less glamorous.

"Come and see me!" Sadat said, and walked on into the gloomy forest.

THE LEADERS ATE in their cabins, but the rest of the delegations were fed in the large dining hall in Laurel Lodge. Somber Egyptians sat at their tables on the lower level, while on the upper level the Israelis chatted quietly, worried about being overheard.

Everyone in the dining hall was in casual clothes, with the exception of Hassan el-Tohamy. Like Begin, he insisted on wearing a suit and tie at all times. The other Egyptians were

alternately amused and embarrassed by Tohamy but also a little cowed. Tohamy's years in intelligence left him with the reputation of a man who had done a lot of dirty work in his time.
He was an intimidating figure with his barrel chest, broad
shoulders, blue eyes, and imposing silver beard. His formality
made him all the more singular among the jeans and sweaters.

Tohamy was known as a kind of guru for Sadat, although
no one grasped exactly what accounted for their intense relationship. He openly spoke of having conversations with genies
or dead saints. When he served as the Egyptian ambassador to
Austria, he suddenly stood up at a dinner party and greeted the
Prophet Muhammad, as if his ghost were physically present in
the room. Such outbursts on his part became legendary in the
upper tier of Egyptian government; he was always spreading
legends of his own prowess, casually mentioning that he had
decided at the last minute not to overthrow the government of
Afghanistan, for instance, or that he had just stopped a revolution in Malaysia. And yet, as the former head of Egyptian intelligence, he did have a history of intrigue. Perhaps Sadat was
under the spell of Tohamy's spiritualism, or enchanted by his
stories. They had been together in the revolution, and conspirators naturally forge links that others fail to see or understand.

At that first dinner in Laurel Lodge with the Egyptians and
several Americans, Tohamy boasted of his mystical powers.
Through sheer force of will, he said, he had trained himself
to control the forces of nature inside and outside of his body.
He used to climb into the lions' cage at the Cairo zoo, he told
his amazed audience, and bring the lions to heel. Eventually,
he was able to leave his body and travel outside of the physical
universe. He had even devised a way to stop his heart from
beating upon command.

This last comment attracted the attention of Menachem Begin's cardiologist, who was sitting with an American doctor at a nearby table. With his enlarged audience, Tohamy related that he had once gone for a physical and the doctor who was taking his pulse suddenly turned pale. "Mr. Tohamy, your heart is not working!" the doctor had cried. "You're dead!" Tohamy apologized, explaining that he had simply forgotten to turn his heart back on.

Hearing the story, one of the incredulous physicians at the dinner table asked Tohamy if he had been able to accomplish this astounding feat through yoga. The question infuriated Tohamy, who said that it had nothing at all to do with yoga! But he refused to divulge his secret technique.

A YEAR BEFORE Camp David, prior to Sadat's trip to Jerusalem, Moshe Dayan had met secretly with Tohamy in Morocco, at the invitation of King Hassan II, in order to broker backdoor peace talks. To keep the meeting secret, Dayan had flown from Paris to Rabat disguised as a beatnik, with a shaggy wig, mustache, and sunglasses.

He must have realized what a monstrous figure he was in the imagination of Egyptian military men such as Tohamy. No Israeli more thoroughly embodied the humiliation they had endured in 1967. Perhaps for this reason, the Moroccan king did not tell the Egyptians in advance whom Tohamy would be meeting, saying that the Israeli representative would be "a figure with status in every Arab state and at a level of responsibility."

When Tohamy entered Hassan's palace in Morocco, he greeted the king and embraced him, but at first he could not bring himself to look at the Israeli. "This is Dayan!" the king finally said.

"No one doubts it is Dayan," Tohamy replied. Finally he addressed the legendary Israeli. "I did not in my life expect to meet you in a parlor. Rather I expected to meet you at any point on the field of battle, where I would kill you or you would kill me."

Tohamy said that he brought a message from President Sadat, which he read aloud in clipped tones, outlining the terms of the Egyptian peace proposal. He repeatedly stressed the need for secrecy; even the Americans could not be told of the meeting, he said—his life depended on it. "His request for secrecy at that time was also prompted by what I can only describe as a crisis of the soul," Dayan later wrote. "For him to be meeting an official representative of the Israeli Government to discuss peace was an emotional shock."

Tohamy was supposed to be laying the groundwork for peace discussions between Sadat and Begin, but his mystical nature kept asserting itself. At one point Tohamy said, "Moshe, you are the false prophet of Israel. There was a prophet before you who was one-eyed, and he was a false prophet."

"Sir, I am not that man," Dayan replied.

When Tohamy got back to business, he stressed that Sadat was serious in his desire for peace. However, Sadat would only consent to meet with Begin and shake his hand once the Israeli prime minister had agreed to total withdrawal from the occupied territories. Guarantees could be established for Israeli security if that principle was agreed upon. That way, Sadat could have peace without surrender.

Tohamy could not refrain from mulling over past defeats. It was inconceivable to him that Egypt, with a population of forty million, together with Syria, Jordan, and other Arab states, had been defeated by Israel, with only three million inhabitants. Tohamy's lips quivered with anger and contempt as he spoke of Nasser, reasoning that Egypt had lost the war in 1967 because Nasser had conspired with the Israelis to bring about defeat. "Otherwise, how could such a catastrophe have befallen us?" he asked Dayan. He went on to say that the economic prosperity and spiritual blossoming of the Middle East had been held back because of the endless wars, but the time was coming for the apocalyptic clash of Gog and Magog, when the sons of light would face the sons of darkness, and the Israeli people would have to choose which side they were on.

The weird encounter between Dayan and Tohamy turned out to be far more consequential than Dayan might have imagined. When Tohamy returned to Cairo, he evidently told Sadat that Begin had agreed to withdraw from the occupied territories. It was on that basis that Sadat went to Jerusalem, believing that only certain details remained to be worked out between the two sides. When he first met privately with Begin and Dayan, Sadat mentioned this secret understanding to withdraw. Dayan denied he had ever made such a commitment; his only purpose in Morocco was to gather information and then report back to Begin.

"But Tohamy said you were ready to withdraw," Sadat protested.

"Mr. President, I did not say that," Dayan responded.

By then, of course, Sadat was in Jerusalem and the focus of the entire world was on him. It is entirely possible that the Middle East peace process was set in motion by the misunderstanding of a madman.

IN THE EVENING, Begin went to Carter's cabin for their first long discussion. They settled into a modest, wood-paneled study where Begin seemed to feel more at home than in the spacious living room. Carter surveyed the issues that would be covered at Camp David, explaining that he would act mainly as the arbiter, putting forward compromises when the two sides couldn't reach agreement.

Of the three leaders, Begin was in the strongest position: he could walk away from Camp David empty-handed with little political damage. His entrenched positions were well known. Even those who strongly opposed him never doubted his principles or his refusal to make any concession that might compromise Israel's security. He was a rock wall. But intransigence brought its own hazards. He realized that there was one thing more valuable to Sadat than peace with Israel: a robust American-Egyptian relationship, mirroring the friendship of Carter and Sadat. Egypt could foreseeably replace Israel as America's closest ally in the Middle East, opening up new diplomatic bridges between the U.S. and the oil sheikhdoms. Meantime, Israel's relationship with the U.S. might look more like the edgy relationship between Begin and Carter. America had provided a comfortable measure of military and economic security for Israel, providing $10 billion of aid since the 1973 war—nearly $4,000 for each Israeli citizen. If Americans came to see Begin as the main obstacle to a genuine Middle East peace treaty, his political career would be finished and Israel might find itself completely friendless in the world.

Begin's main fear was that Carter and Sadat were conspiring against him. He had reason to be concerned. Earlier in the year, Brzezinski came up with the idea of colluding with Sadat in order to put pressure on Begin. The scheme would involve Sadat putting forward an Egyptian plan for the West Bank and Gaza, which would be realistic enough to accommodate Israel's security needs but would also include some points that the U.S. would find unacceptable. That would allow Carter to argue with both Begin and Sadat, whereupon he would produce a "compromise" plan that Sadat had already secretly agreed to in advance. Begin would be placed in a vise. Carter could squeeze him without appearing biased against the Israeli position, bringing to bear all of the power of his office and the acknowledged vulnerability of Israel's dependence on the United States. The Americans were counting on Sadat's theatrical abilities to carry it off. Vance was opposed to the idea, however, and Sadat was really too impulsive to be a trustworthy conspirator. But the American team continued to believe that there would have to be some kind of stratagem in place to pressure Begin if there was to be any hope of pulling off a meaningful peace agreement. If Begin refused to budge, the American goal was to arouse enough domestic pressure against him to bring down his government, with the intention of producing a more flexible partner for peace—Ezer Weizman being the most appealing candidate to replace him.

Begin, however, had a trump card. He brought the actual text of a letter from Carter's predecessor, Gerald Ford. In 1975, Ford's secretary of state, Henry Kissinger, had been trying to broker an agreement in which Israel would withdraw from a portion of Sinai that it had occupied in the 1973 war. During that negotiation, the U.S. made a number of pledges, including the one that Begin brought with him, in which America agreed not to produce any peace proposals without first consulting the Israelis. Little had been gained from this extraordinary commitment, but it had hung over American policy makers ever since. In effect, Ford's pledge gave Begin a powerful veto over any peace proposal and compromised the American posture of being an impartial broker.

"Mr. Prime Minister, we must come out of this conference with an agreement," Carter said, pointing out that if they failed, there was little chance of progress in any foreseeable future. However, here in this isolated environment, with plenty of time, sealed off from the press and protected from the din of partisanship and pressing domestic concerns, the three leaders could change history. Their subordinates didn't have the power or authority to do so, and their successors might never have a better opportunity. Only Begin and Sadat could do it, here and now. Carter added, "The achievement of a peace agreement between Israel and Egypt is more important to me even than my political chances."

Carter began to read from a list of points he thought the two sides agreed upon. He said that Begin's autonomy plan for the Palestinians had been a bold step, as had his willingness to recognize Egyptian sovereignty over the entire Sinai.

Begin stopped him right there. As for Sinai, sovereignty was one thing, but the Israeli settlements there would have to remain.

Sadat would never agree to that, Carter said.

During the discussion, Begin refused to even utter the name "Palestinians." He persisted in calling the West Bank by its biblical names, Judea and Samaria, as if to underline the claim that God had given the land to his Chosen People. "Some people ridicule the Bible," he said. "But not you, Mr. President. And not I."

Israel's continuing presence in Sinai and the West Bank and Gaza was in violation of international law, Carter observed; moreover, "Sadat insists that Israel accept the principle that no land be taken by force."

"Security Council Resolution 242 does not say that," Begin responded. "It says that land is not to be taken by war. Mr. President, the difference is significant. There are defensive wars, too. It's not so simple." The Six-Day War was a defensive response to hostile moves on Egypt's part, not a surprise attack, he added. "If such a principle is accepted, the whole map of Europe would have to be changed." He would only agree to such a formulation if the word "belligerent" was inserted before the word "war" so that Israel could justify hanging on to the occupied territories.

"The United States expects Israel to put an end to the settlements in the occupied territories," Carter said.

"We cannot accept that!" Begin exclaimed. Perhaps he could agree to stop creating new settlements in the Sinai, he said, but not in the West Bank. "It is our absolute right."

Not only did Begin fail to bring any new proposals, he didn't even seem to understand the point of the summit. Yes, it was important to reach an accord with Egypt, he acknowledged, but first Israel would have to work out an agreement with the United States about how to proceed. That alone would take several months. It obviously couldn't be accomplished at Camp David.

Carter was caught off guard by Begin's seeming indifference to the outcome of the summit. "Sadat is impulsive," he warned. "If there's no progress in the negotiations, he is liable to launch a military action."

Begin was unimpressed. Carter began to realize just how

far the Israeli leader was from even the beginning of a negotiation. At eleven p.m. Carter finally called a halt to the pointless discussion. He went back to the bedroom and dejectedly reported to Rosalynn, "I don't think he has any intention of going through with a peace treaty."

BEGIN STROLLED BACK in the dark to his cabin, appreciating the silence. The lights in many of the other cabins were still on as the teams prepared for the first big meeting in the morning between the two delegations. There was a mild autumn chill in the air. "What a paradise on Earth!" he thought.

Members of his own team were waiting for him when he arrived at Birch Lodge. As prime minister, he had never been good at consulting his cabinet, but now he gathered his advisers around on the veranda and filled them in on his conversation with Carter. "We have a tough nut to crack," he told them. "His name is Anwar Sadat."

Day Two

Jimmy Carter, Ezer Weizman, Aliza Begin, Yechiel Kadishai, and Menachem Begin at Camp David

SINCE HIS NAVY DAYS, Carter had awakened each morning at five, a habit he could never break no matter what time he got to bed. This morning he looked over his dictation, and when the sun came up he and Rosalynn played tennis for about an hour. Cy Vance and Zbig Brzezinski joined them for breakfast. Carter kept shaking his head as he described his meeting with the Israeli prime minister the night before. Begin had seemed rigid and unimaginative, parsing every syllable; he was entrenched in the past and unwilling to look at the broad perspective. Carter was already dreading the meeting that afternoon among the three leaders.

Sadat rose at eight, went for his vigorous daily walk, then met with Carter at ten a.m. "My program is ready," Sadat proudly told the president, handing him a draft of the Egyptian position. As Carter read "The Framework for a Comprehensive Peaceful Settlement of the Middle East Problem," his heart sank. It was certainly comprehensive—page after page of uncompromising Arab boilerplate that was bound to torpedo any possibility of an accord; for instance, Sadat was insisting that Israel sign the 1968 Treaty on the Non-Proliferation of Nuclear Weapons, to which Egypt had acceded but Israel had not. All settlements in the occupied territories would be dismantled. In addition to totally withdrawing from Sinai, Israel would have to pay for the oil it had pumped and the damage caused by acts of war to people and civilian installations. Displaced Palestinians would be allowed to return to Israel or receive compensation, and within five years there would be a Palestinian state on the West Bank. Israel would surrender control of East Jerusalem to Arab sovereignty. It was a fantasy. There was almost nothing Israel could agree to.

Sadat said he intended to read aloud the "Framework for Peace" at the afternoon meeting. Imagining Begin's reaction, Carter warned Sadat that it would be a terrible mistake, but it was clear that Sadat wanted a strong initial position that would appease other Arab leaders and make it easier for him to grant concessions in the long run. Then he made a surprising offer. This part of the discussion was to be kept totally secret, Sadat stressed. He produced three typewritten sheets of paper, marked for the president's eyes only, in which he proposed several concessions that Carter could use at his discretion. Sadat would agree to full diplomatic relations, with an exchange of ambassadors and free movement of peoples across the border, routine postal service, free trade—a normal, neighborly relationship, in other words, which was exactly the future that Carter hoped to secure. In addition, there could be a more modest approach to the Palestinian refugees, as well as the establishment of a self-governing authority in the West Bank short of a state. Sadat would also agree to minor modifications in the borders of the West Bank to accommodate Israel's security needs. In Sinai, he would accept the presence of UN peacekeepers. Jerusalem could remain an undivided city. These were all points that Carter thought he could sell to Begin. For the first time Carter caught a glimpse of a possible settlement. But for now, he was the only one who knew of the existence of this secret memorandum. Sadat had even kept his own delegation in the dark.

WHEN SADAT RETURNED to his cabin, he was in high spirits, his foreign minister observed. Mohamed Kamel had known Sadat for most of his adult life, even before they were in prison together. They had been drawn together because of their lifelong hatred of the British, which united them in a sensational conspiracy.

In the summer of 1942, the German tank corps of General Erwin Rommel, the "Desert Fox," had bottled up the British Eighth Army in El Alamein, a seacoast town in northern Egypt. Many fervent Egyptian nationalists thrilled to the Nazi invasion and openly prayed for Britain's defeat. "Germany is the enemy of our enemy, England," Sadat later explained.

Sensing an opportunity to make history, he took it on himself to send a letter to Rommel, proposing that elements in the Egyptian Army would block British soldiers from leaving Cairo so that German forces could have a free hand; in return, Egypt would be granted her complete independence. At the time, Sadat was a twenty-three-year-old captain in the Signal Corps, but he felt entitled to negotiate a treaty between Egypt and one of the most illustrious figures in military history. The letter never actually got to Rommel; Sadat had dispatched a fellow conspirator to fly to El Alamein and deliver the note, but he flew in a British plane and the Germans shot it down.

Soon after that, two Nazi spies contacted Sadat. Their names were Johannes Eppler, who was half Egyptian, and Hans-Gerd "Sandy" Sandstede. They had a damaged transmitter that they hoped Sadat could repair. Sadat saw another chance to communicate his scheme to Rommel, and he readily agreed. The spies were living it up on a houseboat on the Nile belonging to a well-known belly dancer. They boasted to Sadat that a Jewish intermediary had changed more than forty thousand counterfeit British pounds for them. "I was not surprised that a Jew would perform this service for the Nazis because I knew that a Jew would do anything if the price was right," Sadat recalled. "But I was worried on behalf of Eppler and Sandy over this contact with the Jews."

Hekmet Fahmy, the belly dancer, had the face of an ingénue, but she was a fierce Egyptian nationalist, the Mata Hari of Cairo. Eppler used her to lure British officers she met at the Kit Kat Cabaret to the houseboat. While she was occupying the officer in her bedroom, the spies would go through his papers. Sadat began spending nights at the houseboat himself, where the scene became one of mounting depravity. Eppler was obsessed with the legend of "A Thousand and One Nights," and he was constantly playing a recording of Rimsky-Korsakov's *Scheherazade*. He told Sadat, "How happy King Shahryar must have been—getting a fresh virgin every night and then killing her in the morning! That's my ideal life!"

The Nazi spies were caught, and they quickly implicated Sadat. Eppler complained that they had been betrayed by two Jewish prostitutes, who turned them in to British authorities after he had threatened to "slaughter" them during a role playing of "A Thousand and One Nights" while singing "Deutschland über Alles."

Sadat was arrested in September 1942. Two years later, when the war was clearly coming to a close, many Egyptian prisoners who had fallen afoul of the British were freed, but Sadat was not. As a kind of publicity stunt, he and several companions escaped from the lightly guarded prison where they were held, hailed a taxi to the king's Cairo residence, Abdeen Palace, signed the guest book, and then took a cab back to the prison. After this escapade, Sadat went on a hunger strike, and when he was eventually sent to the hospital, he slipped away once more. For the next year, he lived as a fugitive. He grew a beard to disguise himself and tried to find work as a contractor. Sadat was free but destitute. In 1945, his ten-month-old daughter died, apparently of starvation.

It was during this period that he met Mohamed Kamel. Kamel was the leader of an underground organization that stalked and killed British soldiers, usually when they were drunk and alone on the streets of Cairo. The two men met in a coffee shop in Opera Square. Sadat was a striking figure, tall, quite dark, with a mustache and a deep, resonant voice. In Kamel's opinion, Sadat wore "eccentric clothes"—a dark gray suit, a red-checked waistcoat, and an especially notable pair of white leather shoes, quite an outfit for a man on the run.

Sadat immediately understood how he could employ Kamel's little "murder society," as he called it. Shooting a handful of British soldiers was not going to liberate Egypt, but it could be a sort of "limbering up" for the main task: eliminating prominent Egyptians who supported the British—in particular, Prime Minister Mustafa al-Nahhas.

Sadat took the aspiring assassins into the desert, taught them how to shoot, and schooled them in the use of hand grenades. The plan was to hurl the bombs at the prime minister's car as it passed by the American University in Cairo on Qasr el-Aini Street and then riddle him with bullets for good measure. Sadat gave Kamel and the other killers a package containing the grenades and a couple of pistols, and then he waited in the getaway car in front of the university. When Nahhas's car appeared, it suddenly sped up to avoid a tram, and the grenade exploded behind the target. The conspirators scattered. The getaway car was nowhere to be seen.

Sadat quickly produced another candidate for elimination: Amin Osman, a minister in the government who had said that the relationship between Egypt and its British occupiers was "as unbreakable as a Catholic marriage." This time the attempt was successful. Osman was shot as he was entering the Old Victorians' Club, a favored den of the English and a highly symbolic venue for the assassination. "Apart from removing a staunch supporter of colonialism, we had seriously damaged the prestige of the British authorities," Sadat boasted. Within a few days, however, the killer made a confession and the entire murder society was rounded up and jailed.

Kamel came from a wealthy and influential family; in fact,

his father was a prominent judge, which meant that he was granted special favors. His family sent food into the prison, which Kamel generously divided among his codefendants. Sadat loved Kamel's mother's cooking and would boldly request special dishes, such as rice-and-pigeon casserole. Kamel was also allowed out of the prison twice a week, allegedly to go to the dentist. There he would meet his family and some of Sadat's military friends, who would fill Kamel's pockets with goods to be smuggled into the prison.

The trial of what was called "the great political assassinations case" filled the front pages of Egyptian newspapers during the two years that it took place. Sadat's involvement was the main subject of interest; the former military officer was already well known for his attempts to collaborate with the Nazis. His bravado and lurid background, with his handsome looks and natural dramatic flair, made him a tabloid sensation and a hero to Egyptian nationalists. "Condemn me to death if you like," he declared from the cage that enclosed the defendants in the courtroom, "but stop the public prosecutor from praising British imperialism in the venerable presence of this Egyptian court of law."

Although he doesn't write about it in his memoirs, Sadat was twice smuggled out of prison by a group of young military officers who were dedicated to protecting the honor of the king from British humiliation. They called themselves the Iron Guard. Like Sadat, they too hoped to assassinate Mustafa al-Nahhas. Sadat was in a car belonging to the royal palace when shots were fired at the prime minister, but missed. A month later, Sadat was involved in a car bombing of the minister's house, but he was never charged. (The charmed Nahhas lived to be a very old man.)

Sadat and Kamel adamantly lied about their involvement in the political assassinations case and were eventually acquitted. "My efforts at the cross-examination had adequately thrown the case into confusion," Sadat happily concluded. Soon he was able to return to the military, where he joined the conspiracy that Nasser had established to overthrow the king. Kamel went into the Foreign Service, eventually becoming the Egyptian ambassador to West Germany. The two men rarely saw each other in the intervening years, even as they ascended in their government careers.

In December 1977, when Kamel had returned to Cairo for official business, his wife heard on the radio that he had been appointed foreign minister. He was shocked; Sadat had not even bothered to tell him. By making a public announcement, Sadat made it impossible for Kamel to back out without creating a scandal. Two foreign ministers in a row had already resigned because of Sadat's peace overtures. Kamel felt trapped; old ties of loyalty going back to their prison days pulled on him, but in truth he was appalled by any dealings with the Israelis. He believed that once you began to talk, half the battle was lost, because dialogue implied equality. Egypt was too weak to be Israel's equal. The only strength Egypt had was to stand with other Arabs in their refusal to negotiate. Sadat was deaf to his concerns, however. "Do you remember when we were in prison?" Sadat asked him when they finally did talk about the job. "You'll have a place in history with me, Mohamed!"

Kamel arrived at Camp David in a state of great emotional distress, smoking too much, far more worried about success than failure. After some of the previous meetings with Israelis, Kamel had been heard sobbing in his room. Vance had tried to pacify him. The Israelis' historic claim to Arab lands caused him to explode with outrage: "The Israeli attitude rests on an erroneous racist belief, which dominates their thinking and governs their behavior—namely, that they are God's Chosen People. Accordingly, whatever they believe, their rights transcend the rights of others."

AFTER RELATING HIS MEETING with Carter that morning, Sadat suggested to Kamel and other members of his delegation that they take a walk in order to get familiar with the surroundings. Sadat set off in his tracksuit. Along the way they ran into Menachem Begin in a golf cart. It was the first tentative encounter between the two men at the camp.

"How are you, Mr. President," Begin said, as they shook hands. "You are looking well. I hope you are feeling well, too."

"You are looking well, too, Mr. Prime Minister," Sadat replied, sizing up his adversary.

Their health was a subject of constant speculation and scrutiny by all parties. Both men had suffered repeated heart attacks. Of the two, Sadat seemed to be in better condition, although he handled his health like a cracked pot that had to be very carefully used. He usually slept until nine or nine thirty in the morning; upon waking, he ate a spoonful of honey and royal jelly, along with a cup of sweet mint tea. He prayed, bathed, and shaved, then went back to bed to read the papers until breakfast—usually yogurt or papaya and honey. Eventually, he dressed for work, fortified perhaps with a shot or two of vodka as a tonic to stimulate his heart. For the next three or four hours he conducted official business, receiving visitors and reading reports. He believed he got colds very easily and so he forbade air conditioning no matter what the temperature. Whenever needed, an aide supplied a clean white handkerchief to mop the perspiration from his face. For an hour each afternoon, he lay on the floor of his bedroom with a scarf over his eyes. As part of his diet, he had given up eating lunch, although he still smoked a pipe, which was rarely out of his hand. Every day, he would take his vigorous two-and-a-half-mile walk. The only other exercise he allowed himself was Ping-Pong; in addition to his other duties, he was chairman of the African Union for Table Tennis. Exercise was followed by a massage, a bath, and a long nap. He would wake again around seven in the evening. He had another glass of tea, then a light supper. He conducted more business until nine, when he put on his pajamas and sent out a

Anwar Sadat

list of films he wanted to watch—mainly American westerns—which he enjoyed with a nightcap of whisky.

Begin seemed to have an aversion to exercise, although unlike Sadat he had managed to give up smoking. He took a number of medications for heart disease and diabetes, which drained his vitality and undermined his mood. He, too, ate a bland diet, preferring boiled chicken and cottage cheese, but he drank tea constantly—in the Russian style, with a cube of sugar in his mouth. He was frequently withdrawn and depressed. In 1951, after one of his many failed elections, he briefly retired from politics and sailed to Italy with Aliza. It was rumored among his staff that he had spent time in a Swiss sanatorium during that period. Throughout his life he would plunge into dark moods, and even in cabinet meetings he was often listless and unable to concentrate.

There was concern among the Americans that the stress of the negotiations at Camp David could be perilous for both men. Mortality was an unacknowledged guest but always present.

CARTER ASKED BEGIN to come to the three o'clock meeting a little early, and when he arrived Carter appeared extremely nervous. "President Sadat brought a written proposal with him," Carter said, warning Begin in advance that he knew the Israelis would not be willing to accept it. "But I would not want that to break up the conference."

Sadat arrived, now showered and dressed, like Begin, in a coat and tie—neither man was willing to adopt Carter's insistent informality. They sat on the porch of Aspen, around a small wooden table in the mottled afternoon light. Carter intended to participate as little as possible in this meeting, hoping that the two men would get to know each other better and begin to trust one another. At that point, he still saw his role as a facilitator, nothing more.

Begin started by saying, "We must turn over a new leaf." But he added, "Negotiations require patience."

"It's true we need time," Sadat agreed. He wanted a framework for comprehensive settlement, details to be sorted out later by the drafters of the treaty. "I think we will need three months' work." Sadat seemed uncharacteristically ill at ease, fumbling over his words several times as he responded. The tension of the first meeting was affecting each of them.

Begin noted that when the Catholics choose a new pope they say, "*Habemus papam.*" He hoped that at the end of the conference the three of them would all be able to say, "*Habemus pacem*"—we have peace.

After these pleasantries, the moment that Carter had been dreading arrived. Sadat put on his glasses and read from his eleven-page plan. "Further to the historic initiative of President Sadat," he said immodestly, "the initiative that revived the hope of the entire world for a happier future for mankind, and in consideration of the desire of the Middle Eastern peoples and all peace-loving peoples to end the pain of the past . . ." He went on in this high-flown vein until he came to the actual proposal. For the next ninety minutes, he read feelingly, gripping the sides of his chair at times as he made his demands for a Palestinian state, an Arab stake in Jerusalem, the return of Sinai, the elimination of all settlements, and Israel's withdrawal to the 1967 lines. Begin sat stony-faced. Carter sensed the lava rising in the volcanic prime minister. When Sadat finally concluded his presentation, there was a moment of complete silence.

Carter broke the tension by suggesting to Begin that he

could save everyone a lot of trouble if he just signed the document as written. Suddenly, all three leaders burst into laughter. Begin made a surprisingly polite response, saying that he appreciated how hard the Egyptians had worked on their document, but now he would have to read it more carefully and consult with his aides. The three leaders agreed to meet again the following day. Everyone parted in high spirits.

It was odd. Carter had predicted to Rosalynn, "Begin will blow up," but on the contrary, he appeared strangely relieved. So did Sadat.

BEGIN'S MEETING with his advisers on his porch at Camp David became a nightly ritual. His assistant, Yechiel Kadishai, would solemnly draw a chair to the center for Begin, "like a rabbi," Dayan observed. On this chilly autumn evening, as Begin recounted the session with Sadat and Carter, the Israelis were aghast. Begin noted that Sadat had even demanded compensation—as if Israel were the defeated nation, not Egypt. "What chutzpah! What impertinence!" he railed.

"Chutzpah is an understatement," Dayan agreed.

Begin added a bit of uncharacteristic Israeli slang: "If I'm wrong about the Egyptian document, I'm a flowerpot!"

It was clear in Begin's tirade that he felt that Sadat's opening gambit breached the normal boundaries of diplomacy, and that somehow Israel's national honor had been called into question. He was acutely sensitive to such slights. His life and career testify to his ceaseless effort to promote Jewish dignity— the word he used was *hadar*, which actually means glory or splendor, in any case the extreme opposite of the degradation and victimization that Jews had experienced in modern history. His attempt to embody this quality accounted not only for his grandiose manners and love of ceremony but also for his absence of sympathy for cultures that were not Jewish. Such flintiness made him a daunting figure in the underground but a difficult man to reason with at a peace conference. "There is only one thing to which I'm sensitive," he admitted to Carter. "Jewish blood."

THE ISRAELIS REALIZED that there was a relationship between Begin and Kadishai that could not be understood in the usual terms of employment or friendship. It had begun in Tel Aviv in the early days of the Second World War. Kadishai was part of a group of Jews who had joined the British Army. About twenty of them would meet secretly in a cellar under King George Street, trading rumors about what was happening in Europe. They all had families there, and word was spreading that the Germans were massacring Jews. Was it true? What could they do? They had so little information.

One day, the door to the cellar opened and a slender young man—the others at first thought he was a boy—entered. He was wearing round glasses and an army uniform with a Scottish cap and knee shorts with buttons on his socks. On his cap was the emblem of the Polish eagle, signifying his membership in the Anders' Army, made up of former prisoners who had come out of the Russian gulags. After the Nazis invaded the Soviet Union, Joseph Stalin had released the Polish prisoners, including Jews, and allowed them to form their own army under General Wladyslaw Anders. Eventually, the Anders' Army came under the British High Command in the Middle East.

The young man brought appalling news to Kadishai and the Jewish soldiers gathered in the cellar in Tel Aviv. The Jews in Poland—more than three million—were already condemned, the mysterious messenger said. But the Jews in Hungary, Romania, and Bulgaria could be rescued because the Germans had not yet turned their attention to them. "We can save them, but there are no savers," he said. If Great Britain would only open the doors to Palestine, Jews from all over Europe would come pouring in—on bicycles, trucks, they would even walk through Turkey and Persia. But the only way to persuade the British was to cause trouble.

Kadishai—who was nineteen at the time—turned to one of his military comrades. "Who is this boy?" he asked. One of the soldiers replied, "He came now from Siberia. His name is Menachem Begin."

Soon after that, Kadishai signed up to become one of Begin's troublemakers. In 1946, during the Irgun campaign to drive the British Mandate out of Palestine, Kadishai would help blow up the British embassy in Rome. Three decades later, Kadishai was still at Begin's side, attending him with a kind of spousal tenderness that no one questioned or entirely understood. Only those who had been with Begin in the underground grasped the moral cost of his journey, and no one knew better than Kadishai. But who could ever have imagined that it would bring them to this wooded mountain retreat to talk about peace?

IN DECEMBER 1943, when he was thirty years old, Begin became the head of Irgun. The idea of waging a Jewish insurgency at a time when the British were fighting the Nazis seemed like madness to many Jews. However, the British, freshly awakened to the value of oil and hoping to maintain productive relations with Arab countries, agreed to severely restrict Jewish immigration into Palestine. The Irgun was smuggling Jews out of Europe, but British authorities were blocking ships carrying refugees to Palestine and sending them back to the European slaughterhouse.

The organization that Begin took over was nearly defunct; there were about a thousand members in Irgun at the time but only a third of them were trained fighters; between them they had one machine gun, five submachine guns, a number of pistols and rifles, along with a hundred hand grenades and five tons of explosives. With that meager inventory, Begin declared an armed rebellion against the British Mandate. "We shall fight, every Jew in the homeland will fight," he proclaimed. "There will be no retreat. Freedom—or death."

Begin intuitively understood that terror is theater. Murder was not the object, even if it was the inevitable result. His idea was to create a number of showy attacks that would make headlines in London and New York and provoke repressive countermeasures. Predictably, British authorities would resort to mass internments, brutal interrogations, and exemplary executions; the Jews of Palestine would be increasingly alienated and aroused; and Britain's standing in the world community would suffer, as would support for the Mandate in Britain itself. "History and our observation persuaded us that if we could succeed in destroying the government's prestige in Eretz Israel, the removal of its rule would follow automatically," Begin writes.

Thenceforward, we gave no peace to this weak spot. Through all the years of our uprising, we hit at the

British Government's prestige, deliberately, tirelessly, unceasingly.

The very existence of an underground, which oppression, hangings, torture and deportations, fail to crush or to weaken must, in the end, undermine the prestige of a colonial regime that lives by the legend of its omnipotence. Every attack which it fails to prevent is a blow at its standing. Even if the attack does not succeed, it makes a dent in that prestige, and that dent widens into a crack which is extended with every succeeding crack.

Begin's brilliant improvisations created a terrorist playbook that would be followed by groups around the world—including Palestinian organizations—that hoped to emulate his success.

Begin was fortunate in that he was dealing with a weakened and distracted adversary that was still enmeshed in a war with Germany. During its entire history in Palestine, Britain never formulated a coherent policy in fighting Jewish terrorism, which unlike Arab revolt a decade earlier took place largely in the cities, where it was easy for the insurgents to fold back into the surrounding communities. Begin's goal was not to win battles but to prove to the British that Palestine was ungovernable. He concentrated on highly symbolic targets, starting with simultaneous attacks on three British immigration offices, which were in charge of blocking illegal Jewish immigrants. That was followed by similar attacks on four police stations. He raised money through extortion and theft. In January 1945, Irgunists snatched a shipment of diamonds from a post-office wagon in Tel Aviv, which they later sold for forty thousand British pounds. A year later, they stole a similar amount in cash during a train robbery. Weapons were obtained from raids on British arsenals and eventually supplemented by Irgun's own weapons factories. In July 1945, the British placed a reward of two thousand Palestinian pounds on his head. Begin went into hiding. He grew a beard and disguised himself as a Hassidic rabbi named Israel Sassover, with a long black coat and a narrow-rimmed hat. He lived with his family in a small apartment in Tel Aviv, where the terrorism impresario spent much of his time changing diapers and washing dishes. Except for his daily newspaper delivery and his prayers in the synagogue, few other people ever saw him during this period.

One who did meet him was Moshe Dayan, who was by then a trusted officer in Haganah, the Jewish defense organization. Relations between Haganah and Irgun were always fraught. Haganah was working at the direction of the official Jewish Agency, then headed by David Ben-Gurion. Almost from the moment Begin entered Palestine, Ben-Gurion saw him as a rival. Haganah had a history of accommodation with British authorities, which Begin infuriatingly compared to the diffidence of the European Jews during the rise of Nazism. Ben-Gurion had vowed to shut down Irgun at any cost, and he sent his protégé Dayan to deliver a message.

Begin was dazzled by the dashing young officer, his contemporary but his opposite in so many ways. Dayan was a native-born Israeli—a sabra—who embodied the Fighting Jew that Begin had summoned in his imagination. "He had lost his eye in Syria, but he certainly had not lost his courage," Begin observed admiringly. Begin, on the other hand, still had the refined air of a Polish lawyer. Dayan noted that, although Begin was in hiding, he still managed to present a neat appearance. "He has large and parted front teeth and is well dressed," Dayan reported. The message that Dayan came to deliver was that Irgun should stay in line. "You have no right to act without coordination and approval," he said. This was not the time for a freelance insurgency. British Prime Minister Winston Churchill had promised to allow Haganah to form a brigade to fight the Nazis, which Ben-Gurion hoped would form the basis of a future Jewish army. Begin replied that only military force would drive the British out of Palestine. Then he asked, "Are you also in favor of violence against us?"

Dayan said he was a soldier, and would follow orders.

This first meeting was the beginning of a fateful relationship. The two men stood across a wide divide of ideology and tactics that would threaten to bring the Jews to civil war. In November 1944, Haganah cracked down on Irgun and an even more violent splinter group known as the Stern Gang (also known as Lohamei Herut Yisrael or LEHI). Ben-Gurion saw them as a threat to the consolidation of power in the incipient Jewish state and tried to crush them. Irgun members were kidnapped; some were locked up in makeshift dungeons and others turned over to the British. Some were even tortured. Children of Irgun members were expelled from school; Irgun sympathizers were fired from their jobs. Although his followers were howling for revenge, Begin refused to retaliate. He decreed that Jews must not be harmed. His ability to keep his men in line made a profound impression, even among the Haganah. A new picture of Begin was emerging—that of a patriot with a nearly mystical attachment to Jewish lives. If he had chosen to respond in kind to Haganah's attacks, the community would have been torn utterly apart, but his willingness to endure persecution for the sake of peace among Jews lent him and his movement an aura of martyrdom.

When the Second World War came to an end, Europe was

overrun with Jewish refugees, but Western democracies closed their doors to them. In some cases, refugees who had gotten as far as the docks of Palestine were turned around and sent to "displaced persons" centers in Germany right next door to the concentration camps where they had formerly been imprisoned.

In July 1945, Churchill suffered a surprising defeat. Zionists were thrilled because the incoming Labour Party had been so supportive of their cause, but they were quickly disillusioned when the new government decided to maintain the same restrictive immigration policies of its predecessor. In the minds of many Jews in Palestine, Begin—the fanatic, the terrorist—had been proved right.

Ben-Gurion decided that Haganah should temporarily join forces with Begin's Irgun and the Stern Gang in a united resistance against the British. The pace and scale of the attacks ramped up dramatically, and so did the British response. By 1946, there were more than a hundred thousand troops in Palestine—about one British soldier for every adult male Jew in the country. In a single immense sweep on June 29, which came to be called "Black Sabbath," the British picked up three thousand suspected members of the resistance. At that point, Ben-Gurion decided the revolt had become too hazardous. But he had allowed one last operation to be put in motion, the biggest one of all.

The elegant King David Hotel in Jerusalem was not only the center of the country's social life, it was also the headquarters of the British Administration, which had set up offices on two floors of the southern wing of the highly secure building, which the hotel had been designed to withstand earthquakes as well as aerial bombardment. There had been numerous threats made against the facility but the British chief secretary, John Shaw, chose to ignore them. "We must retain, as far as possible, normal conditions," he told his subordinate, "and you can't take a last place of amusement away from the people."

Posing as Arab waiters, Begin's men smuggled seven large milk churns, each packed with seventy pounds of TNT, into the basement through the kitchen of the restaurant. Upstairs, diners were being seated for lunch in the posh Café Régence. At 12:10 p.m., an anonymous woman called the switchboard and said that the hotel had been mined. "Evacuate the entire building!" But somehow the news did not reach the diners or the hotel guests. Begin would later blame the British for not heeding the warning, and in particular, John Shaw. He spread a rumor that Shaw had declared he was there "to give orders to the Jews and not to receive them." Shaw claimed there was no warning at all.

At 12:37, the city was shaken by the blast, which sheared off the southern wing of the once impregnable six-story hotel and left a mound of smoking rubble in the street. The silence that followed the great noise was soon broken by the cries of the wounded. Two weeks later, when emergency workers had finally sorted through the shattered stones, twisted girders, splintered furniture, and the detritus of offices and hotel rooms and kitchenware and plumbing pipes, they counted ninety-one dead, including twenty-eight British, forty-one Arabs, seventeen Jews, two Armenians, a Russian, a Greek, and an Egyptian.

A distraught Begin listened to the report of the casualties on the BBC, which was followed by the playing of a funeral march. One of his aides, concerned about Begin's mental state, removed a tube from the radio so he couldn't listen anymore.

Haganah ordered Begin to take sole responsibility, which

he loyally did. Ben-Gurion then denounced the operation, although according to Irgun he had secretly authorized it. "The Irgun is the enemy of the Jewish people," the prime minister publicly declared. "It has always opposed me."

Begin admitted that the fact that innocents were killed caused him "days of pain and nights of sorrow," but his grief was circumscribed. "We mourn the *Jewish* victims," he said on the radio afterward. "The British did not mourn the six million Jews who lost their lives, nor the Jewish fighters the British have murdered with their own hands. We leave the mourning for the British victims to the British." He neglected to mention the other victims, including the Arabs, who made up the largest number of fatalities.

During the manhunt that followed, Begin hid in a secret compartment in his house for four days without food or water. A wanted poster was circulated by British authorities with a photo of Begin, slightly frowning and staring evenly at the camera with an implacable expression. The poster described him as "5ft. 9in."—he was actually about three inches shorter— "medium build, long hooked nose, bad teeth, wears horn-rimmed spectacles." The search was confounded by the abundance of misinformation in the British files. "He may be a Soviet agent," the British Foreign Office speculated. "He was made 'better-looking' by a German-Jewish doctor in Cairo," a British newspaper asserted. "It is likely the flat feet and bad teeth have also been remedied."

As Begin had hoped, the King David bombing exhausted the will of the British people to continue the Mandate. They were already spending more on Palestine than on their own domestic health and education. In February 1947, Britain announced it was turning the problem of Palestine over to the UN, saying the Mandate had proved "unworkable."

Sensing victory, Begin stepped up the attacks—sixteen on a single day in March, including a bomb in a British officers club that killed twelve. When teenage members of his Irgun gang were arrested and flogged by the British, Begin warned that British officers would be treated in the same demeaning fashion, stroke for stroke. No doubt the childhood memory of Polish soldiers flogging Jews in Brisk flooded his mind. "For hundreds of years you have been whipping 'natives' in your colonies—without retaliation," an Irgun message stated. "Jews are not Zulus. You will not whip Jews in their homeland." Britain stopped this practice after four of its soldiers were captured and flogged. The news of this event went all over the world, in part because of the equivalence in human worth that Jews had dared to make with their British occupiers.

Begin soon posed an even more insulting challenge to British authority. Early on the morning of July 29, the British hanged three Irgunists convicted of terrorist crimes. That very same morning, Begin's men hanged two British soldiers and booby-trapped their dead bodies. Begin, the lawyer, justified the murders by saying that the soldiers, who had been randomly kidnapped, had been court-martialed for "anti-Hebrew activities."

Many Jews were appalled by this action, not only by the murder of the British sergeants but also by Begin's legal sophistry. There was an immediate and virulent eruption of anti-Semitic attacks all over Britain—synagogues burned, shops looted. Outraged British troops went on a shooting spree in Tel Aviv, killing five civilians. And yet Begin's strategy had worked. The hanging of the British sergeants tipped the scale of public opinion in the UK decisively against the Mandate.

Terror was not the only reason that the State of Israel finally came into being, but the Irgun campaign was a critical factor in driving the British out of Palestine. Begin was the first terrorist to grasp the value of publicity in promoting his cause to an international audience. The transformation of terrorism from a primarily local phenomenon into a global one came about in large part because of the success of his tactics. He pioneered techniques that would become basic terrorist strategy, such as simultaneous bombings and the use of improvised explosive devices (IEDs). He proved that, under the right circumstances, terror works. Many years later, American forces would find a copy of Begin's memoir *The Revolt* in the library of an al-Qaeda training camp. Osama bin Laden read Begin in an attempt to understand how a terrorist transformed himself into a statesman.

Begin always disputed that he had engaged in terror. He wrote that his object was "precisely the reverse of 'terrorism,'" because the point of his struggle was to free Jews from their chief affliction—fear. He concludes, "Historically we were not 'terrorists.' We were, strictly speaking, anti-terrorists."

Day Three

Jimmy Carter beside Camp David fish pond

AFTER BREAKFAST on the morning of September 7, Carter and his top aides, Vance and Brzezinski, met with Begin, Dayan, and Weizman. Begin was in full fury. Carter tried to placate him by agreeing that Sadat's proposal was "very tough." He asked the Israelis if they could make some concession that would help change the mood of the summit; otherwise, it would all end very soon. Begin ignored his plea, insisting on going through the Egyptian proposal line by line, treating individual words and phrases as if he were spitting out poison. "Palestinians!" he exclaimed. "This is an unacceptable reference. Jews are also Palestinians." "Conquered territory! Gaza was also conquered by Egypt." Carter pointed out that Egypt was not laying a claim to Gaza, which was now under Israeli control. As Begin continued to tear into the Egyptian document, Carter realized how much the prime minister valued it as a foil to avoid addressing the issues.

"What do you actually want for Israel if peace is signed?" Carter said, nearly shouting in frustration. "How many refugees and what kind can come back? I need to know whether you need to monitor the border, what military outposts are necessary to guard your security." He added, "My greatest strength here is your confidence—but I don't feel that I have your trust."

"We wouldn't be here if we didn't have confidence in you," Weizman protested.

"You are as evasive with me as with the Arabs," Carter responded. He said it was time to stop "assing around" and put their cards on the table. "Throw away reticence. Tell us what you really need." The discussion got out of hand. Carter accused Begin of wanting to hang on to the West Bank, and said that his offer of autonomy was really just a "subterfuge" to keep the territory under permanent control.

Begin bridled at having his integrity questioned. Then he turned again to the Egyptian proposal, claiming it would force Jews to become a minority in their own country. That's the kind of peace Sadat was seeking, he contended—with an Israel doomed by the very terms of his offer.

"Sinai settlements!" Begin continued, in his endless refutation of the Egyptian proposal. "There is a national consensus in Israel that the settlements *must* stay!"

At the outset of the Camp David summit, Sinai had seemed to be the issue most easily resolved, but Carter would come to the conclusion that it was, in fact, the most difficult of all. It was where the trouble all began.

THE BIBLE AND THE QURAN tell very similar stories about the origin of the conflict between the Egyptians and the Israelites. For four centuries, large numbers of Israelites were living and prospering in Egypt, growing into a great nation. Then a new pharaoh arises who is suspicious of the Israelites. Worried that they are becoming too numerous and pose a threat, Pharaoh turns the Israelites into slaves and orders that every male child born among them be thrown into the Nile.

One day, Pharaoh's daughter (in the Quran, it's Pharaoh's wife) discovers a beautiful child floating in a wicker basket among the reeds of the river. This is Moses. The daughter is enchanted and adopts Moses into the royal household. Because the baby refuses to suckle at an Egyptian's breast, the child's actual mother is summoned to act as a wet nurse. Moses is raised as a prince, but he is always aware that he is a Hebrew. When he witnesses one of his enslaved kinsmen being beaten by an Egyptian overseer, he strikes the assailant and kills him. He spends the next four decades in exile, fleeing the wrath of Pharaoh, living as a nomadic shepherd in the land of Midian, across the Red Sea.

While tending his flock at the base of Mount Sinai, he investigates a strange fire on the slope. He finds a bush aflame, and yet it is not consumed by the blaze. "Moses," a voice cries out from the flames, "I am God, the Lord of the Worlds!" The

Lord tells Moses that he has taken pity on the Israelites. For the first time, God has decided to actively shape human history by taking the side of the Jews. "I have come down to rescue them from the Egyptians and to bring them out of that land to a good and spacious land, a land flowing with milk and honey." He appoints Moses to lead his people out of Egypt.

Moses returns from Sinai to confront Pharaoh. "Let my people go," he demands. When Pharaoh refuses, Moses and his brother Aaron cast a spell, turning the Nile into a river of blood. God sends a series of devastating plagues—frogs, boils, lice, flies, wild animals, hailstorms, locusts, and days of darkness—to harry the Egyptians until Pharaoh relents. Again and again, Pharaoh promises Moses, "If you remove this plague from us, we will truly believe in you and let the children of Israel go with you!" The Quran says that each time a plague is lifted, Pharaoh changes his mind and rejects his pledge to free the Israelites. The Bible says that God intentionally hardened Pharaoh's heart, telling Moses that he is doing so in order to make a point, "that you may tell in the hearing of your son and of your son's son how I have made sport of the Egyptians and what signs I have done among them; that you may know that I am the Lord."

Finally God instructs Moses and Aaron to tell their people to slaughter a yearling lamb and smear its blood on their doorways. "I will pass through the land of Egypt that night, and I will smite all the first-born in the land of Egypt, both man and beast," he says. "When I see the blood, I will pass over you, and no plague shall fall upon you to destroy you, when I smite the land of Egypt." In memory of this miracle, Jews celebrate Passover each year. At the Seder, a drop of wine is spilled for each of the ten plagues, to signify that the joy of the Jews because of their liberation is diminished by the suffering inflicted on the Egyptian people.

When Pharaoh awakens to find his own first-born son among the dead, he summons Moses and entreats him, "Go forth from among my people, both you and the people of Israel." The Israelites quickly gather their belongings, but also take the time to demand jewelry and clothing from the ruined Egyptians.

But God isn't finished with Pharaoh and his people. Once again, he hardens the heart of the ruler and causes him to summon his chariot and marshal his entire army. The Egyptian force chases the Israelites and catches up to them on the shore of the Red Sea. The cornered Israelites cry out to Moses, "Is it because there are no graves in Egypt that you have taken us away to die in the wilderness?" Moses responds by lifting his rod, whereupon a great wind rises up, parting the waters of the Red Sea. The Israelites cross into Sinai, but when the Pharaoh and his army pursue them, the Lord causes the waters to return and swallow them up. Not a single soldier survives. Moses and his people stand on the far bank and marvel at the sight, and they sing out,

> *My strength and my refuge is the Lord,*
> *and he has become my savior.*
> *This is my God, I praise him;*
> *the God of my father, I extol him.*
> *The Lord is a warrior,*
> *Lord is his name!*

"We saved the Children of Israel from their degrading suffering at the hands of Pharaoh," the Quran concludes.

For the secular Jews who created modern Israel, the story of the Israelites' presence in Egypt, and the Exodus, and the arrival in Canaan three thousand years ago is a testament to Jewish title to the land. History and archeology combine to tell a different story, however. There may have been Jews in Egypt, but there is no documentation by the ancient Egyptians—scrupulous record keepers—of their presence. It is possible that the biblical chronology is wrong. There was a Semitic people called the Hyksos who invaded and occupied part of Egypt before they were forcibly expelled more than a hundred years before the Exodus is supposed to have taken place; however, Israel is not cited in the inscriptions from the Hyksos period. A national trauma such as the drowning of a pharaoh and his army is not mentioned in Egyptian records.

According to the Bible, the Israelites who followed Moses numbered 603,550 men above the age of twenty, plus their wives and children, livestock, and a multitude of non-Israelites who accompanied them—a horde of at least 2.5 million people. Marching ten abreast, they would have stretched more than 150 miles. That would span the entire width of the peninsula. Many miracles supposedly occur on the journey. In the barren desert, God provides fresh water and provisions—in particular, manna, a divine substance that falls from heaven each night and sustains Moses and his people for the forty years that they wandered in the Sinai wilderness. The Lord instructs them not to eat more than their daily ration, except for the sixth day, when they are to gather enough for two days, so that they can rest on the seventh.

As the Children of Israel attempt to reach the Promised Land, they are set upon by the Amalekites, a tribe of nomads, who prey on the stragglers. The Lord is so infuriated that he instructs the Jews to annihilate the Amalek tribe entirely: "Do not spare him; kill men and women, children and infants, oxen and sheep, camels and donkeys." In Jewish lore the Amalek came to be seen as a mythic enemy of the Jews that is eternally recreated. In the first evening of the Passover service, when Jewish families around the world recite the story of the Exodus, they are reminded that in every generation there is someone that will rise up in order to destroy the Jewish people. Menachem Begin would be guided by this admonition. In his parents' generation, it was the Nazis; for him, it would be the Arabs.

Three months after the Israelites escape from Egypt, God calls Moses to meet him atop Mount Sinai, the place where He first revealed himself in the burning bush. When the Lord descends onto the mount, heralded by lightning and thunder and trumpet blasts, the summit blazes, and the people quiver in fear. The Lord speaks to Moses, issuing the Ten Commandments, followed by a long list of ordinances, such as how to treat slaves and sorcerers and cattle thieves. Twice God reminds Moses to be generous to strangers, "for you were once aliens residing in the land of Egypt." In addition, the Lord promises to send an angel to lead the Children of Israel into the land of milk and honey—which inconveniently happens to be occupied by a number of other tribes. "Little by little I will drive them out before you," the Lord pledges, "until you have grown numerous enough to take possession of the land. I will set your boundaries from the Red Sea to the sea of the Philistines [i.e., the Mediterranean], and from the wilderness [Sinai] to the Euphrates." Elsewhere in the Bible, God specifically awards the land of Canaan to Moses, describing its boundaries as roughly encompassing those of modern Israel, but including much of southern Lebanon and the West Bank of the Jordan River.

The vast migration through Sinai that the Bible describes—millions of people tramping about for forty years—should have left some archeological residue, but not a single scrap of evidence exists to prove that the Exodus ever happened. The archeological record seems to show that the ancient Hebrew people were a Bronze Age tribe native to the Canaan region—a province of Egypt at the time the Exodus is supposed to have taken place, a fact the Bible does not mention. That would give Egypt an equal claim on present-day Israel with that of the Jews, if antiquity is the yardstick used to measure territorial rights.

The Quran accepts the premise that God awarded the Holy Land to the Israelites, but asserts that the people were disobedient and God turned against them, revoking their special status as the Chosen People. "But they broke their pledge, so We distanced them and hardened their hearts," God says of the Jews; "you will always find treachery in all but a few of them. Overlook this and pardon them."

AT TEN THIRTY on the morning of the third day at Camp David, Carter and Begin walked together to Aspen Lodge just in time to meet Sadat coming from the other direction. Begin, with his granitic sense of protocol, refused to enter the cabin before the two presidents, which caused a rather comic and awkward start to the proceedings. Carter began by asking Begin if he could make a generous concession that would respond to Sadat's trip to Jerusalem. The prime minister brushed this overture aside, saying that the Israeli people had already rewarded Sadat by their warm reception. It should not be forgotten, Begin continued, that only four

years before, on Yom Kippur, the holiest day of the Jewish calendar, Sadat had launched his surprise attack, "knowing we
would all be in the synagogues."

"It was strategic deception," Sadat responded.

"Deception is deception," Begin said. He then took up
Sadat's proposal, going through it once again point by point,
ridiculing the language in brutal fashion. The men seemed
unable or unwilling to understand each other. Begin contended
that the Egyptian document laid the groundwork for a Palestinian state. "We will not allow the establishment of a base for
Yasser Arafat's murderers within our borders, including the
redivision of Jerusalem. There can be no agreement on the basis
of these demands."

"No! I said already yesterday that there is no need to divide
Jerusalem," Sadat protested.

"You address us as if we were a defeated nation," Begin
said, talking past him. He clung to Sadat's document like a
prosecutor waving the murder weapon in front of the jury.
"You demand we pay compensation for damages incurred by
Egyptian civilians," he continued. "I would like you to know
that we also claim damages from you."

This set Sadat off. At that very moment, Israel was still
pumping oil from the Sinai wells that properly belonged to
Egypt, Sadat said indignantly. Begin made another provocative remark about being treated like a defeated nation, which
brought up the question of who actually lost the war of 1973.
Carter interceded to say that neither side was claiming to represent a defeated nation. They calmed down for a moment, but
the grievances of both parties were burning hot, and neither
man seemed inclined to hear the other.

Sadat angrily recited the suffering that four wars had

inflicted on the Egyptian people. Carter tried to interrupt, but Sadat waved him aside. "I thought that after my initiative there would be a period of goodwill," he complained to Begin. "We are giving you peace and you want territories."

Begin replied that Israel merely wanted a defensible situation.

"I also want to defend Egypt!" Sadat shouted. Whenever he lost his temper, Sadat tended to call Begin "premier" rather than "prime minister," which irritated Begin. Now Sadat leaned forward in his chair and accused the Israeli leader of not wanting peace at all. Stabbing the air with his finger he exclaimed, "Premier Begin, you want land!"

The two men no longer seemed aware of Carter's presence. Their faces were flushed and their voices unrestrained. Rosalynn was in the next room, and she could hear the leaders screaming at each other. Sadat pounded the table and declared that land was not negotiable. For thirty years, he said, Israel had sought security, an end to the Arab boycott, and full recognition—and here it was, on the table! If Begin continued to insist upon holding on to territory then the discussion was over. "Security, yes! Land, no!" Sadat cried. No Israelis could remain in Sinai. Egyptian territory must be "clean-shaved."

The presence of a few Israeli settlers in Sinai was not an infringement on Egyptian sovereignty, Begin responded, infuriating Sadat even further. All the good feelings his trip to Jerusalem had engendered had gone up in smoke, Sadat said. "Minimum confidence does not exist anymore since Premier Begin has acted in bad faith."

Weirdly, there were moments when Sadat and Begin burst into spells of levity. One of the men referred to kissing Barbara Walters, and wondered if the cameras had been on and his wife was watching. Another time, they bickered about who was responsible for the trade in hashish between Israel and Egypt in Sinai. This struck them both as hilarious.

After three hours of exhausting interchanges, the leaders recessed to consult their advisers in advance of the next session that afternoon. Before they broke up, Carter recited a list of all the problems that remained to be resolved:

Sinai. If it was to be demilitarized, what did that mean? Was it the entire peninsula or could the Egyptians station troops to protect the canal? Would police be allowed in Sinai to maintain order?

Settlements. Begin refused to dismantle any settlements anywhere; Sadat demanded that they all must go, not only in Sinai but also in the West Bank and Gaza and the Golan Heights.

An independent Palestinian state. This was Begin's biggest fear; he would assert that any compromise on the West Bank and Gaza was a gateway to a state for terrorists. Sadat thought an independent state was inevitable, but he preferred that whatever entity emerged be affiliated either with Israel or Jordan. The Palestinians themselves should be allowed to choose. The fact that the Palestinian movement was led by Yasser Arafat, who had been the head of the terrorist organization Fatah, made this issue diplomatically radioactive.

Palestinian autonomy. Begin claimed that Israel would be very generous in granting Palestinians "full autonomy," but in Carter's opinion the evidence was to the contrary. Begin wanted to keep the land and rule over the people through a puppet government that didn't have final authority.

Israeli military presence in the West Bank and Gaza. If the Palestinians were indeed to be given some kind of autonomy, how would Israel guarantee its security without having a military government overseeing the region? Would it be able to station forces in the territories?

The West Bank. Begin maintained that UN Resolution 242 simply didn't apply to the West Bank, because when Israel seized the territory in 1967 it was a defensive war. Thus, he argued, the victor was entitled to keep the land. Sadat was somewhat flexible on borders but not on the principle that the West Bank belonged to the Palestinians.

Jerusalem. Under the 1947 UN Partition Plan, which created the State of Israel, Jerusalem was envisioned to be an international city that was not under the rule of any other entity. Begin, however, was not willing to budge on anything having to do with Jerusalem.

What peace means. In addition to ending the state of war, there should also be trade, open borders and waterways, and an exchange of ambassadors, although Sadat sourly suggested he was reconsidering diplomatic recognition because of Begin's poor attitude.

Refugees. There were approximately 750,000 Palestinians who fled during the war of Israel's creation in 1948, and another 300,000 or so who became refugees in 1967. Many of them and their descendants were living in refugee camps in neighboring countries, stateless, often in squalid conditions. How many of them could return to Israel? How many would even be allowed back into the West Bank? What compensation would be given to those not allowed to return? The fact that the Palestinians were not represented in this summit made it difficult to arbitrate on their behalf.

The Sinai airfields. Israel had ten on the peninsula, only two of them significant. Begin suggested that the U.S. could take over the operation of the bases, allowing the Israelis to continue using them. Sadat adamantly rejected this plan.

There were several other points, regarding participation by other Arab countries and the establishment of a mutual defense treaty between the U.S. and Israel. Both Begin and Sadat were in favor of this because it would eliminate Israel's chronic complaint about security needs, but Carter was reluctant to formally ally himself with one of the partners. It would make it impossible in the future to mediate between Israel and the Arab countries.

When Carter finished reading his list, he was depressed. The problems were overwhelming. There were so few areas of agreement. He had no idea where to go next. These were problems that were built into the creation of Israel itself, thirty years before.

IN NOVEMBER 1947, the UN voted to divide the territory of Palestine into two states, 56 percent for Jews and the remainder for Arabs. Jerusalem would be an international zone, available to all three religions but governed by an independent body. The plan was never given a chance. On May 14, 1948, the British formally left Palestine, and the State of Israel was born. The next day, armies from Lebanon, Syria, Iraq, Transjordan, and Egypt approached from the north, east, and south in an attempt to destroy the Jewish state.

It is interesting to imagine what might have happened if we could have stopped those Arab armies in their tracks, before the cascade of wrongheaded decisions, and let history take an alternative course. None of the surrounding Arab countries favored the creation of Israel, but they were also opposed to a

Palestinian state. King Abdullah of Transjordan had previously sought an accommodation with the Jewish leaders in order to annex the West Bank and Gaza and gain precious access to the Mediterranean, but his rival Arab leaders were determined to prevent the Hashemite king from expanding his domain. Both Egypt and Iraq aspired to replace the defunct Ottoman Empire. Each of these Arab powers was primarily interested in blocking the aspirations of the others, but their predatory instincts were also aroused. The Palestinians themselves were weak and leaderless. Thus, the Israeli-Palestinian problem was Arabized instead of subsiding into a two-party dispute.

In turning against Israel, Arab societies also turned against the Jews in their midst. There were about 800,000 Jews living in Arab countries in 1948, 75,000 to 80,000 in Egypt alone. Mass detentions, bombings, and confiscations of their property prompted the Arab Jews to pack their bags, taking with them their investments, their long history, and the cosmopolitanism that once infused urban centers from Morocco to the Levant. Today, only remnants of the Jewish population exist in Arab countries, where any Jews remain at all. Arab culture and society were profoundly diminished by this modern exodus; and in the absence of actual Jewish neighbors, a simplistic and reflexive anti-Semitism took hold. Many of those refugees found their way to Israel, replacing the Palestinians who fled or were chased out of the contested land.

Egyptian military leaders advised against intervening in the Israeli-Palestinian dispute. The army was weak, poorly trained, and inadequately armed. Egypt was still occupied by the British, and many Egyptian nationalists argued that war in Palestine would be a needless and dangerous distraction; a wiser course would be to strike a deal with the Jews to use their influence with

Britain and the U.S. to support Egyptian independence. But the decadent King Farouk, who pictured himself as the new caliph of the Muslims, decided otherwise, and so he sent his ragged, ill-prepared army into battle. The Egyptian Army officers "didn't think about the possibility of victory or defeat," Sadat would later write. "They thought about one thing only, that a war had been announced in the name of Egypt, and Egypt's army must wage this war as bravely as any army wages war, and its men must die, officers and soldiers, in sacrifice for every kernel of the wealth of the Holy Land, for Arab unity, glory, history, and piety." Those high-minded abstractions were scarcely equal to the commitment of a people who were fighting for their very existence.

Although five Arab countries attacked the new nation, it was not really such a one-sided contest as legend would have it. The total number of Arab troops fielded at the beginning of the war was 25,000, whereas the Israel Defense Forces had 35,000 troops, a number that increased to nearly 100,000 by the end of the war in 1949—about twice the size of its foes. Egypt attacked from the south, through Sinai, getting within twenty miles of Tel Aviv and bombing the city several times before encountering the newly formed Israeli air force. Ezer Weizman had created it with five or six light planes—Piper Cubs and Austin biplanes—commandeered from the Palestine Aviation Club. By the start of the war the corps also included four brand-new Messerschmitts. Weizman himself flew one of them in the air force's first action, strafing an Egyptian armored unit that was bearing down on Tel Aviv. The sky was thick with anti-aircraft fire, and the Messerschmitts had never actually been flown before. "We swung out to sea, climbing to 7,000 feet, and swooped toward the Egyptian column," Weizman recalled. "I must confess I had a profound sense of ful-filling a great mission." That first run was scarcely a success: one of the four Messerschmitts was shot down, and Weizman's cannon jammed; but the Egyptian troops were shocked and sensed that they had already lost control of the air.

The war provided an opportunity for the new Jewish nation to reshape itself, not only geographically but also demographically. Many Palestinians fled the conflict, under the impression that the Arab victory would be swift and they could soon return to their homes. But many others were forced out. Dayan was put in charge of a commando unit, Regiment 89, soon noted for slashing raids into Arab towns, his troops killing indiscriminately, feeding the panic that led to the mass exodus of Palestinians. He led his men into the city of Lydda (near the site of what is today called Ben Gurion Airport), where they shot everyone they saw—more than a hundred civilians in less than an hour. The next day, the Israeli army carried out a systematic massacre of hundreds more and the expulsion of thousands of the town's surviving citizens, many of whom would die on the trek toward the ruined lives that otherwise awaited them. They joined hun-dreds of thousands of others who swelled the refugee camps of neighboring countries, destabilizing those governments and opening an era of terror that continues to find its jus-tification in the loss of a nation that never actually got the chance to exist. The 1948 war would leave Egypt in control of Gaza, and Jordan with the West Bank, including the Old City of Jerusalem. Israel annexed two thousand square miles, giving it three-fourths of the territory of the British Mandate. So much for Palestine.

The Arab defeat would have shattering consequences for

those societies. Humiliated in battle, the soldiers returned to take revenge on their governments. Military coups, one after another, turned the region into a vast barracks state. To justify their continued hold on power, the military rulers had to enshrine a permanent enemy, and the one they could all agree upon was Israel. Peace would ruin everything.

ONE OF BEN-GURION'S MAIN TASKS during the War of Independence was to gain control of the underground movements, especially Begin's Irgun. As Israel's first prime minister, Ben-Gurion did not want his country riven by private militias contending for power. Even though Irgun nominally had been disbanded and its members integrated into the Israeli army, Begin still commanded a fanatically loyal following. His greatest worry was that the Arab countries would accept the partition plan and that the war would end, forcing Israel to remain inside the borders that it had been awarded. That seemed to be its destiny on June 11, 1948. The UN had brokered a cease-fire between Israel and its Arab neighbors. Both sides agreed not to bring in any more arms. UN observers were straining to enforce the ban.

At this delicate moment, a boatload of French arms, purchased by Irgun and valued at more than five million dollars, arrived off the Israeli coast. The *Altalena* dropped anchor at nightfall opposite a village named Kfar Vitkin, north of Tel Aviv. Begin emerged from the underground and greeted the vessel. He was still unused to being in public, and many of his Irgun followers had never actually seen him. Some of them wept to discover their commander standing in front of them.

The shipment was supposed to have arrived before the

cease-fire went into effect. There was an agreement with Ben-Gurion that the Irgun would receive 20 percent of the munitions and the Israeli army would get the rest, the Israeli prime minister suddenly became convinced that Begin intended to stage a coup d'état. He excitedly told his cabinet, "It's an attempt to run over the army and murder the State." He sent Lieutenant Colonel Moshe Dayan to Kfar Vitkin to confiscate the entire shipment.

Dayan found members of Irgun unloading the shipment. He thought it would be sufficient to spread his men around the beach and say, "Enough! You're surrounded." Begin defied the ultimatum, however, instructing his men to continue unloading the cargo. Although guns were drawn on both sides, Begin scoffed at the possibility that violence would break out. "Jews do not shoot at Jews!" he confidently told a subordinate. But then automatic weapons crackled, followed by mortar fire.

Who fired first became a matter of dispute. "Our men called on Irgun to give themselves up," Dayan recalled. "Their reply was a volley of fire in which eight of our men were hit, two fatally." According to Begin, "Suddenly, we were attacked from all sides, without warning." Six of his men were also killed. When Begin refused to leave the beach voluntarily, his followers wrestled him aboard a launch to get him to the *Altalena*. Trailed by Israeli warships, the *Altalena* steamed toward Tel Aviv, where Begin's supporters were gathering in force. So was the Israeli army.

In its panicked flight, the *Altalena* came aground just off the coast of Tel Aviv, in front of the Kaete Dan hotel, which served as the headquarters for the UN as well as a watering hole for diplomats and foreign journalists. They stood on their balconies watching in gape-mouthed astonishment as Israeli forces strafed the stranded ship and even shot at Irgunists swimming toward the beach. The captain ran up a white flag, but Begin demanded that he take it down. "We must all perish here," he proclaimed. "The people will rebel. A new generation will come to avenge us." Then a shell struck the cargo hold, fire engulfed the *Altalena,* and the ammunition stored below began exploding. The captain gave the order to abandon the sinking vessel. Begin, who couldn't swim, was again forced into the launch, while protesting that he wanted to go down with the ship. Sixteen of his men were killed and dozens wounded. Three members of the Israeli Defense Forces were also killed.

Once ashore, Begin rushed to a radio transmitter to convey his account to the Israeli public before the government had a chance to put its stamp on it. He was terribly distraught and in no condition to make a speech. He wept and screamed. At times, he was incoherent. He called the attack "the most dreadful event in the history of our people, perhaps in the history of the world." His speech was a disaster, all the more so because he punctured the legend of mystery that had surrounded him while he was underground. He turned what might have resulted in a national outcry against Ben-Gurion into a bathetic display of self-pity. His career as a leader of an underground movement was over. He went into seclusion, a broken man. It was then that he decided to reinvent himself as a politician.

AT FIVE P.M., the three principals reconvened in Carter's small office. Sadat was still fuming from the morning meeting, insisting that he had nothing more to add. Begin suggested that they return to what he saw as the main issue, Israel's security needs in Sinai. He reminded Sadat that King Farouk, President Nasser, and President Sadat himself had each attacked Israel from Sinai. The settlements there served as vital outposts for Israel's protection.

"Never!" Sadat said adamantly. "If you do not agree to evacuate the settlements, there will be no peace."

"We will not agree to dismantle the settlements," Begin replied stonily. "The opposition in Israel will not agree to it either."

The Egyptian people genuinely long for peace, Sadat argued, but "they will never accept an encroachment on their land or sovereignty." Any remaining Israeli settlements in Sinai would be an absolute insult to Egypt, he said. "I have tried to provide a model of friendship and coexistence for the rest of the Arab world leaders to emulate. Instead, I have become the object of extreme insult from Israel, and scorn and condemnation from the other Arab leaders." He added: "I still dream of a meeting on Mount Sinai of us three leaders, representing three nations and three religious beliefs. This is still my prayer to God!"

It was a characteristic moment for the Egyptian leader. Under stress, his idealism spread its wide wings. He became emotional and took any setback extremely personally. Begin, his opposite in so many ways, became colder and more analytical, marshaling data to try to win debating points while dismissing the broader perspective that Sadat tried to place on the table. "Anyone observing the two men could not have overlooked the profound divergence in their attitudes," Weizman later recalled. "Both desired peace. But whereas Sadat wanted to take it by storm . . . Begin preferred to creep forward inch by inch. He took the dream of peace and ground it down into the fine, dry powder of details, legal clauses, and quotes from international law."

Ignoring Sadat's dream, Begin said that there were only about two thousand Israelis in thirteen settlements in Sinai—so why couldn't Sadat just convince the Egyptian people to accept them as permanent residents who posed no military threat to Egypt and no infringement of their sovereignty?

Sadat had had enough. He said he saw no reason for the talks to continue. He stood and stared sternly at Carter.

Carter was desperate. He had gambled his career on Camp David, but more than that, he had placed a bet on human nature. He firmly believed that men of goodwill, representing the interests of their people and with history looking over their shoulders, would acknowledge that the benefits of peace were so great that they must find a way to achieve it. But war makes its own compelling argument. Hatred is so much easier than reconciliation; no sacrifices or compromises are required. War holds out the promise of victory, and with it the enticing prospect of redemption from the humiliation of the past. Revenge always wants to be satisfied before peace can come to the table. There is a natural human tendency to inflict on others the indignity one has had to endure. Israel and the Arab world were two anguished cultures that could only be healed by making peace with each other; but their wounds preoccupied them. The anger and willful misunderstanding that had characterized the talks so far were the language of war, not peace.

Carter temporized. He outlined areas of agreement, but there were few to point to. He warned that failure at Camp David could lead to a world war. He said he couldn't believe that the Israeli people would prefer settlements in Sinai to peace with Egypt. He suggested to Begin that, if he couldn't bring himself to make the sacrifice, he should go to the Knesset and ask that they make the decision about dismantling the settlements. "I'm sure you will get an overwhelming majority," he said.

The Israeli people would never accept it, Begin replied; moreover, it would spell the end of his government. He would be willing to accept the consequences if he believed that it was the right thing to do, but he absolutely did not believe it.

By now both Begin and Sadat were heading toward the door. Carter physically blocked their path. He begged them for one more day so that he could devise a compromise. Begin agreed. Carter looked at Sadat, who finally nodded his head. Then the two men left without speaking to each other.

THAT EVENING the Carters had arranged a party. They had thought that by now the delegations would be hammering out the final details of an agreement, and this would be a kind of celebratory break. Bleachers were erected around the helicopter landing field, and Marines conducted their famous Silent Drill—marching in close order, with bayonets on their rifles, and performing their intricate movements in total silence. The grim-faced audience in the bleachers also sat in total silence. There was a light mist in the air, which made the blades gleam as the rifles twirled. Moshe Dayan, who had written the training manual for the Israeli army, watched the display with quiet contempt. Such a display belonged in a circus, he thought, not on a military parade ground.

Since the start of the summit, the press had been shuttered miles away from the grounds. Daily press conferences were held at the American Legion Hall in nearby Thurmont, Maryland, which boasted the tenuous claim of being the "goldfish capital of the world." Hundreds of journalists had commandeered every available room in the region. ABC News had secured an entire motel, turning it into a remote bureau, complete with a blimp carrying a satellite dish several hundred feet above the scene. Each day, White House press secretary Jody Powell fed hundreds of journalists little more information than what the delegates had for breakfast and the precise times that they met. The reporters were ravenous for real news. For this one occasion, they were bused to the Camp David grounds and allowed to observe the delegates from a distance. What they saw were the three leaders with fixed expressions, not exchanging a single word, watching a military pantomime. It seemed clear that the talks had broken down.

After the drill, as the Marine Band struck up a medley of patriotic songs from the three countries, the press was ushered back to the buses. Gerald Rafshoon, Carter's media adviser, was checking to make sure everyone was aboard, but he discovered that Barbara Walters was missing. She was finally located, lurking in the ladies' room.

When the press departed, there was a reception with a string quartet for the delegates. The Carters had made a great effort to get the Egyptians and the Israelis to mingle. A buffet was spread on different tables inside Laurel Lodge and on the patio in order to encourage people to circulate. Rosalynn sat with Sadat on the low brick wall around the patio. She had noticed how forlorn he appeared, especially as the patriotic music was playing. Sadat couldn't even bring himself to mention Begin's name. "I've given so much and 'that man' acts as though I have done nothing," he told her. "I have given up all the past to start anew, but 'that man' will not let go of the past." Rosalynn tried to reassure him, reminding him that the whole world admired his courage and was watching Camp David hoping for a breakthrough. She added that sometimes when healing words such as his are said it takes a little time for them to soak in. Sadat was inconsolable. "I would do anything to bring peace to our two countries," he said. "But I feel it is no use."

Carter and his top advisers met with the Egyptian delegation later that evening. It was clear that they were on the verge of leaving. "I know you are all very discouraged," Carter said. The Sinai settlements seemed to be an insurmountable issue. "Our position is that they are illegal and should be removed," he continued. "On this, your views and ours are the same." He admitted that he did not have a solution. He only wanted a little more time.

"My good friend Jimmy, we have already had three long sessions," Sadat replied. "I cannot yield conquered land to Israel, and if sovereignty is to mean anything to Egyptians, all the Israelis must leave our territory. That man Begin is not saying anything that he might not have said prior to my Jerusalem initiative." Sadat pointed out numerous areas where he had been willing to compromise, whereas Begin "haggles over every word, and is making his withdrawal conditional on keeping land. Begin is not ready for peace."

Carter defended Begin as "a tough and honest man." He analyzed the situation from Begin's perspective. "His present control over Sinai was derived from wars which Israel did not start," Carter observed. He reminded the Egyptians of America's special relationship with Israel and stressed that the Israelis really did want peace.

Sadat, annoyed, lit his pipe and exhaled a river of smoke from his nostrils. "It was I who made the peace initiative," he said. "If Begin had really desired peace, we would have had it for some time now." He said he was willing to be flexible, but not on Sinai. "I must have also a resolution of the West Bank and Gaza," he added.

As the Americans auditioned various ideas for the discouraged Egyptians, Carter mentioned the 1972 Shanghai Communiqué, a famous document in the annals of diplomacy, which was crafted by Henry Kissinger, Richard Nixon's national security advisor at the time, and Chou En-lai, the Chinese prime minister. Both the U.S. and China had sought to normalize relations, but they could not find a way to agree on the language that would resolve the central issue, which was China's claim to Taiwan, an American ally. Finally, Kissinger resorted to what he later termed "constructive ambiguity," by inserting the sentence "The United States acknowledges that all Chinese on either side of the Taiwan Strait maintain there is but one China and that Taiwan is a province of China," but avoiding the question of who should govern it. The agreement opened the way for China and the U.S. to overcome decades of hostility. As Carter explained it to the Egyptians, "We both agreed that there was one China, but we did not destroy the agreement by trying to define 'one China' too specifically."

Carter might have employed another famous example of constructive ambiguity with which the delegates were more familiar: UN Resolution 242. The language that had been proposed by the Arab states and the Soviet Union demanded that Israel withdraw from "*all* the territories occupied during the hostilities of June 1967." That was modified to read as just "*the* territories." To further fudge the matter, the definite article was finally removed from the English-language version of the text but was retained in the French version. Since both were official UN documents, the Arabs could say that the resolution bound Israel to withdraw from the lands it had conquered and Israel could say that it agreed to withdraw from some, while not committing to which ones. Of course, finally resolving that ambiguity was one reason for the summit at Camp David.

"Stalemate here would just provide an opportunity for the most radical elements to take over in the Middle East," Carter warned as the meeting broke up. "We simply must find a formula that Egypt and Israel can accept. If you give me a chance, I don't intend to fail."

It was one in the morning when Carter came to bed. For all practical purposes, the summit was over, he admitted to Rosalynn. "There must be a way," he said, again and again. "We haven't found it yet, but there must be a way."

Rosalynn watched him struggle. "When Jimmy's pondering, he gets quiet," she noted in her memoirs, "and there's a vein in his temple that I can see pounding. Tonight it was pounding."

ROSALYNN HAD KNOWN Jimmy all her life; she was actually born in the house next door to his, although Jimmy's family moved to a farm three miles away while she was still a baby. Her father, Edgar Smith, an auto mechanic, a handsome man with dark, curly hair and a prominent dimpled chin, had met Rosalynn's mother, Allie Murray, a strikingly lovely girl, when she was still in high school and he was driving the school bus. They didn't marry until Allie finished college, getting a teacher's diploma from Georgia State College for Women. Eleanor Rosalynn Smith was born the next year, on August 18, 1927. Except for her three younger siblings,

Rosalynn grew up very much alone. There was no movie theater or library in Plains, which had a population of about six hundred and no other girls her age. Rosalynn spent much of her time playing dolls, sewing, reading, and cutting paper dolls out of the Sears, Roebuck catalog.

Her parents were romantic in a way that other adults in Plains didn't seem to be. When Edgar came back from working at his garage, he would whirl Allie around the kitchen and kiss her. Other parents didn't act that way. Edgar was strict with the children, however, and they lived in awe of him. Rosalynn responded by being perfect. Her greatest infraction was "running away"—crossing the street to play with friends. Edgar would spank her and then command her not to cry. She would hold her emotions in check until she got to the outdoor privy so she could weep unseen. She couldn't understand why he wouldn't let her cry. She supposed he only wanted her to be strong, but she also thought that maybe he didn't really love her. "Just having these thoughts troubled me and gave me a guilty conscience for years," she admitted.

In 1939, her parents allowed her to go to summer camp, the first time she had ever been away from home. When she returned, she discovered the reason she had been sent away. Her father had been in the hospital for tests. He was gravely ill. Although Edgar assured Rosalynn he was going to get better, he never did. Assuming that his suffering was because of the mean thoughts she had had about him in the past, Rosalynn did everything possible to show him how much she loved him. She brushed his hair and read the Bible and detective stories to him hour after hour, even as his face grew paler and he fought for breath. In October, he called the children to his bedside. "The time has come to tell you that I can't get well and you're going to have to look after Mother for me," he told them. "You are good children and I'm depending on you to be strong." He said that he had always wanted to go to college, but hadn't been able to. Now he instructed his wife to sell the farm if she needed money for the children's education. His greatest sorrow was that he wasn't going to be around to make sure they all had good lives and opportunities he didn't have. Once again, he commanded them not to shed tears. Afterward, Rosalynn rushed to the privy to cry and cry. "My childhood really ended at that moment," she realized. Later, critics took note of her stoicism, calling her the "Steel Magnolia," but her childhood had hardened her to the blows that life inflicted.

Most of the medical care in Sumter County was embodied in the indomitable figure of Lillian Carter, a registered nurse, who made a practice of treating both the black and the white citizens of Plains and dared anyone to tell her different. When Edgar Smith first contracted leukemia, Miss Lillian checked on him every day, and when the end came she took Rosalynn home and let her spend the night with her daughter Ruth. Rosalynn was thirteen years old.

Rosalynn's mother took in sewing to support her four children and her elderly father. Eventually she got a job as a postmistress. Rosalynn worked as a part-time shampooer in a beauty parlor. She helped as well with her two younger brothers, and her little sister, who was only four when their father died. At night, Allie would read the Bible to her children and assure them that God really did love them. Rosalynn had her doubts. She was haunted by the specter of an angry, vengeful God. She was an outstanding student, always getting As, and graduated as the class valedictorian and the May Queen. She prayed; she went to church practically every time the doors opened; she achieved everything her strict and pious father would have asked of her, except the one, most important thing—to keep him alive.

Rosalynn grew into an attractive young woman, but she was sober and unsmiling. She saw herself as ordinary and painfully shy. She had her mother's wide-set eyes and high cheekbones and her father's dimpled chin—to which was added a small scar when she fell out of a sitting-room window as a child and landed in a rose bush. Ruth Carter, who was two years younger than Rosalynn, became her best friend; and it was in Ruth's bedroom that Rosalynn fell in love with a photograph of a young man with slicked-back hair and a dark, burning gaze that seemed full of intelligence and ambition, looking "so glamorous and out of reach." It was Ruth's older brother, Jimmy. Rosalynn knew him—everybody in Plains knew everybody else—but she rarely saw him. By now she was following her father's last dictate and attending a nearby junior college, hoping to become an interior designer, and Jimmy was off at Annapolis, another universe away. The only time Rosalynn could remember speaking to him was when she bought an ice cream cone from him one summer on Main Street. The photograph in Ruth's bedroom filled her with longing. Jimmy had escaped Plains. He had what it took. Surely her father would have approved of him.

Ruth cooked up the idea of a romance between her idolized older brother and her best friend. She would call Rosalynn whenever Jimmy came home at Christmas or during summer leave, but Rosalynn was so intimidated by the boy in the photograph that she couldn't imagine what she would say to him. Finally, in the summer of 1945, the year the world war ended, Ruth invited Rosalynn to a picnic. Jimmy was there.

He teased her about the exotic way she made her sandwich, on mismatched slices of bread, using salad dressing instead of mayonnaise. He was obviously a perfectionist. After the picnic, the Carters dropped her off at her house, and she thought to herself, "That's that."

Later that afternoon, after church, she was standing with friends when a car drove up and Jimmy got out. He asked if she'd like to go to a movie—a double-date with Ruth and her boyfriend. Jimmy and Rosalynn rode in the rumble seat, and on the way home, under a full moon, he kissed her. That very night he told his mother he was going to marry Rosalynn. He was twenty; she was seventeen. They were married a year later. Jimmy presented her with a manual, called *A Navy Wife*.

Jimmy Carter, in his Navy uniform, and Rosalynn Carter, on their wedding day, July 7, 1946, in Plains, Georgia

She felt liberated the moment she left Plains, although some of their early postings were dreadful. Jimmy was often at sea, leaving Rosalynn to take care of their first child, Jack. In 1948, the year the State of Israel was created, Jimmy was accepted to submarine school in New London, Connecticut. For the first time in their married life, Jimmy had regular hours. They studied Spanish and took an art class together. When Jimmy finished sub school, they got the best news: he was being posted to the USS *Pomfret,* based in Hawaii. Rosalynn sewed aloha shirts and took hula lessons. Jimmy learned to play the ukulele and Rosalynn would dance to "My Little Grass Shack" and "Lovely Hula Hands." Another son, James Earl Carter III, called Chip, was born. Plains, thankfully, was very far away.

The submarines of the era had to surface every twenty-four hours to recharge their batteries, and during Carter's first cruise aboard the *Pomfret,* as an electronics officer, the ship ran into one of the most violent storms ever to strike the Pacific Ocean. Seven ships went down that night, and the *Pomfret* itself was so badly battered that it was reported missing. Carter was violently sick during the tempest, but he was dutifully standing his watch in the middle of the night when a gigantic wave rolled over the ship and swept him out to sea. He floundered inside the wave in utter darkness. In an instant, he had been subtracted from the world he knew and plunged into an obscure and inky grave. Suddenly he was slammed against the five-inch gun behind the conning tower, about thirty feet from where he had been standing. He held on to the cannon with everything he had. It was eerie; no one on the ship had even known he was missing. Fortunately, Rosalynn was visiting in Plains and did not hear the false report that the ship had been lost at sea.

Being a Navy wife suited Rosalynn. She enjoyed the companionship of other wives; there were always children around for her own to play with; and the postings took them to interesting places. So when Carter's father died in 1953, Rosalynn wasn't at all prepared to hear that Jimmy was quitting the Navy and they were moving back to Plains. She cried and screamed. It was the most serious argument of their marriage. She refused to talk to him on the entire drive back. If she needed to stop for the restroom, she would tell Jack, and Jack would tell his dad. When they finally pulled into Plains, Jimmy turned to her with his biggest grin and said, "We're home!" It was as if the prison doors had closed upon her and the best part of her life was over.

The first year Jimmy and Rosalynn were back in Plains there was a terrible drought; the crops failed, and their income that year was less than $200. They lived in public housing. Rosalynn took over the bookkeeping in the peanut warehouse, while Jimmy sold seed and fertilizer. The bank turned them down when Jimmy asked for a business loan. Quitting the Navy appeared to be a colossal mistake. Although they were scraping by, living on savings, they buried themselves in community work. Jimmy got involved with the Chamber of Commerce, the Hospital Authority, and the Library Board, while Rosalynn joined the PTA and the Garden Club. She was the den mother for her boys' Cub Scout pack. The next year the rains finally came and their business began to prosper.

Jimmy was seen as somewhat exotic in Plains because of his education and his spin in the Navy. He quickly took on the role of a community leader, becoming chairman of the county school board at a time when racial integration was ripping the Deep South into bitter factions. In 1962, he tried to consolidate the three white schools in the county, but the white population saw it as a prelude to school desegregation. A homemade sign was placed in front of the Carter warehouse: COONS AND CARTERS GO TOGETHER. Carter's initiative was voted down. As would be true at other times in his life, failure was a spur to Carter's ambition. On the morning of his thirty-eighth birthday, he put on his Sunday pants rather than the work clothes he normally wore to the warehouse. Rosalynn asked where he was going, and he told her he was on his way to Americus, the county seat, to place a notice in the newspaper that he would be a candidate for the state senate. He had not consulted her or anyone else. The election was fifteen days away. Rosalynn was thrilled, although she had never actually met a state senator.

South Georgia in 1962 was a brutal school for political neophytes. Sumter County, where Plains is located, was the largest in Carter's district, and he was well known there. However, Quitman County, on the Alabama state line, was ruled by a bootlegger with a reputation for disposing of his enemies in the Chattahoochee River. His name was Joe Hurst. He exercised almost total control, like a feudal lord, handing out patronage and even passing out the welfare checks for the 50 percent of the county residents who were beneficiaries. He used his fiefdom to become one of the most powerful figures in the state. For the Democratic primary, Hurst refused to set up voting booths; instead, he greeted each voter and told them how to vote—against Carter, with his clean-government agenda. Because there was no Republican candidate, the primary was tantamount to election. When one elderly couple tried to sneak their ballots into the box without Hurst's examination, he threatened to burn down their house.

Carter was leading by 70 votes until Quitman County finally announced its results: 333 voters had somehow cast 420 votes. Some of the dead had risen from their graves to cast ballots, and more than a hundred had managed to vote in alphabetical order. Carter lost the election. He contested the results, precipitating a convulsion in state politics that wasn't resolved until the moment he actually raised his hand and took the oath of office on the floor of the state senate in 1963. Joe Hurst sent Rosalynn a message that the last time people crossed him, their businesses burned down. Rosalynn was terrified. While Jimmy was in Atlanta during the legislative session, she left lights on in their house, pushed the couch against the door at night, slept with their children, and nailed the windows shut.

That year the civil rights movement arrived in Sumter County. Martin Luther King was arrested in Americus. Police beat protesters with billy clubs and shocked them with cattle prods. Hundreds of black marchers were arrested. A white student was killed in one of the demonstrations. Carter was quiet on the subject of race, although in his first substantive speech in the state senate, in his second legislative session, he denounced the thirty questions that were asked of blacks who were attempting to register to vote, which included abstruse matters of law, such as "What do the constitutions of the United States and Georgia provide regarding the suspension of the writ of habeas corpus?" and such nonsense as "How long is a piece of string?" or "How many bubbles are in a bar of soap?" His maiden speech went unreported, however.

In the summer of 1965, Carter finally had to face a moment of truth on the race issue. There was a photograph in newspapers all over the world of a mixed group of blacks and whites praying on the steps of the First Baptist Church in Americus while the pastor stood over them with a riot gun and a bando-lier of bullets across his chest, barring entry. Soon after that, a resolution was introduced in the Plains Baptist Church, where Carter was a deacon, to exclude "Negroes and other agitators." Jimmy and Rosalynn were in Atlanta for a wedding, and she begged Jimmy not to return for the vote in the church. She was exhausted by the controversies and the boycotts of their business; moreover, Jimmy was contemplating a run for the U.S. Congress, and racial politics could easily sink him. Jimmy insisted on speaking against the measure, however. When the vote was taken, the ban passed overwhelmingly. Only six parishioners voted against it—five members of the Carter family and a deaf man who may not have understood what he was voting for.

Carter announced that he was running for the U.S. House of Representatives against Howard "Bo" Callaway, the Repub-lican incumbent, who was a West Point graduate and the heir to a textile fortune. Callaway was popular in the state and had strong support from the extreme-right-wing John Birch Soci-ety. However, when the Democratic candidate for governor suffered a heart attack and withdrew from the race, Callaway decided to run for that office instead, leaving Carter with only token opposition for the congressional seat. Carter tried to enlist another candidate to run against Callaway in order to keep the statehouse from going Republican for the first time in a century, but finally decided to do it himself. With only three months before the primary, he dropped out of the congressio-nal race he was nearly certain to win and entered the guberna-torial Democratic primary. His main opponents were a former governor, Ellis Arnall, thought to be too liberal to beat Calla-way, and the segregationist and archconservative Lester Maddox. Rosalynn was extremely unhappy with Jimmy's decision. It meant that they would not be moving to Washington, which she dreamed of, and that they would also be spending a large portion of their savings on a race that was going to be very difficult to win.

Carter recruited his family and a small circle of friends to travel the state and campaign for him. That included Rosalynn, who was shy and fearful of speaking in public, but she gamely drove all across the state asking people for their vote, sometimes a degrading or humiliating experience. She hated standing in front of Kmarts, for instance, which did not allow soliciting, and she suffered the indignity of being run off from nearly every Kmart in the state. In one small Georgia town she handed a brochure to a man who was standing in the doorway of a shoe shop, chewing tobacco. Rosalynn asked him to vote for her husband. The man responded by spitting on her.

Carter lost the primary by twenty thousand votes. Maddox went on to win a runoff with Arnall and then faced Callaway in the general election. Because of a write-in campaign for Arnall, neither man received a plurality, and under Georgia law the race was decided by the predominately Democratic General Assembly. Maddox became the new governor. Carter had dropped 22 pounds (down to 130), and was deeply in debt. One month later, he started campaigning for the office again.

He roamed the state, meeting people, recording their names on a pocket tape recorder, along with some personal details, such as their job, political philosophy, and likelihood of being a contributor or a worker in the campaign. He kept a running tally of how many hands he shook—600,000 by the end of the campaign. To get the addresses of people he came in contact with he bought every telephone book in Georgia—

more than 150—and then Rosalynn followed up with a thank-you note. She kept his files and clipped newspaper articles for him. To save money, he stayed in the homes of his support-ers. For the last two years of his second run he was away from home nearly every night.

As Rosalynn barnstormed through Georgia, she got an intimate education about the problems that her fellow citizens faced. One day at four thirty in the morning, she was standing in front of a cotton mill, waiting for the shift change, when a woman came out, her hair and sweater covered in lint from her labor during the night. Rosalynn asked if she was going home to bed. The woman said she might get a nap, but she had a mentally retarded child at home, and the expenses were more than her husband's income so she had to work nights to make up the difference. That moment became a turning point for Rosalynn. When she realized that Jimmy was com-ing to the same town later that day, she stood in line to meet him. He reached for her hand before he even realized who she was. "I want to know what you are going to do about mental health when you are governor," she said. The startled Carter replied, "We're going to have the best mental health system in the country, and I'm going to put you in charge of it."

On election day, 1970, Carter won 60 percent of the vote. Maddox, unable to succeed himself as governor, was elected lieutenant governor, with 73.5 percent of the vote.

Carter was seen as a rising figure in Democratic politics, but very few people understood the full scope of his ambition. He gained a reputation as a progressive governor, despite a contentious relationship with the Georgia legislature. Within two years of his election to the statehouse, he decided he would run for president. He would be out of office in 1974, which meant that he could run full-time for the following two years.

Once again, Rosalynn was making the speeches she hated so much. By the end of the presidential campaign she had visited forty-two states, and more than a hundred communities in Iowa alone. On January 20, 1977, on an icy morning in Washington, D.C., her husband was inaugurated as the thirty-ninth president of the United States, and Rosalynn Carter, the lonely little girl from Plains, became first lady. While Jimmy was taking the oath, their predecessors, Gerald and Betty Ford, stood beside them—a ritual of democracy that is perhaps the most powerful testament to the tradition of nonviolent social change. At that very moment, the closets of the White House were being emptied of the Fords' belongings and the Carters' clothes hung there instead.

Rosalynn proved to be an activist first lady, sponsoring significant legislation for mental health and the elderly, and upsetting many Americans by unapologetically sitting in on cabinet meetings. Those close to the president knew that she was always his most influential adviser, and they came to appreciate her political savvy. In 1979, even as Carter's own poll numbers plummeted, Rosalynn topped Mother Teresa in Gallup's poll for the most admired woman in the world.

Camp David had been her idea. However it turned out, she would bear both credit and responsibility.

FOREIGN MINISTER KAMEL WAS unable to sleep. He sat on the edge of his bunk talking to his roommate, Boutros Boutros-Ghali, until late at night. Camp David was a strange place to conduct diplomacy, they agreed. They were used to wearing dark suits and meeting in the marbled offices of state, and here they were in the woods in their pajamas. The main problem for the Egyptians, however, was not the setting but their leader. Whenever they met, Sadat sat silently, inscrutably puffing on his pipe, as his delegation fumed. It didn't seem to trouble him that Carter was not interested in a single principle embodied in the Egyptian project. "And now look where we are!" Kamel exclaimed in his bunk, "Here we have the United States president, without equivocation or ambiguity, coming up with the idea of concluding a strategic American-Egyptian-Israeli alliance, while Sadat does not utter a single word! What can be the matter with him?"

"Maybe he was only absent-minded or tired," Boutros-Ghali responded. He added, "It could be that Carter's aim was to test us by throwing out ideas as trial balloons."

"Didn't you notice Carter's sly remark to Tohamy, to the effect that rumors had it that President Sadat was moderate while his assistants were hard-liners? He means us, of course."

"Anyway, today's meeting was merely preparatory," Boutros-Ghali said. "We shan't know the conclusions they have reached until they finalize their project and submit it to us—then we shall see. So stop worrying until then and let's get some sleep—it's almost dawn!"

Day Four

Zbigniew Brzezinski and Cyrus Vance

AT EIGHT THIRTY A.M., the American team met with Carter and Rosalynn in the president's cabin. They were all deeply pessimistic. Carter now believed that Begin had never intended to agree to anything. The proof was his apparent joy at having Sadat's harsh proposal to hide behind. It was his alibi. When the talks failed, he could wave it in the air and say, "See, this is what they demand."

Jimmy and Rosalynn went to play tennis, but the phone at the court kept ringing with senators on the line, or his defense secretary—there were many other problems in the world demanding the president's attention. Carter asked Rosalynn to cancel the fly-fishing trip they had planned for the next morning. They had hoped to slip away for a few hours during the Jewish Sabbath, but now he had to do something to rescue the talks.

When they got back to the presidential cabin Carter learned that Sadat was preparing to leave and Begin was drawing up a list of reasons why the summit had failed. Carter had no plan except to stall. He asked Begin to meet him at two thirty that afternoon, and Sadat an hour and a half later. He was hoping that by putting Sadat off until late in the afternoon he could hold the Egyptians at Camp David for at least another day. Meantime, he invited Cy Vance to join him and Rosalynn for a drink and lunch. It was time to change tactics.

Vance was often overshadowed by the brash and imaginative national security advisor, Zbigniew Brzezinski. Vance embodied the "establishment" that Carter had run against: Yale, Wall Street, and years at the upper tier of the Washington bureaucracy, serving as secretary of the army under John F. Kennedy and deputy secretary of defense in the Lyndon Johnson administration. Where Brzezinski was an activist with a fondness for covert operations, Vance's experience during the Vietnam era had taught him the virtues of patience and diplomacy over military intervention. Brzezinski focused on the big picture, Vance on the small print. Hamilton Jordan, Carter's political strategist and later chief of staff, analyzed the role each of these men played in the administration. Brzezinski, he decided, was the bold side of Jimmy Carter—the side of him that ran for president when he was still "Jimmy Who?" That was the man who was never afraid to challenge conventional wisdom and to risk everything, just as he was doing now at Camp David. Vance was the more traditional and methodical side of Carter. He got to work before the sun came up, and he was principled to the point of priggishness. His decency earned the trust of everyone he met. According to Jordan's analysis, Brzezinksi was the thinker, Vance the doer, and Carter the decider.

So far, however, the decider had avoided putting forward an American proposal. His strategy had been to allow Sadat and Begin to talk face-to-face, expecting that they would struggle toward their own agreement, perhaps with some American nudging. That had proved to be hopelessly misguided. Carter couldn't even leave them alone together in the same room. The danger of putting forward an American proposal was that, if it failed, both sides could declare that the U.S. had tried to force an agreement on them. Now there was no alternative. "Proceed with the American plan," Carter told Vance at lunch. It had to be fair to both sides, he specified, but it also had to be a document that Sadat could accept and that Begin couldn't use as a foil. "I think we ought to get tough on the Israelis, and the time has come to let them know this," Carter added.

Carter really had nothing to say to Begin when they met, except to beg him again for greater flexibility. "You can go down in history as the great leader who brought peace." But Begin was immune to emotional appeals. He responded by once again taking out Sadat's proposal, which he kept in his breast pocket close to his heart, and fondly reciting the Egyptian positions. At this point, Carter made a critical mistake. He still had the several concessions Sadat had secretly given him to use at his discretion—points that even Sadat's own team was unaware of. Carter did not now call upon any of them, but he betrayed Sadat's confidence by revealing that the Egyptian proposal was by no means Sadat's final negotiating position.

Perhaps this was the only way to persuade Begin to put the Egyptian document back in his pocket; however, Begin now had the important knowledge that concessions had already been made without any corresponding Israeli offers. He could afford to be even more intransigent in his positions and wait to see what was put on the table.

Carter argued that since Sadat had agreed to demilitarize Sinai there would be 130 miles of empty desert between Egypt and Israel—therefore no need for any Israeli settlements to act as a buffer. Begin responded with a lengthy and, by now, wearyingly familiar diatribe about the need for retaining the settlements, but in the middle of his speech, Begin may also have slipped. "I will never personally recommend that the settlements in the Sinai be dismantled!" he exclaimed. This legalistic formulation caught Carter's ear. It was one thing to say he would never permit the settlements to be removed, another to say he would never "personally recommend" such action. Perhaps, if another party were to take responsibility, Begin might not stand in the way. It was the first tiny crack of daylight.

Begin then said that there really had to be two agreements at Camp David. The one between Israel and Egypt was important, of course. But there was a far more urgent contract that must be reached between Israel and the U.S. It would show the world that there were no important differences between the policies of the two countries. His argument was similar to the one Sadat had also been trying to make. Both sides wanted to enlist the U.S. against the other party. The implicit danger that Carter would lean in one direction or the other gave him the only real leverage he had. He wasn't about to surrender that.

"We are going to produce a comprehensive proposal for peace," Carter warned Begin. "I can see no other possibility for progress," he remarked. He intended to present it the next day.

"Mr. President, please do not put this in a proposal to us," Begin pleaded.

"I cannot let you tell me not to discuss the Israeli presence on Egyptian territory," Carter tersely responded.

The two men talked until nearly four o'clock, when Rosalynn sent in a note reminding Carter of his meeting with Sadat. As Begin was leaving, he invited the president and his wife to join him for Shabbat dinner that evening.

Carter rushed over to Sadat's cabin. As they drank sweet mint tea, Carter implored the Egyptian leader to remain at Camp David. "You promised me," Carter reminded him. Slyly using the single advantage he had, he suggested that the Egyptians and the Americans could come to an agreement, even if the Israelis weren't a part of it. Sadat eagerly agreed. "You write it," he said. "You know the issues that are important to me. I will support any reasonable document you put forth."

For the moment, the summit was saved. But Carter's role had changed. He had originally cast himself as a facilitator, the person who could place Begin and Sadat in the same room and let them work out the details of an enduring peace. That idea had failed. If the summit was going to succeed, it would require a catalyst, someone with new ideas, yes, but also someone who was willing to go beyond pleading and persuading to the point of issuing threats. Carter had to be that person. Each side had to believe that it had something vital to lose, which was its standing with the United States.

MENACHEM BEGIN AND HIS WIFE, Aliza, hosted the Shabbat dinner in the Camp David movie theater, which had been converted to a banquet hall for the occasion. Gefilte fish and challah were brought in from Washington for the occasion, along with extra skullcaps.

At the head of the table Rosalynn sat between Begin and Dayan—two of the most compelling men in Israel's history. The evening started with Begin offering the blessing of the wine, saying, "Blessed are You, Lord, our God, King of the Universe, who sanctifies us with His commandments, and has been pleased with us. You have lovingly and willingly given us your holy Shabbat as an inheritance in memory of creation. The Shabbat is the first among our holy days, and a remembrance of our exodus from Egypt. Indeed, You have chosen us and made us holy among all peoples."

The tension of the last few days lifted and there was a convivial, even joyful atmosphere among the guests. Begin reminded Rosalynn that the Bible says you cannot serve God with sadness, and so he commanded everyone to sing. One of the songs was the Israeli national anthem, "Hatikvah," which means "The Hope." It had special meaning for Begin. He said that his father had sung it as he was being led to the River Bug to be drowned by the Nazis.

> *Our hope is not yet lost,*
> *The hope of two thousand years,*
> *To be a free people in our land,*
> *The land of Zion and Jerusalem.*

While Begin was translating the lyrics of one of the songs for her, Rosalynn enviously asked how many languages he knew.

He said he fluently spoke the Slavic languages, including Polish and Russian; also, German, English, Hebrew, and French. He could read Italian and used to teach Latin. He and Aliza, also a Latin scholar, liked to read Virgil aloud to each other, much as Rosalynn and Jimmy read the Bible to each other every night in Spanish.

The Begins' courtship and marriage resembled that of the Carters to a marked degree. Begin had decided to marry Aliza the moment they met, and their union was famous for its exclusiveness and fidelity. Unlike her tempestuous husband, who was often subject to fits of depression or euphoria as well as explosions of fury, Aliza was always controlled and calculating, her huge unblinking eyes behind thick tinted lenses rarely betraying any doubt of the rightness of her husband's calling, even through his years in the underground, in prison, and on the political fringe. Despite her chronic asthma she smoked incessantly, and frequently resorted to the inhaler in her purse. If Carter had been hoping that Aliza would moderate her husband's views, he miscalculated. She was known by the Israeli delegation to be a staunch ideologue.

For three decades before Begin became prime minister the couple lived in a rent-controlled, three-room ground-floor flat in north Tel Aviv, on an income of about five hundred dollars a month. While they were raising their three children, the couple slept on a fold-out couch in the living room. Unlike the wives of previous prime ministers, who sometimes sought power for themselves, Aliza strained to keep out of the public eye. She made her own clothes and loved to cook. Even when her husband was prime minister, she insisted on riding the public bus whenever she traveled between Jerusalem and Tel Aviv. Such austerity was in blatant contrast to many high-ranking politi-

Aliza and Menachem Begin on their wedding day, May 30, 1939, in Truskawiec

cal figures, who lived luxuriously, often benefiting from bribes and favors. Indeed, the election that brought Begin to power was triggered by the downfall of Yitzhak Rabin, the previous prime minister, whose wife was charged with maintaining an illegal bank account in the U.S. Begin's scrupulousness, by comparison, was legendary. In 1977, when he first traveled to Washington to meet Carter, he had only two suits to his name, both of them a decade old, and way too large for him after the weight he lost following his heart attack. His aide Yechiel Kadishai insisted that he get new suits for the trip, but when another of his aides told him what a suit would cost, Begin balked. "I can't afford that!" he exclaimed. "Ask if I can pay it on time."

Kadishai told him the store was intending to give him the suits.

"Absolutely not!" Begin cried. He finally went to Washington with two new suits that he paid for on credit.

Moshe Dayan's single eye was on Rosalynn's side, so she spent most of the evening talking to him. His hearing was poor, and unless he leaned toward his companion he was likely to drift into himself. Despite Dayan's reputation for bluntness and pessimism, Rosalynn found him charming, in part because he flattered her husband. He said that he had been preparing for this summit for thirty years, having been involved in every negotiation since the founding of the State of Israel, but in all that time there had not been a single instance when Middle East countries were actually negotiating for peace. This meeting would never have happened, he said, without Jimmy Carter. He recalled that he had recently seen Rosalynn on television saying, "Jimmy is a fighter and you won't see him giving up." Dayan offered, "If you want me to, or need me to, I can testify to that!" Such a statement would be an incalculable asset for the Carter reelection campaign, especially among American Jews, who had always been leery of the Baptist from the Deep South. Rosalynn replied that Jimmy was always ready to tackle tough issues and never worried about the consequences of his actions, such as whether he could be reelected.

"Oh, he'll be reelected," Dayan assured her.

DAYAN WAS NOT just a hero, he was a riddle, his complexity holding him apart from serious emotional relationships, even with his children. "He was a man made for labyrinths," his often estranged daughter Yael summed up. It was as if behind his black eye patch there was not a ruined empty socket but some ghastly secret he could never share. His rise through the Israeli military ranks was aided by his relationship with David Ben-Gurion, who noted his "almost insane daring balanced by profound tactical and strategic judgment." Dayan was a lodestar; his arrogant self-assurance gave Israelis a sense of relief. They had come to believe that he was unbeatable; nothing bad would happen so long as Dayan was at hand.

Throughout his life, women offered themselves to him, drawn by his fame and mystery. One woman who fell in love with him was the wife of a military officer who was a childhood friend of Dayan's. The officer discovered the affair and wrote to Ben-Gurion, demanding that he publicly distance himself from his protégé. Ben-Gurion responded with the story of Bathsheba, the beautiful wife of one of King David's officers, Uriah the Hittite. King David impregnated her, and then to cover his sin, he sent her husband to the front lines, where he was killed. The message seemed to be that there were some people so important to the Israeli nation that such matters must be overlooked. There was also a hint of a threat that the cuckolded husband might suffer for making such a complaint.

From his birth, Moshe Dayan seemed destined to become the living embodiment of the Israeli experience. His parents had immigrated to Palestine when it was still part of the Ottoman Empire. Moshe's father, Shmuel, a horse-cart peddler from Ukraine, arrived in 1908, and his mother, Dvora, the daughter of a lumber merchant from Kiev, five years later. They married and helped start the very first kibbutz in their new country. It

Aliza Begin, Jimmy Carter, Menachem Begin, and Rosalynn Carter
at a Shabbat dinner hosted by the Israelis

was imagined as a communal workers' paradise, where everything was owned collectively, all the work was shared, and even
the children were raised communally, in separate housing
from their parents. In 1915, Moshe became the very first child
actually born in the kibbutz, which added to the symbolic
weight that would accrue around his life.

When Shmuel Dayan became discontented with the kibbutz system, he moved his family to another experimental
farming cooperative, called a *moshav*—it means settlement—
once again the first in the country, the prototype of the hundreds that would follow. The settlement was called Nahalal; it
was in the Jezreel Valley, near Nazareth.

Although Shmuel taught his children to think of Arabs
as shiftless marauders who were violent by nature, Moshe
mingled with other boys in Arab villages and Bedouin camps,
absorbing their language and customs. "From my boyhood

days, I have found it easy to get along with Arabs," he would later boast. At the age of fourteen, Moshe was initiated into the outlawed Jewish defense organization, Haganah, created to protect settlers in isolated communities. He patrolled the fields, driving away goats belonging to the Arabs that had trespassed on settlement areas. As he grew older, relations between the Jewish pioneers and the native Palestinians grew increasingly tense and violent. In 1932, Arab terrorists threw a bomb into the hut of Dayan's neighbor, killing an eight-year-old boy, a harbinger of what was to come.

Two years later, the settlers in Nahalal cultivated a parcel of land that had been purchased from Arabs by the Jewish National Fund. A Bedouin tribe had been using the area for grazing, and when Jews arrived to turn the field, the Arabs gathered on a hilltop and sullenly watched. Then stones began to fly. A plowman was struck. The settlers fought back. Neighbors on both sides joined in the fray; meantime, Dayan defiantly continued sowing seeds as rocks flew overhead. Suddenly, when he got to the top of a rise, he was clubbed into unconsciousness. He was taken by horseback to a hospital in Jerusalem to convalesce. He returned to Nahalal with a scar on his head but no bitterness toward the dispossessed Arabs. "I could understand their feelings, but I could not assuage them," he writes. "They had been pasturing their flocks on other people's land, and watering them at other people's springs, for generations. But the land then had been untilled, untended, and misused for grazing because it had fallen into disuse. It was ours now."

Open revolt by Palestinian Arabs against mass Jewish immigration started in 1936. Several hundred Jews were killed. The British authorities responded by killing, wounding, or imprisoning more than 10 percent of the adult Arab males in

Palestine. Moshe joined the Jewish Settlement Police Force, working with the British Army to protect an oil pipeline that was a frequent target of Arab saboteurs. This experience taught him the futility of regular troops trying to deal with guerrillas who knew the terrain and easily disappeared into the local population. "It became clear to me that the only way to fight them was to seize the initiative, attack them in their bases, and surprise them when they were on the move," he writes. These were tactics that he would use to devastating effect.

At the outbreak of the Second World War, Dayan was recruited into a unit of the British Army that was preparing for an invasion of Syria, then occupied by the Vichy French. His task was to seize the bridges on the coastal highway to Beirut before the French could blow them up. His patrol came under machine-gun fire while attempting to capture a police station, which turned out to be a regional headquarters for Vichy forces. Dayan stormed the building by himself and tossed a hand grenade through the window, silencing the machine gun. He and his men then took control of the station. When French reinforcements were drawn to the battle, Dayan went up on the roof with the captured machine gun. As he was scanning the landscape to see where the shooting was coming from, a bullet struck his field glasses, shattering the lens and the casing and driving bits of glass and metal into his left eye and socket bones. It was another twelve hours before the Allied troops reached the police station and Dayan was driven back to a hospital in Haifa. Dayan endured the agony with his customary stoicism. An Arab scout named Rashid held his hand throughout the ordeal.

"Who will hire a one-eyed man?" he asked despairingly, when his wife announced she was pregnant with their second child. "I can't support my family." But his reputation as a soldier overcame his disability. He was instantly, universally recognizable, with his round, balding head, and the piratical eye patch. He became an emblem of Israel itself—arrogant, blunt, visibly wounded but undaunted.

DURING THE 1948 WAR, two hundred thousand Palestinian refugees had taken refuge in the Gaza Strip, a narrow ribbon of land twenty-five miles long and only seven miles wide at its widest point, which lies along the Mediterranean Sea at the southern end of Israel. Gaza was an administrative capital of the ancient Egyptian empire and a stop on the caravan route to Syria. The Philistines—thought by most scholars to be the ancestors of today's Palestinians*—conquered the territory in the twelfth century BCE. God seemed to have taken a special dislike to the people and to the land that they occupied. "Gaza shall be forsaken," Yahweh warns in the Old Testament. "I will leave you to perish without an inhabitant!" But whenever he was angry with the Jews, God handed them over to the Philistines. Despite the Lord's partiality to the Israelites, the Philistines had a technological advantage. They had discovered iron, and the Israelites were still in the Bronze Age.

But then, among the Jews there arose a champion who terrorized the Philistines with his bare hands. His name was Samson. He was a kind of monster. In rabbinical literature, he was said to be so mighty he could rub mountains together in the palms of his hands. He married a Philistine woman, but

---

* In Arabic, the Philistines are called "ancient Palestinians" (*filistini qadim*).

then murdered his wedding guests, burned their fields, and slaughtered an army of a thousand Philistines with the jawbone of an ass.

Samson used to visit the whores of Gaza. One night, the Philistines locked the gates of the city, thinking to trap him after his carousal, but at midnight he ripped up the massive gates and carried them away on his immense shoulders. Another Philistine woman named Delilah, from the Valley of Sorek, coaxed him into disclosing the secret of his physical powers. He confided that he was a Nazirite, a kind of Jewish monk, who is commanded never to cut his hair. "If I am shaved, my strength will leave me, and I shall grow weaker and be like anyone else," he confessed. Delilah, who had contracted for eleven hundred pieces of silver from the Philistine rulers to betray her lover's secret, cut off seven locks of his hair while he was sleeping. When he awakened, the spirit of the Lord had left him, and he became an ordinary man. The Philistines gouged out his eyes and put him to work as a draft animal in a gristmill in Gaza.

The Philistines cheered their own god, Dagon, for this wonderful turn in their fortunes. To celebrate, they dragged the blinded Samson into a large stadium before an audience of three thousand people. Samson prayed to God to restore his strength one last time, and with a final exertion he pulled down the pillars of the building, killing the entire host. "Those he killed by his dying were more than those he had killed during his lifetime," the Bible notes approvingly.

In the minds of the Palestinians who suffered Moshe Dayan's wrath, he was a kind of modern-day Samson, a role he readily embraced. He, too, was a famous womanizer and even partially eyeless. Physically, Dayan was not imposing; he was of modest height with a wiry frame; but he noted in one of his memoirs, *Living with the Bible,* an account of his obsession with biblical archeology, "The greatness of Samson lay not only in his physical strength, but in the spirit of freedom that flamed in his breast and inspired him to rise up against the enslavers of his nation." Like Samson, Dayan evinced a quality of remorselessness that was woven into the myth of his invulnerability.

After the 1948 war, Dayan was put in charge of the Southern Command of the Israeli army. "I would leave early in the morning for my headquarters in the south," he writes, "and as I drove down from the cold mountains, crossed Delilah's Valley of Sorek, and reached the coastal belt, I always had the feeling that I had come to another land. It was a land of springtime every day of the year. . . . No wonder Samson loved to walk in the land of the Philistines."

The armistice that ended Israel's War of Independence left Egypt in control of the Gaza Strip. A single furrow in the sand made by a tractor plow marked the border. Dayan would stand beside the furrow and survey the mud huts of the refugees, many of whom had been driven from their former homes by his forces. The squalid, crowded camps, swarming with schoolchildren, looked to him like anthills. "Thousands of youngsters, the boys in blue, the girls in black, poured out like a swollen river, branched into the alleys, and were absorbed by the slums," he writes. At times, refugees would slip into Israel to harvest crops they had left behind or graze their flocks. Some came for revenge, planting bombs or attacking Israelis. The official Israeli army policy was to shoot any Arab who strayed into the territory Israel now claimed.

"We shoot from among the 200,000 hungry Arabs who cross the line—will this stand up to moral scrutiny?" Dayan asked himself. "Arabs cross to collect the grain that they left in the abandoned villages and we set mines for them and they go back without an arm or a leg." Perhaps it wasn't moral, he concluded, "but I know no other method of guarding the borders. If the Arab shepherds and harvesters are allowed to cross the borders, then tomorrow the State of Israel will have no borders."

Dayan's philosophical excuses masked an avidity for killing. He initiated retaliatory raids as a form of collective punishment. In February 1955, when a team of Egyptian intelligence scouts slipped into Israel to reconnoiter military facilities and indiscriminately killed an Israeli cyclist, Dayan, now the military chief of staff, sent two companies of paratroopers into Gaza to attack an Egyptian military post. They massacred the Egyptians in their barracks. A truck carrying reinforcements was rocketed and set afire, burning the troops alive. Forty Egyptians were killed, and eight Israelis. It was the bloodiest clash since the 1948 war, and it would cause Nasser to consider how to respond. In September, he concluded a massive Soviet arms deal with Czechoslovakia. From now on, he said, invoking the immemorial tradition in the Middle East, it would be "an eye for an eye."

That suited Dayan. His strategy was to provoke Nasser into a counterstrike that would give Israel the excuse to wage war before Egypt could put new Soviet weapons to use. After a series of skirmishes along the border, including Egyptian mortar fire toward a kibbutz, Dayan turned the army loose on the Gaza Strip, shelling the marketplace and homes and even a hospital. Fifty-eight civilians, including thirty-three women and thirteen children, were killed; four Egyptian soldiers were also killed.

Under pressure from the UN, Ben-Gurion directed Dayan to halt the border patrols and pull back from the armistice line. Dayan reluctantly obeyed, but in a bitter meeting with his mentor, Dayan told the prime minister that a show of weakness would only encourage the Arab terrorists. Indeed, the Egyptians retaliated with suicide squads, including one that attacked a synagogue near Tel Aviv, where five children were murdered. Although the war Dayan sought eluded him, the inescapable moral calculus of terror had taken hold, as each side cloaked itself in righteousness, allowing blood to flow without discrimination or pity.

One of the victims was Roy Rotenberg, a security officer for the kibbutz Nahal Oz, the closest village to the border of the Gaza Strip. Dayan had met Rotenberg during the siege of Gaza and had been impressed by the charming young man with bright blue eyes. Only a few days after that meeting, Rotenberg spotted some Arabs who were pasturing their flocks in the fields that had been commandeered by the kibbutz. He got on his horse to drive them away, but he was shot, and then his body was dragged across the border. His mutilated corpse was later given to UN soldiers, who returned it to the kibbutz for burial.

Dayan spoke at Rotenberg's graveside. His eulogy became a defiant anthem for the State of Israel as well as a candid and unvarnished lament for the tragedy that encompassed both sides. "Yesterday morning Roy was murdered," Dayan said.

The morning stillness so dazzled him that he did not see those lying in wait for him on the furrow line. Let us not cast blame on his murderers today. It is pointless to mention their deep-seated hatred of us. For eight years they have been sitting in Gaza refugee camps while before their eyes we have been making the land and villages where they and their forefathers had lived our own.

It is not from the Arabs in Gaza that we should demand Roy's blood, but from ourselves. How we shut our eyes to a sober observation of our fate, to the sight of our generation's mission in all its cruelty. Have we indeed forgotten that this young group in Nahal Oz carry on their shoulders—like Samson of old—the heavy "Gates of Gaza"—and that behind those gates live hundreds of thousands of hate-ridden people who pray that we be weakened so that they may then tear us apart . . . ?

We are the biblical generation of the settlement, following the Joshua conquest, and the helmet and the sword are essential requirements. Our children will have no life if we do not dig shelters, and without barbed wire and a machine gun we will not be able to pave roads or drill for water. Millions of Jews who were annihilated without having had a country look to us from the ashes of Israeli history, commanding us to settle and build a land for our people. But beyond the furrow border, a sea of hatred and vengeance swells, waiting for the day that calm will dull our vigilance, the day that we listen to ambassadors of scheming hypocrisy who call on us to lay down our arms. . . .

This is the choice of our lives—to be prepared and armed, strong and resolute or to let the sword fall from our fist and our lives be cut down. Roy Rotenberg, the blond, slender young man who left Tel Aviv to build his home at the gates of Gaza and serve as our bulwark, Roy—the light in his heart blinded him to the gleam

of the knife, the longing for peace deafened him to the
sound of lurking murder; alas, the gates of Gaza were too
heavy for him and they prevailed.

ON JULY 26, 1956, four years after the Egyptian military
overthrew the king, President Gamal Abdel Nasser stood in a
square in Alexandria, a quarter of a million people at his feet.
His speech was being broadcast all over Egypt and the Arab
world, to the millions captivated by Nasser's vision of Arab
unity and rebirth. Through diplomacy, Nasser had already
persuaded the British to abandon their occupation of Egypt,
meaning that his country would soon be free of foreign domination for the first time since the brief interval in the sixth
century BCE when Egyptians overthrew their Persian occupiers.

The phased departure of the eighty thousand British troops
stationed along the canal had come as a great blow to Israel,
which depended on them to act as a barrier against Egyptian
aggression. Nasser was now taking an even more consequential step. "The Suez Canal was dug by the efforts of the sons
of Egypt—120,000 Egyptians died in the process," Nasser
exhorted the crowd.* "Today, O citizens, we declare that our
property has been returned to us. We are realizing our glory
and our grandeur." As of that moment, he announced, he was
nationalizing the Suez Canal. "And it will be run by Egyptians!
Egyptians! Egyptians!"

This stunning action catapulted Nasser into being the hero
of the developing world, a leader with a following that knew

---

* The Suez Canal Company claimed that the number of Egyptian workers who
died was 1,390. Neff, *Warriors at Suez*, p. 268.

no borders. Meanwhile, as Britain and France were recovering from their shock, they started plotting how to seize control of the canal. It was not just Suez that was at stake, it was their status as Great Powers. Although Britain had already lost India and was leaving Egypt, it still ruled over thirty-five colonies, including half of Africa. France had nearly as many—including, most importantly, Algeria, which was falling dangerously under the sway of the charismatic Nasser and his dream of Arab nationalism. In addition, most of the oil going to Britain and France came through the canal; a cutoff could bring their economies to the point of collapse. The fact that one man had his finger on the pinch point of Western power was an earthshaking revelation. Britain and France were suddenly more vulnerable than their colonies; the world order seemed to have been completely upended.

Two months after the nationalization of the canal, Dayan and an Israeli delegation flew to Paris to meet secretly with French officials, who invited the Israelis to be their partner in toppling Nasser and gaining control of the canal. If Israel agreed, the French were certain Britain would join in as well. The only purpose Israel actually served in this plan was to offer a pretext for the two Great Powers to enter a war they didn't want to be seen as starting. The scheme was for the Israelis to capture Sinai, which would give the British and the French an excuse to take over the canal, ostensibly to protect it. The French called their scheme Operation Musketeer, after Alexander Dumas's famous novel, *The Three Musketeers*.

Ben-Gurion, the indomitable prime minister, was short and stocky, with intense dark eyes and tufts of white hair that spread from the sides of his head like pigeon wings. He was suspicious of the plan and insisted that the British commit themselves on paper, not just through vague assurances offered through French intermediaries. On October 21, days before the war was scheduled to commence, Dayan and Ben-Gurion returned to France for more talks. On the flight, Dayan observed the prime minister buried in a volume by Procopius, the sixth-century Palestinian historian. Ben-Gurion excitedly called his aides over and pointed to a passage in which the author mentions a Jewish mini-kingdom in the Red Sea region called the "isle of Yotvat"—an ancient Hebrew name for Tiran, one of a pair of small islands at the mouth of the Gulf of Aqaba. That would become a justification for Ben-Gurion's assertion that Sinai never belonged to Egypt at all—it was once a part of historic Israel, and it must be again.

The Israelis landed at an obscure airstrip southwest of Paris, where they were shuttled to a small private villa in Sèvres, on the outskirts of the capital. There they met with top French officials, including Prime Minister Guy Mollet. Ben-Gurion, who had seemed so reluctant at first to get involved in the conspiracy, now shocked his French counterparts by proposing what he termed a comprehensive solution to the Middle East's problems. It amounted to an entirely new map of the region, one in which Israel would expand its territory significantly and shed the troublesome Palestinian refugees by sending them across the River Jordan. Israel would then annex the West Bank, while British-dominated Iraq would gobble up the remainder of the Kingdom of Jordan. Southern Lebanon would also be folded into Israel, and the predominantly Muslim parts would be handed over to Syria. What remained of Lebanon would become a Christian state. Finally, Israel would also take over the Sinai Peninsula. In this manner, the three musketeers would not only control the canal, they would dominate the Middle East long into the future. The French were cool to Ben-Gurion's scheme, possibly because it had little more to offer them. The canal was enough.

That evening the snappish and disdainful British foreign minister, Selwyn Lloyd, arrived. The contempt the British minister felt for Jews was clear, but in Dayan's opinion it was outweighed by Israel's opportunity to forge an alliance, even a clandestine one, with two such powerful nations. At first Lloyd and his officials sat in a separate room, getting briefed by the French and relaying suggestions to the Israelis—all in the effort of preserving the sham that they were not in collusion. Lloyd even proposed that, during the war itself, the British would indiscriminately bomb both Israeli and Egyptian forces on either side of the canal in order to give the appearance of strict impartiality. One can imagine the Israelis' reaction.

Within a few hours the British deigned to meet face-to-face with the other parties. Lloyd conceded that the Egyptians had already agreed to allow international supervision of the operation of the canal and had even offered guarantees to keep it open. But that was not enough. Nasser had to be taken down. To preserve Britain's precious standing in the world, however, Lloyd required Israel to commit a "real act of war" against Egypt in order to provide moral cover for the Anglo-French invasion.

Dayan offered a plan for a limited raid into Sinai, followed by a paratroop drop behind Egyptian lines, which would be seen as an attempt to seize the canal. The British and the French would then meet, pretend to discuss the matter, and then demand that both sides withdraw their troops ten miles from the canal area. The Israelis would make a show of accepting the proposal while the Egyptians would necessarily reject any ultimatum to withdraw from their own territory. Thereupon, the British and the French would begin their bombing campaign, wiping out the Egyptian Air Force as a prelude to a larger war followed by the overthrow of Nasser and the installation of a puppet government in Cairo. With some modifications, the three leaders agreed to Dayan's proposal. D-day was scheduled for October 29, at five p.m.

That day, a curfew was abruptly imposed on Arabs living inside Israel. Half an hour before it went into effect, the mayor of the village of Kafr Qasim, near Tel Aviv, protested that many of his citizens were out in the fields or working in neighboring towns and had no way of knowing about the new rule. The Israeli Border Police refused to hear his plea and blockaded the village. All the Arabs returning to their homes after five p.m. were shot. Some were murdered as they arrived on donkeys or bicycles, others executed en masse as they were returning on a bus from the olive fields. Within an hour, forty-nine villagers were killed, many of them women, including one who was eight months pregnant. About half of those slain were children between the ages of eight and seventeen.

The war began when four Israeli P-51 Mustangs, flying about twelve feet off the ground to avoid detection, used their props and wings to slice the Egyptian communication lines. Two hours later, Israeli paratroopers dropped into the desert and took up blocking positions. After feinting at Jordan, an armored column, led by the headstrong Ariel Sharon, raced across the desert, sweeping away lightly defended Egyptian outposts.

The next day, the British and the French issued their agreed-upon ultimatum, threatening armed intervention within twelve hours. As expected, Israel nominally agreed to the terms, the Egyptians rejected them, whereupon Israeli forces continued their march through Sinai.

Only two roads crossed the peninsula; the main one leading to the canal passes through a narrow gap in the arid southern mountains called the Mitla Pass. Sharon was under orders from Dayan not to try to take it because the paratroopers had already outflanked the Egyptian defenders. Sharon did so anyway, believing that the defile would be poorly defended, like the forts he had crushed on his way, so why not. When the Israelis were partway through the pass, however, Egyptian troops, who were dug into rifle pits carved into the walls on either side, rained down fire, creating a hellish gauntlet that trapped the invaders. Israeli reinforcements climbed onto the ridges and scrambled down the hillsides in order to root out the Egyptian defenders in hand-to-hand combat. The Israelis finally took the Mitla Pass at a cost of 38 dead and 120 wounded. The Egyptian casualties included 150 killed. After the battle the pass was abandoned; it had been a totally pointless action.

In this war Dayan formed a firm opinion about the fighting qualities of the Egyptian soldiers. "In general, they fought well during the static phase of their combat," he observed. "Dug in and using their anti-tank, field, and anti-aircraft guns from fixed positions prepared in advance, they fought effectively. But they became poor soldiers when we forced them to leave their entrenched posts or change their plans." Some sights made a lasting impression on him. On the morning of November 1, he joined Israeli troops entering the stronghold of El Arish, where a major battle had been fought the day before. The Egyptians had withdrawn during the night. Not even a single nurse remained to take care of the badly wounded men left behind. There was a dead Egyptian soldier on the operating table. His leg had been amputated. "He had been abandoned in the middle of the operation without a doctor or a nurse stopping to bandage him, and he died from loss of blood," Dayan observed.

Some Egyptian snipers held on; one of them killed Dayan's signalman, who was standing at his side. When Dayan departed, in a Piper Cub, his pilot climbed high to avoid the random fire. Dayan could see an Israeli armored brigade headed for the canal and Egyptian soldiers fleeing haphazardly through the dunes. "These troops, abandoned by their officers, immediately shed all they wore and carried which hampered movement—weapons, military pack, uniform, and even their heavy army boots," he wrote in his diary. "From the air these troops looked like an endless procession of pilgrims, their white underwear conspicuous against the background of golden sand."

Meantime, an immense amphibious fighting force was steaming toward the Egyptian shore. The British and French assembled nearly 250 warships carrying 80,000 soldiers, in the company of 80 merchant ships and hundreds of landing craft. The purported objective of the Anglo-French invasion was to impose peace, but Nasser had already agreed to an American-sponsored cease-fire resolution in the UN, and Israel followed on November 5—the same day that it took Sharm el-Sheikh, completing its capture of the peninsula. Still the armada sailed on, despite the absence of combatants and in the face of worldwide condemnation of what everyone now knew was about to happen.

At dawn the next morning, the main act began with a naval bombardment of the beaches around Port Said and Port Fuad, accompanied by an aerial assault. The troops came ashore while the sand was still burning from the intense cannonade. The point of the overwhelming display of force by the Anglo-French invasion was to terrify the Egyptians into immediate surrender. The military planners expected that the people would topple Nasser themselves. Instead, the invaders found themselves fighting the entire town of Port Said. Nasser had called upon all Egyptians to resist the invaders, supplying the citizens of the canal area with assault rifles and grenades. For two days, the people of the isolated desert town kept up their amateur resistance, although much of Port Said was burned to the ground by the fierce assault, which killed 2,700 Egyptians and left tens of thousands homeless.

The Soviet Union, which was savagely extinguishing the Hungarian uprising at the very moment that the Suez crisis was unfolding, unhelpfully proposed an alliance with the U.S. against France, Britain, and Israel. Soviet premier Nikolai Bulganin chillingly pointed out that both the U.S. and the Soviet Union possessed "all contemporary forms of armaments, including atom and hydrogen weapons," which would allow them to impose their will on the region. Bulganin sent similar letters to the French, British, and Israelis, implicitly threatening nuclear war.

It was President Dwight Eisenhower who finally brought the war to an end, without the nuclear rattling of the Soviets. He was incensed by what he saw as the treachery of his allies, who had kept him in the dark about their plot. The fact that the invasion happened to coincide with the final week of his campaign for reelection only amplified his rage. Determined to reverse the outcome, Eisenhower took aim at the fragile British economy, blocking Britain's access to loans from the

International Monetary Fund, which it desperately needed to avoid the collapse of its currency. The British capitulated and agreed to accept the cease-fire and withdraw from Egypt. The French soon followed suit.

The Israelis were harder to deal with. From the outset of the conflict, the Israeli government continually reassured the UN and the Eisenhower administration that it had no aims for territorial expansion; its only goal was to eliminate threats to its security. As soon as the fighting concluded, however, an exultant Ben-Gurion declared to the Knesset, "Egypt has lost its sovereignty over Sinai, which has now become an integral part of Israel." Eisenhower had little support in Congress for his threat to impose sanctions and withhold aid if the Israelis did not withdraw unconditionally, so he took his argument to the American people. "If we agreed that armed attack can properly achieve the purposes of the assailant, then I fear we will have turned back the clock of international order," the president said in a nationally televised address. Ben-Gurion finally bowed to the pressure.

The 1956 war, called the Suez Crisis in the West and the Tripartite Aggression in Egypt, stands as a tombstone for European colonialism. The unintended consequences for the aggressors were shattering. Both the British and the French governments fell within months of their ignominious departure from Egypt, when their countries were made to step back from long-standing roles as leading players on the world stage and merge into the chorus. In any case, the entire concept of Great Powers was obliterated by the emergence of the superpowers, the United States and the Soviet Union, each declaring a vital interest in the Middle East. Britain had been motivated to join the invasion in part to block Soviet penetration of the region, but within the next two years Iraq, Libya, and Syria had joined Egypt as Soviet clients. France's colonial empire, already under siege by revolutionary movements in Algeria and Vietnam, formally came to an end in 1960; after that, France withdrew from the Atlantic alliance into old, unattainable dreams of grandeur. However reluctantly, America had inherited the Middle East portfolio and now was the only real arbiter of peace, if that was ever to come.

Nasser was not toppled; indeed, he emerged as an even more formidable figure as the three musketeers were forced to surrender their prizes. On the other hand, by blocking the canal during the crisis, the Egyptian president had spooked oil suppliers. Within a few decades only a small fraction of Middle Eastern oil passed through Suez; most of it traveled around the African route in supertankers, which were too massive to fit through the canal.

Ben-Gurion stayed in power until 1963, although he was forced to step back from his territorial ambitions. Israel did achieve its goal of forcing Egypt to open the Gulf of Aqaba to Israeli shipping, but it had to accept UN forces along the Israeli-Egyptian border to prevent future clashes. The Arab world was now confirmed in its suspicion that Israel had been created not as a homeland for persecuted Jews but as a base for Western imperialists to maintain their stranglehold on the Middle East. The main lesson Israel learned from the Sinai adventure, however, was that it could not depend on European alliances. There were only two powers that mattered now, and since Egypt and several other Arab countries were in the Soviet orbit, that left only America to turn to.

As a consolation prize for the fiasco, the French agreed to provide nuclear technology and resources to Israel. The remorseful prime minister Mollet confided to an aide, "I owe the bomb to them."

BEGIN SAVORED the company of women, which allowed him to fall into domestic chatter, telling stories about his eight grandchildren, as he did with Rosalynn that Shabbat evening. He shared very few of the pastimes that men might talk about; he had no interest in sports; he didn't care to go drinking; and he had never actually fired a gun in his life, despite serving in the Polish army and leading a terrorist movement. Indeed, he was quite squeamish about blood. Whenever he served as a godfather at a circumcision he would turn his face away at the crucial moment. Like Sadat, he loved American movies, especially westerns, and before he took office he and Aliza went to the cinema twice a week. Sentimental scenes would bring him to tears. At home, the Begins would watch the television shows *Starsky & Hutch, Hawaii Five-O, Kojak,* and their favorite, *Dallas.* So far, the only movie the two of them had watched at Camp David was *An Unmarried Woman,* but he had fallen asleep before the end.

The other side of him was as hard as iron. He relished the bare-knuckled intellectual combat of the Knesset, where his formidable memory and scathing wit made him a dreaded adversary. He became most alive, however, when speaking to crowds. Despite his antiquated, flowery Hebrew, he was a mesmerizing and provocative orator. "He is intoxicated with the love of the masses," one of his old comrades admitted, blaming it on the isolation Begin endured during his years underground. Harkening to the glory of Israel's imagined past, the frenzied crowds would call to him, chanting, "Begin, the King

of Israel!" He had a kind of "magic influence" on his followers, Aharon Barak, one of the Israeli lawyers at Camp David,
observed. "He would talk and they would listen and start to
cry." Begin seemed to be something other than a political
leader; he had a kind of religious authority—"more a pope
than a Caesar," Barak believed.

Begin was implacable when his sense of Jewish honor was
offended. Such was the case when Israel demanded reparations
from Germany in 1951 to compensate it for the cost of absorbing half a million survivors of the Holocaust. Israel desperately needed the money. The young country was struggling to
accommodate both the crush of Jewish immigrants and the
cost of the 1948 war. Begin, however, was outraged. "They say
that Germany is a nation and not what it actually is: a herd of
wolves who devoured our people as prey," he thundered. "How
will we look when our disgrace is exposed, as we turn to our
fathers' murderers to receive money for their spilled blood?"
While the subject was being debated in the Knesset, Begin
incited a mob to stone the parliament and attack the guards
who defended its members—his own colleagues. The next
morning, Begin stood in the Knesset and proudly boasted of
his action. His speech that day would reveal the passions and
themes that guided him throughout his political career:

In Zion Square, to fifteen thousand Jews, I said: "Go,
surround the Knesset, as in the days of Rome. When the
Roman procurator wanted to set up an idol in the Holy
Temple, the Jews came from all corners of the country,
surrounded the building and said, "Over our dead bodies!" And to the Knesset I say, there are things in life that
are worse than death. This is one of them. For this we

will give our lives. We will leave our families. We will say
goodbye to our children, but there will be no negotiations with Germany. I know that you have power. You
have prisons, concentration camps, an army, a police
force, detectives, artillery, machine guns. It makes no
difference. On this matter all this force will shatter like
glass against a rock. I know you will drag me off to a
concentration camp. Today you have arrested hundreds.
Perhaps you will arrest thousands. We will sit together
with them. If necessary we will die together with them
but there will be no reparations from Germany.

None of the dreadful events he forecast came to pass. The
bill to negotiate for reparations passed by a large majority;
and for his actions, Begin was suspended from the body for
three months. German money helped build the electrical and
communications networks in Israel, along with roads, housing, and the national airline. Begin's implicit comparisons
of the Ben-Gurion government to Rome and the Nazis typi-
fied the low demagoguery that he was willing to stoop to, and
the lifelong hatreds he engendered by doing so. He invariably
painted himself against such tragic historical backdrops, as if
the Jewish story were his alone.

AFTER THE 1956 WAR, Begin barnstormed through Israel
campaigning against the withdrawal from Sinai. "Much of the
land remains to be possessed," he said, quoting the Book of
Joshua. It is interesting to consider what a post-Holocaust Jew
such as Menachem Begin made of the biblical account, since
the gift of the Promised Land is tied to the campaign of ethnic
cleansing that Joshua waged.

In the biblical legend, when the Israelites finally emerge from the Sinai wilderness, they camp on the banks of the River Jordan. God draws Moses to the top of Mount Nebo and shows him the Promised Land, which stretches out before him, from the Jordan Valley to the Mediterranean. "This is the land about which I promised on oath to Abraham, Isaac, and Jacob, 'I will give it to your descendants,'" the Lord tells him. "I have let you see it with your own eyes, but you shall not cross over." Moses dies, at the age of 120, having delivered his people to the border, where the land of milk and honey beckoned.

The Lord instructs Joshua, Moses's successor, to take the Israelites into the Promised Land, saying, "Every place where you set foot I have given you." That land was not vacant, however. The Canaanites, Hittites, and many other tribes already occupied the vast tract God awarded to the Israelites. "Be strong and steadfast!" God tells Joshua. "For the Lord, your God, is with you wherever you go."

The River Jordan stops flowing long enough to allow Joshua and the Israeli horde to cross into Canaan, where they pause on the outskirts of Jericho. Before proceeding, the Lord commands Joshua to circumcise all the men; in this way they would be cleansed of the "reproach of Egypt"—in other words, the memory of their enslavement. The Lord advises Joshua to surround Jericho and march around it seven times; then a priest should sound a blast from a ram's horn, whereupon the walls of the city would fall down. "And it came to pass," the Bible says, "that the wall fell down flat, so that the people went straight before him, and they took the city. And they utterly destroyed all that was in the city, both man and woman, young and old, and ox, and sheep, and ass, with the edge of the sword." After looting the valuables, the Israelites burn the city. Joshua then leads his legion to the city of Ai, where all the men and women—12,000, according to the Bible—are put to the sword and the city burned, "made it an heap for ever, even a desolation unto this day." Only the king of Ai is spared, in order to be hanged from a tree.

Word of the massacres spreads. The king of Jerusalem calls together the monarchs of Hebron, Jarmuth, Lachish, and Eglon to band together for mutual defense. The Israelites rout even this great army, aided by a hailstorm the Lord inflicts on the fleeing warriors, killing more of them than the Israelites have done with their swords. At Joshua's bidding, God holds the sun still so that the Israelites can finish the carnage in the daylight.

From there, the Israelites take Makkedah, killing "all the souls that were therein"; and Libnah, once again killing "all the souls that were therein"; and so on, and so on. "Joshua conquered the entire land; the mountain regions, the Negeb, the Shephelah, and the mountain slopes, with all their kings. He left no survivors, but put under the ban every living being, just as the Lord, the God of Israel, had commanded." The twelfth chapter of Joshua has a tally of all the kings that Joshua slew: thirty-one.

But the Lord is not done yet. Even when Joshua is old and "stricken in years," God upbraids him, using the phrase that Begin quoted: "a very large part of the land still remains to be possessed." He provides Joshua with a lengthy list of new territories, including "all the Lebanon," to be parceled out among the tribes of Israel.

When he is close to death, Joshua calls all the elders together and relates the words of God: "I gave you a land you did not till and cities you did not build, to dwell in; you ate of vineyards and olive groves you did not plant. Now, therefore, fear the Lord and serve him completely and sincerely." The Israelites agree to this covenant, and Joshua passes away, at the age of 110.

For many believers, the account of the annihilation of the peoples of Canaan is one of the most troubling stories in the Bible. For Begin, however, Joshua was the original incarnation of the Fighting Jew. Joshua's mission was to carve out a living space for the Israelites, much as modern Jews sought to do in the Arab world. Over the long horizon of Jewish history, so scarred by the pogroms and death camps of Europe and semi-servitude in the regions of Islam, Joshua is a singular and daunting paragon. Begin certainly wasn't the only Israeli leader who believed that spilling blood was a necessary ritual for the unification and spiritual restoration of the Jewish people, and that enacting revenge on the Arabs was a way of healing the traumas of the Jewish experience in Europe and elsewhere. Even many secular Israelis, such as Dayan, saw Joshua as a model for the post-Holocaust new Jewish man. "Look at these Jews," David Ben-Gurion told his biographer, Michael Bar-Zohar, when explaining the policy of massive Israeli reprisals against any Arab attacks that Dayan was carrying out.

They come from countries where their blood was unavenged, where it was permissible to mistreat them, torture them, beat them. They have grown used to being helpless victims. Here we have to show them that the Jewish people has a state and an Army that will no longer permit them to be abused. We must straighten their backs and demonstrate that those who attack them will not get away unpunished, that they are citizens of a sovereign state which is responsible for their lives and safety.

In the modern era, archeologists have excavated nearly all of the cities mentioned in the Old Testament account of Joshua. Neither Jericho nor Ai was inhabited in the Middle or Late Bronze Age (1550 BCE to 1200 BCE), when biblical scholars date the Israelite invasion. Jericho was not a fortified city, so there were no walls to fall down. Ai had been destroyed a thousand years before. Other cities mentioned in the Book of Joshua were either not inhabited at the time or not destroyed. The story was probably derived from earlier Canaanite or Mesopotamian legends, which are replete with similar details. The Egyptian empire firmly ruled over Canaan during the entire period when the Israelites might have invaded, if the biblical account is to be accepted as true. The kings mentioned in Joshua were all vassals of the Egyptian state, which collected taxes and maintained garrisons and administrative centers in the region. In contrast to the absence of archeological support for the Exodus and the Israelite conquest of Canaan, there is a rich trove of evidence of the Egyptian occupation.

The most likely explanation for the origin of the Israelites is that they were themselves the Canaanites. The first time that the Hebrews or Israelites are mentioned in any texts from the ancient world is 1207 BCE, in a stele now in the Egyptian Museum in Cairo. The stele celebrates the many conquests of the Pharaoh Merneptah, including those in Canaan. Israel is scarcely treated as a great power:

> *The Canaan has been plundered into every sort of woe:*
> *Ashkelon has been overcome;*
> *Gezer has been captured;*
> *Yano'am is made non-existent.*
> *Israel is laid waste and his seed is not;*

Hurru is become a widow because of Egypt.
All lands together, they are pacified;
Everyone who was restless, he has been bound.

North of the Egyptian mandate of Canaan, in present-day
Turkey, was another great empire, the Hittites. The Egyptians and the Hittites met in a great battle at a place called
Kadesh in western Syria around 1259 BCE, to determine who
would control the eastern Mediterranean—the same land the
Lord was supposed to have promised Moses and Joshua. The
Egyptians were led by Merneptah's predecessor, Ramses II,
perhaps the most powerful pharaoh of them all, but he was
fought to a standstill by the Hittite king Mutwatallis. They
then signed the oldest written peace treaty known to history,
pledging "peace and brotherhood for all time." A copy of the
text appears above the entrance to the United Nations Security
Council in New York.

Day Five

Menachem Begin and Zbigniew Brzezinski playing chess on the
porch at Camp David

MOST OF THE ISSUES on the table at Camp David were
the unforeseen consequences of Israel's overwhelming victory in the Six-Day War of 1967. Leading up to the war, many
Israelis had decided that the Israel experiment was another
historical trap they had fallen into. There was a sense of
foreboding that led to a rush for the exits. Then the war
came, and Israel defeated three Arab armies in six days. At
once, the country experienced an explosive burst of Jew-

ish immigration, especially from America. Scripture foretold an "ingathering of exiles" in the Land of Israel before redemption: "Thus says the Lord God: I will soon take the Israelites from among the nations to which they have gone and gather them from all around to bring them back to their land. I will make them one nation in the land, upon the mountains of Israel." There was a sense that a miracle had occurred and a prophecy was fulfilled. Forces were set loose in the religious world that would prove to be difficult to contain as the fundamentalists took the floor. Formerly secular Jews were increasingly drawn into the messianic cults of the National-Orthodox, which spearheaded the settler movement. The seizure of the holy places was seen as the prelude to redemption, soon to be followed by the establishment of a theocratic Kingdom of Israel and the rule of Jewish law (Halakha). For Christians as well the war was full of auguries and portents. It seemed that the hand of God had reached out of the Old Testament and once again tipped the scale in favor of his Chosen People, heralding the approach of the End of Days. Surely the Messiah was soon to come.

Many Muslims came to the opposite conclusion. Radical Islam blamed the crushing defeat on the moral decay of modern, secular Arab society. Evidently, God had turned against them. The only remedy was to embrace the pure Islam embodied in the times of the Prophet, which meant a return to Islamic law, jihad, and the tribal codes of seventh-century Arabia. The loss of Jerusalem, in particular, fueled the rise of Islamic extremism and sharpened the hatred of the Jewish state. Other Muslims decried the corruption and backwardness of Arab governments, all of them—excepting fractured Lebanon—in the hands of kings, sheikhs, sultans, generals, dictators, and presidents-for-life, where the voices of democracy and modernism were effectively silenced.

Deception and delusion play a role in every conflict, but especially in the Middle East. The manner in which the Six-Day War was set in motion would place it on an irrational trajectory that its participants seemed unwilling or unable to escape. It began with Anwar Sadat, then president of the Egyptian parliament, making a stopover in Moscow on May 13, 1967, after a goodwill trip to North Korea. His plane was delayed by an hour, so he had a chance to talk with Soviet president Nikolai Podgorny and Vladimir Semyenov, the deputy foreign minister. They gave him the startling news that Israel had moved ten brigades to the Syrian border. Egypt had recently signed a mutual defense pact with Syria. "You must not be taken by surprise," the Soviet president warned in dire tones. "The coming days will be fateful."

He was right about that; three weeks later the map of the Middle East would be redrawn and Egypt would suffer a defeat so rapid and abject that there are few parallels in history. But he was wrong about the Israeli brigades. There was no such movement toward the Syrian border. That fact has subsequently led to abundant speculation about whether the Soviets merely lied to Sadat, perhaps in order to destroy Nasser, or were carelessly passing on misinformation from sources, such as Syria or Israel, with their own agendas, or simply were mistaken. When the Israelis learned of the false report about their troop movements, they invited the Soviets on three occasions to tour the Syrian border region to see for themselves that there were no such troop concentrations. Each time, the Soviets refused, saying that they already knew the facts. Nasser sent a trusted general to Syria to study aerial photographs; the general even surveyed the border from a private plane. "There is nothing there," he reported to Nasser. "No massing of forces. Nothing."

Still, Nasser felt obliged to make a show of force by sending Egyptian troops into Sinai and demanding that some of the UN peacekeepers be removed from their posts. Despite the bellicose speeches that followed, Nasser seemed to be bluffing. He didn't expect all of the UN troops to be withdrawn, although they were. A war with Israel couldn't have come at a worse time for Egypt; the country was already tied down in a war in Yemen, where nearly half of the Egyptian Army was involved. In addition, a third of its planes were unfit for action, as well as a fifth of its tanks. On top of this, the Egyptians had no actual battle plan and no strategy. Nasser's gestures stopped short of pulling the trigger. Then, tired of being heckled by other Arab leaders because of his weak responses toward Israel in the past, he closed the Gulf of Aqaba to Israeli shipping. The Israelis had long warned that this would be an act of war. "If war comes it will be total and the objective will be Israel's destruction," Nasser boasted. He pledged to "totally exterminate the State of Israel for all time." Rhetoric left reason far behind as the logic of war took command. "Nasser was carried away by his own impetuosity," Sadat observed.

Many Egyptians would look back at this moment with fury and shame. They were living inside a bubble that had been inflated by an absurdly self-confident, over-empowered military establishment; a dictator who listened only to the cries of his name in the streets; and a tamed and in any case censored press. Ignorance of the enemy's capabilities and designs led to an exuberant feeling that history was about to bow to the Arabs at last. Egypt, haunted by its ancient grandeur, had found a new champion in Nasser; together they would unify the Arabs and lead them to a resurgent future. Destroying Israel would be only a first step.

The exhilaration in Egypt was matched by a sense of mounting panic in Israel. War loomed on two horizons— in the east, with Syria and probably Jordan as well, and in the south, with Egypt. Other Arab armies would rush into the fray if they thought there was any chance of victory. The Egyptian Air Force, fortified with new MiG fighters, dared to make a reconnaissance flight over the Israeli nuclear reactor in Dimona. The Israelis were also aware that the Egyptian Army had used chemical weapons in Yemen, and the prospect of facing gas attacks resurrected thoughts of the Nazi death camps, inflaming profound psychological wounds. Israel had one of the most potent militaries in the world, but the feeling of invulnerability alternated with a sense of weakness and victimization that was never far from reach. The days leading up to the war were fraught with talk of annihilation, an entirely different discussion than the prospect of defeat. Prime Minister Levi Eshkol faltered and stuttered during an address to the nation, sending chills through the country. The military chief of staff, Yitzhak Rabin, had a nervous breakdown of sorts, fretting that the country was on the brink of catastrophe for which he would be responsible. The Israelis stockpiled antidotes to poison gas and dug trenches in city parks to be used as mass graves.

It was still unclear, however, whether the Egyptian military buildup was a genuine prelude to war or a beating of drums on Nasser's part to elicit cheers from the Arab street. America was urging both Egypt and Israel not to strike the first blow; President Lyndon Johnson promised the Israelis that the U.S. would lead an international flotilla through the Straits of Tiran and pry open the Gulf of Aqaba to Israeli ships again. As it turned out, Johnson was unable to garner the support of other countries to carry out this action, and the Israelis decided they couldn't wait for the Egyptian attack. "We must strike now and swiftly," argued Ezer Weizman, who was Rabin's deputy chief of staff. "We must deal the enemy a serious blow, for if we don't, other forces will soon join him." Israel formed an emergency cabinet, bringing Menachem Begin into the government for the first time in his career as a minister without portfolio. Dayan, who had demonstrated his military genius in the 1956 war, was made the minister of defense four days before the war was scheduled to commence.

Dayan took immediate charge of the planning, deciding to concentrate his forces entirely on the Egyptian front before turning to other adversaries. At the same time, he deliberately gave the impression that Israel was in no hurry to respond to the Egyptian threats. He was sufficiently convincing that Nasser canceled the state of emergency he had imposed on his country. On June 5, just before the war actually began, Israel decided to lie about who started it. A message, which Dayan opposed, was sent to President Lyndon Johnson saying that the Egyptians had fired on Israeli settlements and that an Egyptian squadron had been spotted headed toward Israel. Neither of these statements was true.

Dayan coolly had breakfast with his wife, then coffee with his mistress, and finally he went to his office and began the war. Shortly after seven a.m., the entire Israeli Air Force took to the air. "The whole plan rested on total surprise," Weizman recalled. "All those planes, taking off from different airfields, flying at different speeds, would get into formation as planned and, at precisely the identical moment, they'd arrive at nine

Egyptian airfields. . . . If the scales should tip against us, and we failed to destroy the Egyptian Air Force, only four planes were held in defense of Israel's skies." Within thirty minutes, more than two hundred Egyptian planes had been destroyed. The outcome of the war was effectively decided.

Israel was aided by excellent intelligence—one of its spies was Nasser's personal masseur—and by Egyptian incompetence. The commander in chief of the Egyptian Army, Field Marshal Abd al-Hakim Amir, who had goaded Nasser into the war, was on his way to inspect an air force base near Suez, along with all his top commanders, and he had ordered his anti-aircraft and missile forces to hold their fire for fear they would hit his plane. The skies over Egypt were wide open.

When Sadat awakened that morning, he learned from the radio that the war had started. "Well, they'll be taught a lesson they won't forget," he thought, as he shaved and leisurely dressed. He didn't arrive at the command center until eleven in the morning. Entering Field Marshal Amir's office, Sadat found him standing in the middle of the room, his eyes wandering like an animal that has been stunned by a blow. "Good morning!" Sadat said, but Amir seemed unable to hear him. Other officers whispered that the Egyptian Air Force had been totally wiped out.

When Nasser came into the room, Amir suddenly began to talk. He had come up with the theory that it was the U.S. Air Force, not the Israelis, that had attacked. Nasser sneered at the accusation, but an idea was planted in his mind. Soon afterward, he called King Hussein of Jordan. Hussein was cowed by Nasser. Several days earlier, he had formally entered the war after Nasser lied to him, saying the battle was in Egypt's favor. "Quickly take possession of the largest possible amount of land in order to get ahead of the UN's cease-fire," Nasser had advised earlier that morning. The Israelis had pleaded with King Hussein not to join the war, promising to leave Jordan alone, but once again he cast his vote with the Arabs. In a matter of minutes, he lost his air force as well. Syria had lost half of its planes already. Now, in this desolate moment, Nasser asked Hussein, "Shall we say that the United States is fighting on Israel's side?" He was unaware that his conversation on an unscrambled line was being recorded by Israeli intelligence. "Shall we say the United States and England or only the United States?"

"The United States and England," Hussein replied.

When Radio Cairo broadcast the lie about American involvement in the war, most of the Arab world broke diplomatic relations with the U.S., although Jordan did not. After Israel released the contents of his call with Nasser, Hussein apologized. Meantime, mobs attacked American embassies throughout the region, and Arab oil producers banned shipments to the U.S. and Great Britain.

Sadat, not sure what to do, simply went home, and stayed there for several days, going for long walks. "I was dazed and unable to locate myself in time or space," he admitted. Meantime, he agonized over the Egyptian people, who were being told that they were winning the war. Young men on flatbed trucks roamed the city leading the chorus of cheers. "I wished I could have another heart attack," Sadat wrote. "I wished I could pass away before these good and kind people woke up to the reality."

Jordan had begun its misbegotten war by firing on Israeli positions in Jerusalem. Begin passionately lobbied for the immediate capture of the Old City, which had been off-limits to Jews since 1948. Dayan had not wanted to divert attention from Sinai, but the nearly instant elimination of any air threat made it easier to open another front. He ordered General Uzi Narkiss to surround the Old City in hopes it would fall without a fight.

In the early hours of the following morning, Dayan made another fateful decision. Jordan was shelling Israeli settlements from Jenin, one of the main cities on the West Bank. Dayan ordered the guns silenced. At that point, there had been no discussion of conquering and occupying the territory, but it was in the back of everyone's mind. From the Israeli perspective, the war really had no design beyond the elimination of the Egyptian threat, but it opened up opportunities. As Dayan sat in the operations room of military headquarters, a commander radioed that his forces had surrounded Jenin. Dayan turned to look at the other officers in the room, including Weizman. "I know exactly what you want," he said. "To take Jenin."

"Correct!"

"So, take it!"

In that dizzying, unaccountable, almost thoughtless moment, the decision to seize the West Bank was made. Within a few days, more than a million and a half stateless Palestinians would fall under Israeli control, and the moral burden of becoming an occupying power would fall on the shoulders of the Jews.

Later that same fateful morning, Dayan announced he was going to Jerusalem. Weizman offered to fly him there in an Alouette helicopter. He flew low, so the convoys of Israeli troops could see their instantly recognizable commander. They waved to him in greeting. Weizman set the helicopter down in the parking lot of the Jerusalem convention center. The war was all around them and the smell of cordite seared the nostrils. Dayan ordered General Narkiss to provide a jeep to take them up to Mount Scopus, which looms over the Old City. Although nominally a part of Israeli territory, Mount Scopus had been a demilitarized enclave inside Jordanian Jerusalem since 1948. That war had left the city divided between the new Jewish neighborhoods and the major portion, including the Old City, which Jordan had seized and annexed. Now after nineteen years the prospect of reunifying the holy city was within grasp. "What a divine view!" Dayan declared when they reached the ridgetop. Around him were the hills of Golgotha, the Mount of Olives, Mount Zion—names that echoed in the minds of believers—and before him was the historic Old City behind its crenellated limestone walls. The Temple Mount, with the glorious Dome of the Rock, was at his feet. He was struck by the Old City's air of calm indifference as the sounds of war exploded all around it.

Weizman broke away from the others and entered the old Hebrew University, shuttered for nearly twenty years. His uncle Moshe Weizmann had been a professor of chemistry at the university, and his laboratory was still there. The clock on the wall had stopped. Professor Weizmann's papers were still on the desk, and his handwriting was on the blackboard. It was as if time had frozen and now that other life might just start again.

Narkiss wanted permission to take the Old City immediately. "Under no circumstances," Dayan replied, imagining the international outrage that would follow if any religious sites were damaged. But the following day, rumors of a UN cease-fire prompted Begin to call Dayan. "We must not wait a second more," he said.

For two thousand years, Jews had been promising themselves, "Next year in Jerusalem!" Now that dream was about to be realized. An Israeli tank blasted open one of the giant gates to the Old City, and troops of the 55th Parachute Brigade raced down the Via Dolorosa toward the Temple Mount. As soon as it was taken, Dayan entered the Old City. He ordered an Israeli flag that had been placed atop the spire of the Dome of the Rock taken down. Then he joined the delirious soldiers at the Western Wall, a remnant of the temple that was destroyed by the Romans in 70 CE. Many of the troops were weeping or praying. Following an ancient custom, Dayan took a small notebook from his pocket, wrote a prayer, and stuffed it into a crevice in the ancient rock face. It said, "May peace descend upon the whole House of Israel."

"We have returned to the holiest of our sites, and will never again be separated from it," this avowedly secular man declared. "To our Arab neighbors, Israel extends the hand of peace." The victory was so rapid, so thorough, so mythic, that its architect still couldn't take it all in. It would be at least a generation before the Arabs could mount another military challenge to Israel, Dayan boasted, and who could doubt him?

Afterward, in the helicopter back to General Headquarters, Dayan wrapped himself in his coat and curled up quietly in the corner, contemplating what future he had just created for his country.

HISTORY IS REPLETE with wars, conquests, and surrenders, but negotiated settlements between two ardent antagonists have been surprisingly rare. In the fifteenth century, Pope Alexander VI thoughtfully parceled out the newly discovered world between Spain and Portugal. He drew a line dividing the globe that was intended to give the continents of North and South America to Spain and everything east of that—i.e., Africa—to Portugal. It was later discovered that the bulge of Brazil strayed into the Portuguese sphere, which is why Brazilians speak Portuguese today.

Before Camp David, Hal Saunders, the assistant secretary of state for Near East affairs, paid a visit to the State Department historian to ask if there were any precedents in the history of American diplomacy. The only example the historian could point to was when President Theodore Roosevelt invited emissaries from the warring countries of Russia and Japan to Portsmouth, New Hampshire, in 1905, to resolve their differences. Like Carter, Roosevelt had hoped that they would work it out between themselves, but that proved impossible. His strenuous and imaginative diplomacy provided the breakthrough that ended the war. He became the first American to earn a Nobel Peace Prize.

At Camp David, there were no formal meetings on Saturday, so the American team spent the fifth day drafting the American proposal. The new approach sprang in part from a fortuitous meeting that Cyrus Vance had several weeks before the talks began. At the same time as the Carters were vacationing in the Grand Teton National Park, Vance rented a house in Martha's Vineyard next to an old friend, Roger Fisher, who taught negotiation at Harvard Law School. They played a game of tennis, and afterward, Vance asked if Fisher had any ideas about how to handle the forthcoming summit. Fisher had been hoping he would ask.

Vance was already a veteran negotiator. Lyndon Johnson had chosen him as his personal envoy to settle a dispute between Greece and Turkey over the division of Cyprus. He had been involved in the early peace talks at the end of the Vietnam War, where he was forced to spend much of his time debating the shape of the negotiating table. Both philosophically and morally, he was closer than anyone else in the Carter administration to the president; but Vance was handicapped by a growing suspicion on Carter's part that he couldn't conclude an agreement.

Both Fisher and Vance had fought in the Second World War, losing many friends in that conflict. At Harvard Law School, Fisher put together ideas about how countries could resolve disputes diplomatically rather than through the constant resort to arms. Over cocktails, when Vance asked him if he had any suggestions for the summit, Fisher was able to produce a draft of a book he had just written, titled *International Mediation, a Working Guide: Ideas for the Practitioner.** Still in his tennis duds, Vance sat in a lawn chair on Fisher's terrace and looked it over.

The main idea that Vance took with him was what Fisher called the "one-text procedure." The concept was simple: the arbitrator in a dispute creates a document and then asks each side for its response. Matters that are not contested are counted as agreed upon. Those that are disputed are then addressed in a way that continually narrows the differences. When each side finally concurs on the language, that issue is also marked off. The key, all along, is that the arbitrator controls the document. Whenever the contending parties hit a stalemate, the arbitrator proposes new language. In this methodical manner,

---

* Many of the ideas Fisher developed in *International Mediation* were reflected in a later best-selling book, *Getting to YES: Negotiating Agreement Without Giving In*, which Fisher wrote with William Ury and, in the second edition, Bruce Patton. Fisher went on to found the Harvard Negotiation Project.

Fisher believed, disputes that would otherwise lead to blood-shed, economic ruin, and centuries of enmity could be sanded down by patient negotiation. He was seeking a cure for war.

Carter had his own method of negotiation, which he had first developed during his years on the Sumter County school board, when he had to deal with labor disputes. He would outline in advance what he thought would constitute a fair settlement and then try to bend each side toward his position. When he was governor, rural Hancock County, which had a history of racial violence, became the first county in Georgia in which blacks held all the top offices. That spurred panic among white citizens, who still constituted the majority of the city of Sparta, the county seat. The white mayor ordered machine guns for the city police officers, which led the black-controlled county government to order thirty machine guns in response. An arms race began between the two branches of government that could lead to a kind of civil war. Instead of occupying the county with state policemen or calling out the National Guard, Carter studied the complaints on each side and then composed a list of compromises. He sent a special assistant, Cloyd Hall, to interview both sides and make a presentation to the community. On October 1, 1971, Hall called him, and said, "Governor, I've got a birthday present for you." It was a truckload of machine guns.

Now, at Camp David, both Vance and Carter had the chance to put their experience to the test.

Harold Saunders, the assistant secretary of state, had spent all Friday night into Saturday morning writing what would be the first of twenty-three drafts of an American proposal. Carter listed about thirty items that he called "Necessary Elements of Agreement." They included:

An end to war.

Permanent peace.

Unrestricted passage of Israeli ships through Suez Canal and Gulf of Aqaba.

Secure and recognized borders.

Diplomatic recognition and an exchange of ambassadors.

Phased Israeli withdrawal from Sinai and demilitarization of the peninsula.

An end to blockades and boycotts.

Abolition of the Israeli military government in the occupied territories.

Full autonomy for the Palestinians.

Determination of the final status of the West Bank and Gaza within five years, based on UN Resolution 242.

Withdrawal of the Israeli military into specified security locations.

A prompt and just settlement of the refugee problem.

Definition of the final status of Jerusalem.

An end to Israeli settlements in Sinai.

No new Israeli settlements or expansion of existing ones in the occupied territories until all negotiations are complete.

Formal signing of a peace treaty between Israel and Egypt within three months.

Putting all of this on paper caused the American team to focus on what was really important or realistic to achieve at the summit. When Carter met with his team that afternoon, he made several changes in the proposal. For the time being, he decided to omit the demands to end Israeli settlements because Begin would focus on that issue exclusively.

He amended the clause concerning "secure and recognized borders" to say that the borders might incorporate "minor modifications" that differed from the 1967 armistice lines. He also deleted a provision that linked the implementation of a treaty between Egypt and Israel to the creation of a self-governing authority on the West Bank and in Gaza. Inevitably, he began thinking of two separate agreements. This would lead to what many critics consider to be the failure of Camp David to achieve a comprehensive peace, while others believe that it allowed the summit to achieve anything at all.

"The president was very frank in saying that we should try to get an Egyptian-Israeli agreement started and concluded," William Quandt, who was part of Brzezinski's staff on the National Security Council, wrote in a memo that day. "If there are any delays in negotiation of the West Bank/Gaza agreement, that is somebody else's problem. [Carter] said that he hoped both agreements could move in parallel, but it was clear that the Egyptian-Israeli one took priority, and if nothing happened in the West Bank for ten years he would not really care very much."

Gaza was usually lumped with the West Bank as a single issue, but in fact each side regarded it as a distinct concern. It was physically separated from the West Bank, complicating the design for any future Palestinian entity; it was also home to the densest concentration of Arab refugees in the Middle East. Members of the Israeli delegation privately urged Sadat to take it back under Egyptian dominion, but he didn't want it, and Begin was aghast that Gaza was even on the table, insisting that it was part of the historic Land of Israel.

THE ISRAELIS WERE BEGINNING to chafe at the confinement. Begin was calling Camp David "a concentration camp *de luxe*." They joked about digging an escape tunnel. "It all reminded me of the World War II films about submarines," Weizman recalled. "Here we were, in the enclosed, claustrophobic atmosphere of Camp David, with Captain Jimmy Carter at the periscope." He compared the expected American proposals to depth charges slowly descending upon the Israelis, as they held their collective breath and hoped the bombs would not sink them.

That morning, Weizman set off on his bicycle to conduct his own private negotiation. He was often at odds with his prime minister and appeared to the other delegates to be inappropriately close to the Egyptian president. After Sadat's trip to Jerusalem, Weizman was the only member of the Israeli cabinet who subsequently developed a friendship with him. Whenever Sadat had something he wanted to discuss with the Israelis, it was Weizman he summoned. Carter observed that Weizman was regarded within his own delegation as an adversary or even an enemy.

Foreign Minister Mohamed Kamel happened to be on another long walk with Sadat. Like Begin, the Egyptian president was complaining that Camp David was beginning to remind him of prison.

"What makes things even gloomier is the fact that our intramural colleagues are, of all people, Begin and Dayan, with whom we have to deal!" Kamel said.

"We are dealing with the lowest and meanest of enemies," Sadat agreed, as he led Kamel on his rapid pace through the forest footpaths. "The Jews even tormented their Prophet Moses, and exasperated God!" He added, "I pity poor Carter in his dealings with Begin, with his stilted mentality."

Just then, Weizman approached on his bicycle. Kamel dreaded seeing him, believing that Sadat's obvious affection for Weizman colored his thinking. No doubt Sadat had talked himself into believing that he was using Weizman as a means of gathering intelligence on the Israelis' positions, but Kamel feared it was the other way round, offering the amiable but ambitious Israeli defense minister unfettered access to the mind of the president of Egypt. Sadat had already had one private meeting with Weizman and had given no report to his delegation about what transpired. Kamel shuddered when Weizman asked if he could pay another visit later that afternoon. "Of course," Sadat replied, "it's always a pleasure to talk to you."

A few hours later, however, when Weizman arrived at his cabin, Sadat seemed impatient and distracted. The constant fights with his delegation were extracting a toll on his mood.

"I get the feeling that a lot of things aren't moving for psychological reasons, not practical ones," Weizman observed.

"Of course," Sadat replied. "I'm sure it's ninety percent a psychological problem."

"I suggest you talk to Dayan," Weizman said, bringing up a name that evoked strong feelings in Sadat. "He heard you repeat that you do not trust him because he's a liar."

"This is true," Sadat agreed. "He's a lying man."

Weizman urged him to set his personal feelings about Dayan aside. "He has influence over Begin," he advised. Weizman then probed to see if there was any room for maneuver in Sadat's positions. "There is no argument about the Sinai being your country," he said. "But a lot of things have happened in the course of thirty years. You must understand the mentality of our people. On the one hand, they never believed that an

Arab leader—certainly not the leader of the largest and strongest Arab nation—would come to Jerusalem. But the Israelis are still convinced that any error is liable to bring a disaster upon them." For that reason, the settlements needed to stay in place.

"How can I show my face before the other Arab states if that is the price I pay for peace?" Sadat protested. Even if he agreed to such an arrangement, he said, it would breed new problems in the future. He had already told Begin that he would agree to a phased withdrawal from the peninsula. "I told him other things that he did not understand before. Full recognition? Yes! International waterway in the Tiran Straits? Yes!"

"And the airfields?" Weizman asked hopefully.

"They have to be evacuated within two years!"

Weizman observed that Sadat did not mention full diplomatic and commercial relations, something that Sadat had agreed to in previous conversations between the two men.

"I know I spoke to you about it," Sadat conceded, "and I can tell you that I want it. But Begin said in the Knesset: 'I will not give anything without getting something in return.' I will behave the same way."

"What do you want to achieve here?" the frustrated Weizman asked.

"I want to reach agreement on a framework," Sadat assured him.

Weizman left the meeting feeling that Sadat was not inclined to make any major concessions, but at least he didn't want the talks to break down. The Egyptian proposal was obviously not Sadat's final word. "He may have climbed too far up on his high horse, in which case he would need an American ladder to help him down," Weizman concluded. On his way back to his cabin, he hummed a snatch of the Israeli national anthem, "Our hope is not yet lost!"

WHILE WEIZMAN AND SADAT were conferring, other members of the Egyptian delegation sat around, killing time and chatting about the movies that they had been watching. They noted who was coming out of Begin's cabin and speculated on what might have been said. There was little else to do until the Americans produced their document. Idleness was a part of their forced confinement. Finally, the mysterious Tohamy arrived. Except for the heads of state, Tohamy was the only person at Camp David with his own cabin, which made his status all the more inscrutable. No one knew what he did all day here in the woods, but as soon as Tohamy arrived the other delegates perked up. "He could hardly cross the threshold of the bungalow before all the weariness, gloom and anxiety disappeared like magic, to be replaced by joy, liveliness and jest," Kamel recalled. "And we were all ears!"

Tohamy interpreted their dreams and recounted miraculous tales of his adventures: for instance, how he had been poisoned on a visit to another Arab state, then retreated to his room and bolted the door, touching neither food nor water for three days as he treated himself with a poison antidote that he happened to always carry with him. He provided a fanciful report that Dayan had just now agreed to restore Jerusalem to the Arabs. Turning to address Kamel, he burst out, "Jerusalem has been put in trust with you, brother Mohamed; beware of renouncing it!" Everyone recognized that as a delusion, but it was nice to hear.

When Kamel fretted that he was supposed to meet with his

Israeli counterpart, Dayan, Tohamy told him that all he had to do was tighten his right fist, fix Dayan with a firm gaze, and then suddenly open his hand and shout, "Tohamy!"

Tohamy's attention often turned to the gaunt, patrician figure of Boutros Boutros-Ghali. A figure from the ancien régime, Boutros-Ghali had been born in a hundred-room mansion in Cairo and educated at the Sorbonne, where he took a degree in law. His grandfather, Boutros Ghali, after whom he was named, was the first—and only—Coptic Christian prime minister of Egypt. (In 1910, a Muslim fanatic shot him after he had negotiated an extension on the Suez Canal concession for the British, on terms more favorable to the Egyptians.) Given his talents and the trust Sadat placed in him, Boutros-Ghali should have been made the foreign secretary instead of Kamel. But Boutros-Ghali was not only a Christian; he had compounded his political difficulties by marrying a Jew. High office in Egypt would never be his. (He later became secretary-general of the United Nations.)

Tohamy fixed on the idea that Boutros-Ghali must convert to Islam—here, at Camp David, where it would take on greater symbolic importance. The others in the cabin jokingly offered to take bets on whether Boutros-Ghali would see the light. Later, however, some of them privately begged him to keep talking to Tohamy in order to distract him from the negotiations. Boutros-Ghali agreed. As it happened, he had studied Islamic law and was well versed in the doctrines and teachings of most important Muslim scholars. For the rest of the summit, the two men spent many hours walking through the autumnal forest, discussing fine points of Islamic scholarship as Tohamy continually urged him to accept the true faith. "I felt strange about this, but it was important to draw him away from the others," Boutros-Ghali later confessed. "I was the decoy."

IN THE EVENING, a tense crowd of onlookers gathered on the porch of Begin's cabin to watch the Israeli leader play chess with Zbigniew Brzezinski. It was a highly charged match: two Polish expatriates facing one another, each with a reputation for ruthless strategic brilliance. Begin identified Brzezinski with the Polish feudal lords who had made life so miserable for the Jews back in Brisk. Brzezinski's Catholic father had been a Polish diplomat to Germany during the rise of the Nazi Party and then to the Soviet Union during Joseph Stalin's Great Purge, so the associations were really stark.

Brzezinski was blond and athletic, with steepled eyebrows that gave an immediate impression of intellectual disdain. He was a political innovator, constantly injecting fresh ideas into the discussion. No obstacle seemed insurmountable to his agile mind. Carter appreciated the fact that when all solutions to a problem appeared blocked, Brzezinski could offer five or six fresh alternatives. But at Camp David, perhaps because of the cloud of suspicion that hung over Brzezinski in the Israeli imagination, he was less prominent in the meetings than Vance. The Israelis noticed that Brzezinski chafed at riding in the backseat.

Although he was usually hyperaware of the political currents flowing through powerful personalities, Brzezinski once had been totally surprised by Begin. In one of his first trips to Washington to talk to Carter, the new Israeli leader invited Brzezinski to breakfast at Blair House. Thinking it was a private affair, Brzezinski was surprised to be greeted by reporters and television cameras. Begin appeared, holding a dossier in his hands. He explained to the press that the folder contained information about Brzezinski's father, Tadeusz, helping Jews to escape Germany while he was ambassador. Begin's public praise of his father brought Brzezinski nearly to tears. Despite this emotional moment, Begin still privately condemned Brzezinski as "*ocher Israel*"—a hater of Israel. They were such different men, divided by their common background—"Poles apart!" Yechiel Kadishai cracked.

As the match started, Begin announced that this was the first time he had played chess since September 1940, when he was arrested by the Soviet police because of his Zionist activities. On that fateful day, he had been playing chess with his friend Dr. Israel Scheib. Aliza had calmly invited the detectives to join them for tea. They thanked her but said they were in a hurry, although they allowed Begin to polish his shoes. As he was leaving, he told Aliza, "Don't forget to tell Scheib that I concede that last chess game to him. He was leading, anyway, when they interrupted us."

For a man who hadn't touched a chessboard in nearly four decades, Begin played surprisingly well. Observing the match, Dayan compared the scene to combat. In the first game, Brzezinski recklessly attacked and lost his queen. Begin was also an aggressive player, but more systematic and deliberate. Brzezinski adjusted his strategy and won the second game, but he fell behind in the third. By now, word had spread all over the camp about the match. At one point, Begin's wife appeared and seemed so pleased. "Menachem just loves to play chess!" she exclaimed, confirming Brzezinski's growing suspicion.

Hamilton Jordan sidled up to one of the Israelis in the audience. "Do me a favor and make sure Begin wins," he remarked. "Otherwise Zbig will be unbearable."

Begin did win, three games to one. Later, a lawyer with the Israeli delegation decided that Brzezinski had lost the match on purpose, as part of a larger strategy: "He thought it would put Begin in a good mood, so he would give up the West Bank," said Meir Rosenne. "It did get him in a good mood, and he became more extremist than ever."

THAT NIGHT, Mohamed Kamel and Boutros Boutros-Ghali once again lay in their bunks, talking until late at night as Kamel poured out new worries. Kamel chided his room-mate for talking to the Israelis, especially to the gregarious Weizman. "Did we not agree not to speak to those people?" he demanded. Boutros-Ghali said that negotiating was more than sitting around a table. "It is also a dialogue away from the table." He tried to calm down the agitated foreign min-ister. But Kamel was too overwrought to be reasonable. He was humiliated because he had lost control of his delega-tion. He was also losing control of himself; his passions and his anxieties were running away with him. What did Sadat really want? Kamel wondered aloud. The Egyptian president was so secretive and unpredictable he might say anything! The future of the nation was on the line. Who knows what he might have already pledged without consulting his advisers? But Sadat had burrowed into his cabin and rarely came out, even for meals. Americans visited him—even Israelis did!— but rarely members of his own delegation. He never went to the movies or the pool hall, emerging only to pray in the theater or go for his daily constitutional. The ordinary intelligence one might pick up from such an informal interchange was maddeningly unavailable.

Kamel was particularly worried that Sadat was trying to preserve the legacy of his trip to Jerusalem. A failure at Camp David would make it seem as if that overture had been nothing more than a historic blunder. Boutros-Ghali agreed that Sadat might cut a deal just to save face. They would have to find a way to reassure Sadat that when the talks broke down, there would be other pathways to peace. Finally, Kamel cried, "I cannot go on. My nerves are about to explode."

Day Six

Hassan el-Tohamy, Ezer Weizman, Anwar Sadat, Jimmy Carter, Amy Carter, Menachem Begin, and Moshe Dayan at Gettysburg

BEGIN AWAKENED on Sunday morning in a panic. The Americans planned to submit their proposal later that afternoon, and of course the Egyptians had already presented their intransigent document. So far Israel had not responded in kind. The man who had come to Camp David thinking he had the least to lose now realized he had created a trap for himself. He had nothing new to offer. He had no strategy. The Israeli team had arrived without background materials or alternative proposals and practically no preparation. Convinced that the conference was about to break apart, Begin now wanted something to show that the Israelis had at least made an effort.

At five a.m. he awakened Kadishai and dictated an improvised draft of an Israeli proposal. As much as he tried to cast it in positive terms, the paper was essentially a rejection of everything on the table: no to an end to Sinai settlements; no to withdrawal from Sinai airfields; no to any abridgment of Israeli settlements in Judea and Samaria; and no, no, no to any division of Jerusalem. These were principles for him, not mere positions; compromise and defeat were one and the same. He genuinely wanted peace but his main obstacle was himself and his own history.

When Dayan, Weizman, and Aharon Barak, Begin's main lawyer, appeared at seven thirty that morning, Begin read his draft aloud. Dayan diplomatically suggested that they should wait until the Americans submitted their own report before showing the document to anyone else. There was no way to disguise the uncompromising mind behind the Israeli proposal.

CARTER RECOGNIZED that the delegations were beginning to feel imprisoned at Camp David, so he proposed an outing to the nearby Gettysburg National Military Park that morning after church services. He stipulated that there would be no negotiations during the excursion; it was merely a chance for the delegates to catch their breath and get a change of scenery. Of course, the choice of destination was no accident.

Begin appointed four of his delegation to stay behind and

work on the Israeli document, which was no longer intended to be the basis of a discussion. It was a summary of Begin's non-negotiable positions. Begin told Barak to sit down and write the reasons why the meeting failed, "and then we will go home." Barak and the others packed their belongings and called El Al—the Israeli national airline—to prepare for their departure.

THE SERMON THAT MORNING at Camp David's Hickory Lodge was taken from I Samuel 17:47, the story of David and Goliath. Goliath was the mighty warrior of the Philistines, their own Samson. The Bible describes him as being "six cubits and a span" tall—about nine feet nine inches. Goliath was clad in a coat of mail and a brass helmet, nearly invulnerable to the arrows and spears of the Israelites. David was a shepherd boy, armed only with a slingshot and five smooth stones taken from the river. But in single combat he slew the giant, then drew Goliath's sword from his sheath and cut off his head, scattering the Philistine army in awe and terror. The point that Chaplain Cecil Reed wanted to make is that when God chooses a particular person to do a job, he will enable him to do it.

The David and Goliath story is one of the most resonant biblical tales in modern Israel. Moshe Dayan wrote that the symbolic meaning of little Israel in the vast Arab world was perfectly expressed by the David-Goliath duel. David told Goliath, "You come against me with sword and spear and scimitar, but I come against you in the name of the Lord of hosts, the God of the armies of Israel whom you have insulted." For Dayan, the moral of the story is: "The Arabs come to us with sword, dagger and spear, while we seek to live with them in peace, side by side, on terms of equality. We come to them in the name of the Lord God of Israel."

As a longtime Sunday school teacher, Carter drew his own lesson from the David and Goliath story. Even when David became king, the Israelites were never able to firmly defeat their eternal enemy, nor could they under David's successor, Solomon, during Israel's supposed Golden Age. Despite that legendary combat in the Valley of Elah, the Israelites and the Philistines had to continue suffering each other's presence.

Although it's usually assumed that the Palestinians are the same people as the Philistines, there's an opposing theory, which is that they are actually Jews. David Ben-Gurion, Israel's first prime minister, and Yitzhak Ben-Zvi, its second president, were notable advocates of this line of thinking. In 1918, when the two men were living in New York, they wrote a book, titled *Eretz Israel in the Past and Present*. They noted that, although the Jewish community had undergone catastrophic diasporas in its history, there was a pattern of unbroken Jewish settlement in Judea and Samaria. They proposed that the current inhabitants of Palestine were not Arab migrants but the descendants of Jewish peasants who had been forcibly converted to Christianity or Islam. Ben-Zvi in particular became obsessed with the historical intermingling of Jews with other peoples and what he thought was the loss of their Jewish identity over time. He used to wander in the Arab villages, among his "long-forgotten brethren," and he was struck by the resemblance of Arab place-names to Hebrew ones, and the similarity of religious practices. He and Ben-Gurion entertained the hope that the revelation of their shared ethnic origin would make it easier for the two peoples to unite as one. Archeological finds and genetic studies would eventually bear out their theory.* The Israelites and the Palestinian Arabs both emerged from Canaanite culture. The David and Goliath story actually anticipates later scientific findings. In a Talmudic account, David reminds Goliath that their mothers were sisters, so they are actually first cousins. The intermingling of the tribes in ancient times was no doubt a fact as well as a fancy.

CARTER HOPED THAT, by taking the two leaders to Gettysburg, the men would be reminded of the fateful consequences of a failure at Camp David. The American Civil War was also a fratricidal struggle over land and sovereignty. The Deep South that Jimmy and Rosalynn had grown up in was still shadowed by the bitterness of defeat and the economic deprivation that war leaves in its wake.

Rosalynn Carter and Aliza Begin rode in the presidential limousine along with the three leaders. Carter carefully stationed himself between Begin and Sadat, who stared out opposite windows at the lush Pennsylvania farmland. Carter knew that each of them had spent time in prison, so he broke the

---

* One notable study, by Antonio Arnaiz-Villena et al., "The Origin of Palestinians and Their Genetic Relatedness with Other Mediterranean Populations," *Human Immunology* 62 (2001), pp. 889–900, which appeared shortly after 9/11. It compared genetic samples from Palestinian Arabs in Gaza with other Mediterranean peoples, and found that the Gaza population was closely related to Ashkenazi Jews. Both are descended from the Canaanites. The article concludes that the "rivalry" between Jews and Palestinians is "based on cultural and religious, but not genetic, differences." The European authors referred to the Israeli settlers as "colonists" and asserted that Israel began the war with its neighbors when it was created in 1948. Although the science wasn't in question, the publisher of the journal fired the guest editor and withdrew the article from publication—deleting it from databases—and librarians and subscribers were directed to physically rip the pages out of the journal. See also Israel Finkelstein and Neil Asher Silberman, *The Bible Unearthed*, p. 118.

tension by asking Sadat if he had read much while in confinement. Sadat said that for the first year and a half he had nothing at all to read, and when he was finally allowed to have books, he was so desperate that he read everything he could get his hands on. That initial prison experience, after he was arrested for collaborating with the Nazi spies, was in the Aliens' Jail, which was operated by the British. Sadat requested books in English, and the warden provided a collection of short stories as well as a random book on local government in rural Britain, which made a deep impression on the future president. Sadat was soon transferred to a different prison, where the brother of one of the Nazi spies taught him German. At another prison, a converted villa, he was so bored he began breeding rabbits in an open hallway, which became a handsome source of revenue. The rabbits soon overran the place, until they were all wiped out by an infectious disease.

His next spell in prison was during his trial with Mohamed Kamel in the political assassinations case. Sadat had always yearned to be an actor, and finding himself in confinement once more, with ample time on his hands, he wrote a play in which he played the Caliph Harun al-Rashid, whose exploits became the basis of "A Thousand and One Nights." The performance did not go well. "The audience began shouting at me, 'stop all this nonsense,'" Sadat later admitted. "So I stopped."

Eventually, he was transferred to the grim Cairo Central Prison and locked in solitary, in Cell 54. It was completely bare except for a mat on the floor, a filthy blanket, and a retinue of bugs crawling across the walls. Cut off from the outside world, with no radio or newspapers, he considered the course of his life. One of his first realizations was that he was unhappy in his marriage, so he resolved to get a divorce.

When he was finally given access to reading material, he taught himself French.

During this period, he stumbled upon an article in the popular magazine *Reader's Digest* by an American psychologist, which helped him deal with "certain nervous troubles" that plagued him. The author proposed that the disasters that befall a person are determined by fate and cannot be avoided. God sends trouble just as he does good times; it is a divine way of teaching his creatures how to play the roles for which he created them. Unlike the menacing God that Sadat had been taught to fear in his village religious school, he learned from the *Reader's Digest* article that God is just and loving. Some traumas might be so great as to make a person feel as if all avenues are blocked and that life itself is a prison with a perpetually locked door. The key that unlocks the prison door is faith.

Sadat felt liberated by this news. "My relations with the entire universe began to be reshaped, and love became the fountainhead of all my actions and feelings," he later wrote. "Armed with faith and perfect peace of mind, I have never been shaken by the turbulent events, both private and public, through which I have lived." He would say that the last eight months he spent in prison were the happiest period of his life. But when he finally became president, he had the old prison torn down. He was given a pickax and had the honor of striking the first blow. "The bricks were sodden and easy to break," he recalled. Cockroaches spilled out of the hole he created. After that ceremonial blow, he couldn't stop himself. "I still raised my pickax and hit at the wall, determined and tense, as though I could demolish it all myself." Altogether he had spent five years of his life in various prisons.

Begin said that prison had also been a "university" to him.

When he was arrested in the middle of his chess game in Vilna, he grabbed a couple of books for what he guessed would be an extended stay. He selected the Bible and an English biography of Disraeli. Those would be taken away from him at the dreaded Lukishki Prison, which loomed over the center of the city. Thousands of Jews were sent there; few would ever leave. Begin's cell mates also included generals and high-ranking Polish officials. They passed the time telling jokes and avoiding open talk about politics.

Begin was interrogated, night after night, and forbidden to sleep during the daytime. After several days of this, most prisoners would sign anything just to be allowed to sleep without interruption. Begin, however, actually seemed to relish the interrogation, which turned into a debate, wearing down his Soviet interrogator, whom he was instructed to call "Citizen-Judge," with his legalistic hairsplitting. Begin recalled one evening's exchange when the interrogator tried to make the point that Zionism was another form of imperialism:

> "Citizen-Judge, we were not in favor of a colonial regime," I said; "we demanded a colonization regime and those are two different conceptions entirely."
>
> "What is the difference? Are you trying to influence me by playing on words?"
>
> "No, it is not a play on words. A colonial regime means the rule of a foreign people over a country that is not theirs, and we are returning to our own country. . . . The British want a colonial regime, while what we want is, in fact, anti-colonial."
>
> "Talmudism! Colonial, colonization, it's one and the same thing. You simply want to deprive the Arab farmers of their land."

Although Begin never experienced a mystical conversion in prison like Sadat, he was a humble witness to the power of faith. A young Polish corporal was placed in Begin's cell. He was uneducated, and gradually Begin took him on as a student, giving him lessons in history and languages. The corporal was an atheist, and he took pleasure in relating stories about the hypocrisy of the Catholic priests who violated their vows of chastity. One morning, Begin was astonished to see the corporal sink to his knees in prayer. "I can testify that the revived faith of the corporal helped him, as his imprisonment continued, to overcome the melancholy which is the portion of every prisoner," Begin wrote. "It is a fact—and I saw it with my own eyes—that man in his downfall has nothing to lean on, nothing to solace him, except faith."

While in prison, Begin received a handkerchief from Aliza, smuggled through a friend, with the letters "OLA" embroidered on it. At first, Begin thought it might be a misspelling of Ala, her nickname, but a fellow prisoner suggested it was actually the Hebrew word *olah*, which means immigration to Israel. Aliza was letting him know where to find her if he ever saw freedom again.

Eventually, Begin was convicted, without trial, of being "an element dangerous to society." His interrogator directed him to sign a confession that he was "guilty of having been the chairman of the Betar organization"—the Jewish paramilitary group. Begin said he would sign the document if the Citizen-Judge struck the word "guilty."

"Are you at it again? . . . You said you were the chairman of the Betar in Poland and that is what I wrote."

"Yes, but I am not guilty."

"Ah! Ah! You are guilty all right!"

Finally, the Citizen-Judge scratched out the offending word and Begin signed his confession. As Begin was led back to his cell, the interrogator yelled, "I never want to see you again!"

Begin was sent to a gulag in Siberia, which made him long for the misery of Lukishki. However, he was there only for three months. He would later claim that he spent two years in confinement, but altogether, his prison experience lasted a single year, from September 1940 to September 1941. While he was on his way to Siberia, Germany declared war on the Soviet Union, and soon all the Polish prisoners were released to fight the Nazi allies in the Middle East. The Polish army initially turned Begin down because of his weak heart and poor eyesight, but relented on appeal. The largely Jewish unit he joined was sent to the Middle East in 1942. That's how Begin reunited with Aliza. He never saw action, but soon after he arrived in Palestine he was made the head of Irgun, which was stocked with former Betar members. The Polish army gave him a year's leave and never bothered to call him back to service.

Perhaps if he hadn't been arrested, Begin would have been killed in the Holocaust, like other members of his family. Events carried him along in a powerful tide. Other people might feel helpless in the swell of history, but Begin had the sense of being swept along by destiny, just like Sadat.

In the presidential limousine, the two men seemed to enjoy talking about their time behind bars. By the time they entered the gates of Gettysburg, both Sadat and Begin were in high spirits.

CARTER HAD BRUSHED UP on the history of Gettysburg. He had received a briefing from the historian Shelby Foote a few months earlier, so the park ranger had little to add to Carter's narration. It was here in these green, rolling hills that Confederate General Robert E. Lee intended to take the fratricidal war to the North, only to be blocked by the Army of the Potomac under Major General George Meade. More than fifty thousand men fell in the first three days of July 1863. Although the war lasted another two years, the Confederate cause was doomed at Gettysburg.

Like Carter, who had studied the battle at Annapolis, the other military men on the excursion were quite familiar with the hallowed names where the blood-drenched battle took place: the Peach Orchard, Cemetery Ridge, Little Round Top. They examined the breastworks and admired the mortars and cannons with keen professional interest, remarking how modern the armaments of the time seemed by comparison with the state of medicine in its ability to treat the wounds inflicted by such awful instruments of destruction.

"Moshe, you've been avoiding me," Tohamy said as they traipsed through the battlefield. "Are you angry with me?"

"I certainly am," Dayan replied. Before the summit, Tohamy had given an interview in which he said that Dayan had reneged on promises made about Sinai and Jerusalem.

"Are you the anti-Christ?" Tohamy asked.

Rosalynn noticed Begin standing off by himself, isolated even from his own delegation. Perhaps the somber sight of the battlefield had made him reflective. He had said nothing about the plans that were being made at that very moment to leave Camp David.

One of the monuments on Cemetery Ridge marks the "High Water Mark of the Rebellion." Here the Irishmen of the 69th Pennsylvania withstood an intensive Confederate artillery barrage, followed by one of the most disastrous infantry assaults in military history, known as Pickett's Charge. Twelve thousand five hundred men, many of them farm boys from Georgia, marched across a thousand yards of open terrain, under withering fire from the Yankees. Half the soldiers on both sides fell. The Union line wavered at one point, but reinforcements pushed back the Southern assault. It was relentless, savage combat, cannons giving way to grapeshot, musket fire giving way to bayonets; and finally the Irishmen of the 69th stood their ground with their fists. The defeated Confederates withdrew to Virginia under cover of rain and darkness. Carter proudly added that, even under these conditions, the rebels were without panic and unbroken in spirit.

Dayan had visited the site before, but he was moved by Carter's emotional recounting of the war that tore the young country apart. "He seemed to know every hill and boulder which had served them as cover," Dayan wrote. "And when he told the story of how the tattered, bedraggled and barefoot Southern fighters had an additional incentive to capture Gettysburg upon hearing that it had large stores of boots, he seemed to be talking about his own family."

In fact, Carter's great-grandfather Littleberry Walker Carter had been in the Confederate ranks at Gettysburg, along with his two brothers. They survived the war and then walked home to Georgia, through the devastated South, the plundered towns, the scorched fields, carrying psychic wounds that would blight the region for another century. Thirty percent of the men in the South of fighting age had been killed in the war. Much of civilization had been scraped away and the region rolled back to frontier. The real cost of such devastation can never be measured, but the graveyard at Gettysburg was a somber reminder—row after row of simple tombstones.

Carter observed that it was here at the cemetery where Lincoln made his famous Gettysburg address, when he came to consecrate the resting place of the Union dead.

"Four score and seven years ago our fathers brought forth on this continent, a new nation, conceived in liberty, and dedicated to the proposition that all men are created equal."

Everyone turned in surprise to Begin. His voice was very quiet at the beginning, as if he were reciting the address to himself.

"Now we are engaged in a great civil war, testing whether that nation, or any nation so conceived and so dedicated, can long endure . . ."

Begin's voice gained power, and he continued in his distinct Polish accent:

"But in a larger sense, we cannot dedicate—we cannot consecrate—we cannot hallow—this ground. The brave men, living and dead, who struggled here have consecrated it, far above our poor power to add or detract . . ."

Carter realized that Begin understood Gettysburg in a different way from the military men. For Begin, Gettysburg was not just the site of a significant battle, it marked the spot of one of history's great moments of presidential leadership, when the power of words rose above the military fray and knit together a devastated nation.

"It is rather for us to be here dedicated to the great task remaining before us—that from these honored dead we take increased devotion to that cause for which they gave the last full measure of devotion—that we here highly resolve that these dead shall not have died in vain—that this nation, under God, shall have a new birth of freedom—and that government of the people, by the people, for the people, shall not perish from the earth."

Rosalynn was quivering with emotion. Maybe this was a

turning point, she thought; maybe Begin really did appreciate what peace was and what it could be for his country.

LATE THAT AFTERNOON, back at Camp David, Carter, along with Mondale, Vance, and Brzezinski, met with Begin, Weizman, and Dayan. The time had come to present the American document to each team. "There are phrases in it which both you and Sadat will find difficult to accept—not because they hurt your countries, but because they are different from positions you have taken and statements you have made in the past," Carter warned the Israelis. He deliberately left certain thorny issues—sovereignty on the West Bank and Gaza, Israeli settlements, and withdrawal from Sinai—for later, although they would eventually have to be addressed as well.

Weizman noticed the blood drain from Begin's face as he scanned the American paper—"seventeen pages of high explosive," as Weizman termed it. When he finished, Begin finally looked at Carter. "We would also ask that you defer giving this to President Sadat," he said, invoking Kissinger's 1975 agreement to coordinate any peace proposals with Israel.

"I did not draft this proposal with the idea that either side would alter it substantially," Carter said testily. "I have tried to keep in mind what Israel wants and needs. Most essential is your permanent good relationship with Egypt, which would assure adequate security for Israel."

Begin fixed on the reference to UN Resolution 242 regarding the "inadmissibility of acquisition of territory by war." He said that was unacceptable. "The language applies only to wars of aggression," he said. "The war of 1967 gives Israel the right to change frontiers."

"Do you reject United Nations Resolution 242?" Carter asked, his voice rising. "To delete this phrase would mean that we have no basis for negotiation now or in the future. What you say convinces me that Sadat was right—what you want is land!"

The meeting adjourned till later that night in order to give the Israelis a chance to read the document more carefully. Carter reluctantly sent a message to Sadat that he would not be able to present the document to the Egyptians until the Israelis had had their say.

After the Americans left, Begin remarked, "Gentlemen, the Americans have simply copied the Egyptian plan." He was so angry that Weizman worried he might have another heart attack. But Begin's order to return to Israel was set aside, at least for the moment.

Carter and the Americans returned for another meeting that night at nine thirty. Begin started off by briefly praising certain paragraphs—"a beautiful number on Jerusalem"—but he now insisted on deleting all references to UN Resolution 242.

"This is not the time to beat around the bush," Carter said furiously. If he had known that the Israelis intended to disavow the resolution, he said, "I would not have invited you to Camp David nor called this meeting."

"That has been our position for eleven years," Begin replied.

"Maybe that's why you haven't had peace for eleven years," Carter snapped. "Israel has repeatedly endorsed 242, but now you are not willing to respect the language."

"I am willing to respect it, but not as a basis for what follows in your proposal."

Carter thought this was "gobbledygook." The entire UN resolution consists of a single sentence, he pointed out; it was impossible to excise the objectionable clauses and preserve only the ones that Israel agreed with. If either delegation started throwing out established agreements and resolutions, the summit would be going backward. Besides, the American proposal was flexible; it allowed for the final borders to be negotiated in order to take into account Israel's legitimate security concerns.

"Sadat wants an agreement with Israel on his terms, and these are a danger to Israel," Begin insisted. "We speak here of the very existence of our nation."

Begin invariably spoke in such apocalyptic language, which in Carter's opinion torpedoed rational conversation. Even the other Israelis seemed impatient with Begin's emotionalism. "Let's move on," Weizman urged. But Begin subjected every point on the American proposal to the same agonizing, minute scrutiny.

"Listen, we're trying to help you bring peace to your land," Carter pleaded in frustration. "You would have us feel that we are going out of our way deliberately to be as unfair to Israel as possible."

Hours passed. Food and coffee were sent in. Begin brushed aside a provision for keeping the international waterways open, saying the Egyptians had no right to close Suez to Israeli shipping in the first place, so that was not a concession. Even though Carter had withheld the most contentious issues regarding the West Bank and Gaza, Begin continually objected to every remaining reference to the Palestinians; in Carter's opinion, the Israeli leader was utterly unconcerned with their plight. Begin rejected the reference to their "legitimate rights," saying that it was a tautology and who knows where it might lead.

Carter had incorporated what he thought was Begin's own proposal for "full autonomy" for the Palestinian people, but even here Begin had different language to propose. Yes, the Palestinians would have autonomy, but the Israeli government would approve their laws, install a military governor, and maintain a veto over decisions made by the Palestinian governing council.

"What you want to do is make the West Bank part of Israel," Carter concluded. "No self-respecting Arab would accept this. It looks like a subterfuge." It certainly wasn't "full autonomy."

"Autonomy doesn't mean sovereignty," Begin said.

Carter concluded that Begin was offering the appearance of self-rule, but Israel would remain totally in charge. "If I were an Arab, I would prefer the present Israeli occupation to this proposal of yours," he said.

Voices were raised, including Carter's. When Dayan was allowed to speak, he said that the Israelis would reconsider some of their objections to the proposal. "We are not after political control," he said. "If it seems that way to you, we will look at it again." He openly ridiculed Begin's idea of inserting the phrase "Jerusalem, the capital of Israel" in the text, because Sadat would never sign such a document. Carter began to realize that he had allies on the Israeli team. Both Dayan and Weizman would occasionally speak in Hebrew to Begin, apparently urging him to be more receptive to Carter's proposal.

It was nearly three in the morning when Begin circled back to the language of 242 concerning the occupation of territory by force. "We will not accept that!" he declared.

"Mr. Prime Minster," Carter responded impatiently, "that is not only the view of Sadat, it is also the American view—and you will have to accept it." Weizman noticed that Carter's lips were tightly compressed and his blue eyes blazed with fury. He crumpled up the papers on the table and threw down his pencil. "You will have to accept it!" he said again.

"Mr. President," Begin said. "No threats, please."

AFTER THE MEETING concluded in acrimony, Carter asked Dayan to walk with him back to his cabin. He vented his anger over what he saw as Begin's obstructionism and asked for Dayan's help.

They sat on the terrace of Carter's cabin, speaking in low tones to avoid waking Rosalynn. Dayan said that Carter was misreading Begin. He really did want peace, but the issue of the Sinai settlements was standing in the way. It was a matter of principle with Begin that Jews should be allowed to live anywhere. On the eve of Camp David, Begin had pledged to his own delegation that he would never withdraw the settlements from Sinai, and if he was pressured to do so he would walk out. In the face of that, Dayan suggested, Carter might propose that Sadat allow Israelis to continue living there, at least temporarily, as they might in Cairo or Alexandria. If Sadat agreed, that might satisfy Begin.

Before Dayan left, Carter went into the cabin and emerged with a bag of peanuts. They were from Georgia, he said proudly. They had been allowed to soak in salt water, unshelled, which was what gave them their special flavor. Dayan was touched by the simple gesture.

It was nearly dawn, but still dark, and Dayan was a bit disoriented as he made his way back to his cabin. After losing his left eye in battle, his lifelong fear was that he would lose sight in his remaining eye; and now, although he tried to hide the fact, he truly was going blind. When he turned around to head back to his cabin, he walked directly into a tree. Carter ran to help him. Blood was streaming out of Dayan's nose. Carter guided him to the main path.

When Carter finally climbed into bed, Rosalynn asked, "What happened?" It was nearly four in the morning. "We had to do a song and dance with Begin over every word," he said wearily. "I'll tell you about it in the morning." If Dayan or Weizman were prime minister, there would be a peace treaty by now, Carter believed, but he was beginning to have doubts about Begin's sanity. Just before he fell asleep, he added that Begin was a "psycho."

Day Seven

Anwar Sadat with his advisers, *left to right:* Osama el-Baz, Sadat, Mohamed Ibrahim Kamel (with his back to the camera), and Hassan el-Tohamy

DAYAN'S CABINMATES WERE WORRIED about him. Even before he ran into the tree he was obviously in pain. The famous warrior was sixty-three years old and in poor health. He hated going to doctors, so he may already have been suffering from the cancer that wouldn't be diagnosed until several months later. He kept up a stoic front, but he moaned in his sleep. Moreover, he had never fully recovered from an

accident he had experienced ten years before, during a land-
slide at a prehistoric burial cave near Tel Aviv, in which he had
suffered cracked ribs and several broken vertebrae.

In Israel, archeology is a national passion, but Dayan was
a fanatic. Perhaps because he was secular, and the theological argument for Israel's existence was not persuasive, the evidence buried in the ground of Israel's past existence became
a religious substitute. He pursued it with the zeal of the most
fervent believer. He turned his home in the military suburb of
Zahala into an archeological garden, filling it with priceless
artifacts he had discovered—or looted—from sites all over
the country. He frequently broke into protected sites and even
used the army to cart off his treasures. His hobby had become
a national disgrace. He came to be seen more as a grave robber
than an avid hobbyist. In addition to purchases from antiquar-
ian dealers, Dayan dealt with thieves and smugglers. People
would be shocked to find him in their backyards with a shovel,
prospecting for likely sites. He spent any spare time alone in
his studio, gluing potsherds together for his collection. These
were his happiest moments.

When the Six-Day War ended, Dayan put himself in charge
of the holy places of Jerusalem. For a man who was responsible
for more Arab deaths than perhaps any other Israeli, Dayan
proved an amazingly progressive and openhanded administrator. On the Saturday after the war, he met with Muslim leaders, including the mufti of Jerusalem, at the Al-Aqsa
Mosque. He respectfully removed his shoes and sat on the
carpet. The Muslims received Dayan with trepidation. They
knew that many Jews had longed for the moment when the
mosques on the Temple Mount could be torn down and the
temple erected once more on this site; and if that time was ever

to come, surely it was in the aftermath of their lightning victory. Instead, Dayan informed them that although Jews would now have access to the Temple Mount, there would be no other changes. He asked the Muslim leaders to resume their Friday sermons.

He tore down all the barricades and anti-sniping walls that had divided Jerusalem, and instead of sealing off the Arab communities on the West Bank, he ordered free passage in either direction, without checkpoints or special permits. Despite the protests of Jewish leaders and the handwringing of police officials, it was a remarkably peaceful transition. "There is a festive air in the city," Teddy Kollek, the mayor of Jerusalem, wrote Dayan the day after the barriers were removed. "Kudos! You were right; all the Arabs are at Zion Square and all the Jews at the bazaars." A pleased Dayan observed, "The only thing the police had to do was to try to unsnarl the traffic jams."

Even more dramatically, Dayan instituted an "open bridges" policy, so that people in the West Bank could move freely across the Jordan River. In this manner the Arab citizens could commute to universities or meet with friends and family members. He hoped that the open bridges would bring Israelis and Arabs in touch with each other. Arabs were allowed to work in Israel, which created an economic boom in the West Bank and Gaza. But Dayan's expectation that the free movement of people would lead to peaceful coexistence between the Israelis and Palestinians in the occupied territories proved to be illusory. The Arab countries did not reciprocate by allowing Israeli citizens to visit them, and the occupation only increased Palestinian radicalism, which led to acts of terror and harsh Israeli reprisals.

It had been Dayan's decision to seize the West Bank, but in the process he created an enduring political problem, for which his idealism was no match. His policy of spreading Jewish settlements in the territories stood in the way of peace. Perhaps that was always his goal. In September 1967, right after the end of the war, he announced that one of his principal aims was to block the possibility of a future Arab majority in the occupied territories. This was at a time when not a single Jew lived there.

SADAT SHOWED no patience for Dayan's compromise. He told Carter it was out of the question for Israelis to remain in the Sinai settlements, even if the land was returned to Egypt. Carter asked if he would permit Jews from any nation, including Israel, to live in other Egyptian cities, such as Cairo or Aswan.

"Of course."

Then it wasn't logical, Carter explained, that he would forbid them living in Sinai.

"Some things in the Middle East are not logical," Sadat informed him.

While they were talking, the revised American proposal, incorporating the Israeli changes, finally arrived. Sadat looked it over and offered surprisingly few changes, except for one: he wanted Egyptian and Jordanian forces to be allowed in the West Bank and Gaza, so that it didn't appear that he was consenting to exclusive Israeli military occupation. Carter suggested that he amend the document to include diplomatic recognition and an exchange of ambassadors as a gesture of goodwill, but Sadat choked, saying he couldn't do that until Begin left office.

Carter then brought up Jerusalem. He knew how important it was to the Egyptians, but this was one issue Carter wanted to take off the table—for Sadat's sake. Any compromise would be subject to attack by the radicals on both sides; it was just too dangerous for Sadat to try to resolve by himself. Carter advised him to wait and involve King Hussein and others so that he didn't bear the responsibility alone. Sadat listened but didn't respond.

"Sadat is smarter than I am," Carter told Rosalynn at lunch. He related that in the first fifteen minutes of their meeting that morning, Sadat had told him four things about Begin:

1. He does not want or intend to sign anything while he is here.
2. Camp David will expose him.
3. He wants land.
4. Camp David is a trap for him.

"I think he is right on all four," Carter said.

WHILE JIMMY AND ROSALYNN were having lunch, the anxious Egyptian delegation finally met privately with Sadat. All morning the Egyptians had been watching their Israeli counterparts running or cycling over to Holly Lodge, where the Americans were furiously incorporating the Israeli objections into the new draft. The Israelis would hand over a few pages, then race back to their cabin. Soon, an American would hop on a bicycle and take new pages over to the Israelis. The level of suspicion in the Egyptian delegation was naturally quite high, and they deeply resented the unbalanced relationship of the three parties—two against one, in their opinion.

But the Egyptians were not just negotiating with the Americans and the Israelis; the real problem was their own president. Until now, Sadat was the only member of his team to have seen the American proposal. He finally presented it and asked Boutros-Ghali to read the document aloud, before opening the floor for comments. It immediately became obvious to the frustrated delegates that he was paying no attention to their remarks. Whenever Sadat became distracted he would stare into space and fiddle with his pipe. He readily consented when Mohamed Kamel suggested that the delegation be allowed to withdraw and discuss the proposal privately.

Kamel believed that the American document was thoroughly contaminated by Israeli ideas. The right to Palestinian self-determination and the return of the refugees had been made impossibly vague. There was no demand for Israeli withdrawal from Sinai and the West Bank. The document seemed to be created to respond to Israel's security needs at the expense of all other issues.

When the rest of his team returned to give their reactions, Sadat's mood had radically changed. It was as if a storm had blown in. He raged against Begin's intransigence, complaining that the American proposal called for the return of Sinai to Egypt in stages rather than all at once. The delegates cheered him; they all felt the same way. Then Sadat announced that he was withdrawing from the talks and leaving Camp David the next morning.

What? Leaving? Boutros-Ghali delicately suggested that walking away from Camp David with nothing in hand would place Sadat's government in jeopardy. Sadat snapped at him, "You don't understand anything about politics!" Then he ordered everyone out so he could take a nap.

The dazed Kamel wandered over to the dining hall with Tohamy. What were they to do now? Were they really leaving, or was this another bit of Sadat's theatrics? On the way the two men ran into President Carter on his bicycle. He greeted them and expressed hope that they would be able to reach agreement in the next few days. "I am sorry to say I don't share your optimism, Mr. President," Kamel responded. "The Israeli attitude is as obdurate and unyielding as ever. And the U.S. project submitted to us falls far short of the minimum we can accept."

Carter explained that the text was subject to negotiation; the point was to reach an agreement acceptable to both parties.

"Our problem is that we are not entitled to make any concessions on the occupied Arab territories," Kamel said. "We can be very flexible on security arrangements and peace relations. However, it is obvious that this is not what Israel is after." He begged Carter not to pressure Sadat any further. The other Arab states would not approve of a pact that included territorial concessions. "If you want this conference to succeed, an agreement which provides for Israeli withdrawal from the West Bank, Gaza and Arab Jerusalem must be reached. This will induce the other parties to join in the peace process."

"It seems to me you fail to realize my aim," Carter said icily. "I don't think it would be fair to ask President Sadat to bear the whole responsibility for the Arab-Israeli conflict." He confided that he intended to ask for the support of the kings of Jordan and Saudi Arabia as well.

"There we go again!" Kamel exclaimed. "Neither King Hussein nor King Khalid will agree to join the talks unless these were to be based upon Israel's withdrawal from the West Bank and Jerusalem."

Carter turned his bicycle around and rode away, leaving Kamel feeling even more frustrated and isolated from the negotiations.

Kamel went immediately to Sadat and reported the conversation with Carter. He found the Egyptian president sitting alone, bored and lonely. With the Americans now taking the lead in the negotiations, neither Sadat nor Begin had much to do except to wait anxiously for the next draft. Each of the leaders relapsed into a kind of nervous passivity, while Carter drove himself endlessly.

As Kamel was giving his account, the phone rang in Sadat's cabin. It was King Hussein. Sadat told the Jordanian monarch that he was not optimistic about reaching an agreement because of Begin's determined resistance to new ideas. He begged Hussein to join the summit, but the king refused, saying that he could not do so until Israel guaranteed a total withdrawal from the West Bank. It was just as Kamel had warned Carter. Sadat was in this alone. He would pay the price.

When Kamel returned to his cabin, Boutros-Ghali tried once again to calm him down. Kamel said he felt betrayed by the Americans, who had obviously folded in the face of Israeli pressure. It was a trap, he believed; at every step the Egyptians would be negotiating not with the Israelis but with their American partners. The grand Egyptian design for Camp David was to create a deeper alliance with the Americans, no matter what the outcome of the talks with Israel. Now Sadat was risking Egypt's relationship with the U.S., and there was nothing Kamel could do about it. Sadat was negotiating behind their back.

Boutros-Ghali pointed out that they were only present to support Sadat. "We must offer *al-Rayyis* our advice," he said, using the Egyptian term for chief, "but the final decision is his."

"But *al-Rayyis* is possessed!" Kamel cried.

AFTER LUNCH, the weather turned chilly and a light rain fell, reflecting the dampened spirits of the delegates. Like everyone else, Weizman was exhausted, and he seized the opportunity to return to his cabin for a nap. He stripped off his clothes and plopped into bed. Suddenly, he was awakened by Carter's voice: "Mr. Weizman!"

Weizman was startled to see the president standing in his doorway. Horrified, Weizman jumped up and put on his pants. "I would like to talk to you," Carter explained, with an awkward smile, staring into the middle distance as Weizman got dressed. Then the two of them went for a stroll.

Weizman had previously been struck by the precision of Carter's thinking. He never uttered a single superfluous syllable, sounding as though his thoughts had been programmed by a computer. "That's the way an engineer thinks," Weizman reminded himself, "in squares and rectangles."

Carter made it clear that the talks had reached a critical juncture. The Americans had offered their proposal. Neither side had accepted it. Somebody was going to have to bend. Weizman had no doubt who that somebody was supposed to be.

By now the Americans had figured out the roles that the two top Israeli advisers played in their delegation. Weizman was there to maintain contact with the Arabs, especially Sadat, who brightened whenever the Israeli defense minister came into the room. His charm and ebullience was a welcome contrast to the dour Begin. By comparison, Dayan was a blunt instrument. Dark and pessimistic by nature, he was also a creative thinker and the one most likely to coax Begin into making a concession. Carter sent for him. Dayan agreed to meet after dinner, but he wanted to bring someone with him.

The man who accompanied Dayan was Aharon Barak, one of the Israeli lawyers, who had just been appointed to Israel's supreme court. He spoke to Carter with surprising candor. He explained that the Sinai issue was important to Begin mainly because he feared that removing the settlements in Sinai would set a precedent for the West Bank and the Golan Heights. For Carter, this was an epiphany. He also learned that Begin had pledged when he came into office that he would retire in one of the Sinai settlements, so the issue was a matter of honor to him as well. And honor was the very core of Begin's personality.

Carter aired his frustration about some of the latest Israeli responses to the American proposal, and a surprised Dayan pointed out that the changes weren't nearly as drastic as he imagined. Barak and Dayan also confided that Begin was not going to totally reject the American proposal. There were three possible routes of action on each issue. One was for Begin to simply approve the matter; another was for him to approve but to refer it to the Knesset or the cabinet for confirmation; and finally, for him to disapprove the item and recommend against acceptance, but still send the matter to the government for a final decision. This was the most likely destiny for the Sinai issue.

Carter was chagrined to realize that, in his fatigue, he had inflated the importance of some of these issues. There were so many genuine obstacles in the path to peace; he certainly didn't need to be inventing new ones. What he gleaned from his conversation with Dayan and Barak was that Begin was not going to be the one to say no to peace. Obviously, the Israeli delegation had been working on him relentlessly. Carter went to bed a little after midnight, exhausted but hopeful for the first time in seven days.

Day Eight

Anwar Sadat and Jimmy Carter on the porch of Aspen Lodge

CARTER AWAKENED EARLY, as usual, and went for a long bicycle ride around the sleeping camp. The hopes that he had taken to bed with him the night before seemed far out of reach in the chilly light of the morning. He had budgeted three or four days for the summit; now he was entering the second week with no actual progress to report. He had come face-to-face with his own limitations as a negotiator. First of all, he was overly ambitious. He wanted to fix the entire problem of the Middle East. That was naive. He wasn't certain now that he could solve even a tiny portion of the conflict. His original vision—that Sadat and Begin could find their own solution to their problems—had failed. Their hatred and distrust for each other really did seem to be three thousand years old. The American proposal was also a failure. Both sides were using it to attack the other, demanding that unworkable formulations be inserted in the text for no clear reason other than to alienate the other side. Carter had an engineer's conviction that any problem can be solved if it is attacked with conviction, intelligence, and persistence. Those were qualities he had in abundance, but he was beginning to see that human problems have their own irrational logic, which might be more responsive to the touch of a magician or a psychiatrist than an engineer.

As a result of his ambition, Carter had done a poor job of setting priorities. Everything was on the table, but what was most important? Should he divide the issues into different categories; for instance, setting aside Gaza and the West Bank? Carter's inability to delegate authority was also beginning to take its toll. While others could rest, or go to the movies or play Ping-Pong, Carter felt that his presence was essential. But he was wearing down, getting only a few hours of sleep a night, and exhaustion was clouding his mind.

His impatience was a problem as well. If Carter let his restlessness run away with him, the project was certainly doomed, but there was a midterm election coming up in two months, and Carter should be out campaigning. The tide was still out on the economy, the prime rate was 20 percent, energy prices were peaking, and the shah of Iran was about to be pushed off his Peacock Throne by a radical cleric. Rapacious political opponents in Carter's own party were sharpening their knives. How long could the president of the United States be away from his office? Or, for that matter, the president of Egypt or the prime minister of Israel? If Sadat and Begin failed to get an agreement they could live with, Carter's impetuous decision to hold the summit could bring them all down. He was going to have to come up with a new strategy. It had to be today. He couldn't hold these men here even a few more hours unless he could offer them a new pathway to peace.

When he passed Sadat's cabin on his way back from his bicycle ride, Carter was reminded of the danger he had placed him in. They were supposed to meet later that morning for Sadat to provide the Egyptian response to the American proposal, but as he rode past Carter saw Sadat on the porch of his cabin engaged in a violent argument with his top advisers. It was a very disturbing scene. Carter returned to Aspen Lodge with a feeling of foreboding.

When Sadat finally arrived for the meeting later that morning, he was pale and shaken. He had a paper in his hand, but it was not the American proposal. Instinctively, Carter felt that Sadat had come to tell him that the negotiations were over. Stalling, Carter suggested that they sit beside the swimming pool, in hopes that a different environment might lighten the mood. He didn't want Sadat to say the words that were on his tongue or perhaps even scripted for him on that paper that he gripped so anxiously.

Carter was closer to Sadat than to any other world leader— indeed, he felt almost like a brother to him. That relationship was also at stake. He could only imagine the pressure that Sadat was under. Instead of talking about the proposal,

Carter painted a portrait of Egypt at peace. Right now, Sadat had five army divisions lined up against Israel, which handicapped Egypt in fulfilling its natural role as the leader of the Arab world and the most important country on the African continent. Once Carter and Sadat put the Israeli-Egyptian dispute to rest, the two of them could move on to other problems besieging the region—in Yemen, Afghanistan, Libya, Ethiopia.

Sadat dreamed of such a partnership. He prided himself on his astuteness in world politics; but this morning he would not take the bait. Israel had no intention of signing a peace agreement, he said; meantime, in the process of trying to appease Begin, the Americans and the Egyptians were putting forward proposals that would alienate the Arab world and inevitably push Egypt and America into separate camps.

Thankfully, Sadat never read the paper he had in his hand, but he still seemed upset and uncertain when he left. One of the lessons that each party to the talks was beginning to learn was that, like war, making peace has unforeseen perils. The most important thing that Egypt hoped to gain from the summit was a closer relationship with the U.S., drawing upon the friendship of Sadat and Carter; but in the process of trying to achieve that, they might inadvertently sabotage the basis for any relationship at all.

Unbeknownst to the Americans, Begin had ordered his delegation to issue a declaration that the talks were at an end, but worded in such a fashion as to suggest that the Israelis weren't pulling the plug themselves, and stating that they were "ready to continue with negotiations anytime, anyplace." Weizman and Dayan realized that, no matter what language they used, deserting Camp David now would leave Carter's initiative and perhaps his presidency in ruins. What would that do to Israel's relationship with the U.S.? How long could Israel endure without American political, military, and economic support? "This is going to end with us clearing out of here," Weizman warned his fellow Israelis. "But Sadat will remain—and that's the worst thing of all."

Begin was unyielding. He had given up on the summit. "I shall ask for a meeting with Carter today," he told his delegates. "I'll present our views to him and tell him what we intend to tell the Israeli people and world public opinion."

Dayan left the meeting of the Israeli delegation with all hope bled out of him. On his way to his cabin, he ran into Sam Lewis, the astute American ambassador to Israel. "There's no sense to these meetings and negotiations," Dayan told Lewis curtly. He said he was leaving for Israel right away. Of all the members of the Israeli delegation, Dayan had been the most creative. Now he was walking out on the proceedings. The one person who seemed most invested in getting agreement had surrendered.

Weizman followed Dayan to his cabin. The foreign minister was squatting on the floor, packing his suitcase.

"Moshe," Weizman said. "Don't be hasty. I still have faith."

Vance also rushed over to the Israeli cabin to plead for patience. Dayan advised him to abandon the big issues—such as the Sinai settlements—and find some limited item they could agree upon to save face. Vance rejected this idea. The whole point of Camp David was to resolve the main problems standing in the way of peace, not to produce a symbolic gesture that would leave the situation essentially unchanged. Dayan shrugged. He said he had done his best. History would show that the conversation between the two of them was the last chance to salvage something, he told Vance, and that had failed.

———

WEIZMAN RESPONDED TO the president's summons and found Carter poring over a giant map of Sinai. The White House had requested a map of the peninsula that was fifteen feet by twenty-two feet—the exact dimensions of the Camp David billiards room. Carter had spread it out over the floor and spent a considerable amount of time on his knees examining every wadi and oasis in the region. He told Weizman that he had decided to break the American proposal into two parts: one was to be the grand bargain he hoped would resolve the Middle East conflict; the other would specifically deal with the Sinai settlements in order to achieve a separate peace treaty between Israel and Egypt. From the beginning, the Israelis had hoped to separate the two issues; the trick for Carter would be in linking them in a way that would be acceptable to Sadat.

Carter took his yellow legal pad and spent thirty minutes drafting a proposal to resolve the Sinai dispute. Then he walked over to Sadat's cabin. Sadat read the six-page document in Carter's precise and legible handwriting. It was titled "Framework for a Settlement in Sinai."

"In order to achieve peace between them, Israel and Egypt agree to negotiate in good faith with a goal of concluding within three months of signing this framework a peace treaty between them," the draft began. "All of the principles of UN Resolution 242 will apply in this resolution." The outstanding issues of Sinai, including the "full exercise of Egyptian sovereignty up to the internationally recognized border between Egypt and mandated Palestine," as well as the disposition of the airfields and the stationing of military forces, "will be resolved by negotiations between the parties." The ambiguity of the document was obvious—the framework only said that the problems would be negotiated—but Carter wanted an explicit declaration by each party that if they settled these issues, there would be peace between the two countries.

After less than twenty minutes, Sadat made two small changes in the text, both of which favored the Israeli position. "It's all right," he told Carter.

Evening arrived, and so did the rain. Carter trudged through the mud to Begin's cabin, where the Israelis were gathered. Carter did not intend to show them the Sinai draft yet, in part to slow things down, but he made a point of shaking hands with each member of the delegation, promising that an important new American draft would be given to them the next day. He then offered an inspired and unconventional notion. "Let me suggest that one Israeli and one Egyptian delegate sit down with me for the drafting," he said. Acknowledging the personal hostility that had poisoned the talks so far, Carter was effectively cutting Begin and Sadat out of the process. Carter, however, would remain. This was unprecedented. Even at Camp David, when members of the delegations met, they convened with their peers—Vance would meet with Kamel or Dayan—but the idea that the president of the United States would negotiate with anyone other than a head of state was hard to fathom. Carter already had an idea of the Israeli he wanted to work with: Aharon Barak, who was there simply as a lawyer, not even a member of the Begin government. As for the prime minister himself, Carter suggested that they postpone the meeting that Begin had requested for that evening.

Begin took immediate exception to that. "I beg your pardon, Mr. President," he said. "I have asked to meet you tonight for a very important discussion, maybe the most important I have ever had in my life."

Carter had been intending to eat dinner with the Israeli delegation, but Begin now stood up and announced, "I am going to shave for my meeting with the president. The others can go and watch a movie."

"In that case," Carter said, "I must also go and shave."

HASSAN EL-TOHAMY CONTINUED to pursue Boutros Boutros-Ghali. He confided that he had been up all night, "in communication."

"With whom?" Boutros-Ghali asked.

"Up," Tohamy said, pointing to the heavens. Once again he pressured his fellow delegate to turn to Islam.

"Such a grave decision requires much deliberation," Boutros-Ghali replied.

Sadat was amused to learn of Tohamy's missionary efforts. "Do not underestimate Boutros, Hassan," he said. "You will convert to Christianity before he converts to Islam!"

Tohamy continued to cast a spell over Sadat that the other delegates could not account for. During the heated discussion on his porch that morning, Sadat blurted out, "It could be really great if we could swing this idea of one square mile!" When Mohamed Kamel asked what he meant, Tohamy jumped in to explain his scheme. Israel would withdraw from one square mile of Jerusalem and an Arab or Islamic flag would be hoisted over that territory. When Tohamy finished, he turned to Sadat. "There's one thing I ask of you, *Rayyis,* namely that you fulfill your promise of appointing me governor-general of

Jerusalem," he said. He fantasized riding into Jerusalem on a white steed. "This is my life's dream, and I pray to God you will make it come true before I die!"

Kamel recoiled. Imagine Tohamy ruling over Jerusalem!

At the beginning of the conference, there had seemed to be a consensus on all sides that Jerusalem should remain united, with unimpeded access to the holy places and complete freedom of worship. An independent authority would govern the city itself. This was very much what the UN had in mind for Jerusalem when it partitioned Israel and Palestine in 1947. But the more the Egyptians and the Israelis talked about Jerusalem, the less they agreed. The one issue they thought they could resolve became radioactive because of the conflicting religious claims to the city. The Americans and the Israelis wanted to put the matter off until the end of the summit, but it refused to go away because of Tohamy's emphatic campaigning and his inexplicable influence over Sadat.

Within the rising element of Islamic radicals, Jerusalem played a powerful emotional role. Sadat's trip there had already sent a jolt through the entire Muslim world. Jerusalem was a symbol of the Palestinian movement; pictures of the golden Dome of the Rock were everywhere as a reminder of the claim that Arabs had on the city. Jerusalem had also become a kind of marker for Islam's standing in history. Control of the religious sites had passed back and forth from pagan to Jewish, followed by the Romans, the Crusaders, the Ottomans, the British, and the Arabs. Each of these powers had promoted and exploited the city's cult of holiness. The Old Testament repeatedly asserts that Jerusalem is where God lives and where his power is most efficacious. That promise has drawn pilgrims to the city for centuries. Muslims also endorse the idea that whoever prays in Jerusalem—or *al-Quds*, as it is called in Arabic, the Holy Place—has all his sins absolved and becomes as innocent as a newborn child. Each of the three religions believes that Jerusalem will be the scene of the Last Judgment. Evangelical Christians and Jews say that the Messiah will appear on the Mount of Olives and enter the Old City through the Golden Gate. In Islam, there is a belief that, on that last day, the Kaaba—the holiest place in Mecca—will be spiritually transported to Jerusalem and that the dead will rise and greet each other in jubilation on the streets of the city. Because such legends are believed to be the literal truth, the struggle for Jerusalem never ends.

These dangerous currents created a charge that made Jerusalem almost untouchable at the summit. Genuine, comprehensive peace in the Middle East of the sort that Sadat and Carter envisioned would sap the radical Islamist trend; on the other hand, complete failure would appease the naysayers and allow Sadat to return to the Arab embrace. It was in the middle area of compromise where real peril lay.

Sadat knew that he was mixing highly volatile materials, but these same disparate elements were a part of his own personality. He had always been attracted to Islamist politics, and in his youthful revolutionary days, he had met several times with Hassan al-Banna, the founder of the Muslim Brotherhood, a clandestine organization that was destined to shape the political climate of the entire Arab region and give birth to even more radical spin-offs in the future. Eventually Sadat served as a conduit between the Brothers and Nasser's underground junta-in-waiting, the Free Officers. Sadat even arranged a back channel between Banna and the palace, through the king's private doctor.

Following the mortifying defeat of Egypt and other Arab armies in the 1948 War of Independence, the clandestine Muslim Brotherhood boomed in membership. The population of Egypt at that time was about eighteen million, and as many as one million of them were in the Brotherhood. Some of Sadat's fellow coup plotters in the military also joined the Brothers, swearing allegiance on a Quran and a revolver. The terrorist arm of the organization, called the secret apparatus, bombed theaters, harassed Jews, and turned on the government, assassinating prominent officials. The king himself felt sufficiently threatened by the Muslim Brothers that the palace had Banna killed in 1949. But the Brotherhood survived its founder's death.

When Nasser's revolution took power in 1952, he tried to work with the Brotherhood, appointing its premier propagandist, Sayyid Qutb, as an adviser to the Revolutionary Command Council. But the Brothers and the Free Officers had practically nothing in common. Nasser's dream was to unite the Arabs, with Egypt at the center of a secular, socialist republic. The Brothers had a similar but wholly incompatible goal: to recreate a Muslim theocracy, called a caliphate, which had been dormant since the collapse of the Ottoman Empire. The tension between these opposing utopian ideals would roil Egypt for decades to come. Nasser came to wage an unending campaign against the Brotherhood, imprisoning its leadership and, in 1966, hanging Qutb, who had been convicted of plotting to overthrow the government.

After Nasser died in 1970, Sadat looked to the Islamists for allies, calculating that they would stand with him against the Nasserites and Communists. He began a dialogue with the imprisoned Brotherhood leaders, which ended with the new president allowing the Brothers back into society as long as they renounced violence. Sadat didn't realize that there had been a generational split among the Islamists. Radical new groups were already forming, which reached far beyond Egypt's borders. He had granted the Islamists freedom, but they were watching him, and waiting.

AT EIGHT P.M., a clean-shaven Begin appeared at Carter's cabin. "This is the most serious talk I have ever had in my life, except once when I discussed the future of Israel with Jabotinsky," Begin said, invoking his political mentor. Then he proceeded to reject everything in the American proposal.

The first subject on Begin's agenda was UN Resolution 242. Yes, Israel had signed it, he admitted, but he was unwilling to cite it in the "Framework for Peace." To bolster his case, the prime minister pulled out a number of old press clippings from different countries about the resolution that omitted the telltale phrase "inadmissibility of acquisition of territory by war." To Carter, the yellowed clippings seemed weirdly beside the point, but Begin insisted that Israel could not agree under any circumstances to sign a document that included this language.

Then for the next hour, Begin spoke passionately about Sinai. He referred to a conversation he had had with an Egyptian general, who told him it would take only seven hours for the Egyptian Army to cross the Suez Canal and move to the border of Israel. "Seven hours!" Begin stressed to Carter. "When we evacuate Sinai there won't be one Israeli soldier, or one Israeli tank, between that Egyptian Army on this side of the Suez Canal, and on the other, to stop them. And in seven hours they can be on our southern border and threaten the civilian population of our country." It was all the more reason that the Israeli settlements would have to remain. "Mr. President, do we ask for one square kilometer of Sinai?" he asked. "Didn't we produce a peace plan in accordance with which all the peninsula will go to Egypt?" Under Israel's proposal, however, those thirteen settlements must remain; nothing else stood in the way of a hypothetical blitzkrieg move by Egyptian forces. Begin vowed that he would resign before agreeing to withdraw from them. "I will not surrender to Sadat's ultimatums or threats."

Begin turned to the West Bank—"Judea and Samaria"—and Gaza. They were a part of Greater Israel, Begin insisted, "the land of our forefathers, which we have never forgotten during exile, when we were a persecuted minority, humiliated, killed, our blood shed, burned alive. . . ." Israel would be perfectly entitled to declare its sovereignty over these regions, but Begin had chosen to find an alternative solution. "We wracked our brains and wounded our hearts, and we found a way," he said. "Let the question of sovereignty remain open. And let us deal with the human beings. With the peoples on both sides. Let us give the Palestinian Arabs autonomy and the Palestinian Jews security, and we shall live together in human dignity."

By "autonomy" Begin meant that the Palestinians would be given nominal authority to rule themselves, but Israel would retain a veto and military control over the districts. Since Israel was not formally annexing the land in Judea, Samaria, and Gaza, Begin contended, the whole question of the "acquisition of territory" was moot.

Carter brought up the proposal of an Arab flag on the Temple Mount. The Saudis were also pressing for this symbolic gesture. "Never!" Begin cried. "What will happen when the Messiah comes? After all, that's where we are supposed to build the Temple, and agreeing to an Arab flag would mean giving up our faith." He cited the Book of Psalms, 137:5–6, saying, "If I forget you, Jerusalem, may my right hand forget. May my tongue stick to my palate if I do not remember you, if I do not exalt Jerusalem beyond all my delights." It is a phrase every Jewish male cites at his wedding when he breaks a glass in memory of the torment the city has endured since the glorious days of King David, who established the city as the eternal capital of the Jewish nation three thousand years ago. (Begin neglected to quote the end of that Psalm, a paean to revenge and enduring hatred: "Blessed the one who seizes your children and smashes them against the rock!")

Jerusalem was simply nonnegotiable.

Finally, Begin reached in his pocket and pulled out the declaration he had prepared. Carter braced himself. There was no way to stall Begin, as he had done with Sadat. The statement had been softened with bland expressions of gratitude for Carter's initiative, but essentially it declared the summit was at an end. When he finished reading, Begin added that he sincerely wished he could have signed Carter's proposal, but he had to represent the will of the Israeli people.

By now, Carter was truly furious. He had suffered through Begin's repetitive, contentious lecture for an hour and a half. He pointed out that public opinion polls in Israel repeatedly showed a substantial majority favoring peace, even if it meant an end to the settlements and the surrender of large amounts of the West Bank then under Israeli control. Carter said that he represented the Israeli people's position better than Begin.

The meeting turned so nasty and personal that Carter

finally stood up for Begin to leave. He accused the prime minister of being unreasonably obsessed with the question of settlements. Was Israel really willing to give up peace with its only formidable enemy, included unimpeded access to the Suez Canal and the Straits of Tiran, free trade and full diplomatic recognition from Egypt, an end to the economic boycott, Arab acceptance of an undivided Jerusalem, permanent security for Israel and the approbation of the entire world—all to keep a few illegal settlers on Egyptian land?

Begin responded enigmatically, saying that Israel did not want any territory in Sinai or the West Bank *for the first five years*. Carter had no idea what he meant. Later, Begin's team explained he was saying that he would agree to "decide" the future of the West Bank after five years, rather than simply to "consider" it, as he had previously said.

It was late, and both men were tired and angry. The meeting had ended on an inconclusive note. Each of them had said things they regretted but were unwilling to call back. Was the summit over? As Begin wandered back in the dark to his cabin, it wasn't clear what the next day would bring.

Day Nine

Aharon Barak, Moshe Dayan, and Menachem Begin

IT IS STRIKING THAT, in a region as intimate as the Middle East, cultural ignorance and political miscalculation have played such perverse roles. By attacking the new country of Israel in 1948, the Arabs lost the chance to create an entity for Palestine. Through its policy of expulsion of the native population, Israel destabilized its neighbors and created a reservoir of future terrorists that was continually refreshed by new wars and population transfers. In 1956, the Israelis waged a proxy war for the European imperial powers that stoked the paranoia of the Arabs and gave Egypt a plausible reason for its enmity. In 1967, the Six-Day War was set off by actions and rhetoric on Nasser's part that were bound to elicit a belligerent response from Israel, although Nasser was blind to the consequences. Israel asserted that its borders weren't defensible, but even so it rapidly dispatched Egypt, along with Jordan and Syria, seizing the West Bank, Gaza, the Golan Heights, and Sinai, and setting the stage for the next conflict.

Immediately after the Six-Day War, Israel considered withdrawing to its former international boundaries in Sinai and the Golan Heights in exchange for demilitarization of those regions. Israel wanted to keep Sharm el-Sheikh in order to ensure its access through the Straits of Tiran. The West Bank would not be a part of the offer, however. The Arab leaders responded at a summit in Khartoum with a unanimous declaration of no peace, no negotiations, and no recognition of the State of Israel. Abba Eban, the eloquent Israeli foreign minister, remarked that it was "the first war in history in which the victor sued for peace and the loser called for unconditional surrender." In any case, Israel never formally presented its offer because its enemies had been so thoroughly crushed and posed no real threat.

Egypt and Israel now faced each other across the Suez Canal in entrenched positions. Although it is not often counted in the tally of bloodshed between Egypt and Israel, the constant artillery duels for two years after 1968, called the War of Attrition, took a toll on each side—Israel suffered about 3,500 casualties and the Egyptians perhaps 10,000. Impatient with the state of affairs, the Israelis embarked in January 1970 on a series of deep-penetration bombing raids, aiming to bring the war home to the Egyptian people and cause them to rise up against Nasser—the same mistaken psychology employed by the French and British in 1956, with the same result: the Egyptians rallied behind their leader. Nasser then turned to the Soviets for help; they supplied him with weapons, troops, trainers, Soviet pilots, and an advanced missile system, setting the stage for the war to follow. The Nixon administration negotiated a nominal end to the hostilities, but Israel continued to believe that the only route to peace was through total military domination. The Israelis were aided in this illusion by the support of the Americans, who implicitly encouraged the tactic of trying to bomb the Egyptians into submission—even though the strategy had been proved worthless so far in Vietnam.

In October 1971, Sadat went to Moscow to demand more weapons. He had already declared 1971 as the Year of Decision. "We shall not allow 1971 to pass without deciding the issue, whether through peace or war—even if it means sacrificing one million lives," Sadat had grandly announced that summer. But his fateful pledge rested on the promise of the Soviet Union to supply Egypt with additional modern arms, and his very public declaration placed him in a quandary as the calendar was moving forward to call his bluff.

The Soviets had already supplied Egypt with sophisticated anti-aircraft missile batteries and other armaments. The country was overrun with Soviet political aides, intelligence agents, foreign service officers, and more than fifteen thousand combat troops. Their domineering presence had begun to remind the Egyptians of the days of the British occupation. The Soviets were also uneasy. It was the first time they had placed their own troops in jeopardy in a non-Communist country. That made the White House nervous, especially after the Israeli Air Force shot down four aircraft flown by Russian pilots.

Sadat felt that Soviet military aid was designed to keep Egypt just far enough behind Israel that it wouldn't be tempted to actually use the weapons. Despite his repeated entreaties to the Soviets to fulfill commitments they had already made, the additional arms never seemed to arrive, and Sadat began to look increasingly feckless in the eyes of his countrymen. He returned from Moscow that fall with a guarantee of missile-equipped aircraft, along with Soviet experts to train Egyptian crews in how to operate them. Sadat desperately wanted the new weapons in place before the end of the year, but two months later, he still had nothing to show for the promises made in Moscow. The Year of Decision ended and the Year of Derision began.

The Soviets were in the middle of a much more important secret negotiation—détente with the United States—and the arms buildup in the Middle East was a concern to both superpowers. There was no place on the globe more likely to set off a catastrophic confrontation between them. Each had vital interests in the region that they believed had to be defended at all costs, but the continual skirmishing between their allies, and the increased sophistication and destructiveness of the weapons available to belligerents, meant that the fate of the United States and the USSR wasn't entirely in their own hands.

In May 1972, Nixon visited the Soviet Union, and the first declaration of the newly revealed détente emphasized the need for military relaxation in the Middle East. Sadat was beside himself. He thought he would never get his weapons now. He summoned the Soviet ambassador. "I have decided to dispense with the services of all Soviet military experts," he told the stunned envoy. "They must go back to the Soviet Union within one week from today."

This apparently rash action turned out to be one of the most brilliant maneuvers in Sadat's career. In a single stroke he upended the diplomatic structure of the Middle East and the strategic balance of the superpowers. It was one of America's greatest victories in the Cold War, and yet it was completely unexpected. By pulling Egypt out of the Soviet embrace, Sadat was able to steer his economy away from the socialist model that had retarded its development. Moreover, the chastened Soviets began speeding up the arms shipments, hoping to regain Sadat's favor. The U.S. found itself with a new ally in its lap—and new responsibilities. Camp David would not have been possible if Sadat had not thrust his country into America's zone of influence.

An added benefit, as far as Sadat was concerned, was that all parties misinterpreted his reason for Soviet expulsion. Israel, the Soviets, and the West all concluded that Sadat had thrown out the Soviet military because he had decided against going to war. In fact, he realized that he could not fight a war so long as the Soviets exercised a restraining hand.

"Why has he done us this favor?" Kissinger asked his aides. "Why didn't he demand all kinds of concessions first?" To compound the confusion, the Americans got a note from Cairo in September explaining that Egypt was not seeking any special consideration from the U.S. because of its action. While deploring American partiality to Israel, the letter expressed a willingness to reopen the Suez Canal, which had been closed since the 1967 war, and set no preconditions for talks with the U.S. "It was all, as I would come to realize, vintage Sadat,"

Kissinger later recalled. "His negotiating tactic was never to haggle over detail but to create an atmosphere that made disagreement psychologically difficult." Sadat perceived that agreement on broad concepts was more important than were complicated formulations in a treaty destined to be ignored or disavowed. "I cannot say that I fully understood Sadat's insight then," Kissinger admitted. "Great men are so rare that they take some getting used to."

ERIK BRIK WAS BORN in the Lithuanian city of Kovno (now called Kaunus), in the year 1936. His father was a lawyer who headed the local Zionist office; his mother was a teacher. In June 1941, the same month that the Nazis occupied Begin's hometown of Brisk, they also marched into Kovno. "I remember machine guns mowing down Jews," he would later tell Israeli journalist Ari Shavit. "I remember the Jews of my hometown being murdered en masse by the Nazis." He was five years old.

The Nazis didn't have to do all the work themselves. This was early in the project of mass extermination, and in Kovno, a center of Jewish culture and learning, the Nazis found that they could stand aside and let the citizens of the city beat their former neighbors to death. Thousands of Jews were shot or bludgeoned while people gathered to watch or take a hand in the slaughter. Similar homicidal orgies took place in other Lithuanian cities and in the Ukraine. But the deepest reaches of depravity were still to be fathomed.

For the next three years, the Brik family lived in the Kovno ghetto. Erik was one of 1.6 million Jewish children in the territories occupied by the Nazis. By the end of the war, more than a million of those children would be dead. In the final months, the Nazis decided to eliminate all the Jewish children, because they were "useless eaters" who contributed no labor. German soldiers went from house to house in the ghetto, rounding up everyone under twelve. Erik's mother hid her eight-year-old son, but after the slaughter was over, he had to dress up with elevator shoes and a hat, pretending to be adolescent. Eventually, his father was able to smuggle Erik out of the ghetto in a canvas sack tossed onto a horse cart. His mother escaped soon after. For six months they lived behind a double wall in the cottage of a family that gave them refuge, coming out only at night. During the days, as they sat in the dark behind the wall, Erik's mother made him her only student, teaching him math, Latin, and history.

Erik's father continued to labor in the ghetto until the end of the war, when he was finally reunited with his wife and son. Like many survivors, the Brik family then made a long journey through the wreckage of Europe, being robbed by Russian soldiers along the way and abused by anti-Semites in Poland and Hungary, until they arrived in the British zone in Austria, where they were met by soldiers of a Jewish brigade. It was like a dream. The soldiers spoke Hebrew, a language Erik didn't yet know.

Finally they boarded a ship to Haifa. Erik's aunt was waiting for them. She bought him Israeli clothes—khaki shirt, trousers, and sandals. "When I took off my old clothes I shed the past, the Diaspora, the ghetto," he said. "I was a new person. An Israeli."

He also took a new name: Aharon Barak.

Barak quickly learned Hebrew and assimilated into Israeli society. He became the youngest faculty member at Hebrew

University's law school; he was dean at the age of thirty-eight, and Israel's attorney general three years later. He had a reputation for integrity and toughness; it was he who had indicted the wife of Prime Minister Yitzhak Rabin, which opened the door to Begin's eventual election over Rabin's replacement, Shimon Peres. Barak brought an end to the official tolerance of political corruption that had characterized the country until that point.

Even in high office, Barak still gave the impression of a professor with his head buried in abstruse legal theorems. His fingers were covered with ink stains, his pants did not always match his jacket, and his hair grew shaggy from neglect. He seemed to be a man who never looked in the mirror. During cabinet deliberations he was remarked for his doodling and the occasional sigh. Just before Camp David, he had been appointed to the Israeli supreme court, the youngest justice in the country's history. Begin had to make a special appeal to the court to allow him to join the delegation.

In this new stage of the Camp David negotiations, Barak was matched with Osama el-Baz, a fellow prosecutor—he had been appointed the district attorney of Cairo, after graduating at the top of his class from Cairo University's law school. Slight, almost elfish, with a sallow complexion and a raspy voice, Baz was easily mistaken for a teenager, but his intellect was impossible to miss. One of nine children, Baz came from a distinguished academic family. His father had been a well-known Islamic scholar. One of his brothers, Farouk, was a geologist who worked on the Apollo lunar landings. Osama himself spent six years at Harvard Law School, gaining two advanced degrees. While there, he studied with Henry Kissinger and Roger Fisher—the same man who had helped Cy Vance prepare for Camp David.

Carter considered Baz to be the most extreme of all the Egyptian delegates. He had been head of the Harvard Society of Arab Students and had written Sadat's assertive speech in Jerusalem. Despite his zealous reputation, Baz had had a Jewish girlfriend while he was studying in the U.S.; in fact, he had asked a member of the Israeli delegation to bring a menorah to Camp David so he could send it to her.

Sadat had appointed Baz to be Vice President Mubarak's chief political officer, with the instruction to teach "the future president" what he had learned at Harvard. As Mubarak's right-hand man, Baz was one of the most influential figures in the Egyptian government, but the cherished perks of his job never interested him. He maintained a defiant simplicity, riding the bus to work and eating the humblest Egyptian fare—*ful* and *falafel*—in everyday restaurants. He had a horror of social events and tended to hide in his work. Even at Camp David, he would sit quietly at dinner, wary and solitary, picking at his food; but during conferences he would spring to life, often with slashing responses that betrayed both his unyielding ideology and his mastery of the material. Sadat trusted Baz more than anyone else in his delegation. At times, he would bring Baz into meetings, ostensibly as a translator and notetaker. They had a prearranged code: when there was something put forward in a meeting that Baz didn't agree with, he would subtly raise his head, then look back down at his notes. At this signal, Sadat would table the proposal.

CARTER'S EXPERIMENT with the two proxy negotiators began at eight that Wednesday morning. Without Sadat or Begin in the room, there was a different atmosphere, although one that placed their two delegates in a very awkward spot.

They were the two most brilliant legal minds at Camp David, but instead of arguing a case in a courtroom they were negotiating the future of their countries with the president of the United States.

Baz and Barak met with Carter and Vance for eleven hours that day. Carter began by attacking the issue of Resolution 242, which the Israelis had objected to because of the phrase "inadmissibility of acquisition of territory by war" in the prologue. To avoid setting a precedent for the West Bank if Israel withdrew from Sinai, Barak came up with an ingenious formulation. Israel would agree that Resolution 242 applied to the West Bank, but once the autonomy agreement was in place and the Palestinians had secured political control, the territory would no longer be formally "occupied." Therefore the question of withdrawal was moot. Carter responded by saying Barak could be a justice on the U.S. Supreme Court. Carter went on to suggest deleting the contentious phrase from the main text of the agreement while noting that both parties agreed to Resolution 242 "in all its parts." The entire text of the resolution would be stuck in an appendix. Barak agreed to this stratagem, but Baz hesitated. Resolution 242 was a central plank in the Egyptian platform, and the degree to which it appeared to be downgraded to accommodate Begin meant that it came at the expense of Egyptian priorities. Carter disarmingly offered to let Baz delete any phrase in that part of the text that he did not like. Baz pointed to the sentence "They have both also stated that there shall be no more war between them." He reasoned that if Israel did not withdraw from Sinai, another war might be necessary. When Barak posed no objection, the first concrete agreement of the Camp David summit became a reality.

Another seemingly small but intractable problem was

solved when it was decided to use the term "West Bank" in the
American and Egyptian versions of the agreement, and "Judea
and Samaria" in the Israeli text. On the question of the Sinai
settlements, however, Barak said he could not even discuss it
because Begin felt so strongly about the issue. That very day
Begin had vowed to Brzezinski, "My right eye will fall out, my
right hand will fall off, before I ever agree to the dismantling
of a single Jewish settlement."

In that case, Baz said, Egypt would not commit to open
borders and full diplomatic recognition.

By now night had fallen. The men were discussing the
problem of refugees when Baz asserted that Israel could not
be a part of deciding which Palestinians could return to the
West Bank. Carter set his pen down and stared at Baz. In such
moments, Carter doesn't shout, but his blue eyes blaze and
his fury is clearly apparent. He said that he had previously
talked to Sadat about this very issue. Had Sadat now reversed
himself?

Baz finally admitted that he had not actually talked to
Sadat about the matter; it was actually his idea, but he thought
Sadat would agree with him.

"Reaching agreement with you has become impossible,"
Carter said. "I want to talk to President Sadat." He then stood
up for Baz to leave.

Aharon Barak was a bit shaken by the flash of presidential anger. "When he gets furious, he's really furious!" Barak
recalled. On the other hand, the basic framework of an agreement seemed to be taking shape. "Now I have faith in Israel's
sincere desire for peace," Carter told him.

Barak went back to the Israeli cabin and briefed the others on what had transpired. Despite all the progress that had

been made, the summit was coming down to a single issue: the Sinai settlements. Weizman had spoken to Sadat earlier that day to see if there was any way to soften his opposition. "I won't give up a single inch of my land!" Sadat had declared.

Later, Carter went looking for Begin and found him in the projection room watching a movie. The president described the Sinai agreement that Vance and Brzezinski would present to Dayan and Weizman. Once again, Begin said he would not sign anything that called for the removal of the settlements, and Carter replied that there would be no agreement without it. The success of the summit balanced on this issue.

"It is out of the question," Begin said.

SADAT WAS WATCHING television when Osama el-Baz arrived to tell him of his disastrous encounter with Carter on the issue of the returning Palestinian refugees. "You're right," Sadat replied. "It is impossible for me to agree to an article like that. But you know my strategy, Osama. We want to gain Carter for our side. I know he's a weak man, but let's be patient."

"It's not his right to talk in your name," Baz grumbled. "I'm the one representing you."

"We must make do," Sadat said. "What will Carter do now?"

"He will call you, sir."

"I won't talk to him now. I want to think." Sadat told Baz to turn off the light as he left so Sadat could pretend that he had retired. "Tell the secretary I am sleeping and no one is to contact me at all."

When word came to Carter that Sadat was unavailable, he

grew suspicious. He knew the Egyptian president was a night owl, and it seemed out of character for him to go to bed at nine thirty p.m.

When Rosalynn returned from a day in Washington, she found Jimmy reading in bed. He told her it had been a fairly good day; matters had gone better than expected with the Israelis but abysmally with the Egyptians. When they went to sleep, he was still feeling upbeat.

Suddenly, in the middle of the night, Carter awakened with a horrible premonition. Suspicious things were happening with the Egyptians, he believed. He recalled the violent argument he had observed on Sadat's porch the day before. The strange behavior of Baz in the meeting today. The lights out in Sadat's cabin hours before he normally retired. All of these moments crowded together in a worrisome conspiracy and kept him from falling back to sleep.

Rosalynn stirred and then woke when she realized Jimmy was up. It was four a.m., and he was clearly agitated. "I don't know exactly why, but I have an uneasy feeling about Sadat's safety," he admitted. He roused Brzezinski, who came over in his pajamas, along with the head of the Secret Service detail. "Zbig, I am very much concerned for Sadat's life," Carter said.

Day Ten

Hassan el-Tohamy, Mohamed Ibrahim Kamel, and Ahmed Maher confer with Jimmy Carter

AT EIGHT A.M., Jimmy and Rosalynn looked out the window of Aspen Lodge and saw Sadat setting out for his morning constitutional. Immensely relieved, Carter rushed out to join him.

Sadat kept a brisk, military pace as they marched through the forest paths. Carter was in an expansive mood, although he didn't tell Sadat about his apprehensions of the night before. Sadat confided that since the trip to Gettysburg, he had seen

Carter in a different light—as someone who could understand the ravages of war, not just the damage to material things but to the spirit of a defeated people as well. They talked about how long it was taking America to get past the psychic wounds of the Vietnam War. Sadat wondered whether the people of the Middle East would ever recover, even if they made peace at Camp David.

Carter came back to Aspen and went directly to his study. He wanted to work on the latest American draft before Aharon Barak arrived. Rosalynn was headed to Washington again that morning for a luncheon, and before she left she looked in to see what Jimmy's mood was. When he saw her, he pushed back his chair. "Come here," he said. Rosalynn sat in his lap. "I think it's all coming together now," he said cheerfully.

FROM THE BEGINNING of the conference, Weizman had been urging Sadat and Dayan to meet. He thought that the two of them could break through the psychological obstacles that blocked a settlement. Carter also thought it was important for Sadat and Dayan to talk, because the Israeli foreign minister was the most creative member of the team and also the one most familiar with the West Bank. And yet both men had resisted. Sadat loathed and feared Dayan because he was the architect of the Six-Day War. No Arab could look at Dayan without experiencing once again the flood of shame that followed that overpowering defeat. Moreover, Dayan's blunt and unsparing manner grated on Egyptian habits of formality and indirection, in which difficult conversations were buttered over with social pleasantries.

For his part, Dayan owed the destruction of his legend to

Sadat. He had been minister of defense when Sadat sent the Egyptian Army across the Suez Canal in 1973, shattering the sense of invulnerability that Israel had cloaked itself in. It was Israel's Pearl Harbor. Dayan had been Israel's greatest hero, but he got the largest dose of the blame. Before the war, he had been a figure on the cover of magazines around the world, adored by women and courted by statesmen, but after 1973 he was shunned even by people he had never respected—all because of Sadat.

A meeting between the two men was bound to stir up powerful conflicting feelings, even though they were seeking the same goal, perhaps more ardently than anyone else at Camp David. Under pressure, Sadat finally agreed to talk to Dayan, "for Carter's sake." That phrase would become an inside joke with the Egyptian delegation, because just when the summit seemed to be on the verge of finding a path to peace, the meeting that neither man wanted would bring everything crashing down.

THE ILLUSION THAT led to Israel's greatest military setback, and was the source of Dayan's disgrace, was the Bar-Lev Line. It was one of the great defensive fortifications in military history. Erected after the 1967 war, and stretching a hundred miles along the eastern bank of the Suez Canal, the line presented a sheer, seventy-foot-high sandy rampart facing the Egyptian troops on the western bank, like a mountainous man-made fault line. Buried inside the cliff face were thirty-six Israeli outposts built of reinforced concrete, meant to withstand direct hits from artillery or bombs of more than a thousand pounds. Each fort was equipped with machine-gun emplacements, anti-aircraft weapons, and mortars. In the basement of the multistory forts, there were large containers of oil that could be spewed onto the surface of the canal in order to set the water ablaze. In the intervals between fortifications there were three hundred firing positions for tanks. A second line of defense ran six to eight kilometers to the rear, which included airfields, underground command centers, long-range artillery positions, and anti-aircraft missile bases. All of these positions were encased in multiple circles of barbed wire and studded with minefields and booby traps. Israelis saw the monumental barricade as their first line of defense, but to the Egyptians, the Bar-Lev Line represented Israel's attempt to confiscate the entire Sinai.

In 1973, Dayan, then minister of defense, took an American diplomat, Nicholas Veliotes, on a tour of the fortifications. They stood atop the mountainous rampart and looked across the canal, two hundred yards wide, at the Egyptian encampment. As usual, the Egyptian soldiers were playing soccer, fishing, and swimming in the canal. Veliotes asked what would happen if Egyptian forces attacked without warning. "The Egyptian Army today is like a ship covered with rust while anchored in harbor and unable to move!" Dayan said dismissively. He was reflecting the consensus of the Israeli defense establishment. Peace no longer seemed necessary or even desirable. Dayan was already drawing up plans to enlarge the State of Israel even more, stretching from the Jordan River to the canal and fortified by new Jewish settlements. "There is no more Palestine," he told *Time* magazine in July. "Finished."

The euphoria of the 1967 victory had blinded Israel to

the possibility that Arabs were still capable of inflicting real damage. One after another the Israeli commanders published memoirs and went on television describing their brilliant tactics in the last war and forecasting endless Israeli dominance. An attack by the Arabs was unthinkable, they agreed, suicide.

But as much as the Six-Day War marked a peak moment in the Israeli experience, it was also a turning point for Egyptian society. The defeat acted as a spur to modernization, especially in the military. Before the war, the Arab world treated Israel as if it didn't exist. Customs officers ripped out pages in imported books that mentioned Israel, including the Larousse French dictionary and *Encyclopaedia Britannica*. After the war, the Egyptian leader became obsessed with knowing his enemy. Nasser got tapes of the chest-thumping Israeli generals on television, and he watched them for days on end trying to decipher the secret of their success. Obviously, surprise was key; whoever struck first had a decided advantage. Another reason for the Israeli victory was their superior equipment, and so Nasser persuaded the Soviets to resupply the Egyptian forces with better munitions. But those weren't the only advantages the Israelis enjoyed; their soldiers were simply more capable and better motivated than the Egyptians. Nasser concluded that there would have to be a transformation of the armed forces. University graduates were recruited into the officer corps and encouraged to study Hebrew. Soviet advisers trained the Egyptian troops. Even with all these changes, Nasser had little hope of achieving victory.

When Sadat came to power in 1970, he received a tentative overture from Moshe Dayan for an interim solution: both sides would withdraw outside of artillery range and allow the Egyptians to resume operation of the canal. Sadat responded a few months later with a far more ambitious initiative to declare a cease-fire and sign a peace agreement with Israel through the UN. His price was the return of Sinai to Egyptian sovereignty. Israel could maintain a security presence at key points, such as Sharm el-Sheikh. The Palestinians would be assured of either a state of their own or affiliation with the Kingdom of Jordan. In a secret overture to the U.S., Sadat's envoy confided to Kissinger that there was a deadline for beginning peace negotiations: September 1973, shortly before the Israeli elections. By that time, Israel would have to make a partial withdrawal from Sinai as a good-faith deposit on the future treaty. Prime Minister Golda Meir rejected the deal. She pressured Kissinger to stall Sadat's peace overture and maintain the political deadlock until after the elections. In return, Kissinger extracted a fateful promise that Israel would not initiate another war.

With the failure of his initiative, Sadat announced that "the stage of total confrontation" was about to begin. "Everything in this country is now being mobilized in earnest for the resumption of the battle—which is now inevitable," he told *Newsweek* in April 1973. "The time has come for a shock." Nobody believed him. In Egypt, he had become a laughingstock. The complacent Israelis ignored the buildup of troops along the canal that fall, which they accounted as another pointless maneuver by the feckless Egyptian leader. After all, without the Soviets, Egypt would have to fight on its own, or with another weakened Arab state. The assumption was that, because the Arabs would lose, they wouldn't start a war. This idea was so sensible that the Israelis were deaf to any other argument. Menachem Begin warned of the need to counter the movement of a large number of Egyptian tanks near the canal, but he was a lone voice. The canal itself was the greatest tank trap ever devised, Israeli defense specialists observed, to say nothing of the formidable Bar-Lev Line. Even as the experts told themselves this, however, Israel was gradually scaling down its canal defenses. About a third of the outposts were sealed with sand and left as dummy fortifications, and troop levels were reduced in those that remained.

Dayan had threatened that, in the event of war, "I don't rule out planning to reach the Nile." He had always viewed war as an opportunity to expand Israel's borders, and as the secret September deadline approached, he began boldly speaking of "a new Israel, with wide borders, not like in 1948." He advocated for more settlements in Sinai and Golan to consolidate Israel's occupation. He announced the construction of an Israeli port in northern Sinai, in Egyptian territorial waters. All this confirmed in Sadat's mind that the Israelis were never going to willingly surrender Egyptian territory. War was the only recourse.

Egyptian military planners spent years studying the challenge before them. First, they had to get their troops across the canal. That objective was broken down into discrete tasks, such as backing trucks up to a water barrier and braking so abruptly that the momentum hurled segments of a pontoon out of the truck bed into the water. Twice a day for four years crews worked to unload the trucks in exactly this manner; meantime, other crews trained to bolt the floating segments together to form a bridge. Once the first wave got across, Israeli tanks would be waiting to greet the infantry; in order to blast through that armored barrier, Egyptian teams that would be operating the new handheld Soviet Sagger anti-tank missiles trained every day in a simulator. Endless repetitions made such actions second nature, even among soldiers who doubted they would ever be put to use.*

But the biggest challenge facing the attackers was the formidable Bar-Lev Line. The Russians had told them that only an atom bomb could destroy it. Neither conventional bombs nor artillery could blast open passages in the rampart; the sand just collapsed and filled in the hole. Finally, Egyptian engineers came up with an ingenious solution: they discovered that high-pressure fire hoses connected to turbine-driven German pumps, capable of spewing a thousand gallons a minute, could melt the sand away with seawater drawn right from the canal. Replicas of the barricade were built and blasted down day and night, until the teams could punch a twenty-foot-wide corridor through the wall of sand in the space of five hours. After that, the infantry and the tanks would pour through. Sadat labeled the plan Operation Badr, a reference to the siege of Mecca in 624 CE, by the Prophet Muhammad, in which the Quran says he was assisted by three thousand "havoc-making" angels.

Many considerations went into the timing of the invasion—for instance, the tide should be low and the sun in the eyes of the defenders. Syria planned to attack simultaneously, but there was a possibility of snowfall in the Golan Heights in the late fall. October was the optimum time, with its long nights and moderate weather. As it turned out, the Israelis would also be in the middle of its parliamentary election, and the Americans were hypnotized by the Watergate scandal. October

---

* In an Israeli survey of eight thousand Egyptian prisoners captured during the war, only one said he knew that an actual war was imminent three days before the battle, and 95 percent of the soldiers said they learned of it the day of the actual invasion. Herzog, *The War of Atonement*, p. 39.

that year was also Ramadan, the fasting month for Muslims, which would make an invasion seem less likely to Israelis but which only enhanced the religious significance of the occasion for the Egyptians. There was one date that leaped out to the military planners: Yom Kippur, the Day of Atonement, which fell that year on October 6. Ordinary activity in Israel would come to a near-total halt—no buses, no radio, no television— meaning it would be difficult to call up the reserves. The moon that day would shine from sunset to midnight.

On October 4, the remaining Soviet families in Egypt and also in Syria were evacuated—another clear signal that war was imminent. The next day, Israeli aerial reconnaissance discovered five Egyptian divisions poised on the western bank of the canal, along with mobile bridge units and an additional fifty-six batteries of artillery; even in the face of all this, the Israeli cabinet still refused to believe that the Arabs would actually attack. Perhaps the memory of the Egyptian soldiers fleeing in their underwear in 1956 still played in Dayan's mind, blinding him to the blow that was about to fall. But he wasn't alone. Israeli military leaders largely agreed that the likelihood of war breaking out was "the lowest of the low."

The night before the invasion, Egyptian frogmen swam across the canal to sabotage the fuel lines that were meant to incinerate any assault vessels that attempted to cross. Syria had already moved up missile batteries within range of Golan. That same evening, Israel sent a message to Kissinger assuring him that war was unlikely.

Then, in the very early morning of October 6, Israeli intelligence notified military authorities that they had gotten word from a well-placed and trusted spy—actually, Nasser's son-in-law and Sadat's confidant, Ashraf Marwan—that the Egyptian forces were going to invade at six p.m. that evening. A meeting took place in Dayan's office before dawn. He still opposed a general mobilization or a preemptive air attack. Mindful of Israel's secret pledge to Kissinger not to start a war, he argued that Israel's regular army should be able to absorb a first strike and quickly organize a massive retaliation; later that morning, however, Meir overruled him and authorized the mobilization of 100,000 troops. It would still take at least twenty-four hours for them to reach the Egyptian front.

The Egyptians were puzzled by the lack of response on the Israeli side; their intentions had been obvious since the spring, when Sadat had publicly spelled out exactly what was going to happen. And yet, on the day the war began, on the Bar-Lev Line itself there were only 436 Israeli soldiers, 3 tanks, and 70 artillery pieces, with an additional 8,000 men and 277 tanks in the rear. They were facing 100,000 Egyptian troops and 1,550 tanks on the western shore.

At 2:05 p.m., the Egyptian artillery—nearly two thousand guns—opened up, raining more than ten thousand shells per minute on Israeli positions. Fifteen minutes later, eight thousand commandos and engineers burst over the western bank and jumped into rubber dinghies. Each of the 750 boats had been numbered and color-coded to avoid confusion. Meantime, low-flying Egyptian jets struck Israeli air bases, anti-aircraft missile batteries, command centers, and radar stations. Simultaneously, from the east, seven hundred Syrian tanks charged toward Israeli positions on the Golan Heights.

When the Egyptian commandos reached the eastern bank of the canal, they scaled the massive barricade of the Bar-Lev Line on rope ladders and planted Egyptian flags atop the fortifications. Water pumps began blasting through the sand.

Within a few hours, sixty passages had been opened in the line. Five infantry divisions crossed in a continuous flood—on bridges, boats, some soldiers even swam. "My God," an Israeli radioman reported to the rear defenses, "it's like the Chinese coming across."

The Israeli Air Force, slow to get off the ground, arrived two hours later, but they were knocked out of the sky by heat-seeking SA-6 missiles, which took out twelve Phantom jets before the stymied Israelis turned back. Israeli tank squadrons—so devastating in the previous war—rushed from their rear-guard positions toward the canal to relieve the surviving defenders. Egyptian commandos were waiting for them with wire-guided Sagger missiles. The Israeli tanks were wiped out. Eight bridges were in place by ten thirty p.m., and by midnight the first five hundred Egyptian tanks had crossed to the eastern shore. In Cairo, the fundamentalists passed out pamphlets claiming that the angels of havoc were once again fighting with the Muslims. Sadat had to remind his countrymen that the first Egyptian general to cross the canal was not a Muslim but a Copt.

The Arabs now had better weapons, but the soldiers themselves were also different, Dayan realized: they were well trained and disciplined, and they did not run away. Moreover, they had the crucial advantage of striking first. That evening, however, Dayan went on television to reassure his fellow citizens that he had the situation under control. "In the Golan Heights, perhaps a number of Syrian tanks penetrated across our line," he conceded, but it was nothing to worry about. As for the canal, Dayan said, the Egyptian attack "will end as a very, very dangerous adventure for them." The truth, he knew, was that Israel was fighting a war on two fronts and losing both of them. Within twenty-four hours, the Arabs had destroyed two hundred Israeli tanks and thirty-five aircraft, and several hundred troops had been killed.

Shaken out of his complacency, Dayan underwent a personal transformation. He was forced to acknowledge that the Arabs were his equals; and if that was true, the very existence of Israel was at stake. Israel could not match losses with those of Egypt and Syria, which had combined forces of more than a million troops. The entire population of Israel was only three million.

The mission of the Arab armies was to recapture the territory lost in 1967. The Syrians sought to take the Golan Heights and hold their positions for four or five days—long enough for the Egyptian forces to capture the mountain passes in Sinai. Sadat hoped that the shock of the attack would then allow for diplomatic flexibility on all sides, which was impossible as long as the Arabs felt immobilized by humiliation and the Israelis comforted by the status quo. But the Israeli leaders did not believe the Arabs would fight a war for limited aims; the rhetoric of Arab leaders in the past still rang too loudly in the Israeli imagination—of being wiped off the map, thrown into the sea—and so they panicked. Once again, it wasn't war they feared, it was extinction.

On the morning of the second day, Dayan urged the air force to concentrate on stopping the Syrian advance in the north, where Israel was most vulnerable, but the Israeli planes failed to take out the anti-aircraft missiles, and seven aircraft were shot down. Dayan warned Golda Meir that a catastrophe was unfolding; it was necessary for Israeli forces to withdraw from the Golan Heights and pull back in Sinai to the mountain passes, and then "hold on to the last bullet." The prime minister and the cabinet were shocked by his forecast, but on the third day, when the Israeli counterattack in Sinai began, Israeli military leaders showed themselves to be disoriented, frightened, and at odds with each other about how to counter the Egyptian thrust. Israeli losses by the end of the day reached forty-nine aircraft and five hundred tanks. The situation seemed even worse than Dayan had described.

Dayan said he intended to go on Israeli television and level with the Israeli public on the perilous state of affairs, but Meir begged him not to. They huddled that night in the huge underground command center. If the nightmare that the Israelis imagined came true, and the vast Arab armies broke through their defenses, then the final line of defense would come into play: nuclear weapons. Israel had never admitted to having such weapons, but it was widely known that it had a small arsenal—perhaps as many as twenty-five bombs—that could be deployed in such a case. Dayan had suitably titled the apocalyptic strategy the "Samson Option."

What happened that night is still unclear. The Israelis may have decided to arm several nuclear bombs in case of a total military collapse. There was also the possibility of using the threat of a nuclear response as a way of coaxing Washington into resupplying the Israeli forces. William Quandt, who was later at Camp David, was the lead staff member of the National Security Council at the time; he recalls seeing a report that Israel had activated its Jericho ballistic missile batteries, which he presumed would be for nuclear weapons because of their rather poor accuracy.

Meir offered to come to Washington to beg the U.S. to immediately resupply Israel with arms, but a shocked Henry Kissinger rejected the idea at once. That Meir would consider leaving Israel leaderless at such a critical period of time showed both the degree of Israel's desperation as well as its abject dependence on the U.S. It also demonstrated the gulf between the American and Israeli perceptions of the danger that Israel actually faced. Kissinger never doubted that the Israelis would ultimately prevail, but he didn't want to see the Arabs thoroughly humiliated again, and he certainly wanted to avoid a superpower confrontation. Total victory left little room for peace negotiations, as the previous war had proved. He readily agreed to resupply the Israeli forces, but in so doing he hoped to manage the scale of the Israeli triumph. The best course, he believed, was to let Israel "bleed a bit but not too much." Meantime, the Soviets began resupplying Syria and Egypt. The involvement of the superpowers dangerously raised the stakes.

By October 11, Israel had gained the advantage on the Syrian front, with Dayan threatening to send his forces into Damascus. Hoping to relieve his Syrian ally, Sadat hurled an Egyptian force of fifteen hundred tanks against a comparable Israeli force in Sinai. It was one of the largest tank battles in history, and one that the Israelis, backed by anti-tank missiles fired from helicopters, decisively won. The Egyptians had ventured outside their umbrella of air support and lost 250 tanks in a single day.

Immediately following that victory, the Israelis launched a counterattack, led by Major General Ariel Sharon, against a much larger Egyptian force near the southern part of the Suez Canal at a place called the Chinese Farm, because the agricultural equipment had markings that the troops took to be Chinese (in fact, it was Japanese). The goal was to break through the Egyptian line and cross the canal—a brilliant and totally unexpected strategy, one that would leave the Egyptian forces stranded on the eastern bank.

The Israeli assault started the morning of October 15, meeting no initial resistance, but it soon developed into the bloodiest encounter of the war; with armor, infantry, and air support, each side was horribly mauled for three days and nights. Finally, at dawn on October 18, the Israelis managed to place a pontoon bridge across the canal and their forces streamed across. The war took a decisive turn.

Dayan flew to the Chinese Farm to view the carnage. Arab and Israeli soldiers lay side by side, their weapons and personal equipment strewn all over the battlefield. There were hundreds of burned-out and mutilated vehicles, still smoking, and destroyed Israeli and Egyptian tanks that were frozen in place only yards away from each other. "I am no novice at war or battle scenes," Dayan recalled, "but I had never seen such a sight, neither in action, nor in paintings nor in the most far-fetched feature film. Here was a vast field of slaughter stretching all round as far as the eye could see."

Sadat stopped eating, living only on fruit juice. He saw his chances of recapturing Sinai slipping away. He grew pale and gaunt and began urinating blood. He just learned he had lost his younger brother Atif in the first five minutes of the war, when his jet was shot down over the canal. Jehan Sadat couldn't bring herself to deliver the news for four days. The only time she had ever seen her husband cry before this was when his mother died. "All those who died for our country, who sacrificed themselves, are my sons," he told her. "Even now my own brother."

On October 17, a new and strikingly modern element of warfare came into play. Arab oil producers met in Kuwait and announced an immediate cut of production by 5 percent, with similar reductions every month until Israel had withdrawn from all the occupied territories. Moreover, they embargoed the sale of any oil at all to the United States. Three days later, Kissinger flew to Russia.

Once in Moscow, he struggled to confine the agenda to a proposed cease-fire, which the UN Security Council passed early in the morning of October 22 and Egypt accepted at once. Nixon had impulsively dashed off a letter to Soviet leader Leonid Brezhnev reviving the old notion that the superpowers simply impose peace on the Middle East. With the Watergate scandal in full blaze, Nixon yearned for a foreign policy triumph that would confound his critics, and peace in the Middle East was the biggest prize imaginable. Brezhnev was enthusiastic, but the last thing Kissinger wanted was for the Soviets to find a way to recapture their eroding influence in the region.

Kissinger then flew to Israel. Over a tense and emotional lunch with Meir and her cabinet, Kissinger observed the psychological damage that the war had inflicted on the Israelis, made especially acute by their previous complacency. Kissinger's sympathetic eye fell on the melancholy figure of Moshe Dayan. They had known each other for nearly twenty years. No other Israeli so impressed him with his imaginative and nimble intellect. Although Dayan was famous for his military genius and his punitive raids against Arabs, he also stood out among his colleagues because of his sympathy for their plight. In Kissinger's opinion, he was the Israeli statesman best suited to lead the country to peace, and yet Israelis were now treating him almost as a traitor. Three thousand Israeli soldiers had already perished in this war. There were pickets carrying signs with his iconic face on them, but they were inscribed "MURDERER."

The Israelis wanted revenge, as if that could restore their reputation for invincibility. But the crossing of the Suez Canal by Egyptian forces had shattered that illusion. Sadat had turned the tables on them, and the rage that the Israelis felt rendered them unable to restrain themselves. Meir complained that the cease-fire came too soon; she demanded another three days of fighting in order to surround and destroy the Egyptian Third Army, which was stranded on the east bank of Sinai at the southern end of the canal. Kissinger wouldn't sanction that, but he added, "You won't get any violent protests from Washington if something happens during the night, while I'm flying. Nothing can happen in Washington until noon tomorrow."

While Kissinger was flying back to Washington, Brezhnev sent an alarming note to the White House, resurrecting Nixon's suggestion of an imposed peace by U.S. and Soviet forces; if that didn't happen, he warned, the Soviet Union would act unilaterally. Three Soviet airborne divisions were placed on alert and a naval flotilla was actually on its way to Egypt, intent on liberating the Third Army. Nixon—under siege, distraught, drinking heavily—was entirely preoccupied by Watergate. Kissinger worried that the Soviets were trying to take advantage of this chaotic moment in American politics. If they returned to the Middle East in the role of the savior of the Arabs, they would be able to influence the oil producers and threaten world economies. To block that scenario, Kissinger was willing to steer the superpowers to the brink of nuclear war.

The threat level in the U.S. is denominated by five defense

readiness conditions. The lowest, DEFCON 5, represents a state of calm; the highest, DEFCON 1, is all-out thermonuclear war. Kissinger decided to send an urgent and unmistakable message to the Soviets, and—without involving the president—he and members of the National Security Council raised the threat level to DEFCON 3—the highest it had been since the 1962 Cuban missile crisis. He also put the 82nd Airborne Division on alert—troops were actually loaded onto transports and were waiting on the runway for the order to fly to Israel. He then sat back, expecting the Soviets to blink, but the flotilla continued toward Egypt.

In a totally unexpected reversal of the forces at play, Sadat saved the superpowers from the clash they were drifting toward. He asked the UN Security Council to provide an international force—one that excluded the United States and the USSR—to oversee the cease-fire. Without a willing client, the Soviets finally backed off, but Israel still refused to take its hands off the throat of the Third Army, which was withering in the Sinai desert, without food or water or even medical supplies.

Once again, Sadat rescued the situation. He suddenly announced that he was willing to engage in direct talks with Israel at the 101-kilometer mark on the Suez–Cairo road—the first time any Arab country had agreed to such an arrangement since the State of Israel was born. In return, Israel finally agreed to let a single convoy of nonmilitary supplies reach the Third Army.

Kissinger had come to deeply admire Sadat without ever having met him. Until the outbreak of the war, he had regarded the Egyptian president as "a buffoon, an operatic figure," but again and again Sadat had surprised him, not only with his vision and courage but also with his adroit moves in the complex game of international chess of which Kissinger was the acknowledged master. Few leaders on the world scene played at a level that even interested him, but now he recognized in Sadat an instinctive genius for the bold stroke that could change history.

Kissinger had never actually visited an Arab country, but on November 6 he landed in Cairo to negotiate a truce between Israel and Egypt. Sadat began by taking the American into his office and showing him some situation maps outlining a proposed disengagement scheme. "It can be called the Kissinger Plan," Sadat said coyly. He proposed that the Israelis withdraw halfway across the Sinai Peninsula. Kissinger observed that unilateral withdrawal was not a feature of the Israeli diplomatic vocabulary. Sadat puffed on his pipe, his eyes narrowed and unfocused. Kissinger went on to suggest that the key was to build up confidence so that the Israelis could trust in the outcome. The problem was mainly psychological, not diplomatic, he said. The best course of action was to leave the Third Army where it was—trapped—but with a steady source of supply, while the U.S. worked to disentangle the forces.

Kissinger was asking Sadat to trust an American he had never met, one with no experience in Middle East diplomacy, while keeping his army cut off in the desert for weeks or possibly months. If anything went wrong—if Kissinger couldn't deliver, if the Third Army cracked under pressure—then Sadat would be ruined and Egypt humiliated once again. Sadat simply accepted, surprising Kissinger once again.

It would take heroic personal diplomacy on Kissinger's part—shuttling back and forth between Israel and Egypt in mid-January 1974—to finally achieve the agreement that he promised, requiring each side to pull back from the canal and thin out their military forces along the front. The basic recipe for negotiating peace between Egypt and Israel was a bold Egyptian leader willing to talk, a cautious Israeli leader still willing to trust, and tireless American diplomacy to press them to make the peace that they couldn't achieve on their own. But real peace was not yet in view.

CARTER'S PLEA WORKED. Sadat sent Tohamy to issue the invitation to Dayan to visit his cabin for tea at three p.m. When Carter found out about the meeting, he asked Dayan not to discuss the issues. He worried that each man would become more entrenched in his position and the conference would once again become deadlocked. The only goal of the meeting should be to reduce the tension between them. Dayan pledged to talk only of "camels and date-palms."

Sadat received Dayan with a polite smile. As his manservant served honeyed mint tea, Sadat accused the Israelis of destroying the summit because of their stubborn refusal to give up the Sinai settlements, the most notable of which was Dayan's pet project—a proposed new city in northern Sinai, complete with high-rises and movie theaters, projected to have a quarter-million inhabitants within twenty years. Ground had been broken and bulldozers were at work at that very minute. "What did you think, that we would resign ourselves to its existence?" Sadat asked testily.

Dayan forgot all about his promise to Carter. He recalled Nasser's rejection of the Israeli offer to return Sinai after the 1967 war in exchange for peace. "What was your reply?" he asked. "What was taken by force, you said, would be recovered by force." He added, "What did you think we would do, sit with folded arms, while you announced that you were not prepared to reconcile yourself to Israel's existence?"

"If you want peace with us, the table has to be cleared," Sadat said. He was willing to make a full peace with Israel, despite the opposition of the Arab states, "but you must take all your people out of Sinai, the troops and the civilians, dismantle the military camps and remove the settlements."

"If anybody told you that any Israeli government could give up the Sinai settlements," Dayan said, clearly referring to Tohamy, "they were deluding you." The settlements formed a security belt to protect the Jewish homeland, not only against Egypt but also against Palestinian guerrillas, who infiltrated Israel from the refugee camps in the Gaza Strip. If the Egyptians did not agree to the terms, Dayan said imperiously, "We shall continue to occupy the Sinai and pump oil."

Sadat exploded. "Convey this from me to Begin!" he cried. "Settlements, never!"

Right after this disastrous meeting, Carter dropped off the draft of a new American proposal. Sadat glanced at it and said he would only negotiate on *when* the settlements would be withdrawn, not *if*. All his previous flexibility had boiled away in his wrath at Dayan.

At this juncture, Carter had no idea how to bridge the gap between the two sides. He went to Dayan and asked for his advice. The unrepentant Dayan told him the best approach was to draw up a list of the differences that remained on both sides to show that ten days of work had not been totally in vain. Dayan himself had given up on further progress.

The Egyptian delegation also wondered where Sadat now stood. Kamel went to see him, and found Sadat lying on his couch in his pajamas watching television. "Hi, Mohamed, take a seat!" he said, without getting up. He continued to watch the show. In a little while, other members of the delegation, including Tohamy and Boutros-Ghali, joined them. They were speaking about matters far from Camp David, and Kamel's mind had wandered, when suddenly he heard Sadat shouting, "What can I do? My foreign minister thinks I'm an idiot!" Then he ordered everyone out of his cabin.

Kamel started to leave, then turned to Sadat. "How can you allow yourself, in front of all these people, to accuse me of considering you an idiot? Would I work with you if I thought you were?" He then announced that he intended to resign as soon as they returned to Cairo.

"Wait, Mohamed," Sadat said. "Come and sit down."

Kamel remained standing.

"What's the matter with you, Mohamed?" Sadat asked. "Don't you know what I'm going through? If you don't bear with me, who will?"

"I feel what you feel, but that was no reason for you to address me in such a manner in front of anybody—I wouldn't take it from my own father!"

"I really am sorry, it's all the fault of this cursed prison we find ourselves in," Sadat said. "Why don't you sit down?"

"It is midnight and I feel like a walk," Kamel said, still steaming.

ROSALYNN HAD SPENT the day in Washington. When she left that morning, success was in the air. All during a White House luncheon for a local community foundation, she had to fight down a smile. Any emotion could give a hint of how the talks were going, so she remained as poker-faced as possible. When she returned to Camp David that afternoon, she was surprised to see Carter, Brzezinski, and Hamilton Jordan in the swimming pool. The men were laughing in a way that struck Rosalynn as odd. She immediately knew something was wrong.

The talks are over, they told her.

"You're teasing," she said desperately. "I know you're teasing me."

"No," Carter said. "We've failed. We're trying now to think of the best way of presenting this failure to the public."

Carter directed Vice President Mondale to clear his calendar in order to help him manage the political damage. Vance came by the Carter cabin later for martinis. He consoled Carter, saying that he had accomplished everything he could have expected, but feelings on both sides just ran too deep to achieve any major breakthroughs. That night, as Dayan advised, Carter sat down and made the list of items that separated the two sides. It was heartbreaking to see how insignificant the differences really were when measured against the enduring advantages of peace.

Day Eleven

Rosalynn Carter, an exasperated Jimmy Carter, Menachem Begin, and Yechiel Kadishai

FOR THE LAST TWENTY-FOUR HOURS, Ezer Weizman had sat in the theater at Camp David, watching one movie after another. He watched George C. Scott in *Patton* five times. He was too anxious to sleep—or perhaps too afraid to confront the truth. Israel's future was at a crossroads; on one side was peace, on the other, endless prospects for war. Weizman used to believe that war was the only path for Israel's survival. Then, in 1970, during the bloody standoff that followed the end of the 1967 war, his son, Shaul, had been shot between the eyes by an Egyptian marksman on the banks of the Suez Canal. Shaul somehow survived, but he was permanently disabled. He had once been so bright and promising, but the bullet in his brain pulverized the future he might have had. After he got out of the hospital, his thoughts were scattered and his emotions raged out of control. He became a heavy drinker. Every day, when Weizman looked at Shaul, he was reminded of the human cost of the conflict. The experience had gradually turned him into a dove. So many other sons and daughters were also dying and suffering similar horrible injuries—for what? If peace was really achievable, wasn't it immoral to fail? The agreement that seemed tantalizingly close at hand now was slipping further away, and to a large extent it was all Weizman's fault.

Wealthy, indiscreet, vain, and outrageous, Weizman was a kind of Israeli prince, both because of his relation to Israel's first president, Chaim Weizmann, and because of his role in creating the legendary Israeli Air Force. He and Dayan constantly vied for the informal title of most popular man in Israel, until Dayan fell from grace. Weizman still looked up to Dayan, who was his former brother-in-law (they had married sisters). Dayan, on the other hand, never bothered to hide his disdain for the younger man, whom he considered a playboy and a ne'er-do-well who failed to take life seriously.

In 1969, Weizman stunned his family and friends by joining Begin's small Herut party. He called it Menachem Begin's Sculpture Garden because the party was filled with unquestioning loyalists from their days in the underground. One election loss after another underscored their small franchise on the fringe of Israeli politics. People paid a price for being in a party of outcasts. There were no perks, no spoils, only quizzical looks from outsiders and damning editorials in the newspapers. Begin was thrilled to have landed such a popular and prestigious general. He was always drawn to military figures, and Weizman provided an imprimatur that the party badly needed.

The contrast between the men was extreme, and not to Begin's advantage. At six foot two, the robust and handsome Weizman loomed over Begin, who was a head shorter but seemed even more diminished because of his physical frailties. Weizman personified the hip and secular political class that dominated Israeli society, while the austere Begin always had about him the bookish aspect of a yeshiva boy. Both were known as extreme hawks, but where that quality was respected in Weizman as a well-earned lesson from his military background, in Begin it was widely seen as a reflection of racism and what many called his fascist politics. Begin, the Polish lawyer, was stiff and abstemious, but Weizman flaunted his sabra informality, often showing up at morning staff meetings in a T-shirt with a beer in his hand. The exasperated Begin called him "my charming naughty boy."

Soon after he joined Herut, Weizman decided to take over the party, but he badly underestimated the extent to which it was a one-man show. Begin booted him out. In 1977, a chastened Weizman returned, and this time he was put in charge of political strategy. Because Begin's party had gone through eight elections without a victory, Weizman combined Herut with a coalition of opposition groups to form Likud, the bloc that would come to dominate Israeli politics. In the campaign, Weizman downplayed Begin's radical past; instead, he presented the grandfather, the patriot, the incorruptible public servant living in the little three-room flat in Tel Aviv—a telling contrast to the high-living grafters who embodied politics in the minds of so many Israelis. This new Menachem Begin found a responsive constituency in younger, disaffected voters, and with Sephardic Jews, who identified with his outsider status. The posters showed a bald, smiling man with a new pair of fashionable glasses, over the legend "FAMILY MAN AND DEMOCRAT."

Begin campaigned against withdrawing from Sinai, saying that the Israeli-Egyptian disengagement agreement that Kissinger had crafted was a bad deal that compromised Israel's security. "Such withdrawals could only bring the enemy to our doorstep," he warned. His policy was simple: "The West Bank, the Golan Heights, the Gaza Strip, and Sinai are all ours."

Something else was at work in that election, however. Before the 1973 Yom Kippur War, the Holocaust was a subject rarely treated in Israeli daily life. There was an attitude of embarrassment about Jews who had gone so unresistingly to their deaths—like sheep to slaughter, as was often remarked—as if their submissiveness would contaminate the new Jewish nation. It was exactly such passivity that the nation of Israel was created to overcome. From its inception, the country had been run by bold pioneers and brawny sabras untainted by exposure to genocide. European Jews, like Begin, who carried the Holocaust inside them, were held somewhat apart—separated by an experience that native Israelis wanted to see as alien to them. Israelis were different. Israelis were strong, not weak; aggressive, not passive. Their hands were callused and they had dirt under their nails. They could take apart a machine gun or pilot a jet. Jews, on the other hand, were haunted, complicated, neurotic. They were not always good "human material," to use a phrase that Dayan and others sometimes invoked—not the kind of people needed to build a muscular new society.

The Yom Kippur War changed that. The sense of peril that Israelis experienced in the first days of the conflict unleashed the horrifying realization that had always stalked their imagination but which they had refused to acknowledge: it could happen to them. Just because they were Israelis they had not transcended the possibility of extinction that encircled the Jewish people. In this moment of rage and vulnerability, Menachem Begin's voice began to sound more reasonable. The fact that he had survived the Holocaust and the gulag promised that the Jewish people would survive this threat as well. Without being especially devout he was far more at home with believers than most Israeli politicians, and this also linked him to a cultural tradition that many felt was being lost. The psychological wounds that he carried with him were now seen as ennobling, not crippling; his ferocity and intransigence appeared to be appropriate responses to the dangers Israelis faced. Weizman succeeded in softening Begin's image, but Israelis knew that under the surface of the kind old Polish grandfather with his baroque manners there was a man who would stop at nothing to save the Jewish people. His rage was a shield against catastrophe.

One other factor played a role in Begin's election. The Americans had just picked Jimmy Carter to be their president, a man scarcely known in Israel. He spoke about Israel in a worrisome way. When he talked about establishing "secure and recognized borders," it awakened the anxiety many Israelis felt about defining borders at all. The eventual size and shape of the country was still in flux and subject to bitter arguments about the very nature of the state. To have it be a matter of interest to a naïf from Georgia was unsettling, especially when he mentioned two months before the Israeli election that "there has to be a homeland provided for the Palestinian refugees who had suffered so many, many years." No American president had ever advocated for the Palestinians.

In the middle of the campaign, Begin suffered a heart attack. When he came out of the hospital and resumed his campaign several weeks later, pale and haggard, Weizman's main concern was how to persuade voters that Begin was sufficiently healthy and in command of his faculties to carry out the duties of office. The opportunity came two days before the election in the form of a debate with the favored candidate in the race, Shimon Peres, one of Ben-Gurion's protégés, who had served in government almost since the beginning of the state. Peres was urbane, witty, and deeply knowledgeable—a formidable opponent, but one who seemed ready to inherit the office as a matter of right. He arrived at the debate accompanied by a motorcycle police escort; Begin appeared unannounced in his small car with his immediate family and a single aide. Peres adopted the casual look typical of the sabra political class—jacket, open shirt, no tie—whereas Begin was typically attired in his dark suit, looking more statesmanlike. There was one critical addition to Begin's meager wardrobe: a blue shirt, thought to be more suitable for television, which would also make him appear less pallid. All the other shirts in his closet were white. Although the debate was scored a draw, the fact that Begin was able to hold his own helped many voters make up their minds.

Begin's victory shocked Israelis, who simply didn't believe he would ever actually win. His election was dubbed "the Reversal," a vote against decades of Israeli political history. "Tonight, the history of the Jewish people and the Zionist movement took a turn, the likes of which we have not known for forty-six years, since the seventeenth Zionist Congress, in which Jabotinsky proposed that the goal of Zionism was to establish a Jewish state in our time," Begin said. Then he put on a black silk yarmulke and read from the Book of Psalms. Later, a stunned Peres summed up the results: "The Jews beat the Israelis."

Weizman had engineered a brilliant victory. Although he enjoyed the credit for Begin's election, Weizman subsequently encouraged speculation that he might replace him because of the latter's ill health and depression. On occasion he had disrespectfully referred to Begin as the *manoach*—meaning "the deceased." Ever since Sadat's trip to Jerusalem, Weizman had grown increasingly disillusioned with Begin's hard line. Many in Israel agreed with him, which had boosted Weizman's popularity over the prime minister's. Six months before Camp David, without consulting Begin, Weizman had even proposed creating a national "peace coalition" government— a poor gamble on his part, which Begin easily brushed back. Now, at Camp David, it seemed to Weizman that the bitter result of his success in getting Begin elected marked the end of any real chance for peace.

CARTER WOKE UP on the eleventh morning knowing that the situation was hopeless. He absolutely could not afford to spend any more time away from the White House. He told the Egyptians and Israelis to prepare their final position papers and instructed his advisers to outline a speech he would make to Congress on Monday, explaining why the summit had failed.

While Carter was working with his defense secretary,

Harold Brown, Cy Vance suddenly burst into the presidential cabin, his face totally white. Carter had never seen him so shaken. The first thought that came to mind was that the Soviets had attacked Egypt.

"Sadat is leaving," Vance said. "He and his aides are already packed. He asked me to order him a helicopter!"

The last bit of hope Carter held on to was that the delegations would at least part in an orderly and dignified fashion. Instead, the summit was going to blow to pieces.

Carter asked Vance and Brown to leave him alone. He went to the window of the little office where he had been working and stared out at the Catoctin Mountains, pondering the fallout. There would be no way to cover up the discord, the hopeless rifts that remained. It would be an international and historic fiasco. The Israelis would blame him for the failure. American ties to the Arab world—and its oil producers— would be shredded. The Soviets would be back in the game. And, of course, his own political career would be destroyed. He prayed, asking God to prevent Sadat from leaving and to somehow open up a pathway to peace. Then he changed out of his T-shirt and jeans and put on a suit and tie.

He was angrier than he had ever been in his life. It came rushing in on him. Sadat had deceived him. Until that moment, Carter had thought they were as close as brothers. They had walked together almost daily during the last eleven days, and Sadat had never confided anything that would lead him to believe that he would desert him in this fashion.

When Carter found Sadat, he was dressed for travel; his baggage was waiting on the porch of his cabin.

"I understand you're leaving," Carter said flatly.

"Yes," Sadat said defiantly.

"Have you really thought about what this means?" Carter asked, not waiting for an answer. "Then let me tell you. It will mean first of all an end to the relationship between the U.S. and Egypt. There is no way we can ever explain this to our people. It would mean an end to this peacekeeping effort, into which I have put so much investment. It would probably mean the end of my presidency because this whole effort will be discredited. And last but not least, it will mean the end of something that is very precious to me: my friendship with you. Why are you doing it?"

Sadat swallowed hard. Carter's cold blue eyes were only twelve inches from his. He said that Begin never intended to make peace. "We are wasting our time with this man!"

Carter accused Sadat of violating his pledge to stay till the end of the summit. He said Sadat had betrayed him. Sadat had lied to him. The responsibility for the failure of the conference would be placed entirely on Sadat. After this, Egypt would be cut off from America and reeled back into the Soviet orbit. More radical elements would be in control. Sadat's reputation as a peacemaker would be ruined, and his trip to Jerusalem would be seen as a historic dead end. His enemies in the Arab world would crow that they were right all along.

Sadat said he didn't know what else he could do.

"What you could do is stay here and let me be the one to decide when it's over," Carter said sternly. He promised that if Sadat remained, the U.S. would support the Egyptian position on settlements.

Sadat finally revealed what had caused him to decide to leave. Dayan had convinced him that Begin would never agree to any further changes at Camp David, so it was pointless to go on. Dayan had also said that the Israelis would meet with

Egyptians at a future date and start negotiations all over again. Sadat envisioned that any concessions he made at Camp David would be pocketed by the Israelis, who could then say, "The Egyptians have already agreed to all these points. Now we will use what they have signed as the original basis for all future agreements." Sadat felt cornered, he told Carter; his only escape was to go home.

Carter pledged to write a letter saying that if either party rejected a portion of the accords, the entire agreement would be null and void.

Sadat was quiet for a long time; then he said, "If you give me this statement, I will stick with you to the end."

WHILE CARTER confronted Sadat, the Egyptian delegation waited anxiously in another cabin. They didn't know if they were leaving or staying. They argued about whether Sadat was just making a show of his displeasure in order to extract some unknown compromise. They knew that Sadat was capable of staging a purely theatrical tantrum. They were alarmed by the latest American draft, which proposed that the entire Sinai Peninsula would become a demilitarized zone monitored by UN forces; thus it would be Egyptian in name only. Tohamy was furious that there was nothing in the draft about Jerusalem being returned to the Arab world. They feared that behind those closed doors Carter would wring another irreparable concession from Sadat, but they also worried that in his hotheaded state Sadat would damage Egypt's relations with the U.S. Nothing good could come from this.

Half an hour later, Sadat sent for his delegates. He met them on the patio of his cabin. He was lively and happy—completely transformed from the man they had just seen. "President Carter is a great man," he informed them. "He solved the problem with the greatest of ease." He explained that Carter suggested that any agreement arrived at during the summit could be made dependent on the approval of the People's Assembly in Egypt and the Knesset in Israel. If either party rejected the agreement, all commitments would be canceled and not binding in any future arbitration. Then he added, "I shall sign anything proposed by President Carter without reading it."

The shocked delegates were quiet for a moment. One of them finally spoke up. "Why, *Rayyis,* sign without reading? If it pleases us, we sign; otherwise, we do not."

"No," said Sadat, rising defiantly to his feet. "I shall sign it without reading it." Then he retreated to his cabin.

Kamel was distraught. The president was a cipher to him. If Sadat were merely the head of a small family, Kamel thought, perhaps the court could revoke his legal competence. But he was the head of the entire Egyptian family, and the fate of forty million people rested on whatever decision might erupt from his fevered mind.

As the Egyptians were stewing over what to do next, Begin appeared at their lunch table with an invitation to the Israeli Philharmonic in Washington the following day. This seemingly simple invitation filled the Egyptians with new alarm. What could that possibly mean, they asked themselves. Was Begin implying that the summit was over? Why wasn't anyone telling them anything?

After lunch, Kamel went for a long walk with Boutros-Ghali. Kamel unburdened himself. He spoke about the special friendship he had shared with Sadat in prison. Out of loyalty he had agreed to become foreign minister, a post he never sought, but now he found himself compromised by a president who was making decisions behind his back. "Sadat agrees to something in the morning, and an hour later he rejects what he had previously agreed to, and then in the afternoon he agrees to the same thing again!" Kamel seemed close to a nervous breakdown.

Sadat's masseur arrived with a message that the president wanted to see Kamel in his cabin. When he arrived, Sadat was on the phone with his wife in Paris. Kamel heard Sadat telling her that there was a good possibility that an honorable agreement could be reached soon. How could that be? Then Sadat spoke to his grandson. "Sherif, you bad boy!" he said several times as he laughed and bantered with the child. Finally, the president hung up and turned his attention to his waiting foreign minister. He triumphantly produced a handwritten note from Carter and asked Kamel to read it aloud.

Kamel read that Carter intended to close the conference on Sunday, and that each side should submit its final comments. Carter himself would draw up a prospective "Framework for Peace"; in the meantime, neither side should publicly comment. That was it.

"Well, what do you think now?" Sadat asked.

"Think about what?" Kamel said. "It deals with matters of procedure and is completely worthless."

Sadat grabbed the paper out of his hands. "No, it's a very important document, and in Carter's handwriting, too," Sadat said. "I intend to take it with me and lock it away in my private safe until the time is ripe."

"Excuse me," Kamel said in a panic; then he rushed out of the room.

When he got back to his cabin, everyone was waiting to hear what the president had wanted. "Nothing important," Kamel said. Then he drew aside a couple of trusted friends. They wandered into the woods until they came to the stump of an enormous tree. Kamel said that he had finally given up. The real problem of Camp David was not Begin's intransigence or America's partisan attitude toward Israel. The problem was Sadat. He was in thrall to Carter, who had surrendered entirely to the Israeli demands. Kamel could no longer be party to an agreement that he was unable to influence in any fashion. He was going to resign.

His colleagues suggested that he think about it overnight, then go see Sadat the next morning. He could point out to the president the dangers in signing any agreement that did not meet the minimum goals the delegates had agreed upon. If Sadat failed to listen, Kamel could resign at that time, knowing he had done everything he could.

"Yes, I'll do it," Kamel said.

BEGIN WAS APPROACHING the moment of truth. Carter had decided to end the conference on Sunday, two days hence, and the following day the president would be speaking to Congress. The story he was going to tell was that the summit failed because of Begin.

The Israelis met in a crisis session to discuss how to end the summit to their best advantage. Weizman implored Begin to make some effort to compromise. There was going to be no way to disguise the fact that Israel had chosen to keep its settlements in Sinai rather than make peace with Egypt. Dayan agreed that Israel could not afford to be the cause of the failure of the talks. It wasn't just a question of peace with Egypt; Israel's relationship with the U.S. was also at risk. Some concession had to be offered. But Begin could not be moved.

Perhaps he had in mind the pledge he had made that when he left office he would retire to a Sinai community settled by his old comrades in Betar. His devotion to the settlements was not theological—Sinai was not necessarily part of the compact that God made with the Jews, as far as Begin was concerned. Mondale, whom the Israelis saw as a far more sympathetic figure than Carter, spent hours with Begin appealing to his image of himself as a historic figure, but to little avail. For Begin, the question of Sinai was existential. The peninsula was the buffer that lay between Israel and its historic enemy. No matter what paper was signed, it would never replace 130 miles of mountains and sand standing between Israel and the Suez. Sinai had been the margin of salvation in the Yom Kippur War. The settlements were the vital outposts that would slow the enemy's advance. History had been cruel when Jews put their trust in others.

The crisis meeting among the Israelis ended with no solution. Afterward, General Avraham Tamir, the Israeli military adviser at Camp David, quietly approached Weizman with a plan to contact General Ariel Sharon, the chief architect of Israel's settlement program. Begin was a great admirer of the bold and ruthless warrior; moreover, Sharon's Polish grandmother had been the midwife at Menachem Begin's birth. No one was more hawkish than Sharon. If he of all people could be convinced that peace with Egypt was more important than the Sinai settlements, perhaps he could influence Begin. It was a desperation move, but Weizman agreed. A few hours later, Begin called his delegation together again. Deeply moved, he told them that Sharon had phoned him to say that if the settlements were the last remaining obstacle to a peace agreement, "I see no military objection to their evacuation." Sharon's blessing meant that Begin now had the political cover to make the decision to compromise, but to the frustration of the Israeli delegates he still chose not to.

"Evacuation of the settlements is essential if we want peace," Weizman implored.

"I heard you!" Begin snapped.

In the middle of this heated discussion, a message arrived: "President Carter requests that Dayan and Barak come and see him for a further talk." Weizman went along. Carter knew that these men were his best hope to influence Begin. He made a final plea. The gap between the Israelis and the Egyptians wasn't wide, he said; couldn't the Israelis come up with something to salvage the talks—even something symbolic, like a Jordanian flag on the Dome of the Rock in Jerusalem? A few symbolic gestures could make a difference. So much of the deadlock had to do with words, not substance. Surely the Israelis could find a way of phrasing the agreement that Begin would find acceptable.

There was one nonnegotiable concession that Carter demanded: "You must agree to evacuate the Sinai settlements to achieve a peace treaty."

"Such a thing cannot be agreed upon here," Dayan said. "It can't be done without the consent of the whole cabinet and Knesset."

That wasn't the same as saying it couldn't be done at all.

ROSALYNN SPENT another whole day in Washington, scarcely able to concentrate on anything except the dismal prospect for the summit that she had left behind. When the helicopter ferried her back to Camp David that evening, however, she found that the mood among the Americans had once again completely swung around. "We're closer than we've ever been," Vance assured her. Sadat had proved willing to stick it out, and the Israelis were worried that the U.S. and Egypt would sign an agreement without them, so they were finally showing some flexibility. "I think each side [has] decided it could happen," Vance told Rosalynn.

There seemed to be no emotions available at Camp David other than total gloom and utter exhilaration. Rosalynn found Carter and Mondale in Sadat's cabin drinking mint tea and watching the Muhammad Ali–Leon Spinks boxing match for the heavyweight championship. Sadat was a great admirer of Ali's, and after the fight, Carter placed a call to Ali to congratulate him on his victory, but Ali didn't call back until one thirty a.m., after Sadat had already retired.

William Quandt, Brzezinski's colleague on the National Security Council, was in his cabin writing the speech that Carter would give on Monday if the talks collapsed. The president would outline the progress that had been made and the many concessions that Sadat had been willing to offer. Only two issues blocked the agreement, the speech would state: Begin's refusal to give up the settlements in Sinai and his refusal to accept UN Resolution 242 as the basis for the final negotiations on the status of the West Bank and Gaza. Carter would then make a direct appeal to the Israeli people to repudiate their leadership. The political fallout would be unimaginable.

Meantime, the Israeli delegation was celebrating its second Shabbat at Camp David. This time, there were no guests at dinner. The Israeli Philharmonic expedition was canceled. The delegates were emotionally wrung out, except for Begin, who seemed determined to lift everyone's spirits. He insisted that they sing songs from the underground, but the only other person who knew the words was Yechiel Kadishai. The two of them sang one tune after another as the demoralized delegates waited for the dinner to end.

Mohamed Kamel went to bed, but he couldn't sleep. He smoked continuously as his mind swirled with fears and misgivings. Here he was, thousands of miles from home, trapped in a forest on a mountaintop in Maryland—in what was in fact a military compound, once you stripped away the trees—forced to be a member of a delegation that had no influence on Sadat's decision but which would nonetheless be held accountable for the disaster that was bound to follow. In his imagined crystal ball, the agreement that the Americans were urging upon them would bring on a new era of chaos in the Arab world. Egypt would be set adrift from its neighbors, while Israel would be regnant, unconstrained by the threat of Arab reprisals. He envisioned Israel as a beast waiting to devour the confused and weakened Arabs, plundering their wealth and massacring anyone standing in its way.

What was going to happen to him if he resigned? Egypt is a very intimate country, but it could be cruel to people in disfavor. Kamel was an ambitious man. He already held one of the highest posts available; it wasn't beyond possibility that the office of the presidency would be open to him one day—if he encouraged Sadat in desperate quest to salvage his peace overture. So why not close his eyes and go along, rather than throw away his career and who knew what else?

When he finally did sleep, he was beset by nightmares. The

CIA and Mossad, the Israeli spy organization, captured him. They tortured and killed him and made it look like an accident. In another dream he was stranded at Camp David after everyone left, without his passport, unable to prove who he was.

And who was that? In his half sleep, he thought about his father, the judge, who died when Mohamed was only nineteen—a third-year law student who was in prison at the time. His father's words came flooding in upon him: "Never sell or humiliate yourself, my son. . . . You must always be brave and say what you feel, doing only what your conscience and honor approve."

That night Kamel resolved that he would never be accused of being a coward who had held his tongue at the moment that Egypt faced its great calamity. "Tomorrow," he told himself, "I shall speak quietly, firmly, and in all honesty to the president. Maybe he will come to his senses and return to the path of righteousness. Otherwise, well, what will be will be: I have met my obligations, relieved my conscience and obeyed my father's recommendation. . . . I put my trust in God, who is unfailing."

Day Twelve

Menachem Begin on the porch of Birch Lodge

IN THE MORNING, Carter went for another walk with Sadat, then walked over to Holly Lodge, where the American and Israeli teams were conferring. Dayan said that he was personally willing to let the settlers leave Sinai after twenty years but warned that Begin would never accept any deadline that committed to their departure. As for the West Bank, Dayan would agree to no new settlements but not to withdrawal of existing ones. He appealed to Carter to meet with Begin that evening, at the end of Shabbat, since the prime minister was beginning to feel a little left out of the negotiating process. It was true that Carter was avoiding him.

At nine a.m., Brzezinski, Mondale, and Vance joined Carter to go over the latest proposal. Rosalynn sat in. Vance had met with the Israelis the evening before. He reported that Begin was upset by some of the latest changes, and that the American team then spent most of the night preparing a new draft with somewhat different language. The process had become one of laboriously shaving down the differences through increasingly subtle word choices. Begin still had a problem with the phrase "legitimate rights of the Palestinian People." Was there such a thing as illegitimate rights? he argued. Moreover, Jews were also Palestinians. Begin preferred the phrase "Arabs of the Judea and Samaria districts." He would be willing to accept the phrase "people of Palestine" rather than "Palestinian People." The lowercased "p" emphasized the distinction that he wished to make: they were Arab inhabitants within the Land of Israel, and not a people living in their own nation.

Some words had such a charge at Camp David that they couldn't be used without evoking strong reactions, especially from Begin. When Carter had described the prime minister's autonomy plan as a "subterfuge," Begin was enraged, and he continued to bring it up as if it were a personal insult. Similarly, when Brzezinski told Begin that the Arabs considered Israel to be a colonialist enterprise, Begin had taken umbrage, as if that were Brzezinski's personal opinion. In meetings with the Americans, Begin would sarcastically repeat, "We are colonialists, and we are trying to plan subterfuges." Of course, if anyone used the term "that man," it was immediately understood to be a reference to Sadat's inability to say Begin's name aloud.

KAMEL FAILED to appear at breakfast. Two members went to check on him and found him still sleeping. He said he had been smoking cigarettes all night and didn't feel like eating. One of his young assistants insisted on bringing him a tray of fruit and cheese sandwiches. At eleven, Kamel finally went to Sadat's cabin. "I want to have a talk with you, not as a foreign minister speaking to the president of the Republic, but as a friend and younger brother," he said.

"Tell me what you have to say straight out," Sadat said.

Kamel replied that he had read Carter's latest draft of the "Framework for Peace." It wasn't what Sadat sought to accomplish when he went to Jerusalem. It certainly wasn't comprehensive. "The American project leads to a separate peace between Egypt and Israel which would be completely independent of what might happen in the West Bank and Gaza," Kamel said. Israel would have peace with Egypt but then would be free to impose its schemes for annexing the occupied territories. "All Israel needs is a few years in order to bring the land under its control," he warned. "You know how all-powerful Israeli propaganda is." He said that the Israelis would enlist the treaty to justify their occupation. He begged Sadat not to sign such a "ruinous document," which would surely turn Egypt's Arab allies against them.

"You know nothing about the Arabs," Sadat responded. "If they are left to themselves, they will never solve the problems, and Israeli occupation will be perpetuated. Israel will end by engulfing the occupied Arab territories, with the Arabs not lifting a finger to stop them, contenting themselves with bluster and empty slogans, as they have done from the very beginning."

"What you say is not entirely true," Kamel said. The Arabs stood behind Sadat during the 1973 war, he pointed out. "Now that American impotence and its abandonment of the search for a just and comprehensive peace is clear, do you not see that you should go back to the Arabs again?" Kamel promised that the Arab nations were only waiting for a sign from Sadat, whereupon "the differences will be dissipated like a summer cloud."

But the agreement that Carter was proposing gives the Palestinians autonomy, Sadat protested. It abolishes the Israeli military government in the West Bank and Gaza. "Carter has assured me that he feels a moral obligation to do something for the Palestinians, and that he will be in a position to do this when he is reelected," Sadat said. Moreover, Kamel failed to appreciate the reality of Egypt's predicament. The economy was horrible and the public utilities were near collapse. Egypt needed peace in order to turn all its attention and resources to development. It could only help the Palestinians if Egypt was strong. An Egypt weakened by endless conflict could do no one any good.

"If you consider that our internal conditions are such that we are compelled to reach an immediate interim agreement, then announce that openly," Kamel said. It would at least be a way of explaining Egypt's capitulation.

Oh, how the Soviets and the Arab naysayers would gloat over such a statement, Sadat said. "I know what I'm doing and will go through with my initiative to the very end."

"Very well, then," Kamel said. "Please accept my resignation."

Sadat was not surprised. He asked Kamel to keep his decision a secret until they were back in Egypt. "Calm down and relax," Sadat advised him. "Everything will come all right in the end."

"HOW DOES the president feel?" Mondale asked Rosalynn when he arrived in the afternoon to meet with Carter and Vance. Rosalynn said that everything seemed to be all right for the moment, but it couldn't be counted on to last. "Good heavens, this is nerve-racking," Mondale said. He had been back and forth to Washington and had not really kept up with the emotional oscillations.

Indeed, when the meeting broke up, Jimmy despondently told Rosalynn he was skeptical that either side would accept the new proposal. It was too much for Rosalynn. She went off looking for a tennis partner. She thought she was going to be sick if she stayed in the cabin another moment.

Sadat arrived with Baz to review the new language about the settlements. Carter began by reviewing what Sadat stood to lose if the summit failed: the possibility of having Israel accept Resolution 242 in all its parts; the end of Israeli military occupation; the acceptance of the principle of withdrawal in the West Bank and Sinai; autonomy for the Palestinians for five years, after which there would be a permanent resolution of the Palestinian issue; and full peace with Israel, including the economic benefits and international acclaim that would come with that.

Sadat agreed to accept the very limited language in the draft about Jerusalem, which Carter decided was too hot a topic to resolve at Camp David. In return, Carter promised that there would be an exchange of letters in which each side stated its position. The U.S. would reconfirm its long-standing policy that East Jerusalem was part of the occupied territory of the West Bank. Sadat stipulated that the Wailing Wall would always be exclusively Jewish.

There was one sticking point, however. The previous draft had stated that the parties would negotiate "the time of the withdrawal." Begin had demanded "the time of" stricken, because he wouldn't commit to a time when the Israelis would withdraw. Sadat insisted that he was willing to negotiate the *time* of the withdrawal, but not *if* there was going to be a withdrawal. There was no moving him on this.

Vance took the new draft to the Israelis. The question of UN Resolution 242 was still a land mine. Dayan floated the notion that withdrawal from territories occupied by war only applied to states, and since the Palestinians didn't have one, the resolution had no place in the discussion.

The subject of the Palestinians had scarcely been talked about at all. The issue had been parked while the discussion focused on Sinai. Now the clock was running out. Carter had only twenty-four hours left.

Vance and Barak came up with the idea of having two sets of negotiations over the West Bank and Gaza: one between Israel and Jordan, and the other between Israel and the Palestinians. The paragraph would state that the principles of Resolution 242 applied to "the negotiations." What that actually meant would be left up in the air. Egypt and the U.S. could say that it referred to the negotiations with the Palestinians, but Israel could claim that it only included negotiations with Jordan, where the matter of the boundaries would not be an issue, since Begin rejected the idea that Jordan had any valid claim to the West Bank. The Americans rewrote the draft accordingly, although once again adding the phrase that the negotiations should address the "legitimate rights of the Palestinian People." It would still have to be sold to Begin. And for him, the Palestinians posed a daunting dilemma—and the blackest mark in his terrorist career.

MOST TRAGEDIES EXIST in a small moment of consciousness. They create heartaches, they capture headlines, but history doesn't change. Even very ghastly wars may turn out to be inconsequential in retrospect, interesting only to future academics. The fading of memory is one reason life moves on and generations don't dwell forever on the same ancient quarrels. But there are other tragedies that have consequences far beyond the butcher's toll, when one history ends and another begins.

Deir Yassin was one such moment.

On April 9, 1948, Deir Yassin was a Palestinian village of several hundred residents perched on a piney hilltop on the outskirts of Jerusalem. Under the UN partition plan that had been put forward five months earlier, Deir Yassin was scheduled to be part of the international zone for Jerusalem and its immediate environs. But Jerusalem was the great prize, and neither the Arabs nor the Jews were willing to let it escape their grasp.

The inhabitants of Deir Yassin made their living largely from quarrying the famous honey-colored Jerusalem limestone. Aware of their vulnerability, they forged a nonaggression pact with a neighboring community of ultra-Orthodox Jews, Givat Shaul, and they ejected Arab fighters seeking to use their village as a base. But nothing could shield them from the fact that Deir Yassin stood above a strategic roadway into the city, linking Jerusalem and Tel Aviv. In Begin's mind—as well as Ben-Gurion's—the little village of Deir Yassin represented a strategic threat to the new Jewish nation and its claims on the holy city.

Jerusalem itself was in the middle of a war between its Arab and Jewish residents, with Arab mobs looting shops and expelling Jews from the Old City, while Begin's Irgun was bombing Arab military outposts and public facilities. Arabs killed fifty-two people in Ben Yehuda Street, and Irgun shot ten British soldiers. Refugees from both sides were streaming out of the city for safety. Jewish forces drove out the inhabitants of a Palestinian village named Qastel, on the road from Jerusalem to Jaffa, but it was recaptured by Arab militiamen, who slaughtered fifty Jewish prisoners and mutilated their corpses. The attack on Deir Yassin occurred the following morning.

A force of about 120 men, two-thirds of them from Irgun, and the rest from the Stern Gang, was sent to expel the Arabs from the village. Begin instructed that they were not to kill prisoners or women and children. At four thirty a.m. the attackers sent a sound truck to warn the villagers that Deir Yassin was about to be taken and they should run for their lives; however, the truck overturned in a ditch and apparently went unheard. In any case, a sentry saw the attackers and fired. The attackers had expected the villagers to flee; instead, those who had rifles or pistols began firing out of their windows into an onslaught of machine-gun fire. Enraged by the unexpected resistance, the attackers slowly advanced on the village from three sides, going from house to house, lobbing grenades through the doors and windows and dynamiting the houses. Villagers who now attempted to flee were shot down. Haganah, the official Jewish defense organization, reinforced the attackers with mortar and machine-gun fire. The fighting was over before noon, but the mopping up continued for several hours more. A Haganah officer described what followed as a "disorganized massacre" of the survivors. "Groups of men went from house to house looting and shooting, shooting and looting. You could hear the cries from within the houses of Arab women, Arab elders, Arab kids. I tried to find the commanders, but I did not succeed. I tried to shout and to hold them, but they took no notice. Their eyes were glazed. It was as if they were drugged, mentally poisoned, in ecstasy."

It was only when the ultra-Orthodox Jews of neighboring Givat Shaul, with earlocks and wearing traditional Haredi dress, appeared and started yelling at the attackers, calling them *gazlanim* (thieves) and *rozchim* (murderers), that the massacre ended. "We had an agreement with this village," they cried. "It was quiet. Why are you murdering them?" Haganah intelligence said that many of the victims were robbed and that Irgun men may have raped some of the Arab girls. About two hundred of the survivors, including old men, women, and children, were loaded on trucks and paraded through Jerusalem, where they were jeered at, spat upon, and stoned, then set free outside the Old City walls. Others—twenty to twenty-five men—were lined up in a quarry and shot.

Among the attackers, the toll of that awful day was five killed (all Irgun) and thirty-one injured—more than a quarter of the total force. The number of victims from the village was harder to determine. Immediate reports by Haganah, Arab officials, Irgun, and British Mandate officials put the figure at 254 killed. Later assessments are less than half that number, between 100 and 120. As Israeli historian Benny Morris would observe, each party had an interest in publicizing lurid stories about widespread rapes and mutilation, along with the exaggerated death toll: Haganah wanted to discredit the underground militias (even though it had authorized and participated in the attack); Irgun and Stern wanted to terrorize the Arabs and run them out of the country; and the Arabs and the British wanted to blacken the image of the Jews. In the event, all parties succeeded beyond expectations.

Ben-Gurion absolved himself of blame, calling the attack on Deir Yassin the work of "dissidents." Begin, however, crowed over the "splendid act of conquest." He wrote his commanders, "Tell the soldiers: you have made history in Israel with your attack and your conquest. Continue thus until victory. As in Deir Yassin, so everywhere, we will attack and smite the enemy. God, God, Thou has chosen us for conquest."

Later he would defend the massacre by saying that some of the villagers who attempted to flee wearing women's dress were later revealed to have Iraqi military uniforms underneath. He provided no evidence to support that statement.

Deir Yassin was a decisive moment in the collapse of Palestinian society. The slaughter spread panic among Palestinians and led to the mass exodus that soon followed. In the month before the attack, 75,000 Arabs had left their homes; by two months later, 390,000 had fled. Jewish soldiers remarked on the eerie sight of untilled land and vacant farmhouses, and of the unattended shops filled with merchandise before the plunderers arrived. The Palestinians left behind ghost towns that would be blown up and bulldozed, or occupied by Jews, or—in the case of the more picturesque villages—turned into artist colonies. Most of the Palestinian refugees fled into neighboring Arab countries—and into a state of brokenness and resentment that lingers decade after decade. By the end of the war, when forced expulsion had become the policy of the new Jewish state, there were as many as 750,000 refugees. About four hundred Palestinian villages and towns were evacuated, most of them destroyed by Jewish forces. The goal was to scrape away any evidence of the presence of the Arab population and eliminate the possibility of their return. Place names—the roadways, valleys, mountains, wells, and wadis—were Hebraized, turning Aqir to Ekron, Asdud to Ashdod. Biblical names, some of doubtful provenance, were stamped on places that were designed to evoke the continuity of Jewish settlement. As for Deir Yassin, the remains of the village were turned into an Israeli psychiatric hospital called Kfar Shaul, with offices and patient rooms in what were formerly Palestinian homes.

AFTER SUNDOWN, Begin and Brzezinski played a final game of chess. This time Begin lost. At eight thirty p.m., he came to Carter's cabin with Barak and Dayan. Vance was also present. Carter had said this would be the final session. As he did with Sadat, Carter listed the benefits to Israel if Camp David was successful: diplomatic exchanges, economic cooperation, the end of the Arab boycott, adequate security on all fronts, buffer zones with UN participation, a strong voice in the future of the West Bank, improvement of Israel's relations with the Palestinians, guaranteed rights of Israelis to live and work on the West Bank, free passage through the Suez Canal and the Straits of Tiran, a better relationship with the U.S., and full peace with the only Arab country that posed a real threat to Israel.

Begin filled the air with protestations. He said that he

would be willing to negotiate for another three months, and if the talks were successful in every other respect, then he would go to the Knesset for permission to move the settlements. Sadat would never accept that, Carter said; he wanted an agreement to remove the settlers now—*before* the negotiations were concluded. "Ultimatum!" Begin cried. "Political suicide!"

As painful as this discussion was for Begin, his options were narrowing. None of the appealing items on Carter's list would be available to Israel if language could not be found that would allow Begin to surrender Sinai. Everyone in his delegation had been pressing him on the settlements. Sharon had called and given him his blessing. There was only one thing standing in the way, and that was Begin's entire history. Finally he said he would agree to present to the Knesset within two weeks the following question: "If agreement is reached on all other Sinai issues, will the settlers be withdrawn?"

"That's what I can do, no more," Begin pleaded.

"Mr. Begin, what do you plan to say to Knesset members?" Carter asked.

"I haven't decided yet," Begin said. "I might not say anything." However, he agreed to allow members of his party to vote their conscience. Carter knew that without Begin's opposition, the question would surely pass. It proved to be a critical breakthrough.

The discussion continued late into the night. Rosalynn sent in crackers and cheese. They finally came to paragraph 1(c), the proposed resolution of the Palestinian question. Begin seemed resigned to the fact that there was going to be an agreement of some sort, and a few of the linguistic obstacles he had erected began to drop away. Just before coming to see Carter, for instance, he had wrestled with the phrase "recognition of the legitimate rights of the Palestinian People." It contained a moral judgment that no Israeli leader had ever agreed to. Now the most unyielding prime minister in the country's history was being asked to concede that the rights of the Arab inhabitants of Palestine had been infringed and should be addressed.

"What is the ultimate importance of the term 'legitimate rights'?" Begin had pondered aloud before his delegates, musing on the inherent redundancy. "If it is a right—that means it is legitimate. Can a right be illegitimate?" With Carter, Begin continued to balk until Barak proposed one other small change: adding "also" before the phrase about the legitimate rights of Palestinians. That allowed Begin to persuade himself that other rights mattered as well, such as Israel's security claims in the West Bank. "By such verbal acrobatics," Weizman observed, "Begin managed to come to terms with reality."

In return for acknowledging the rights of Palestinians, however, Begin wanted substantial concessions. The text at that point said that "the results of the negotiations" would be based on UN Resolution 242. The principles of the resolution were listed, including withdrawal from territory acquired by war. Begin insisted that the phrase be changed to say merely that "the negotiations" should be based on 242, not the "results"—the difference being that the final agreement would not necessarily reflect the principles of the resolution. Begin also asked Carter to strike from the text the list of the principles of 242, thus eliminating the word "withdrawal" from the crucial paragraph. Carter conceded. These decisions would weaken the framework for future negotiations, but of course there were no Palestinians present to pose objection.

Midnight was approaching. Everyone was bleary and on edge. Because Carter had decreed that this would be the last negotiation at Camp David, they pressed on, into the knotted areas where no agreement had yet been found. There was one particular clause that Carter insisted upon having in the document: "After the signing of the Framework Agreement and during the negotiations, no new Israeli settlements will be established in the area, unless otherwise agreed. The issue of further Israeli settlements will be decided and agreed by the negotiating parties." This was the fundamental link between the two agreements that Carter hoped to forge—the Egyptian-Israeli treaty and the eventual comprehensive settlement of the Palestinian problem. Begin objected strenuously. He said he might agree to a three-month suspension of settlement construction, but Carter was emphatic that the freeze would stay in effect for as long as negotiations continued.

In the process of hammering out the final terms of the agreement, the two sides agreed to deal with several controversial issues in an exchange of letters that would state the policy of each government without actually forming part of the main text. The side letters had no legal standing; mainly, they served to dodge irresolvable questions that stood in the way of an overall agreement. For instance, Begin drafted a letter containing his interpretation of the words "Palestinians" and "West Bank." Carter had already promised Sadat a letter restating the American position on Jerusalem—a seemingly innocuous move that would prove to be another time bomb.

Perhaps they should have waited until morning to address these issues, when heads were clearer. Near the end of the marathon session, Carter thought that Begin had finally agreed to his demand that there would be no new settlements in the West Bank and Gaza as long as negotiations with the Palestinians continued, and that he would state so in a side letter accompanying the final agreement. Based on that understanding, the Americans agreed to remove the crucial language of the settlement moratorium from the proposed accord.

There were five men in the room—Carter and Vance on one side; Begin, Dayan, and Barak on the other. Their memories of what was actually agreed to that night are at odds. Begin and his Israeli colleagues insist that the prime minister consented only to a three-month freeze. Begin later told the American ambassador to Israel, Samuel Lewis, that he had said he would consider Carter's proposal overnight and give him an answer in the morning. In any case, when the meeting finally broke up shortly before one in the morning, Carter believed that he had brokered a peace agreement between Israel and Egypt that was linked to a comprehensive resolution of the Palestinian problem. Begin's supposed moratorium on settling the occupied West Bank would have given the Israelis a strong impetus to bring the dispute to an end. But that was not to happen.

Day Thirteen

Menachem Begin and Yechiel Kadishai holding photos from the peace talks, given to them by Jimmy Carter on their last day at Camp David

AT SEVEN FIFTEEN A.M., Rosalynn was preparing to return to the White House for a reception for the Hispanic community and a concert by the Russian cellist Mstislav Rostropovich. Jimmy came into the bathroom where she was dressing. "I think we've gotten everything we wanted," he told her. "I'm going to try to get Begin and Sadat together today. They haven't seen each other since we went to Gettysburg."

The news surprised her. She had nearly been physically ill when Jimmy told her just the day before that a Sinai agreement was out of reach, and she was still feeling unwell on this final morning. The emotional battering was almost unbearable, even when the news was positive. As she left, Carter reminded her, "Don't smile because they'll think we're gonna get an agreement, and don't frown because they'll think we're not gonna get the treaty." That was the same tightrope she had been treading for nearly two weeks.

Carter brought the happy news to Sadat on their morning walk. "I got the settlement freeze," he said. He reassured Sadat that the Knesset would approve the withdrawal of the settlers from Sinai, as long as Begin didn't stand in the way. "Okay, let's go ahead and sign," Sadat said. Carter went back to his cabin to compose the final American draft.

When Mohamed Kamel came out of the dining lodge after breakfast, he noticed an unusual amount of activity in the conference room next door. A long table was set up with three chairs in front of the flags of the three nations. Hermann Eilts, the American ambassador to Egypt, told Kamel that the signing ceremony by the foreign secretaries was to take place that afternoon.

Kamel blurted out, "I have a problem!"

"What is it?" Eilts asked.

"I have resigned."

"Good God, what happened?"

"You can guess what happened because I made it clear several months ago that I would do so unless we reached an acceptable agreement," Kamel said. "The problem is not my resignation, but rather that I have promised Sadat not to announce it at present. And I insist on not attending the signing ceremony. I don't know what to do!"

Eilts said he would think it over and promised not to tell anyone else. An hour later, he called to say that the ceremony was now going to take place later that day in Washington, not at Camp David. Kamel's absence would be even more conspicuous.

Sadat summoned Kamel to his cabin, where other members of the delegation had assembled. The president greeted him warmly and indicated that he should sit next to him. Despite Sadat's apparently upbeat mood, a gloomy sense of impending catastrophe hovered over the Egyptian delegates. Nabil el-Arabi, the legal director of the Foreign Ministry, observed that there were many obligations for Egypt in the agreement and no written commitment from Begin about withdrawing from the West Bank. He urged Sadat not to sign.

"I heard you," Sadat said. He was smoking his pipe, which always gave him an aspect of serenity, as he retreated behind clouds of tobacco in some remote psychic hideaway. But now he grew petulant. "I don't want you one day to claim I didn't listen," he continued. "All you said went in this ear and out the other. You know why? Because all of you are plumbers! You don't do anything with anything! I am a statesman. I know my objective. I want to release territory. If I don't, your grandchildren will be fighting in Sinai, and there will be war after war."

One of the delegates observed that the Palestinians would be disappointed by the vague definition of their right to self-government.

"It was not possible to do otherwise," Sadat said. "President Carter confided to me that this phrase would, in his words, 'cost me my job.'"

"And this is the president of the most powerful state in the world?" Kamel loudly exclaimed. "Is this the saint who claims that the defense of human rights, principles, and values are the cornerstone of his policy? Is he willing to sacrifice the fate of a whole people in order just to remain president of the United States for eight years rather than four? If so, he is indeed an insignificant and despicable creature."

There was a shocked pause in the room, and then suddenly Sadat laughed. He put his hand on Kamel's shoulder. "You are no politician, Mohamed!" he said in his booming voice.

"If this is politics, then it is an honor for me not to be a politician!" Kamel bitterly replied.

At this, Sadat angrily rose to his feet and the delegates took their leave.

WORD WAS SPREADING in the camp that there was an agreement, but few knew the final terms. When Weizman learned that Israel was going to be required to demilitarize a small portion along its own borders, he hurried directly to Sadat to see if he could be more flexible.

"How many battalions do you want?" Sadat asked him.

Weizman suggested three.

"All right, Ezer," Sadat replied. "For you—four battalions. Ever since the October war, I have no more complexes."

All three delegations were packing their suitcases; they couldn't wait to get out of there. Carter paid a call on Dayan, who was brooding in his cabin and seemed certain that the talks were still going to fail. Dayan had enclosed himself in a dark fatalism that was well known to his colleagues but new to Carter, who had depended on the foreign minister's imaginative mind. Now Dayan said that the Knesset would never agree to withdraw the settlers from Sinai before a treaty with Egypt was concluded. Carter didn't believe that. Perhaps Dayan, who had worked so hard at Camp David for peace, couldn't accept that it was here in front of him. Or perhaps this man of war knew that the price of peace had not been fully paid.

Once again, Ezer Weizman was embarrassed to find the American president standing in the door of his room. His bed was unmade, his clothes were lying on the floor, and liquor bottles and newspapers were scattered about. Carter enlisted Weizman's promise to campaign for the Knesset vote to remove the Sinai settlers, even if the prime minister didn't support it. Weizman relished the idea of fighting Begin on this issue. It could finally open the door for him to occupy the prime minister's office.

Carter directed his staff to prepare the signing ceremony for three p.m. at the State Department, where the three foreign secretaries—Dayan, Kamel, and Vance—would sign the formal documents. He didn't know that Egypt no longer had a foreign minister. In any case, his media adviser, Gerald Rafshoon, was beside himself at the idea that the president would stand aside at the moment of his greatest triumph. The signing would be in the White House during prime time, he insisted, and the leaders themselves would sign. Carter seemed surprised by the idea, but he agreed.

At noon, Vance delivered a draft of the American side letter on Jerusalem, so that the Israelis could see it before it was delivered to Sadat. It drew upon previous statements of former U.S. ambassadors to the UN concerning the established American policy that East Jerusalem was occupied territory. Following the Six-Day War, Israel had unilaterally declared that Jerusalem was its capital—an action that the U.S. government "does not accept or recognize," as Ambassador Arthur Goldberg said in the General Assembly at the time. Two years later, Ambassador

Charles Yost said that the United States "regrets and deplores" the expropriation and confiscation of land in the occupied territories, including Jerusalem. "We have consistently refused to recognize those measures as having anything but a provisional character and do not accept them as affecting the ultimate status of Jerusalem." In 1976, Ambassador William Scranton echoed his predecessors' complaints, saying "substantial resettlement of the Israeli civilian population in occupied territories, including East Jerusalem, is illegal."

American policy on this matter was well known to the Israelis. To Carter, the side letter was innocuous; he wouldn't have thought it necessary if Sadat hadn't requested it. But with this letter, the fumes of doubt that had been gathering in the Israeli delegation exploded into a ball of rage. "We can pack our bags and go home without another word," an indignant Begin declared. It wasn't just Begin; the furor infected everyone in the Israeli delegation. Jerusalem touched a nerve that until now had not been fully exposed.

Carter was upended by the outburst of rage. He pointed out that he was not asking the Israelis to sign the letter. Each of the parties was expected to submit their own position statement on Jerusalem. That didn't mollify the Israelis. If the Americans had planned to make such a declaration, Dayan said, the Israelis would never have come to Camp David in the first place. Jerusalem is the seat of the Israeli government, but the Americans still refuse to recognize it as the capital of Israel. To deny that fact one would have to rewrite the Bible and reject three thousand years of Jewish prayers!

Begin sent word to the Americans that he would not sign a document that contained any letter at all about Jerusalem. He ordered his delegation to immediately withdraw from the summit.

Here it was, hours before Carter expected to be signing the agreement. Rafshoon had already alerted the networks to be prepared to interrupt their programming for a presidential address. Was it possible that the two sides could come so close, only to have the summit detonate in a last-minute, intensely public walkout by an infuriated Israeli delegation? If Carter retracted the letter, he would lose Sadat. If he did not, he would lose Begin. There was no way out.

Carter's secretary, Susan Clough, brought him a batch of photographs of the three leaders for Carter to sign. Begin had previously asked for these souvenirs for his grandchildren, whom he was constantly talking about. Clough had thoughtfully called Israel to get their names. Carter could hardly stand the idea of seeing Begin again, but for some reason, instead of signing his usual, "Best wishes," he added "with love," and inscribed the name of each child. He walked over to Begin's cabin, intending to drop off the photos, no more. The feelings of anger, frustration, and heartbreak were almost overwhelming.

For Carter, the engineer, the frustration was magnified by the absence of logic. He had made the point again and again that each side had so much to gain from peace. Every night as he sketched out the latest draft of the proposed agreement on his yellow legal pads, the simple math screamed at him. It was so obvious, he kept telling both sides. And yet emotions weighed heavily into the discussion, and here Carter was at a disadvantage. His own emotional range was narrow. Although he respected the powerful feelings that the Israelis and the Egyptians brought to the table, his personal style was direct and sincere and not really suited to cajoling. He was no therapist. He was too impatient to respond to the endless litany of slights and insults, whether real or imagined, that each side had. He had thought that Camp David was going to be a meeting of three serious men dedicated to fixing a problem that everyone had an interest in resolving. In the back of his mind there was always the sense that God was also present. But if God wanted peace in the Middle East, so far that wasn't evident.

Each of these three men had met at this crossing point in life. For good or ill, each would be remembered by the decisions he made on this day. No one else could choose for him what to do. History would train its unsparing eye on his actions and sum up his accomplishment or his failure. The true loneliness of leadership is found in such moments, when great gains and great losses await a decision and there is no way of tallying in advance the final cost.

The prime minister was sitting on the porch, surrounded by several aides, obviously distraught because of the failure of the talks. When Carter appeared, Begin was cool and dismissive. His characteristic bluster was gone. He could scarcely permit himself to speak except in brief formalities.

"Mr. Prime Minister, I brought you the photographs you asked for," Carter said.

"Thank you, Mr. President."

Carter handed Begin the photographs and the prime minister coolly thanked him again. Then he noticed that Carter had signed the top photograph "To Ayelet."

Begin froze. He looked at the next one. "To Osnat." His lip trembled and tears suddenly sprang into his eyes. One by one, he said their names aloud, weeping openly. "Orit." "Meirav." "Michal." There were eight of them altogether.

Carter also broke down. "I wanted to be able to say, 'This is when your grandfather and I brought peace to the Middle

East,'" he said. The scale of their failure had never been more evident.

Begin asked the other Israelis to leave them alone, and then he drew Carter into the cabin, closing the door behind them. Once they were alone, Begin was quiet and sober and even friendly, a different man than Carter had seen so far, emptied of the histrionics that had become so familiar. And yet the message had not changed. Begin said that the Jerusalem letter was fatal. He recounted the story of a Jewish sage in tenth-century Germany named Rabbi Ammon of Mainz. The rabbi was such a prize that the local bishop repeatedly demanded he convert to Christianity. Again and again the rabbi rejected the bishop, but finally he said, "Give me three days to consider the matter." When the rabbi returned to his home, he was wracked with guilt. "What have I done? What have I done? That I allowed the bishop to think for a split second that I am prepared to convert?" After three days, when Rabbi Ammon failed to appear, the bishop sent his guards to drag him to the palace. The bishop demanded that Rabbi Ammon tell him what punishment would be appropriate for failing to keep his promise. The rabbi said that his tongue should be cut out because he did not refuse the bishop at once. "Not your tongue, but your legs, which did not bring you at the agreed time," the bishop replied. The rabbi's legs and arms were amputated, and salt rubbed into the wounds. Then he was carried to the synagogue. It was Rosh Hashanah. The rabbi was laid before the congregation, where he recited the hymn "Unetanneh Tokef Kedushat Hayom" ("Let us tell the mighty holiness of this day"). Then he died.

"I am not like the Rabbi of Mainz," Begin told Carter. "I don't need three days to consider the matter. I tell you here and now that Jerusalem is the eternal capital of the Jewish people, and even cutting off my hands and feet will not make me change my position!" The only way the summit could succeed was for Carter to withdraw his letter. Carter replied that the peace negotiations depended on the trust each side had in him to maintain his integrity. He said he was willing to let the talks fail rather than violate his promise to Sadat.

Perhaps Begin had been looking for a way out of the agreement; certainly, that's what Carter believed. But in spurning the possibility of peace because of a side letter that had no legal standing in the accords, Begin was endangering Israel's relationship with the U.S. and no doubt his own political future. Whether it was a bluff or a cry from the heart, Begin had placed everything on the line. Either he would sign the accords or he would walk away empty-handed. And how would history judge his decision?

As he was leaving, Carter added that he had rewritten the draft of the side letter with Barak. Now it simply said, "The position of the United States on Jerusalem remains as stated by Ambassador Goldberg in the United Nations General Assembly on July 14, 1967, and subsequently by Ambassador Yost in the United Nations Security Council on July 1, 1969"—without actually quoting the language those ambassadors had used. Nothing of substance had changed, but perhaps the prime minister could read it with an open mind and let Carter know what he decided to do. Then the president walked back to Aspen, feeling desolate and hopeless. Within hours the whole world would know of the terrible failure—his failure—at Camp David. The consequences would gallop to the front, armed and ready for the unending battles that were bound to follow.

Sadat and Baz were waiting for him, both of them dressed

to go to Washington for the signing. Carter had to break the news to Sadat that Begin was not going to sign.

Just then, the phone rang. "I will accept the letter you have drafted on Jerusalem," Begin said.

CARTER WAS ON GUARD against letting his emotions surge, but surely this was the last obstacle to the agreement.

In the East Room of the White House, Rosalynn had been sitting with Aliza Begin, listening to Rostropovich perform the Shostakovich Cello Sonata, accompanied by his daughter Elena on the piano. During the ovation that followed the recital, Rosalynn slipped away long enough to call Jimmy. "Should I come back?" she asked. "I want to be there when anything happens." Carter told her that a few "obstacles" remained, but if there was to be a signing it would be at the White House.

"If they agree, you ought to get their names on the line immediately and not take a chance on having them change their minds between Camp David and the White House!"

"Don't worry," Carter told her, "we'll have the agreements initialed before we leave." He promised there were going to be no celebrations until "the names were on the line."

Rosalynn said that Aliza Begin was eager to get back to Camp David.

"Don't come back yet," Carter said. "Just stall, but don't let anybody know why."

As Carter was drawing up a schedule for the signing ceremony, Barak presented him with the letter from Begin about the moratorium on settlements in the West Bank. It stated that there would be a freeze on settlements during the three

months allotted for the Israeli-Egyptian peace treaty negotiations. Carter told Barak that this was not what they had
agreed to. He read to Barak from the draft they had worked
on so laboriously the night before. There were two sections,
one having to do with Egypt and Israel, the other concerning the framework for an agreement between the Israelis and
the Palestinians, to be concluded within five years. The crucial
paragraph about restraining settlements came in that second
section. It had nothing to do with the negotiations with Egypt.
Barak agreed that Carter's minutes were accurate. "Go back
and get the right letter," Carter said. "I want you to write that
as long as negotiations go on with the Palestinians there will
not be settlements." He agreed to receive the letter the next
day, after the framework agreements had already been signed.

Perhaps Carter should have waited until Barak produced
the letter he was expecting. Perhaps he should have personally
gone to Begin with the letter he wanted and gotten his signa-
ture then and there. If Begin had pledged—as Carter thought
he had—no more settlement construction during the negotiations with the Palestinians, it is possible that the picture would
look quite different than it does today, with about 350,000 Jewish settlers in the West Bank and 200,000 in East Jerusalem.
On the other hand, those close to Begin say he would never
have signed such a pledge. If Carter had insisted on getting
the letter in hand before the signing, there might have been no
peace between Egypt and Israel. In any case, Carter believed
that he had cleared up the matter with Barak and proceeded
to arrange for the signing ceremony without the crucial letter
in hand.

Carter went to Sadat's cabin to go over the final document
with him and Baz. A terrible storm was arising with thunder

and occasional flashes of lightning in the mountains. Sadat was grim and subdued, and Baz was obviously miserable. Vance and Brzezinski then met with Carter in Aspen Lodge to make sure that all the other issues were nailed down. After twenty-three drafts of the American proposal, there was nothing more to add. At five thirty p.m., Vance turned to the president and said, "That's it." Carter sat back in his chair. They had it. He had forged a peace between Israel and Egypt. He had created a framework for an agreement between Israel and the Palestinians. It was done.

Camp David was over. The page turned almost immediately. Bags had to be packed. Television appearances had to be planned. There weren't enough helicopters, and the storm was now rolling across the top of the forest. There was no sense of jubilation. For Carter, the thirteen days had contained some of the most unpleasant moments he had ever experienced. He needed to call the leaders of Congress, but first he phoned Rosalynn, who was still at the White House. "We're coming home!" he told her. "The agreements are initialed and we'll sign in the East Room tonight!" Rosalynn burst into tears.

A few minutes later, Begin gathered his delegates and said, "Children, we've reached an agreement."

The world outside Camp David was still completely in the dark about what was happening inside the gates. Three of the most prominent leaders in the world had disappeared for thirteen days, unheard, unseen, and somewhat forgotten. Even the reporters who were still hanging around the American Legion Hall in Thurmont had no idea what was happening. They had been filing stories on the local goldfish farms.

Mohamed Kamel was packing when Vance invited him to drop by for a drink. By now it was hailing and the lightning was practically on top of the camp. Kamel waited for the fiercest part of the storm to pass, then waded through the rain with an umbrella. The weather replicated his fury and confusion.

"President Sadat told me you had resigned this afternoon, and I am very sorry to hear it," Vance said as he served the drinks. Kamel was not appeased. He spilled out his anger. "You have drafted your project in accordance with whatever was accepted or rejected by Begin," he said bitterly. "You will live to regret this agreement, which will weaken Sadat and may even topple him. It will affect your position in the moderate Arab states, who are your friends, while all the Arab peoples will resent you. As for Egypt, it will be isolated in the area. . . . All that will happen is that it will allow Begin a free hand in the West Bank and Gaza with a view to their annexation. Far from providing a solution to the Arab-Israeli dispute, the agreement will only add fuel to the fire."

As the storm abated, Carter called political leaders and cabinet members to let them know that an agreement had been reached and invited them to the ceremony that evening. The White House staff began setting up the East Room for the signing, and the kitchen prepared wine and cheese for the reception afterward. Word leaked out that an agreement had been achieved. That Sunday night, as the presidential helicopters flew back to Washington, people who lived below the flight path turned on their house and yard lights, providing an eerie path of illumination that grew more intense as the aircraft entered a bright penumbra of television lights waiting on the South Lawn. The Egyptian and Israeli embassies brought their employees, who waved national flags as the three leaders disembarked. The men seemed a little startled by the delirium that awaited them. When Begin saw his wife, Aliza, he cried out, "Mama, we'll go down in the history books!"

THREE HAGGARD MEN SAT shoulder to shoulder at a small desk in the East Room, with the flags of their nations behind them. Sadat appeared solemn and distant. He looked into the audience for members of his delegation, but empty chairs marked the places where many of them would have been sitting. Even those who attended the ceremony were visibly worried, fearing that their participation in the agreement could cost them their lives.

"When we arrived at Camp David the first thing we agreed upon was to ask the people of the world to pray that our negotiations would be successful," Carter said. "Those prayers have been answered far beyond any expectations." He described the two documents that the men would be signing. The first, called "Framework for Peace in the Middle East," dealt with the West Bank and Gaza, "and the need to solve the Palestinian problem in all its aspects." It envisioned a five-year transitional period, "during which the Israeli military government will be withdrawn and a self-governing authority will be elected, with full autonomy." Israeli forces would remain in specified locations to protect Israel's security. At the end of the five years, Palestinians would determine their own future in negotiations to resolve the final status of the West Bank and Gaza. "These negotiations will be based on all the provisions and all the principles of United Nations Security Council Resolution 242, and it provides that Israel may live in peace within secure and recognized borders," Carter said.

"The other document is entitled 'Framework for the

Conclusion of a Peace Treaty between Egypt and Israel,'" he continued. "It provides for the full exercise of Egyptian sovereignty over the Sinai. It calls for full withdrawal of Israeli forces from the Sinai, and after an interim withdrawal—which will be accomplished very quickly—the establishment of normal, peaceful relations between the two countries, including diplomatic relations.

"Together with accompanying letters, which we will make public tomorrow, these two Camp David agreements provide the basis for progress and peace throughout the Middle East."

Carter added that the Knesset would vote within the next two weeks on the issue of removing the settlements so that the final peace negotiations could begin.

Sadat praised Carter for his courage in undertaking the summit. "Dear friend, we came to Camp David with all the

Sadat, Carter, and Begin sign the Camp David Accords at the White House, September 17, 1978.

goodwill and faith we possess, and we left Camp David a few minutes ago with a renewed sense of hope and inspiration," he read in his resonant voice. "Let us pledge to make the spirit of Camp David a new chapter in the history of our nations."

Begin spoke without notes. "The Camp David conference should be renamed," he said. "It was the Jimmy Carter conference." Carter beamed. "And he worked," Begin continued. "I think he worked harder than our forefathers did in Egypt building the pyramids." He looked around the room with a dazed grin. "When I came here to the Camp David conference, I said perhaps, as a result of our work one day people in every corner of the world will be able to say '*Habemus pacem*,' in the spirit of these days. Can we say so tonight? Not yet. We still have to go a road until my friend President Sadat and I sign the peace treaties. We promised each other that we shall do so within three months." Begin turned to Sadat. "Mr. President, tonight at this celebration of this great historic occasion, let us promise that we shall do it earlier."

"Right!" Sadat said, smiling broadly.

Immediately after the ceremony, an elated Begin told a friend, "I have just signed the greatest document in Jewish history!"

Epilogue

SO MANY NEGLECTED ISSUES had piled up while Carter had devoted himself to making peace in the Middle East. The shah of Iran was overthrown and replaced by a radical Shiite theocracy. Inflation was running out of control, and unemployment remained persistently high. Even Carter's accomplishments—normalizing relations with China, advancing human rights, creating an energy policy, cutting the federal deficit, signing the Panama Canal treaties—were overshadowed by the extended turmoil of the Camp David process.

Begin made things worse by publicly disclaiming aspects of the agreement and complaining about the pressure Carter had placed upon Israel. The prime minister "began to treat this peace we had struggled for as something banal, almost despicable," Weizman observed. Weizman was also embarrassed by the way in which Carter was disparaged. "As far as I know, no American president has ever helped Israel as much as Jimmy Carter."

The morning after the signing ceremony in the White House, Begin sent Carter the letter he had demanded about stopping the construction of settlements. It was exactly the same as the letter Carter had rejected the day before. Begin immediately started making statements to Jewish audiences and on television that Israel would continue building new settlements. He told an Israeli reporter that the Israeli army would remain in the West Bank and Gaza indefinitely. On the Monday after the signing ceremony, Carter was to make a report to Congress, with Begin and Sadat seated in the balcony of the House of Representatives. Just before the speech, Carter confronted Begin about his statements and the letter concerning the settlement halt. Begin was evasive. Carter then told the Congress, "Israel has agreed, has committed themselves, that the legitimate rights of the Palestinian people will be recognized. After the signing of this framework last night, and during the negotiations concerning the establishment of Palestinian self-government, no new Israeli settlements will be established in this area." Begin had no intention of yielding to such pressure.

Begin returned to Israel to be greeted by a large crowd at the airport, although some members of his own party showed up carrying black umbrellas and shouting, "Munich!" in reference to Britain's accommodation with the Nazi German government. Begin honored his commitment to bring the agreement to a vote before the Knesset. He assured the parliament that even after the five-year transitional period Israel would continue to assert its right to sovereignty over Judea, Samaria, and Gaza—in other words, the autonomy talks would go nowhere. As for surrendering the Sinai settlements, he said that Israel could not have allowed the summit to fail on this one matter. "The State of Israel could not stand up in the face of this," he said. "Not in America; not in Europe. Not before American Jewry. Not before the Jews of other lands. We could not have faced this. All blame would have befallen us." At four in the morning, after seventeen hours of debate, the Knesset approved the agreement by a two-thirds majority, the nays coming mainly from Begin's party. Right after that, he announced plans to "thicken" Israeli settlements on the West Bank. Carter was outraged. "Begin wanted to keep two things," he concluded: "the peace with Egypt—and the West Bank." Sadat threatened to withdraw from negotiations.

A month after the Camp David summit, Sadat and Begin were awarded the Nobel Peace Prize.* "Sadat deserved it," Carter noted tersely in his diary. At that point, it had become clear to the Carter White House that Begin was actively working to defeat Carter for reelection. Moreover, Begin seemed uninterested in pursuing a signing anytime soon. The longer he delayed, the more leverage he had. He accurately gauged that Carter and Sadat both needed the treaty more than he did.

In the middle of this extremely tense denouement, Carter was hit with an excruciating case of hemorrhoids. The news got into the press when he had to cancel his appointments. Carter learned on Christmas Day, 1978, that the Egyptian people were praying he would be cured of this affliction, and the following day he was—the first instance, perhaps of divine intervention since the entire peace process began.

In a final act of desperation, Carter decided to go to the Middle East that March to try to force the two sides to resolve their differences. The professionals in the State Department

---

* Carter would win the Nobel Peace Prize on his own in 2002, for his work in human rights and social welfare. At that time, the chairman of the Nobel Prize committee admitted that Carter should have been honored previously with Begin and Sadat.

were embarrassed for their president, who seemed to be taking a swan dive into who knows what. Carter and Rosalynn flew to Cairo, along with Brzezinski and the secretaries of state and defense; essentially, the entire foreign and defense policy leadership of the administration was riding on Air Force One, along with Carter's hopes of leaving behind a historic legacy.

Sadat welcomed them and took them on a train ride to Alexandria. They were overwhelmed by the response—"the largest and most enthusiastic crowds I have ever seen," Carter told Sadat. He was clearly far more popular in Egypt than he was in his own country. "Perhaps we should move to Cairo," Rosalynn remarked.

Carter arrived in Israel on a Saturday evening just after Shabbat, as Sadat had done on that historic trip to Jerusalem only fifteen months earlier. Then, peace had seemed a simple matter, but now the world had turned over several times. Carter went directly to a private meeting with Begin, who brusquely informed him that there was no way to bring negotiations to an end anytime soon. Carter felt it was a personal attack, another way of undermining his prestige and reducing his chances of reelection. He stood up and asked if it was necessary for him to stay any longer. For the next forty-five minutes the bitterness that had developed between the two men poured out. Carter said he doubted whether Begin wanted peace at all, because he was doing everything possible to obstruct it, "with apparent relish." Begin put his face inches away from Carter's and said that he wanted peace as much as anything in the world; however, "the fate of a nation hangs in the balance."

It was nearly midnight when Carter left, convinced that Begin would do anything he could to block the treaty and avoid living up to the commitment he had made at Camp David to provide full autonomy to the Palestinians on the West Bank. Once again, he was struck by the absence of any sympathy on Begin's part for the plight of the refugees.

The next day, Begin took Carter to Yad Vashem, the Holocaust memorial, and then to Mount Herzl to visit the graves of Theodor Herzl and Vladimir Jabotinsky. It was a journey into Begin's roots. The lesson Begin drew from his life was that Jews cannot trust their security to anyone. "It was not only the Nazis and their friends who regarded the Jews as germs to be destroyed," he writes in his memoir. "The whole world which calls itself 'enlightened' began to get used to the idea that perhaps the Jew is not as other human beings. . . . The world does not pity the slaughtered. It only respects those who fight." This was his credo. Herzl had summoned up the vision of a Jewish state, but Jabotinsky had enlarged it and prophesied the problems it would have with its Arab inhabitants and neighbors. Begin saw himself as the natural heir of these two thinkers, the man who would manifest their visions into an impregnable Jewish state.

After this guided tour, Carter went on his own to a service at a Baptist church. He reflected on the fact that Jerusalem had seen more wars than any city in the world, and he prayed that it would never see another one.

On Monday, Carter addressed the Knesset, saying that the people of Israel were ready for peace, but the leaders had not shown that they had the courage to take a chance for it. When Begin got up to speak, he was subjected to whistles and shouts—Israeli democracy at its most riotous. He seemed to enjoy the hurly-burly, grinning with pleasure whenever invective was hurled at him and glancing meaningfully at Carter to make sure he appreciated what he was up against. In fact,

Carter did feel closer to Begin. His own presidency wasn't so easy, either.

After the Knesset meeting Begin told the Americans that the talks were over. He suggested that they issue a joint communiqué saying the usual—progress made, some questions unresolved. In fact, he produced the text, which had already been prepared.

Carter returned to the King David Hotel—the same one that Begin had blown up during the British Mandate—thoroughly exhausted and disgusted. He ordered that Air Force One be prepared for immediate departure. He didn't want to spend a single additional night in Israel, but it was late and getting all the luggage of the presidential party together would take time. He reluctantly agreed to stay till morning. Meantime, the press who were traveling with Carter drew their conclusions. Walter Cronkite, the anchor for CBS, announced that the peace treaty had failed. Both NBC and ABC followed suit.

That night Weizman and Dayan visited Vance and told him they were both ready to resign if Begin continued to obstruct the peace treaty. One of the sticking points was that the Israelis refused to give up the Egyptian oil. Dayan came up with a formula, in which Egypt would promise in principle to supply Israel with oil, and the U.S. would guarantee Israel's petroleum needs for fifteen years. He urged Carter to make one last attempt.

The next morning, Carter invited Begin to breakfast. The prime minister arrived with his wife, who ate with Rosalynn. The two men stood for a few moments looking out the window at Old Jerusalem. The blood spilled on these ancient streets had painted the city red many times over.

There was still the matter of the Palestinians, the only serious issue remaining. Carter agreed to drop all references to Gaza, and Begin promised to treat the president's request to improve the atmosphere on the West Bank "sympathetically." Without actually committing himself to any specific action, Begin said he would provide the Palestinians some degree of peaceful political activity. Both men accepted the deal.

After breakfast, as the Begins and the Carters descended to the lobby, the elevator malfunctioned, jerking to a stop six feet above the ground floor. Hundreds of reporters and diplomats were waiting in the lobby to hear the result of the breakfast meeting. After twenty minutes of fruitless efforts to restart the elevator, the door was torn off and the two couples had to climb down a ladder, "with our butts showing," as Carter later recalled. "That's the way we got the peace agreement."

ON MARCH 26, 1979, a breezy, sunny day in Washington, the flags of three nations fluttered behind an empty table. All of official Washington was gathered on the lawn. While they waited, Begin was in the Oval Office making one last request. As a gesture of friendship to Mrs. Begin, he said, he asked Carter to forgive the debt on the $3 billion in aid that the U.S. was extending to Israel. Several times he repeated the phrase "as a gesture for Mrs. Begin." Carter looked at Brzezinski, who was present at the meeting, with a stunned look on his face, and then he simply burst out laughing.

At two p.m., Carter, Begin, and Sadat took their places and signed the formal treaty. Palestinian protestors could be heard chanting slogans across the street. "During the past thirty years, Israel and Egypt have waged war," Carter said in his opening statement. "But for the past sixteen months, these same two great nations have waged peace. Today we celebrate a victory—not of a bloody military campaign, but of an inspiring peace campaign." There were still outstanding differences, he conceded. "Let history record that deep and ancient antagonism can be settled without bloodshed and without staggering waste of precious lives." Sadat praised Carter as "the best companion and partner along the road to peace." Each of the three men quoted Isaiah, "And they shall beat their swords into plowshares and their spears into pruning hooks."

"I have signed a treaty of peace with our great neighbor, with Egypt," Begin said. "The heart is full and overflowing. God gave me the strength to persevere, to survive the horrors of Nazism and of the Stalinite concentration camp and some other dangers, to endure, not to waver in nor flinch from my duty, to accept abuse from foreigners and, what is more painful, from my own people, and even from my close friends. . . ." He stared into empty space as the memories of his uncompromising life flooded in on him. "Therefore it is the proper place and the appropriate time to bring back to memory the song and prayer of thanksgiving I learned as a child, in the home of a father and mother that doesn't exist anymore, because they were among the six million people—men, women, and children—who sanctified the Lord's name with the sacred blood which reddened the rivers of Europe from the Rhine to the Danube, from the Bug to the Volga, because nobody, nobody came to their rescue, although they cried out, 'Save us, save us'—*de profundis*—from the depths of the pits and agony. That is the Song of Degrees, written two millennia and five hundred years ago, when our forefathers returned from their first exile to Jerusalem and Zion."

At this point, Begin put on a black yarmulke and read in Hebrew from Psalms 126:

When the Lord restored the captives of Zion, we thought
we were dreaming. Then our mouths were filled with
laughter, our tongues sang for joy. Then it was said
among the nations, "The Lord had done great things for
them." The Lord has done great things for us. Oh, how
happy we were!

Restore our captives, Lord, like the dry stream beds
of the Negev. Those who sow in tears will reap with cries
of joy. Those who go forth weeping, carrying sacks of
seed, will return with cries of joy, carrying their bundled
sheaves.

The ceremony lasted only a few minutes. After the signing, Sadat came over to greet Ezer Weizman and his son Shaul,
whose wound from an Egyptian sniper was evident. Sadat
warmly embraced the young man as Weizman held Shaul's
hand. For Weizman, that was the end of the wars.

Moshe Dayan was sitting with Vance and his wife, Gay, at
the gala dinner that followed. Leontyne Price sang, and the
Israeli violinists Itzhak Perlman and Pinchas Zukerman per-
formed. Dayan detested ceremonies. The fatigue of his last
great campaign was rolling in, on top of his illness, still unde-
tected. "You look tired and bored," Gay observed. Dayan took
the opportunity to excuse himself and walk back to the hotel.

On the way he recalled the long debate that had taken
place in the Knesset only a few days before to decide whether
to agree to the treaty that Carter had put before them. Dayan
was the last to speak in the debate. Typically, he shunned the
high-flown rhetoric that infects conversations about peace.
The treaty, he said, was not the fulfillment of Isaiah's vision
of swords beaten into plowshares. It was a military treaty containing clauses for the construction of air bases and guaran-

tees for Israel's security. It was also a political treaty, designed to establish relations between two neighboring countries long at war. It was an honest treaty, because it did not paper over the differences between them. And it was a realistic treaty, because it allowed Egypt to reconcile itself to the idea of Israel's existence.

TWO MONTHS LATER, Begin and Sadat met again at the town of El Arish, the administrative capital of Sinai, where the Israelis formally transferred the peninsula back to Egyptian control. The national anthems played and a bugle sounded as the Israeli flag was lowered and the Egyptian one raised in its place.

A caravan of buses arrived from either direction, leaving long trails of dust in their wake. Begin had invited wounded soldiers from each side to meet in this desert oasis in an act of reconciliation. The veterans, about 150 of them altogether, disembarked in a painful display of war's cruel toll. Blind, lame, disfigured, they hobbled or were guided past the honor guards and military bands. They sat across from each other on opposite sides of the hall where refreshments were served. There was an awkward silence, a standoff. The stress was so great that some of the broken warriors asked orderlies to take them out of the room. Begin's speechwriter, Yehuda Avner, was sitting next to a blind Israeli veteran who had brought his son, who was eight or nine years old. "*Kach oti eilehem*," he told the child: Take me to them. The boy was scared of the wounded men across the hall, but he guided his blind father to the middle of the room. An Egyptian veteran in a wheelchair rolled himself forward and took the Israeli's hand. A few men clapped, then the room erupted in loud applause as the others came together and embraced.

Amid cries of *Shalom! Salaam!* Sadat and Begin entered the room, greeting each of the disfigured veterans, asking them where they had fought and where they had been maimed. Avner noticed the child of the blind soldier, his face filled with fear and confusion. For as long as the boy could remember, he had been escorting his father, blinded by this very enemy. "Don't be afraid, my son," his father told him. "These Arabs are good."

When the two leaders returned to the uncomfortable military plane that had brought them to El Arish, Begin—always fastidious about his appearance—noticed that his shoes were dusty from the sand, so he took out a handkerchief and polished them. Then he offered the handkerchief to Sadat, who politely declined.

THE EGYPTIAN GOVERNMENT built a parade ground to commemorate the 1973 war, when the country recaptured its pride by crossing the Suez Canal. Each year, on October 6, the anniversary of the start of the war, Sadat attired himself in splendid regalia and invited his top officials, foreign diplomats, and international correspondents to attend the annual celebration. In 1981, Sadat wore a field marshal's uniform, which had just arrived a few days before from his tailor in London—jodhpurs with knee-high black boots, a cap with gold braid on the bill, and a blue-gray jacket, which he covered with the green Sash of Justice across his chest and the Star of Sinai medal at his neck. He decided not to wear his bulletproof vest.

The "Hero of the Crossing," as he liked to be called, sat in the first row of the large marble reviewing stand next to Vice President Mubarak. A thousand others gathered to watch, including the American and Israeli ambassadors and other dignitaries. Sadat's wife, Jehan, and their grandchildren sat in a glassed-in box high above. There was a band and fireworks. The stately Camel Corps passed by, looking like a vintage postcard. Parachutists landed on targets only a few yards from the stand. Tanks and armored personnel carriers moved in practiced precision before the dutiful spectators. As a formation of French-made Mirage jets passed overhead, performing aerobatics and trailing streams of colored smoke, one of the troop trucks in the parade slammed to a halt and several soldiers leaped to the ground carrying automatic rifles and grenades. One of them, Khalid al-Islambouli, raced toward the reviewing stand. Sadat abruptly stood up and saluted.

Perhaps he thought the young lieutenant and the others were paying tribute to him. He had brought peace to Egypt, after all. For eight years, the armed forces had been spared from combat. Egypt's economy was still suffering, although boosted by the $2.1 billion, most of it in military aid, that the U.S. provided each year after Camp David. There was reason to imagine that Egyptians—and especially soldiers—would be grateful.

Or perhaps he saw Death coming to collect him. The treaty with Israel had set loose the furies within radical Islam. One of Sadat's first acts as president had been to release the political prisoners that Nasser had imprisoned, most of them members of the Muslim Brotherhood. Sadat had thought that this act of clemency, along with his own very conspicuous piety, would immunize him against the radicals, but they never trusted him to implement their demands—namely, the imposition of strict Islamic law and the mandatory covering of women. Sadat responded with a crackdown on student religious groups. During parliamentary elections, he banned discussion of the peace treaty; he made himself president for life and prime minister for good measure. He passed a law permitting women the right to divorce and banned the *niqab*—the face mask for women favored by Islamic fundamentalists—from the universities. In the summer of 1981, he jailed three thousand people, including the Supreme Guide of the Muslim Brothers and many political opponents, including everyone who had publicly criticized the Camp David agreement.

Sadat ruled his people as an autocrat, as they had always been ruled. He explained to a leading Egyptian intellectual, Saad Eddin Ibrahim, that his critics misunderstood the Quran, which afforded special standing to the ruler of Egypt. When God sought to free the Children of Israel from their Egyptian bondage, he did not speak to the Egyptian people; instead, God advised Moses and Aaron to plead with the leader. "Go, both of you, to Pharaoh, for he has exceeded all bounds. Speak to him gently so that he may take heed, or show respect." If Moses, one of the strongest prophets, was instructed to speak politely to Pharaoh, Sadat reasoned, certainly his intellectual critics should treat him with similar respect.

Egypt, however, had turned against Sadat. It wasn't just the radicals and the intellectuals. The peace he had given his people was not embraced. Peace did not bring the complete resolution that one seeks in war. The allure of conquest and rectification still cast a spell despite the thirty years of conflict that had brought so much misery, poverty, and humiliation. Whenever Egypt was bleeding, other Arab countries egged it on to greater and greater sacrifices, but now that it was at peace, the Arab nations imposed an economic boycott and barred Egyptian planes from their airspace. The Arab League, which was founded and headquartered in Cairo, expelled Egypt and moved its offices to Tunis. Every Arab country except Oman and Sudan severed diplomatic relations. The isolation that Mohamed Kamel had envisioned was a reality. Sadat lashed out at the "cowards and dwarfs" in the Arab world who shunned him. Their criticism of his peace with Israel was no more than "the hissing of snakes," he said. "He was saying things that may be true, but weren't necessary," Carter later recalled. "I tried to get him to shut up."

Sadat responded to the furor, as usual, by turning inward, retreating from social contact. He had never cared much for food, but now he ate only soup and boiled vegetables. He often spoke of death. "It was as if he were set on some sort of divine mission that no one could interrupt," Jehan Sadat observed.

Sadat's assassin responded to his salute by hurling a grenade, which failed to explode, then he and the other soldiers began firing their automatic weapons into the reviewing stand. The first shot hit Sadat in the neck. Islambouli boldly walked directly to the stands and fired into Sadat's body, emptying his magazine. For the first thirty seconds, the presidential bodyguards seemed to freeze in place. Sadat's private secretary, Fawzi Abdel Hafez, tried to shield him with a chair, but Hafez was shot as well, absorbing more than twenty bullets (he somehow survived). By the time the shooting was over, Sadat and eleven others had been murdered. The Coptic bishop lay dead in his official robes. The Cuban ambassador was also dead. Twenty-eight people were wounded. The Belgian ambassador was shot twice. Blood cascaded down the steps of the reviewing stand. One of the assassins was killed and three others injured and then arrested. "I have killed the Pharaoh!" Islambouli crowed.

Osama el-Baz, who was seated near Sadat when the attack began, disappeared. Mubarak refused to announce the president's death until his closest aide could be found. It was hours later that Baz was discovered, walking the streets of the suburb of Heliopolis, many miles away, in a state of shock.

The attack was supposed to have been the prelude to the takeover of the Egyptian government by the plotters, but that plan was thwarted by the dragnet that immediately followed, pulling in members of the numerous radical groups that had proliferated in the Islamist underground. A future leader of al-Qaeda, Ayman al-Zawahiri, was snapped up on his way to the airport. He had conspired to bomb Sadat's funeral, where many foreign leaders would be present, among them Jimmy Carter and Menachem Begin.

SADAT'S FUNERAL WAS on Saturday, five days after his assassination. Because strictly observant Jews abjure using automobiles on the Sabbath, Begin chose to walk to the event from the nearby country club where he had found quarters. He was surrounded by Israeli security men, carrying automatic weapons inside attaché cases. Cairo was fortified and on edge. The leaders of eighty nations came to pay their respects, but Arab delegations were conspicuously absent. All over the city there were sandbagged gun emplacements in hotel lobbies and on apartment balconies. The *whomp-whomp* of low-flying helicopters reverberated in the streets. Soldiers in battle dress stood guard in every major intersection. The hysterical displays of grief that had overtaken Cairo when Nasser died were absent, however. Instead, there was massive indifference.

Moshe Dayan was not present to say farewell to Sadat. He had resigned from the cabinet when he realized that Begin was avoiding implementing autonomy for the Palestinians. Convinced that the Israeli military occupation was destroying the moral fiber of Israel, Dayan had formed his own party, but gained only two seats in the Knesset. By then, the cancer that may have been plaguing him during Camp David had been detected. He immediately sensed that it was fatal. "I had an interesting life until the age of sixty-four," he said with characteristic dispassion. He died six days after Sadat's funeral.

Ezer Weizman was also absent. He, too, had quit the cabinet because of the delay in the autonomy talks and the aggressive expansion of settlements in the West Bank. After tendering his resignation, Weizman furiously ripped a peace poster off the wall of the prime minister's office. "No one here wants peace," he shouted. Begin felt betrayed and refused to allow Weizman to be a part of the Israeli delegation to Sadat's funeral, although no one in Israel had been closer to Sadat.

The dignitaries gathered on the same parade ground where Sadat had been killed. The blood had been washed from the reviewing stand, but the bullet holes were still evident. Carter walked with the American delegation, which included former presidents Nixon and Ford. He, too, was now a former president. Any chance for reelection perished in the failed effort to rescue the hostages held in the American embassy in Tehran after the 1979 Iranian revolution.

Carter and Begin did not talk.

The monument to Sadat at the parade ground where he

died bore the Quranic epitaph he had chosen for himself before his fateful trip to Jerusalem, in case he was assassinated by the Jews: "Do not think of those who have been killed in God's way as dead. They are alive with their Lord, well provided for." In the end, it was his own people who killed him.

FREE OF CONCERN about an Egyptian response, Begin aggressively expanded settlements in the West Bank, and in short order bombed an Iraqi nuclear reactor near Baghdad and extended Israeli law to the Golan Heights. Then, in June 1982, he sent the Israeli army into Lebanon, in order to root out the Palestinian Liberation Organization. The country was home to 300,000 Palestinian refugees, who had tilted the demographic balance in a country that had once been dominated by pro-Western Maronite Christians.

Begin acknowledged that it was a "war of choice," unlike all of Israel's previous conflicts, but he promised that the war would bring "forty years of peace" to Israel once the job had been done. The master plan, envisioned by Ariel Sharon, was to force the Palestinians out of Lebanon into Jordan, which would effectively turn that country into a Palestinian homeland and allow Israel to absorb the West Bank. Begin promised President Ronald Reagan that Israel would not need to go farther than forty kilometers from the border.

Whatever limitations on the plan that the government had imposed were left aside as soon as Sharon moved his army into Lebanon. The Israelis conspired with a Christian warlord, Bashir Gemayel, of the Maronite Phalange party, to expel the Palestinians, defeat the Syrian forces in the country, and make Gemayel president of Lebanon. The Israeli army quickly accomplished those objectives. Yasser Arafat and the leaders of the PLO left Beirut on a ship bound for Tunisia. Gemayel became president of Lebanon that August. A month later he was blown to pieces by a Syrian bomb.

Without a Lebanese partner to clean up the PLO machinery still left in place, the Israeli army then invaded West Beirut. "Two targets in particular seemed to interest Sharon's army," Thomas Friedman, then a young correspondent for *The New York Times* in Beirut, later wrote. One was an archive of old Palestine—books, land deeds, photographs of Arab life, and maps that marked every Arab village that stood before the State of Israel was created. Friedman observed the graffiti the Israeli soldiers left behind in the room where the archives had been kept. *Palestinian? What's that?* And *Palestinians, fuck you.*

The other targets were the two Palestinian refugee camps called Sabra and Shatila. Sharon contended that militants were still hiding there. His troops sealed off the camps and then let the Phalangists enter and take revenge for the death of their leader. Over the next three days they killed nearly everyone in the camps. The Israelis had a clear view of the slaughter from the rooftop of the Kuwaiti embassy, which they occupied. To assist the Phalangists in their work, the Israelis provided illuminating flares at night, and let them supervise their operation from the Israeli command post across the street. When the killers finally left, journalists and diplomats found among the mutilated corpses babies and toddlers who had been ripped apart and thrown into trash cans, boys who had been castrated, people who had been scalped and Christian crosses carved into their bodies. The Red Cross estimated the number of dead between eight hundred and one thousand. Other sources put the number of dead much higher, but because the

Phalangists disposed of many of the bodies it is impossible to have an accurate count. Friedman saw no evidence that any of the victims strewn around the camps were PLO fighters; they had left before the camps were assaulted.

The United Nations condemned it as an act of genocide. Shamed and outraged by the massacre and the miasma of the war, 400,000 Israelis—more than 10 percent of the country's population—went into the streets to demand an accounting. The official inquiry that eventually followed held Sharon personally responsible for the atrocity, but Begin refused to fire him. (Sharon did resign as minister of defense but remained in the cabinet without portfolio.) The world began to take a serious interest in the Palestinian cause, and Egypt once again united with the Arabs in outrage.

Begin had thought the war would last only forty-eight hours, with negligible casualties, but war makes its own calculations. According to the Lebanese government, more than thirty thousand Lebanese were killed during the Israeli invasion, most of them civilians. In the narrow ancient streets of Beirut, where much of the fighting took place, a fourth of the victims were under fifteen and a third were adults over fifty—children and grandparents. The Israeli Defense Ministry says that 1,217 Israeli soldiers died in the conflict. Even worse than the war was the legacy it left behind. Lebanon was already a dysfunctional country, but its fragile democracy was shattered and civil war reignited, destroying a society once noted for its arts, commerce, and lighthearted materialism. When Israeli forces finally began to withdraw, unilaterally, in 1985, the Syrian army that was supposed to have been defeated and expelled returned to assume its brutal management of a desolated country. The space that the PLO left in southern Lebanon was replaced by Hezbollah, which was created to oppose Israeli occupation. Israel finally completed its withdrawal from Lebanon in May 2000, eighteen years after the war began.

Peace had given Begin a free hand, which he overplayed. The war in Lebanon, and the death of his beloved wife, Aliza, broke him. He grew frail, and stopped dying his hair. His mood alarmed everyone who knew him. Intimates shielded him from interviews and the public. On August 28, 1983, Begin was supposed to receive the new German chancellor, Helmut Kohl. One more thing that Begin couldn't bear was to shake hands with a German. When Kadishai came into the prime minister's office that morning, Begin told his old friend, "Today I will quit my job." He explained to his cabinet that he was seeking "forgiveness, absolution, and atonement. Whether it will be granted to me, I do not know."

Afterward, Begin's friend and cabinet secretary Dan Meridor demanded, "Menachem, why did you do it?" Begin listed his physical weakness, the lack of privacy, and the demonstrations that opponents of the war held across the street from his house around the clock. He couldn't sleep for the noise they made. The protestors kept a sign with a running total of Israeli casualties every day. Begin couldn't bring himself to look at it. The police had offered to sweep the protestors off the street but he insisted on their right to demonstrate.

Begin went to his apartment on Zemach Street in Jerusalem and closed the door on the world. For the next nine years he rarely ventured out, except to visit his wife's grave. He developed a skin rash that kept him from shaving. He wore his pajamas during the day or a pair of trousers and a robe when the rare visitor was permitted to call. In the mornings, Kadishai would bring him the newspapers, as he always had, and Begin spent his time reading or listening to the radio. He had gone back underground. From his window he could see the Jerusalem Forest, and beyond that, Deir Yassin.

In 1987, on the eighth anniversary of the signing of the Camp David peace treaty, Jimmy and Rosalynn Carter were in Israel. Begin refused to receive them. Carter was being honored at a luncheon at the home of President Chaim Herzog, along with the Israelis who had been at Camp David. Everyone was there except for Begin. When Carter saw Kadishai, he asked once again to speak to his old partner in peace. "Okay, I'll put you on the phone," Kadishai said. He dialed the number and told Begin, "Mr. President Carter is here, he would like to speak to you."

"Please give him the phone," Begin said.

Carter said, "Hello, Mr. Begin."

"Hello, President Carter. How's Rosalynn?"

"She's fine."

Then Begin abruptly said good-bye. He died in March 1992.

WHEN BEGIN RETURNED, triumphant, from Camp David, the president of Israel, Yitzhak Navon, asked him, "How did you succeed where previous prime ministers have failed?"

Begin replied, "It's all in the timing."

One of the lessons of Camp David is that timing had little to do with it. Yes, each side had incentives to seek peace in 1978, but those incentives were always present, even as Israel and Egypt collided in one war after another. The Yom Kippur War had shaken Israel out of its smug reverie of unchallenged dominance and changed the context, but peace had been available as an alternative to war from the beginning of the conflict in

1948. There were no insoluble issues standing between Egypt and Israel. Egypt chose to identify with the Arabs who rejected a small Jewish state, and so it gambled on war as a more definitive solution than peaceful negotiation. The Arabs lost that bet, and Israel grew larger and became an even greater threat. Each war planted the seeds for the next one. Each defeat made the Arabs more resolute, more defiant. Peace became contemptible. But in the case of Egypt and Israel, it was always a possibility. Egypt had to decide whether to act in its own interests or as the champion of a larger Arab cause. Israel had to sacrifice territory that provided a buffer against a sudden attack but also enlarged the imagined final borders of Greater Israel.

The dispute between the Israelis and the Palestinians is different, and that's why it remains unresolved, although Camp David was supposed to have brought that conflict to a permanent end. The War of Independence in 1948 expanded the territory that the new Jewish state claimed, including nearly 60 percent of the area designated for the stillborn nation of Palestine, the remainder being taken over by Jordan. Arab refugees flooded into neighboring countries, and Israel locked the door behind them. Instead of being digested by other Arab societies, the refugees became a destabilizing presence and a source of radicalism and terror that plagued the whole world. Except for Jordan, the Arab states have avoided absorbing the Palestinian refugees in order to keep the conflict alive. The numerous attempts to bring this conflict to an end have failed because of the absence of political courage on both sides to accept the sacrifices that peace would entail.

Isolation allowed the negotiators to work creatively, explore alternatives, concentrate on a single task, and take risks that might not be ventured in the public eye. Carter had thought that the cloistered environment would allow trust to develop between the two leaders that would cause them to brush aside small obstacles in order to reach the larger goal. In this, he was quite wrong. The intimacy of Camp David amplified the hostility between Begin and Sadat, which repeatedly threatened to torpedo the talks. And yet, neither man could leave without paying a terrible political price. They were trapped. As the days passed, isolation became a stronger incentive to reach a deal simply because they couldn't stand being there any longer. Despite the shuttered environment they worked in, each of these three men knew that the bright light of history was shining on them, and that what they did or failed to do here would outweigh any other measure of their extraordinary lives.

Camp David was unusual in that it was conducted by the leaders of each country and not by subordinates. Nothing had been agreed to in advance. The risk that these men took reflected the courage that they brought to the negotiation. Their personal prestige was on the line. There was no guarantee of even partial success; indeed, it began to seem that the impending failure of the talks was only going to make things worse. But it was crucial to the success of the summit that these men had the authority to make a deal. Every concession was consequential. This alarmed the Egyptian foreign minister, Kamel, who ran out of ways to bridle Sadat. "With Carter leading the United States delegation to Camp David, the confrontation was no more between Sadat and Begin only but rather involved some sort of confrontation between Sadat and the United States President," he wrote. "The success or failure of the Conference, in the eyes of the world, added up to success or failure for Carter." He worried that Sadat and Begin would wind up conceding what didn't belong to them—the rights of the Palestinians—in order to placate the American president.

There would be no peace treaty without Carter's unswerving commitment to bring this conflict to an end. He was fueled by his religious belief that God had put him in office in part to bring peace to the Holy Land. Egypt and Israel simply could not make peace without the presence of a trusted third party; and in truth, there was no other candidate as sufficiently powerful and impartial as the United States to fill that role. And yet, until Carter, no American president had been willing to risk his prestige and perhaps his office to pursue such a distant goal.

The American team incorporated the idea of a single negotiating text, which Carter controlled. This allowed him to lock in gains and gradually pare down the points of disagreement. Carter also schooled himself in the history and geography of the region. His obsession with minutiae had become a subject of ridicule—notably, he was said to monitor which staff members signed up for the White House tennis courts—but in the case of Camp David his ability to absorb information allowed him to see past the hazards and ruses that such bare-knuckled negotiations often employ.

However, Carter came to Camp David under the spell of an illusion, seeing his role as that of a facilitator, a kind of camp counselor helping two quarreling parties understand each other better. He had thought that the leaders would discover the inherent goodness in each other and would willingly work out their differences. That illusion shattered within minutes of the first meeting of the three men. Carter floundered, stunned by the open hostility. Unable to referee the argument, he had to separate the Egyptian and the Israeli. They could not escape the history that had created them in order to see into the soul of the other. Only Carter could do that. His role had to change, which meant that he, too, had to change. He had to free himself of his Christian-inspired conception of human nature and accept a more tragic, Old Testament view of behavior. They needed him to be stronger than they were. He would have to force them to make the peace they both wanted but couldn't achieve on their own.

The change in Carter's role became evident on the sixth day, after the trip to Gettysburg, when Carter presented the first American draft of an agreement. He quite forcefully stated that Begin would be blamed if the talks failed. Similarly, on the eleventh day, when Sadat had ordered a helicopter to take him and his team back to Washington, Carter brought the weight of his office down hard, threatening to break off relations with Egypt and end their personal friendship. Carter made it clear to both men that if either of them deserted the process, they would have a problem with the United States—a problem neither man could afford. By taking an aggressive stance as a full partner to the negotiations, Carter allowed each side to make concessions to the U.S. that they couldn't make to each other.

Carter was aided by a unified American delegation that never broke into factions. Vance and Brzezinski, in particular, had many territorial spats during their time in the Carter administration, but none of that was on display at Camp David. The entire delegation was focused and tireless, in the model of their leader. The Egyptian and Israeli delegations, on the other hand, were disparate examples of the societies they represented. Sadat ruled over a team that was powerless but mainly united against him. The Israeli team was divided, reflective of the diverse and contentious Israeli political system, but its members were largely more in favor of peace than their leader was. Begin may have chosen them for that quality. They helped him overcome his lifelong antipathy to making any concession at all.

Ambiguity played a double role at Camp David. Careful language was the key to making peace between Egypt and Israel, but vague phrases about negotiations with the Palestinians opened up escape clauses that Begin exploited. Carter successfully employed constructive ambiguity to overcome Begin's horror of UN Resolution 242 by simply taking it out of the main text and placing it in the appendix, where it was still a formal part of the treaty. Similarly, in the side letter on Jerusalem, Carter invoked the policy statements of two American ambassadors without actually quoting their language. When Carter traveled to Israel to try to finish the agreement, Begin implied that he would be open-handed in dealing with Palestinian demands, but refused to be specific. The Israelis did concede that the Palestinians had "legitimate rights" and should be given "full autonomy," but they refused to accept the term "self-determination" in connection with Palestinian rights. Vance believed that was about as much as could be hoped for. The failure to make a more explicit link between the comprehensive peace treaty, encompassing the West Bank and Gaza, with the separate peace between Israel and Egypt would essentially doom Palestinian national aspirations. "Sadat has sold Jerusalem, Palestine, and the rights of the Palestinian people for a handful of Sinai sand," Yasser Arafat commented bitterly. (Arafat proceeded to boycott the autonomy talks, ensuring that the Palestinians would not be able to influence their future, but neither the Israelis nor the Americans wished to have them involved.) Sadat's ambivalence on the subject of the Palestinians made it difficult for Carter to prosecute their case more forcefully, although he would come to regret the abandonment of the Palestinian cause by all parties to the agreement, including Egypt.

There was no fixed deadline at Camp David when it began; but, of course, no one expected that it would drag on for thirteen days. Begin was particularly opposed to deadlines. He was a master of pulling small matters to the surface and dwelling on them while the hour hand made its leisurely circles. By the eleventh day, a Friday, Carter decided that he could not invest more time on the summit. He asked Begin and Sadat to prepare their final suggestions, as the summit would end on Sunday no matter what the outcome. The deadline forced the delegations to concentrate on getting to a final agreement, but in the crush of negotiation on Saturday night a crucial mistake was made. Either through misunderstanding or deceit or sober second thoughts, Begin did not produce the letter on halting settlement construction that Carter thought he had agreed to. Alone among the participants at Camp David, Aharon Barak suggested that the negotiators remain until the Palestinian issue was resolved and the comprehensive peace that Carter sought had been achieved. That would have required the Israelis to commit to withdrawing from the occupied territories and permitting free elections and a Palestinian self-governing authority with real control. It seems unlikely that Begin would have committed to such steps, no matter how long he was confined on that woodsy hilltop in Maryland. Instead, he ran out the clock.

Of the three men, perhaps only Carter genuinely believed from the beginning that a peace agreement could actually be achieved. Sadat was negotiating mainly to supplant Israel as

America's best friend in the region. Peace was a highly desirable outcome, but if the talks failed because of Israeli intransigence, that would boost Egypt's standing with the most powerful nation in the world. "This will end in Begin's downfall!" Sadat predicted to his delegation. The Israelis really didn't understand what they were getting into. Begin arrived at Camp David expecting it to last two or three days at most, and to end with no more than a promise for future talks. No one in the Israeli delegation imagined that they would wind up surrendering Sinai settlements and fully withdrawing from the peninsula. Begin's main goal was to avoid the blame for failure. In the end, the only way he could do that was to allow the summit to succeed.

Sadat got back Sinai, including the oil fields, which he had not been able to do through war. Egypt did endure the shunning of its neighbors, but that didn't last. "The Arabs cannot isolate Egypt," Sadat observed haughtily; "they can only isolate themselves." He was right about that. By 1984, the Arab embassies began to reopen in Cairo, although Sadat was not alive to see his prophecy come true. Begin was seen as the stronger negotiator at Camp David, but the Israelis had to surrender something valuable and tangible—land—in return for something ephemeral and reversible—peace. Israel counted as victories things that were not a part of the treaty: for instance, there was no mention of a Palestinian state or self-determination; there was no insistence on Israeli military withdrawal from the West Bank and Gaza; there was no agreement on Jerusalem. Begin's fierce tactics at Camp David and beyond ensured that Israel would continue to occupy the West Bank and that the settlements would never stop. It also meant that the comprehensive peace that might have been achieved at

Camp David would continue to elude Israel. The Palestinians got little except for a vague promise to respect their "legitimate rights." In signing the treaty with Israel, Egypt severed its link to the Palestinian cause. Without a powerful Arab champion, Palestine became a mascot for Islamists and radical factions who could only do further damage to the prospects of a peaceful and just response to the misery of an abandoned people.

The unresolved issues of Camp David have not gone away, but the success of the summit is measured by its durability. Since the signing of the treaty between Israel and Egypt in 1979, there has not been a single violation of the terms of the agreement. It's impossible to calculate the value of peace until war brings it to an end.

Acknowledgments and Notes on Sources

This book had an unusual genesis. In 2011, I received a call from Gerald Rafshoon, who had been the communications director in the Carter White House, asking if I would be interested in writing a play about the thirteen days of the Camp David summit. I had lived in Georgia when Carter was governor and ran for president; I was teaching at the American University in Cairo when Nasser died and Sadat took office; and I later spent a considerable amount of time reporting from Israel. Naturally, the project appealed to me. Rafshoon persuaded the Arena Stage in Washington, D.C., to commission the project, whereupon he and I went to Plains to interview the Carters and then to Egypt and Israel to talk to surviving members of those delegations. Molly Smith, the artistic director of the Arena, staged the production of *Camp David* in April 2014. It was one of the most rewarding experiences of my life.

As it turned out, I wasn't finished with Camp David. There was much more story and there were many more interesting characters than could be fitted into a ninety-minute stage play. Except for William B. Quandt's valuable account, *Camp David: Peacemaking and Politics,* there were few books devoted exclusively to one of the great diplomatic triumphs of the twentieth century. It is perhaps because Carter was so unpopular when he left office that his signal achievement has been largely ignored. And yet, speaking as a longtime observer of the Middle East, it would be difficult to imagine what that region might be like without it. That is not to say that the treaty is beloved. Both Egyptian and Israeli politicians routinely denounce the sacrifices that their countries made to achieve it. Indeed, Carter told me that Prime Minister Benjamin Netanyahu personally blamed him for forcing Israel to surrender Sinai. These complaints demonstrate how painful the compromises were, even today. The Palestinians continue to feel betrayed, both by the accord negotiated in their name and by the fact that it hasn't been honored.

In these pages I have taken the liberty of regularizing the spelling of some of the quoted material and adopting common transcriptions of Arabic and Hebrew names.

This book is both a work of history, in that it draws upon the texts of the past, and a work of journalism that required the cooperation of a multitude of individuals in three different countries. The Carters very generously lent me their personal diaries of Camp David. The Jimmy Carter Library in Atlanta was always a valuable resource. I want to particularly thank Jay Hakes, Jay Beck, and Phil Wise for their time and thoughtful input. Yechiel Kadishai, Begin's longtime friend and assistant, took me through the Irgun museum in Tel Aviv; and Dan Pattir, Begin's former press secretary, provided additional memories. Aharon Barak was particularly insightful on the details of the summit, as were Meir Rosenne and Elyakim Rubinstein. Many other sources patiently added their thoughts and recollections. Iris Berlatzky and Rami Shetivi at the Menachem Begin Heritage Center in Jerusalem were extremely helpful in guiding me through their material and providing archival materials. One of the continuing tragedies of the Arab world is that such historical material is much less available to scholars; however, I was generously assisted in Cairo by Ahmed Abul-Gheit, Nabil al-Arabi, and Abdul Raouf al-Reedy.

During the process of researching this book, I was reminded on several occasions that I had gotten to these sources just in time, but in other cases, I was regrettably too late.

I owe particular thanks to those who read part or all of this book in manuscript: Yossi Alpher, Seth Anziska, Louise Fischer, Jay Hakes, Stephen Harrigan, Steven Hochman, William Quandt, Gerald Rafshoon, Ziv Rubinovitz, and Harold Saunders. The book is far better because of their thoughtful remarks; whatever errors of fact or judgment that remain are my own responsibility.

Michal Baer and Paul Cuno-Booth provided translations from Hebrew and Arabic. My assistant, Lauren Wolf, contributed additional research and much valuable help with the manuscript. My agent, Andrew Wylie, has been a steady friend throughout the process.

This is my sixth book with my editor, Ann Close, a partnership spanning three decades. She has been a wonderful partner, and it is to her that this book is lovingly dedicated.

Notes

PROLOGUE

4 "exalted" people: Interview with Jimmy Carter.
Rosalynn wept at: Interview with Rosalynn Carter.
He had studied: Bourne, *Jimmy Carter*, p. 32.

5 The question of what: Sachar, *A History of Israel from the Rise of Zionism to Our Time*, p. 669; "Demographics of Israel," Jewish Virtual Library, www.jewishvirtuallibrary.org/jsource/History/demographics.html.

6 should be conquered: Interview with Yechiel Kadishai; Shilon, *Menachem Begin: A Life*, p. 147; Hasten, *I Shall Not Die!*, p. 241.
a crank, a fascist: Sachar, *A History of Israel from the Rise of Zionism to Our Time*, p. 450.
"Begin is a distinctly": Shilon, *Menachem Begin*, p. 174.
"Teachers were beaten": Isidore Abramowitz et al., "New Palestine Party," *New York Times*, Dec. 4, 1948.
Arabs from the West Bank: Sachar, *A History of Israel from the Rise of Zionism to Our Time*, p. 707.

7 about 1,500 Jewish settlers: Figures for the settler population in 1972 were 1,182 in the West Bank, 700 in the Gaza Strip, 8,649 in East Jerusalem, 77 in Golan Heights, for a total of 10,608. "Israeli Settler Population 1972–2006," Foundation for Middle East Peace, http://www.fmep.org/settlement_info/settlement-info-and-tables/stats-data/israeli-settler-population-1972-2006.
The governor began speaking: Glad, *Jimmy Carter*, p. 340 fn.
Walter Mondale: Interview with Walter Mondale.

Former Secretary of State: Interview with Gerald Rafshoon.

8 Carter's closest advisers: Carter, *We Can Have Peace in the Holy Land*, p. 20; interview with Walter Mondale.

in his office safe: Steven Hochman, personal communication.

"Heavy support": Hamilton Jordan memorandum to President Carter, June 1977.

10 "shining light": Carter, *Keeping Faith*, p. 283.

"dearest friend": Brzezinski, *Power and Principle*, p. 24.

"It was like talking": Interview with Jimmy Carter.

"President Carter knows": "Begin Bars a Return to '67 Borders," *New York Times*, May 23, 1977.

11 The profiles Carter was studying: Jimmy Carter speech, "The Role of Intelligence in Preparing for Camp David," President Carter and the Role of Intelligence in the Camp David Accords, a conference at the Carter Center, Nov. 12, 2013.

The resulting profiles: Jerrold Post, "Personality Profiles in Support of the Camp David Summit," *Studies in Intelligence* (spring 1979). The actual CIA profiles are still classified, but both Carter and Jerrold Post, who prepared the profiles, were helpful in describing the general features of the analyses.

The CIA noted his: Post, "Personality Profiles in Support of the Camp David Summit."

12 They had each spent: Begin claimed he spent two years in the Vilna prison and in a "Soviet concentration camp." According to Temko, his actual confinement lasted about a year, from September 1940 to September 1941; two-thirds of his incarceration was spent in Vilna. Temko, *To Win or to Die*, p. 64. Sadat spent five years in prison.

He was struck by: Carter, *An Hour Before Daylight*, p. 26.

13 "If I drown": "The World: Sadat: The Village Elder," *Time*, Nov. 28, 1977.

She was chosen: Heikal, *Autumn of Fury*, pp. 8–9.

Umm Mohamed: Sadat, *My Father and I*, p. 3.

14 occasionally beaten: Heikal, *Autumn of Fury*, pp. 10-11.

"How I loved": Sadat, *In Search of Identity*, p. 3.

15 According to the oral: See for instance the poem by Salah Abdel Sabur, "The Execution of Zahran," in Aida O. Azouqa, "Frederico García Lorca and Salah 'Abd al-Sabur as Composers of Modern Ballads: A Comparative Study," *Journal of Arabic Literature* 36, no. 2. (2005).

"The ballad dwells": Sadat, *In Search of Identity*, p. 6. Sadat's account of the incident is somewhat at variance with modern sources. See Turner, *Suez 1956*, pp. 39–40; Mustafa Bassiouni, "A Modern-Day

Dinshaway in Egypt?" *Al Akhbar English,* http://english.al-akhbar
.com/node/2887.

"the odious sight": Sadat, *In Search of Identity,* p. 10.

16 "nothing but a scrap": Quoted in Yunan Labib Rizk, "Gandhi in
Egypt," *Al-Ahram,* Dec. 19–25, 2002.

"I began to imitate": Sadat, *In Search of Identity,* p. 13.

Sadat's obsession with: Ibid., p. 21.

17 "I was in our village": Ibid., p. 13.

"My Dear Hitler": Israeli, *Man of Defiance,* p. 19.

18 They were the only whites: Jimmy Carter remarks at the Civil Rights
Summit, LBJ Library, April 8, 2014.

19 "The constant struggle": Carter, *An Hour Before Daylight,* p. 230.

20 "Believer President": Wright, *The Looming Tower,* p. 39.

He was baptized into: Glad, *Jimmy Carter,* p. 113.

21 "nigger lover": Balmer, *Redeemer,* p. 8.

"Sir, I stood 59th": Carter, *Why Not the Best?,* p. 59.

22 "He would ask me": Carter, *First Lady from Plains,* p. 34.

She would note that: Ibid., p. 35.

"God did not intend": Bourne, *Jimmy Carter,* p. 81.

the only white man: Carter, *Why Not the Best?,* p. 66.

23 "I could not believe": Carter, *An Hour Before Daylight,* p. 264.

"our kind of man": Balmer, *Redeemer,* pp. 30–31.

24 Carter himself was not linked: Glad, *Jimmy Carter,* pp. 134–35.

"I am not a land baron": Ibid., p. 136.

25 "What's the matter?": Oral History of Jimmy Carter, Georgia
Political History Program, May 4, 1993; Godbold, *Jimmy & Rosalynn Carter,* p. 166. Rabhan later spent time in an Iranian prison—as
a hostage, Carter claimed—and then was convicted of bank fraud
and served four and a half years in U.S. federal prison. "Despite His
Shady Record, USDA Backed Borrower," Gilbert M. Gaul, *Washington Post,* Dec. 4, 2007.

26 In 1972, he expelled: Kissinger, *White House Years,* p. 1295. Kissinger puts the number of Soviet troops expelled as fifteen thousand, whereas Ezer Weizman estimates twenty thousand. Weizman,
The Battle for Peace, p. 243.

The Israelis were convinced: Weizman, *The Battle for Peace,* p. 67.

"I am ready to travel": Boutros-Ghali, *Egypt's Road to Jerusalem,* pp.
11–12; "I Knew Sadat," Al Jazeera English, Sept. 28, 2009. The translations of the two accounts vary slightly.

27 the first in Israel's history: Richard Steele et al., "Sadat in Israel,"
Newsweek, Nov. 28, 1977.

Ten thousand soldiers: Elias Shourani, "The Reaction in Israel to the Sadat Initiative," *Journal of Palestine Studies* 7, no. 2 (winter 1978).

in addition to the: Eliahu Ben Elissar in Alterman, ed., *Sadat and His Legacy*, p. 25.

Without sheet music: Ibid.

Sharpshooters were stationed: Quandt, *Camp David*, p. 147.

28 **Sadat's enemies were:** Weizman, *The Battle for Peace*, p. 142.

"Madame, I've waited a long time": Shilon, *Menachem Begin*, p. 288.

"Oh, no, sir": Steele et al., "Sadat in Israel"; Shilon, *Menachem Begin*, p. 288.

Sadat was convinced: Ibid., p. 288. Heikal suggests that this conjecture derived from a comment Secretary of State Henry Kissinger made to Sadat shortly after the 1973 war. Heikal, *Secret Channels*, pp. 223–24.

29 **"to the Kaaba to pray":** Heikal, *Autumn of Fury*, p. 98. Elsewhere, Heikal discusses the taboo against Israel extensively. Heikal, *Secret Channels*.

As the presidential motorcade: Shilon, *Menachem Begin*, p. 288.

The Israelis had no: Interview with Samuel W. Lewis, Foreign Affairs Oral History Collection of the Association for Diplomatic Studies and Training, http://www.loc.gov/item/mfdipbib000687.

All along the way: Ronald Koven, "Sadat Jokes, Laughs with Golda," *Washington Post*, Nov. 22, 1977.

Across the street: Gervasi, *The Life and Times of Menahem Begin*, p. 61.

30 **"All that construction!":** Ibid., p. 26.

One of Sadat's bodyguards: Haber, Schiff, and Yaari, *The Year of the Dove*, pp. 73–74.

"Take these out": John 2:16.

31 **One witness describes:** Armstrong, *Jerusalem*, p. 274.

"The Crusades have now ended": Montefiore, *Jerusalem*, p. 439–40.

32 **At the End of Days:** Angelika Neuwirth, "The Spiritual Meaning of Jerusalem in Islam," in Rosovsky, ed., *City of the Great King*, pp. 113–14.

33 **"Sadat, what":** Hirst and Beeson, *Sadat*, p. 266.

"a *kippah*": Haber, Schiff, and Yaari, *The Year of the Dove*, p. 65.

"All this befell us": Ibid., p. 66.

34 **Some were shot:** Gervasi, *The Life and Times of Menahem Begin*, p. 107.

"A day of retribution": Shilon, *Menachem Begin*, p. 5. Shilon says that Begin's sister, Rachel Halperin, related a different story. "Some time before the mass murders, her father decided to sneak out without approval from the area where the Jews had been gathered in order to properly bury one of the town's most prominent Jews. . . . When Ze'ev Dov was approached by a Nazi officer who questioned him, he answered, 'This is what I have to do.' In response, the officer shot him." Ibid., pp. 5–6.

"May God guide our": Ronald Koven, "Sadat's Day in the Holy City," *Washington Post,* Nov. 21, 1977.

"We have to concentrate": Boutros-Ghali, *Egypt's Road to Jerusalem,* p. 21.

"Every side wants": Cohen, *Culture and Conflict in Egyptian-Israeli Relations,* p. 133.

36 permitted to applaud: Haber, Schiff, and Yaari, *The Year of the Dove,* p. 66.

"Ladies and gentlemen": Anwar Sadat address to Knesset, Nov. 20, 1977.

37 "We have to prepare for war": Weizman, *The Battle for Peace,* p. 33.

38 "No, sir": Menachem Begin remarks in Knesset, Nov. 20, 1977.

"His IQ is probably": Interview with Jimmy Carter.

39 "Begin is absolutely": Weizman, *The Battle for Peace,* p. 193.

"up the wall": Shilon, *Menachem Begin,* p. 304.

"He exhibited a rich": Samuel Lewis, "The Camp David Peace Process," in Sha'al, ed., *The Camp David Accords,* p. 57.

40 "Against the eyes": Temko, *To Win or to Die,* pp. 17–18.

In private, Begin was: Shilon, *Menachem Begin,* p. 165.

He devoutly believed: Interview with Yechiel Kadishai.

award citizenship to every Arab: Shilon, *Menachem Begin,* p. 219.

He went to temple: Interview with Zev Chafets; Shilon, *Menachem Begin,* p. 154.

41 "Is this not a startlingly accurate prophecy": Avner, *The Prime Ministers,* p. 396.

42 "There were only 650,000 Jews": "President's Meeting with Prime Minister Begin of Israel," in Howard, ed., *Foreign Relations of the United States, 1977–1980,* vol. 8: *Arab-Israeli Dispute, January 1977–August 1978,* pp. 336–52; Avner, *The Prime Ministers,* pp. 421–22.

43 "Peasants after all": Ibid., 336–52.

44 "new specimen of human being": Begin, *The Revolt,* p. xxv.

"It is axiomatic": Ibid., p. xxvi.

45 his earliest memory: Temko, *To Win or to Die,* p. 21. Temko says that Begin was not actually present when the soldiers flogged two Jews, one of whom died afterward. The doctor who attempted to save him was the Begins' downstairs neighbor, who himself died of a heart

attack a few days later. The event caused a great deal of distress in the Begin household, which is probably what Begin recalled.

"It was a popular sport": Avner, *The Prime Ministers*, p. 436.

46 "to beat those who beat us": Temko, *To Win or to Die*, p. 32.

47 Even as a precocious: Ibid., p. 34.

In 1929 Begin experienced: Shilon, *Menachem Begin*, p. 10. Shilon gives the date of Jabotinsky's visit to Brisk as 1929; Temko, *To Win or to Die*, p. 37, makes the date 1931. Begin himself says that he joined Betar at age fifteen, which makes the Shilon date more likely. Begin, *White Nights*, p. 53.

48 "Jabotinsky became God": Temko, *To Win or to Die*, p. 37.

"Emotionally, my attitude": Jabotinsky, "The Iron Wall," Nov. 4, 1923, http://www.jewishvirtuallibrary.org/jsource/Zionism/ironwall.html.

49 Begin later admitted: Carter, *White House Diary*, p. 151.

"All you journalists": Heikal, *Autumn of Fury*, p. 104.

"It was as if a messenger": "Sacred Mission," *Time*, Nov. 28, 1977.

"The Middle East after": Sadat interview with ABC, Nov. 27, 1977.

Palestinians in Athens: Alfred L. Atherton and Harold H. Saunders, "Analysis of Arab-Israeli Developments," U.S. Dept. of State, no. 295, Nov. 19, 1977.

50 That was too much: Quandt, *Camp David*, p. 102.

"It's a very interesting plan": Weizman, *The Battle for Peace*, p. 120.

51 "Not a single Israeli settlement": Ibid., p. 147.

If the Israelis: Ibid., p. 195.

He made it clear: Zion and Dan, "Untold Story of the Mideast Talks," Part II, *New York Times*, Jan. 21, 1979.

52 "Everyone who went": "Cairo Expels Envoys of Cyprus in Dispute over Airport Battle," Associated Press, Feb. 20, 1978.

Sadat responded by: Kamel, *The Camp David Accords*, p. 125; Weizman, *The Battle for Peace*, p. 295.

The first person they: Weizman, *The Battle for Peace*, p. 268.

Most of them were: Dayan, *Breakthrough*, p. 121.

53 "Those who killed Jews": Henry Kamm, "Begin Hints Strongly at Reprisal for Raid That Killed 37 Israelis," *New York Times*, Mar. 12, 1978.

Carter was appalled: Carter, *Keeping Faith*, p. 311.

"wounded in the heart": Ibid., p. 311.

"not willing to withdraw": Ibid., p. 312.

54 Begin's intransigence had destroyed: Brzezinski, *Power and Principle*, p. 247.

He told his aides: Zion and Dan, "Untold Story of the Mideast Talks."

"nothing for nothing": Ibid.

55 "pygmies": Quandt, *Camp David,* p. 265.

"my economy": Post, "Personality Profiles in Support of the Camp David Summit."

"If the Middle East": "I Knew Sadat"; Sabry, *Al-Sadat,* pp. 447–48.

56 "If I had to choose one": James Fallows, "The Passionless Presidency," *Atlantic,* May 1, 1979.

Carter made lists: Glad, *Jimmy Carter,* p. 483.

He would take the time: Interview with Philip J. Wise Jr.

57 "I felt that God wanted peace": Interview with Jimmy Carter.

58 In July 1978: Interview with Rosalynn Carter; Carter, *We Can Have Peace in the Holy Land,* p. 36.

"It's so beautiful here": Interview with Rosalynn Carter; Carter, *First Lady from Plains,* p. 238.

His vice president: Carter, *First Lady from Plains,* p. 239.

59 For Carter to invest: Interview with Samuel W. Lewis, Foreign Affairs Oral History Collection of the Association for Diplomatic Studies and Training, http://www.loc.gov/item/mfdipbib000687.

"If you fail, we're done": Walter Mondale comments, "Camp David 25th Anniversary Forum."

"Our main objective": Cyrus Vance, "An Overview of the Camp David Talks," undated memo to the president.

"First Egyptian-Jewish peace": Quandt, *Camp David,* p. 220.

"We wait for peace": Jeremiah 8:15.

DAY ONE

62 "Cuba is absolutely lousy": Nelson, *The President Is at Camp David,* p. 20.

"I couldn't for the life": Quoted in Walsh, *From Mount Vernon to Crawford,* p. 281.

"I don't know what": Ibid., p. 282.

Carter, a tight-fisted: Gerald Rafshoon, personal communication.

63 "Cabins," Carter responded: Gulley and Reese, *Breaking Cover,* pp. 270–71.

"A sort of Presidential": Walsh, *From Mount Vernon to Crawford,* p. 40.

Six miles from Camp: Ted Gup, "Underground Government: A Guide to America's Doomsday Bunkers," *Washington Post,* May 31, 1992. Other estimates of the size of Site R are much larger.

The staff would: Walsh, *From Mount Vernon to Crawford,* p. 296.

64 "bullshit artists": Interview with Jimmy Carter.

65 A number of policemen: National Intelligence Daily Cable, Jan. 19, 1977.

The CIA warned Carter: "National Intelligence Estimate, Egypt—1977," undated CIA document.

In Israel, steep inflation: "Economic Consequences of a Middle East Peace Settlement: The Best Case," unsigned CIA memorandum, July 1, 1977.

"What can I do?": Weizman, *The Battle for Peace*, p. 307.

66 "There was a curious": Carter, *Keeping Faith*, p. 323.

67 Anwar and Jehan argued: Carter, *First Lady from Plains*, p. 241.

Even talking to: Interview with Abdul Raouf al-Reedy.

68 "His knowledge of the": Boutros-Ghali, *Egypt's Road to Jerusalem*, p. 49.

"He has something godly": Baha' al-Din, *Muhawarati ma'a as-Sadat*, p. 149.

Tohamy was constantly: Kamel, *The Camp David Accords*, p. 194.

"We all thought": Boutros-Ghali, *Egypt's Road to Jerusalem*, p. 134.

"What we are after": Kamel, *The Camp David Accords*, p. 283.

"here in my pocket": Carter, *Keeping Faith*, p. 328.

69 "Israel has to withdraw": Interview with Jimmy Carter.

"We can do it": Rosalynn Carter diary of Camp David.

"It will be like a resort": Haber, Schiff, and Yaari, *The Year of the Dove*, p. 220.

70 "like a bunch of boy scouts": Weizman, *The Battle for Peace*, p. 342.

"prima donnas": Brzezinski, *Power and Principle*, p. 237.

reflective of the intimate and contentious style: Cohen, *Culture and Conflict in Egyptian-Israeli Relations*, p. 141.

no more than a couple of days: Iris Berlatzky interview with Elyakim Rubinstein, Menachem Begin Archives.

71 "I'm glad to see you": Weizman, *The Battle for Peace*, p. 344.

"Mayflower generation": Ibid., p. 140.

72 "We were seasoned": Weizman, *On Eagles' Wings*, p. 12.

"As for the Egyptians": Weizman, *The Battle for Peace*, p. 11.

"Imagine that you're Arabs": Weizman, *On Eagles' Wings*, p. 163.

73 "It was only after": Ibid., p. 52.

He always thought: Tamir, *A Soldier in Search of Peace*, p. 37.

"Come and see me!": Weizman, *The Battle for Peace*, p. 344.

74 Tohamy's years in: Interview with Nabil el-Arabi. Arabi says that the "dirty work" included arresting General Mohamed Neguib, the figurehead leader of the 1952 Free Officers coup, driving him into the desert, and threatening to kill him.

a kind of guru: Interview with Dan Pattir.

He openly spoke: Interview with Abdel Raout al-Reedy.

When he served as the Egyptian: Heikal, *Secret Channels*, p. 255.

he was always spreading: Boutros-Ghali, *Egypt's Road to Jerusalem*, p. 134.

just stopped a revolution: Kamel, *The Camp David Accords*, p. 323.

75 "Mr. Tohamy": Interviews with Nabil el-Arabi, Ahmed Abul-Gheit, and William Quandt.

Hearing the story: Boutros-Ghali, *Egypt's Road to Jerusalem*, pp. 135–36. Ghorbal, *Su'ud wa inhiyar*, p. 140.

To keep the meeting: Dayan, *Breakthrough*, p. 43.

"a figure with status": Auda, *Hasan al-tuhami yaftahu malaffatuhu min ihtilal filistin ila kamb difid*, pp. 120; Arabi, *Taba, Camp David, al-jidar al-'azil*, p. 94.

76 "This is Dayan!": Auda, *Hasan al-tuhami yaftahu malaffatuhu min ihtilal filistin ila kamb difid*, pp. 122–23.

"His request for secrecy": Dayan, *Breakthrough*, p. 45.

"Moshe, you are the": Heikal, *Secret Channels*, p. 257.

Sadat would only consent: Dayan, "Highlights from Meeting of September 16, 1977, 21.00," Prime Minister's Official Israel State Archives, http://www.archives.gov.il/archivegov_eng/publications/electronicpirsum/sadatvisit/sadatvisitdoclist.htm.

77 "Otherwise, how could such": Dayan, *Breakthrough*, p. 52.

He went on to say: Haber, Schiff, and Yaari, *The Year of the Dove*, p. 11.

"But Tohamy said you were": Heikal, *Secret Channels*, p. 262. Hermann Frederick Eilts adds that Tohamy apparently told Sadat, after the first Morocco meeting with Dayan, "I've gotten Jerusalem for you!" Eilts in Alterman, ed., *Sadat and His Legacy*, p. 40. Elyakim Rubinstein, who was Dayan's aide at the time of the Tohamy talks, says that Dayan told Tohamy he would report the request for a full withdrawal to Begin but could not guarantee it. Elyakim Rubinstein interview, conducted by Dr. Nina Sagie, May 5, 1994, Menachem Begin Heritage Center; Rubinstein, *Darkey Shalom*, p. 14.

78 Egypt could foreseeably: Brzezinski, *Power and Principle*, p. 236. Prince Turki al-Faisal, the former Saudi intelligence chief, reflects the opinion of many Arabs when he writes that Sadat only went to Jerusalem after Tohamy was assured by Dayan that "Israel would withdraw from every last inch of Egyptian territory in return for peace." Al-Faisal, "Land First, Then Peace," *New York Times*, Sept. 12, 2009.

America had provided: Brzezinski, "Strategy for Camp David," memorandum for the president, Aug. 31, 1978.

79 Brzezinski came up with the idea: Quandt, *Camp David*, p. 171.

79   **American team continued:** Ibid., p. 203.

If Begin refused to budge: "Camp David: The Consequences of Failure," CIA briefing book for Camp David, Aug. 31, 1978.

He brought the actual text: The letter states, "Should the U.S. desire in the future to put forward proposals of its own, it will make every effort to coordinate with Israel its proposals with a view to refraining from putting forward proposals that Israel would consider unsatisfactory." Letter from President Ford to Prime Minister Rabin, Sept. 1, 1975.

80   **"Mr. Prime Minister":** Haber, Schiff, and Yaari, *The Year of the Dove*, p. 222.

"Some people ridicule": Ibid., pp. 222–23.

81   **"Sadat insists":** Ibid., p. 222.

"If such a principle": Weizman, *The Battle for Peace*, p. 346.

"The United States expects": Haber, Schiff, and Yaari, *The Year of the Dove*, p. 223.

"Sadat is impulsive": Carter, *First Lady from Plains*, p. 244.

82   **"What a paradise":** Haber, Schiff, and Yaari, *The Year of the Dove*, p. 224.

"We have a tough nut": Weizman, *The Battle for Peace*, p. 346.

DAY TWO

83   **Begin had seemed rigid:** Brzezinski, *Power and Principle*, p. 255.

84   **"My program is ready":** Haber, Schiff, and Yaari, *The Year of the Dove*, p. 225.

As Carter read: Carter, *Keeping Faith*, p. 341.

85   **"Germany is the enemy":** Anwar Sadat, *Pillar of Fire* interview.

86   **"I was not surprised":** Sadat, *Safahat Majhula*, p. 62.

Hekmet Fahmy: Pamela Andriotakis, "The Real Spy's Story Reads Like Fiction and 40 Years Later Inspires a Best-Seller," *People*, Dec. 15, 1980.

Sadat began spending nights: Sadat, *Safahat Majhula*, pp. 77–78. Jorgensen, *Hitler's Espionage Machine*, p. 177; Pamela Andriotakis, "The Real Spy's Story Reads Like Fiction and 40 Years Later Inspires a Best-Seller," *People*, Dec. 15, 1980. The "best-seller" in question was Ken Follett's *The Key to Rebecca*. The Nazi spies used an English-language version of Daphne du Maurier's novel *Rebecca* as the source book for their code.

87   **his ten-month-old daughter:** Sadat, *My Father and I*, p. 19.

It was during this period: Heikal, *Autumn of Fury*, p. 20.

"eccentric clothes": Ibid.

88   **"murder society":** Mitchell, *The Society of the Muslim Brothers*, p. 59.

"limbering up": Sadat, *In Search of Identity*, p. 58.

"as unbreakable": Sullivan, *Sadat*, p. 30.

"Apart from removing": Sadat, *In Search of Identity*, p. 60.

89   "Condemn me to death": Sadat, *A Woman of Egypt*, p. 74.

the Iron Guard: Heikal, *Autumn of Fury*, p. 21.

90   "My efforts at the": Sadat, *In Search of Identity*, p. 92.

once you began to talk: Boutros-Ghali, *Egypt's Road to Jerusalem*, p. 152.

"Do you remember when": Kamel, *The Camp David Accords*, p. 265.

Kamel arrived at Camp: Interview with Abdul Raouf al-Reedy.

Vance had tried to pacify: Interview with Samuel W. Lewis, Foreign Affairs Oral History Collection of the Association for Diplomatic Studies and Training, http://www.loc.gov/item/mfdipbib000687.

91   "The Israeli attitude rests": Kamel, *The Camp David Accords*, p. 303.

"How are you, Mr. President": Haber, Schiff, and Yaari, *The Year of the Dove*, p. 226.

He usually slept: Hirst and Beeson, *Sadat*, pp. 213–14; Heikal, *Autumn of Fury*, pp. 171–72; Ibrahim, *I'adat al-I'tibar lil-ra'is al-Sadat*, pp. 45–47. *Time* magazine also noted Sadat's occasional violation of the Islamic prohibition against alcohol, saying that he enjoyed "an occasional glass of wine, preferably an Egyptian red called Omar Khayyam." "The Underrated Heir," *Time*, May 17, 1971; Sadat, *A Woman of Egypt*, p. 179.

93   It was rumored among: Interview with Zev Chafets; Shilon, *Menachem Begin*, p. 164.

Throughout his life: Shilon, *Menachem Begin*, p. 215; Weizman, *The Battle for Peace*, p. 307.

"President Sadat brought": Haber, Schiff, and Yaari, *The Year of the Dove*, p. 227.

94   "We must turn over": Ibid.

"*Habemus papam*": Carter, *Keeping Faith*, p. 344.

"Further to the historic": Haber, Schiff, and Yaari, *The Year of the Dove*, p. 228.

95   "Begin will blow up": Carter, *First Lady from Plains*, p. 245.

"like a rabbi": Interview with Elyakim Rubinstein.

"What chutzpah!": Weizman, *The Battle for Peace*, pp. 353–54.

the word he used was *hadar*: Avner, *The Prime Ministers*, p. 403.

96   "There is only one": Haber, Schiff, and Yaari, *The Year of the Dove*, p. 257. Sam Lewis noted Begin's lack of empathy; Lewis, "The Camp David Peace Process," in Sha'al, ed., *The Camp David Accords*, p. 58. Yechiel Kadishai told me, "He loves everyone. Jews he loves more than others."

97   "We can save them": Kadishai, *Yad Yemino*, p. 54.

"Who is this boy?": Interview with Yechiel Kadishai.

98　The organization that Begin: Shilon, *Menachem Begin*, p. 49. Other accounts have different measures of Irgun's strength at the time; e.g., Gervasi says Irgun encompassed only six hundred men. Gervasi, *The Life and Times of Menahem Begin*, p. 153. The same figure is repeated in Bell, *Terror Out of Zion*, p. 107. Shilon relied on actual minutes of Irgun proceedings.

"We shall fight": Gervasi, *The Life and Times of Menahem Begin*, p. 152.

"History and our observation": Begin, *The Revolt*, p. 52.

99　Begin's brilliant improvisations: Bruce Hoffman notes, "The Irgun's campaign . . . established a revolutionary model that thereafter was emulated and embraced by both anticolonial- and postcolonial-era terrorist groups around the world." Hoffman, *Inside Terrorism*, p. 46.

a shipment of diamonds: Joseph Kister, personal communication.

100　In July 1945, the British: Rami Shetivi, personal communication.

Begin went into hiding: Gervasi, *The Life and Times of Menahem Begin*, p. 166.

"He had lost his eye": Shilon, *Menachem Begin*, p. 57.

"He has large and parted": Ibid.

101　"Are you also in favor": Ibid., p. 58.

Irgun members were kidnapped: Haber, *Menachem Begin*, p. 141.

102　In some cases, refugees: "Exodus, 1945–1947," in Lossin, *Pillar of Fire*.

more than a hundred thousand troops: Gervasi, *The Life and Times of Menahem Begin*, p. 170.

about one British soldier: Hoffman, *Inside Terrorism*, p. 50.

103　"We must retain": Hoffman, *Anonymous Soldiers*, p. 263.

"Evacuate the entire": Gervasi, *The Life and Times of Menahem Begin*, p. 177.

"to give orders": "Smear Campaign Charged by Begin," *New York Times*, Nov. 30, 1948.

Shaw claimed there was: John Shaw, *Pillar of Fire* interview.

Haganah ordered Begin: Temko, *To Win or to Die*, p. 92.

104　Ben-Gurion then denounced: Louise Fischer, private communication.

"The Irgun is the enemy": Gervasi, *The Life and Times of Menahem Begin*, p. 178.

"days of pain": Gordis, *Menachem Begin*, p. 52.

"We mourn the *Jewish*": Temko, *To Win or to Die*, p. 93.

"5ft. 9in.": photo inset, Neff, *Warriors at Suez*.

"He may be a Soviet": British Foreign Office telegram to Washington, Nov. 13, 1948, in the Menachem Begin files of British Intelligence.

"He was made 'better-looking'": Undated newspaper clipping in Begin files of British Intelligence, probably summer of 1946.

They were already spending: Turner, *Suez 1956*, p. 80.

"unworkable": Gervasi, *The Life and Times of Menahem Begin*, p. 187.

105 Sensing victory, Begin: Temko, *To Win or to Die*, p. 102.

"For hundreds of years": Jake Eyre, "The Story of Irgun: Terrorism, Propaganda, and the State of Israel," thesis, Norwich University, Nov. 16, 2010, p. 18.

"anti-Hebrew activities": Temko, *To Win or to Die*, p. 106.

The hanging of the British: Hoffman, *Inside Terrorism*, p. 53.

106 terror works: See, for instance, Bruce Hoffman, "The Rationality of Terrorism and Other Forms of Political Violence: Lessons from the Jewish Campaign in Palestine, 1939–1947," *Small Wars & Insurgencies* 22, no. 2 (May 2011): 258–72.

Many years later, American: Wright, *The Looming Tower*, p. 303.

Osama bin Laden read: Bruce Hoffman, personal communication; Al-Bahri, *Guarding Bin Laden*, p. 77.

"precisely the reverse": Gervasi, *The Life and Times of Menahem Begin*, p. 150.

DAY THREE

107 "very tough": Haber, Schiff, and Yaari, *The Year of the Dove*, p. 236.

108 "Palestinians!": Carter, *Keeping Faith*, pp. 347–48.

valued it as a foil: Interview with Jimmy Carter.

"What do you actually want": Carter, *Keeping Faith*, p. 348.

"assing around": Rosalynn Carter diary of Camp David.

"Throw away reticence": Carter, *Keeping Faith*, p. 349.

"Sinai settlements!": Ibid., p. 347.

109 "Moses": Quran 28:30.

110 "I have come down": Exodus 3:7–8.

"Let my people go": Exodus 7:15.

"If you remove this plague": Quran 7:133.

"that you may tell in": Exodus 10:2.

"I will pass through the land": Exodus 12:6–13.

111 "Go forth from among": Exodus 12:31.

"Is it because there are no graves": Exodus 14:11.

"My strength and my refuge": Exodus 15:2–3.

"We saved the Children": Quran 44:30-31.

112   **There may have been Jews:** Sand, *The Invention of the Land of Israel*, p. 118.

Israel is not cited: Finkelstein and Silberman, *The Bible Unearthed*, p. 57.

According to the Bible: Numbers 1:46; Exodus 12:37–8.

Marching ten abreast: Cline, *From Eden to Exile*, p. 74.

113   **"Do not spare him":** 1 Samuel 15:3.

In his parents' generation": Haber, *Menachem Begin*, p. 20.

"for you were once aliens": Exodus 22:20; 23:9.

"Little by little": Exodus 23:30–33.

114   **The vast migration:** Cline, *From Eden to Exile*, pp. 85–89.

"But they broke": Quran, 5:13.

Begin, with his granitic: Rosalynn Carter diary of Camp David.

115   **"knowing we would all be":** Haber, Schiff, and Yaari, *The Year of the Dove*, p. 237.

"We will not allow": Ibid., p. 238.

116   **"I thought that":** Carter, *Keeping Faith*, p. 351.

screaming at each other: Interview with Rosalynn Carter.

"Security, yes!": Carter, *Keeping Faith*, p. 351.

"clean-shaved": Interview with Ahmed Abul-Gheit.

"Minimum confidence does not": Carter, *Keeping Faith*, p. 353.

Weirdly, there were moments: Ibid.

120   **There were about 800,000:** Fischbach, *Jewish Property Claims Against Arab Countries*, p. 3.

75,000 to 80,000: Beinin, *The Dispersion of Egyptian Jewry*, p. 2.

Egypt was still occupied: Aly, Feldman, and Shikaki, *Arabs and Israelis*, p. 75.

121   **"didn't think about the possibility":** Sadat, *Safahat Majhula*, pp. 185–86.

The total number of Arab troops: Shlaim, *The Iron Wall*, p. 35. At the time of the second truce, on July 18, 1948, the CIA estimated total Arab forces, including irregulars, at 27,000, with another 19,800 "near Palestine." By comparison, it listed the forces of Haganah at 85,000, Irgun at 12,000, and Stern Gang at 800. "Possible Developments from the Palestine Truce," Enclosure B, Central Intelligence Agency, July 27, 1948.

"We swung out to sea": Weizman, *On Eagles' Wings*, p. 67.

122   **That first run was scarcely:** Morris, *1948*, p. 240.

killing indiscriminately: About Dayan's raid on July 11, 1948, Benny Morris writes, "The troops appear to have shot at everyone in their path." Ibid., pp. 289–90.

He led his men into: Shavit, *My Promised Land*, p. 107.

123   His greatest worry: Temko, *To Win or to Die*, p. 109.
five million dollars: Gervasi, *The Life and Times of Menahem Begin*, p. 251.
Some of them wept: Temko, *To Win or to Die*, p. 120.

124   "It's an attempt to run": Haber, *Menachem Begin*, p. 222.
"Enough! You're surrounded": Teveth, *Moshe Dayan*, p. 148.
"Jews do not shoot": Temko, *To Win or to Die*, p. 120.
"Our men called on Irgun": Dayan, *Story of My Life*, p. 96. Whether Dayan was actually present at the exchange of gunfire is unclear. His account suggests that he was; however, he had turned over the command to a subordinate, and other reports differ. Cf. Teveth, *Moshe Dayan*, p. 148; Haber, *Menachem Begin*, p. 220.
"Suddenly, we were attacked": Begin, *The Revolt*, p. 173.
In its panicked flight: Gordis, *Menachem Begin*, p. 90.

125   "We must all perish": Temko, *To Win or to Die*, p. 120.
Begin, who couldn't swim: Gordis, *Menachem Begin*, p. 90.
Sixteen of his men: Temko, *To Win or to Die*, p. 122.
Three members of the: Gordis, *Menachem Begin*, p. 91.
"the most dreadful event": Temko, *To Win or to Die*, p. 122.

126   "Never!": Carter, *Keeping Faith*, p. 358.
"I still dream of": Ibid.
"Anyone observing the two": Weizman, *The Battle for Peace*, pp. 136–37.

128   "I'm sure you will get": Haber, Schiff, and Yaari, *The Year of the Dove*, p. 241.
That evening the Carters: Carter, *First Lady from Plains*, p. 248.
Such a display belonged: Dayan, *Breakthrough*, p. 170.

129   "goldfish capital": Haber, Schiff, and Yaari, *The Year of the Dove*, p. 243.
ABC News had secured: Kays, *Frogs and Scorpions*, p. 122.
Barbara Walters was missing: Interview with Gerald Rafshoon.
"I've given so much": Rosalynn Carter diary of Camp David; Carter, *First Lady from Plains*, p. 248.

130   "I know you are all very": Carter, *Keeping Faith*, p. 363.
"It was I who made the peace": Kamel, *The Camp David Accords*, p. 307.

131   "I must have also": Carter, *Keeping Faith*, p. 361.
As the Americans auditioned: Ibid., p. 363.

132   "Stalemate here would just provide": Ibid.
"There must be a way": Carter, *First Lady from Plains*, p. 247.
Rosalynn had known Jimmy: Ibid., p. 9.

133   "running away": Ibid, p. 13.

"Just having these thoughts": Ibid., p. 14.
"The time has come to tell": Ibid., pp. 16–17.

134 "My childhood really ended": Ibid., p. 17.
Rosalynn's mother took in: Ibid., p. 19; B. Drummond Ayres, "The Importance of Being Rosalynn," *New York Times,* June 3, 1979.

135 "so glamorous": Carter, *First Lady from Plains,* p. 22.
By now she was following: Kaufman, *Rosalynn Carter,* p. 8.

136 "That's that": Carter, *First Lady from Plains,* p. 23.

137 The submarines of the era: Interview with Jimmy Carter; Bourne, *Jimmy Carter,* p. 66.

138 If she needed to stop: Kaufman, *Rosalynn Carter,* p. 12.
"We're home!": Carter, *First Lady from Plains,* p. 36.
The first year Jimmy: Carter, *Why Not the Best?,* p. 65.
Jimmy was seen as: Interview with Philip J. Wise Jr.

139 COONS AND CARTERS: Carter, *First Lady from Plains,* p. 49.
The election was fifteen: Carter, *Turning Point,* p. 56.
Rosalynn was thrilled: Carter, *First Lady from Plains,* p. 50.
When one elderly couple: Bourne, *Jimmy Carter,* p. 119.

140 Carter was leading by 70: Ibid., p. 120.
Joe Hurst sent Rosalynn: Carter, *First Lady from Plains,* p. 52.
"What do the constitutions": Carter, *Turning Point,* p. 24.
"How long is": Bourne, *Jimmy Carter,* p. 144.

141 "Negroes and other agitators": Ibid., p. 147.

142 every Kmart in the state: Carter, *First Lady from Plains,* p. 68.
The man responded by spitting: Ibid., p. 60.
Carter had dropped 22 pounds: Carter, *Why Not the Best?,* p. 98.
He kept a running tally: Jimmy Carter remarks at "The Civil Rights Summit," LBJ Library, April 8, 2014.

143 "I want to know what you": Carter, *First Lady from Plains,* p. 73.

144 By the end of the presidential campaign: Bourne, *Jimmy Carter,* p. 264.
Those close to the president: Interviews with Gerald Rafshoon and Walter Mondale.
Rosalynn topped Mother Teresa: Kaufman, *Rosalynn Carter,* p. ix.

145 "And now look where we are!": Kamel, *The Camp David Accords,* p. 314.

DAY FOUR

147 "See, this is what": Rosalynn Carter diary of Camp David.

149 According to Jordan's: Jordan, *Crisis,* p. 47.
"Proceed with the American": Carter, *First Lady from Plains,* p. 249.
"I think we ought": Rosalynn Carter diary of Camp David.

"You can go down": Carter, *First Lady from Plains*, p. 250.

150 **Begin now had the important:** William Quandt states that, from this moment, Begin's position on settlements in Sinai became unyielding; but, as we have seen, he was already intransigent on this issue. Quandt, *Camp David*, p. 225.

"I will never personally": Carter, *Keeping Faith*, p. 365.

151 "We are going to produce": Ibid., p. 367.

"Mr. President, please do not": Ibid., p. 366.

"You promised me": Carter, *First Lady from Plains*, p. 250.

152 **Gefilte fish and challah:** Gordis, *Menachem Begin*, p. 172.

He said that his father: Shilon, *Menachem Begin*, p. 269. Begin's sister, Rachel, claims this story is not true.

153 **liked to read Virgil:** Gervasi, *The Life and Times of Menahem Begin*, p. 326.

She was known by: Interview with Elyakim Rubinstein.

raising their three children: Gervasi, *The Life and Times of Menahem Begin*, p. 326.

Aliza strained to keep: Haber, *Menachem Begin*, p. 300.

She made her own clothes: Ibid., p. 301.

Even when her husband: Ibid., p. 302.

Such austerity was: Interview with Zev Chafets.

154 "I can't afford that!": Ibid.

155 "Jimmy is a fighter": Rosalynn Carter diary of Camp David.

"Oh, he'll be reelected": Ibid. According to Gerald Rafshoon, Dayan never did make such a testimony, but Weizman traveled with the Carter campaign in its last week.

"He was a man": Dayan, *My Father, His Daughter*, p. 249.

156 "almost insane daring": Bar-On, *Moshe Dayan*, p. 109.

Ben-Gurion responded: Ibid., pp. 111–12.

157 **In 1915, Moshe became:** Dayan notes that another child, Gideon Baratz, was the first kibbutz child, but he had actually been delivered in another community. Dayan, *Story of My Life*, p. 27.

When Shmuel Dayan: Ibid., p. 30.

"From my boyhood days": Ibid., p. 31.

158 "I could understand": Ibid., pp. 37–38.

Several hundred Jews: Morris, *Righteous Victims*, p. 160.

The British authorities: Rashid Khalidi, "The Palestinians and 1948: The Underlying Causes of Failure," in Rogan and Shlaim, *The War for Palestine*, p. 26.

159 "It became clear to me": Dayan, *Story of My Life*, p. 41.

At the outbreak of: Ibid., pp. 66–71.

An Arab scout named Rashid: Bar-On, *Moshe Dayan*, p. 24.

"Who will hire a": Ibid., p. 26.

160 "Gaza shall be forsaken": Zephaniah 2:4–5.
   In rabbinical literature: Sotah 9b.
161 "If I am shaved": Judges 16:17.
   "Those he killed": Judges 16:30.
162 "The greatness of Samson": Dayan, *Living with the Bible*, p. 129.
   "I would leave early": Ibid., p. 131.
   "Thousands of youngsters": Ibid., p. 165.
   The official Israeli army: Morris, *Righteous Victims*, p. 272.
   "We shoot from among": Ibid., p. 275.
163 "an eye for an eye": Ibid., p. 283.
   His strategy was to provoke: Ibid., p. 286.
   Fifty-eight civilians: Ibid., p. 287.
164 "Yesterday morning Roy was": Bar-On, *Moshe Dayan*, pp. 74–76;
   Dayan, *Living with the Bible*, pp. 165–66.
166 The phased departure of: Neff, *Warriors at Suez*, pp. 55–56.
   "The Suez Canal was": Turner, *Suez 1956*, p. 180.
167 Although Britain had: Neff, *Warriors at Suez*, p. 18.
   The scheme was: Dayan, *Story of My Life*, p. 202.
168 That would become: Grief, *The Legal Foundation and Borders of Israel under International Law*, p. 233.
   Finally, Israel would: Ibid., p. 215; Neff, *Warriors at Suez*, pp. 342–43;
   Sand, *The Invention of the Land of Israel*, p. 238.
169 Lloyd even proposed that: Sachar, *A History of Israel from the Rise of Zionism to Our Time*, p. 491.
   "real act of war": Dayan, *Story of My Life*, p. 219.
   Dayan offered a plan: Neff, *Warriors at Suez*, p. 348.
170 Within an hour: The soldiers who killed the villagers were sentenced to lengthy prison terms, but all were pardoned. The commander who ordered the slayings was convicted and made to pay a fine of 10 prutot, equivalent to a penny. The tally of victims killed varies between forty-seven and forty-nine, with the higher number being the more recent figure. Yoav Stern, "President Peres Apologizes for Kafr Qasem Massacre of 1956," *Haaretz*, Dec. 21, 2007; Yoav Stern, "50 Years after Massacre, Kafr Qasem Wants Answers," *Haaretz*, Oct. 29, 2006; Neff, *Warriors at Suez*, p. 368. The Jerusalem District Court found that the orders were patently illegal and should have been disobeyed. Louise Fischer, personal communication.
   About half of those: Shira Robinson, "Commemoration under Fire: Palestinian Responses to the 1956 Kafr Qasim Massacre," in Makdisi and Silverstein, *Memory and Violence in the Middle East and North Africa*, p. 105.
   The war began when: Dayan, *Story of My Life*, p. 236.

171   The Israelis finally took: Neff, *Warriors at Suez*, p. 381.
"In general, they fought": Dayan, *Story of My Life*, p. 246.
172   "He had been abandoned": Ibid., p. 248.
"These troops, abandoned by": Quoted in Turner, *Suez 1956*, pp. 340–41.
The British and French assembled: Neff, *Warriors at Suez*, p. 313.
173   The troops came ashore: Ibid., p. 408.
which killed 2,700 Egyptians: Heikal, *Secret Channels*, p. 111.
and left tens of thousands: Varble, *The Suez Crisis 1956*, p. 90.
"all contemporary forms": Letter from Prime Minister Bulganin to President Eisenhower, Nov. 5, 1956, http://history.state.gov/historical documents/frus1955-57v16/d505.
It was President Dwight Eisenhower: Eban, *An Autobiography*, p. 212.
174   The Israelis were harder: Ibid., pp. 215–19.
"Egypt has lost its sovereignty": Gamasy, *The October War*, pp. 13–14.
"If we agreed that": Neff, *Warriors at Suez*, p. 434.
Britain had been motivated: Ibid., p. 438.
175   France's colonial empire: Eban, *An Autobiography*, p. 233.
Within a few decades: Varble, *The Suez Crisis 1956*, p. 12.
176   "I owe the bomb to them": Hersh, *The Samson Option*, p. 43.
Begin savored the company: Interview with Rosalynn Carter.
he didn't care to go: Shilon, *Menachem Begin*, p. 43.
Whenever he served as: Ibid., p. 100.
Sentimental scenes would: Interview with Zev Chafets.
At home, the Begins: Gervasi, *The Life and Times of Menahem Begin*, p. 24; Silver, *Begin*, p. 182. Zev Chafets told me that when the cast of *Dallas* came to Israel to promote a new season, Begin pulled Larry Hagman, the actor who played J. R. Ewing, aside and asked if he could confide who shot J.R.
So far, the only movie: Edward Walsh, "At the Summit's End, Two Intractable Issues . . ." *Washington Post*, Sept. 20, 1978.
"He is intoxicated with": Shmuel Katz quoted in Shilon, *Menachem Begin*, p. 175.
"Begin, the King of Israel!": Carter, *The Blood of Abraham*, p. 8.
177   "magic influence": Interview with Aharon Barak.
"They say that Germany": Shilon, *Menachem Begin*, p. 169.
"In Zion Square": Ben-Gurion, *Israel*, p. 400.
178   German money helped build: Gordis, *Menachem Begin*, p. 112.
"Much of the land": Begin speech to Knesset, Nov. 7, 1956.
179   "This is the land": Deuteronomy 34:4.

"Every place where you set foot": Book of Joshua 1:3.
"Be strong and steadfast!": Book of Joshua 1:9.
"reproach of Egypt": Book of Joshua 5:9.
"And it came to pass": Book of Joshua 6:20–21.

180 "made it an heap": Book of Joshua 8:28.
"all the souls that": Book of Joshua 10:40.
"a very large part": Book of Joshua 13:1.
"all the Lebanon": Book of Joshua 13:5.
"I gave you a land": Book of Joshua 24:13–14.

181 For Begin, however: Interview with Zev Chafets.
"Look at these Jews": Quoted in Neff, *Warriors at Suez,* p. 46.

182 Neither Jericho nor Ai: Finkelstein and Silberman, *The Bible Unearthed,* p. 82.
The story was probably: Cline, *From Eden to Exile,* pp. 96–98.
The most likely explanation: Finkelstein and Silberman, *The Bible Unearthed,* p. 118.
The first time that: Cline, *From Eden to Exile,* p. 116.

DAY FIVE

186 "Thus says the Lord": Ezekiel 37:21–22.

187 "You must not be taken": Oren, *Six Days of War,* p. 54.
But he was wrong: Richard B. Parker has an extensive analysis of this question in *The Politics of Miscalculation in the Middle East.* Nutting, in *Nasser,* makes the case for an Israeli trap to draw Egypt into war, pp. 397–98; while Oren, in *Six Days of War,* p. 54, simply concludes that the reasons are "obscure." Lyndon Johnson, in *The Vantage Point,* p. 289, says that the Soviets manufactured the lie in order to pressure Egypt into supporting Syria.
Each time, the Soviets: Parker, *The Politics of Miscalculation in the Middle East,* p. 8.

188 "There is nothing there": Oren, *Six Days of War,* p. 64.
Still, Nasser felt: Nutting, *Nasser,* p. 408, suggests that Nasser was convinced he could "ride out the storm" if he offered no further provocation.
nearly half of the: Ibid., p. 383.
In addition, a third: Oren, *Six Days of War,* p. 93.
"If war comes": Ibid.
"totally exterminate": Sachar, *A History of Israel,* p. 633.
"Nasser was carried away": Sadat, *In Search of Identity,* p. 173.

189 The Israelis stockpiled: Yossi Alpher, personal communication.

190 "We must strike now": Oren, *Six Days of War,* p. 87.

Dayan took immediate charge: Bar-On, *Moshe Dayan*, p. 130.

A message, which Dayan: Oren, *Six Days of War*, p. 169.

Dayan coolly had breakfast: Bar-On, *Moshe Dayan*, p. 131.

"The whole plan rested": Weizman, *On Eagles' Wings*, pp. 222–23.

191   one of its spies was: Oren, *Six Days of War*, p. 171.

The commander in chief: Ibid., pp. 171–74; Sadat, *In Search of Identity*, p. 174.

"Well, they'll be taught": Sadat, *In Search of Identity*, p. 174.

"Good morning!": Ibid., p. 175.

"Quickly take possession": Oren, *Six Days of War*, p. 185.

192   "Shall we say that": Ibid., p. 226.

After Israel released: Telushkin, *Jewish Literacy*, p. 310.

Meantime, mobs attacked: Oren, *Six Days of War*, p. 217.

"I was dazed and": Sadat, *In Search of Identity*, pp. 175–76.

193   "I know exactly what": Weizman, *On Eagles' Wings*, p. 244.

Within a few days: Gordis, *Menachem Begin*, p. 128.

194   "What a divine view!": Lawrence Wright, "Forcing the End," *New Yorker*, July 20, 1998.

Professor Weizmann's papers: Weizman, *On Eagles' Wings*, p. 246.

"Under no circumstances": Oren, *Six Days of War*, p. 232.

"We must not wait": Ibid., p. 242.

195   "May peace descend": Dayan, *Story of My Life*, p. 16.

"We have returned to": Ibid.

It would be at least: Chafets, *Heroes and Hustlers, Hard Hats and Holy Men*, p. 38.

196   Before Camp David: Interview with Harold H. Saunders.

197   suspicion on Carter's part: Interview with Jimmy Carter.

The main idea that: Bruce Patton, personal communication.

198   "Governor, I've got a": Interview with Jimmy Carter; "To Cool Arms Race in Ga.," *Gettysburg Times*, Oct. 2, 1971; Randall H. Harber, "Georgia's Arms Race," UPI, Nov. 6, 1971.

"Necessary Elements of Agreement": Jimmy Carter handwritten notes.

200   "The president was very frank": Quandt, *Camp David*, p. 228.

it was also home: Neff, *Warriors at Suez*, p. 29.

Members of the Israeli: Aharon Barak told me, "I myself suggested many times to Sadat, 'Take Gaza! Take Gaza!' He said, 'I don't want Gaza.'"

but he didn't want: Shilon, *Menachem Begin*, p. 293; Iris Berlatzky interview with Elyakim Rubinstein, Menachem Begin Archives.

201   "a concentration camp *de luxe*": Silver, *Begin*, p. 191.

"It all reminded me": Weizman, *The Battle for Peace*, p. 359.

Carter observed that Weizman: Interview with Jimmy Carter.

"What makes things even gloomier": Kamel, *The Camp David Accords,* pp. 321–22.

202   "I get the feeling that": Weizman, *The Battle for Peace,* p. 359.

"He heard you repeat": Sabry, *Al-Sadat,* p. 451.

"There is no argument": Weizman, *The Battle for Peace,* p. 362.

204   "He could hardly cross": Kamel, *The Camp David Accords,* p. 323.

"Jerusalem has been put": Ibid.

205   "Tohamy!": Ibid., p. 196.

A figure from the ancien régime: Michael Lind, "Alboutros," *New Republic,* June 28, 1993.

In 1910, a Muslim fanatic: Turner, *Suez 1956,* p. 41.

Given his talents: Heikal, *Autumn of Fury,* p. 105.

"I felt strange": Boutros-Ghali, *Egypt's Road to Jerusalem,* p. 141.

206   Begin identified Brzezinski: Weizman, *The Battle for Peace,* p. 363.

He was a political innovator: Interview with Jimmy Carter.

207   He explained to the press: Avner, *The Prime Ministers,* pp. 439–40.

"*ocher Israel*": Sidney Zion and Uri Dan, "Untold Story of the Mideast Talks," Part II, *New York Times,* Jan. 21, 1979.

"Poles apart!": Avner, *The Prime Ministers,* p. 439.

"Don't forget to tell": Begin, *White Nights,* p. 19.

Observing the match: Silver, *Begin,* p. 192.

"Menachem just loves": Haber, Schiff, and Yaari, *The Year of the Dove,* p. 246.

208   Begin did win: Interview with Yechiel Kadishai; Haber, Schiff, and Yaari, *The Year of the Dove,* p. 246. Brzezinski maintains the score was actually a 1–1 tie. Brzezinski, *Power and Principle,* 259.

"He thought it would": Interview with Meir Rosenne.

"Did we not agree": Boutros-Ghali, *Egypt's Road to Jerusalem,* p. 139.

DAY SIX

211   The Israeli team had: Sofer, *Begin,* p. 191.

212   Dayan diplomatically suggested: According to Louise Fischer, the draft was not meant as a serious proposal but a rebuttal of the Egyptian plan, if it were to be published. Louise Fischer, personal communication.

213   "and then we will go": Interview with Aharon Barak. Louise Fischer believes this did not happen until September 12, but Barak has a clear memory of not being allowed to go to Gettysburg.

The point that Chaplain: "Chaplain Reed Is Now the Person Who Preaches to Carter the Most," *Sarasota Herald-Tribune,* Feb. 24, 1979.

"You come against": 1 Samuel 17:45

"The Arabs come to us": Dayan, *Living with the Bible*, pp. 185–87.

214 "long-forgotten brethren": Ben-Zvi, *The Exiled and the Redeemed*, p. x.

215 In a Talmudic account: Masechet Sotah 42b, *Babylonian Talmud*. There is an intricate and confusing commentary in various rabbinical sources about the possible relationship of David's and Goliath's mothers, or else David's mother and Goliath's great-grandmother.

216 Sadat said that for: Rosalynn Carter diary of Camp David.

"The audience began shouting": Heikal, *Autumn of Fury*, p. 24.

217 "certain nervous troubles": Sadat, *In Search of Identity*, p. 76.

"My relations with the": Ibid., p. 77.

He would say that: Ibid., p. 85.

"The bricks were sodden": Ibid., p. 70.

a "university" to him: Carter, *First Lady from Plains*, p. 253.

218 When he was arrested: Begin, *White Nights*, p. 19. According to Begin's biographer, the prison protocol says that he arrived with the Disraeli biography and a German-English dictionary. Shilon, *Menachem Begin*, p. 31.

They passed the time: Rosalynn Carter diary of Camp David.

"Citizen-Judge, we were": Begin, *White Nights*, pp. 74–75.

219 "I can testify that": Ibid., p. 48.

While in prison: Gordis, *Menachem Begin*, pp. 32–33.

"guilty of having been": Begin, *White Nights*, p. 95.

220 "I never want to see": Silver, *Begin*, p. 29.

He would later claim: Temko, *To Win or to Die*, p. 64.

221 remarking how modern the armaments: Interview with Jimmy Carter.

"Moshe, you've been": Haber, Schiff, and Yaari, *The Year of the Dove*, p. 249.

"Are you the anti-Christ?": Boutros-Ghali, *Egypt's Road to Jerusalem*, p. 140.

222 Carter proudly added that: Dayan, *Breakthrough*, p. 171.

"He seemed to know": Ibid.

Carter's great-grandfather: Littleberry Walker Carter survived the war only to be stabbed to death at the age of forty-two by a business partner in a quarrel over a merry-go-round they jointly owned. Bourne, *Jimmy Carter*, p. 10.

223 Maybe this was a turning point: Interview with Rosalynn Carter.

224 "There are phrases in": Carter, *Keeping Faith*, p. 372.

"seventeen pages of high": Weizman, *The Battle for Peace*, p. 363.

"We would also ask that": Carter, *Keeping Faith*, pp. 373–74.

225   "Gentlemen, the Americans": Weizman, *The Battle for Peace*, p. 364.
"a beautiful number": Carter, *Keeping Faith*, p. 375.
"This is not the time": Ibid., pp. 374–76.

226   "Listen, we're trying": Carter, *First Lady from Plains*, p. 255.

227   "What you want to do": Carter, *Keeping Faith*, pp. 376–77.
"We will not accept": Weizman, *The Battle for Peace*, p. 365.

228   On the eve of Camp David: Interview with Elyakim Rubinstein conducted by Dr. Nina Sagie, May 5, 1994, Menachem Begin Heritage Center.
Before Dayan left: Dayan, *Breakthrough*, p. 156.

229   directly into a tree: Interview with Aharon Barak; Carter, *White House Diary*, p. 231.
"What happened?": Carter, *First Lady from Plains*, p. 254.
"psycho": Brzezinski, *Power and Principle*, p. 262.

DAY SEVEN

231   Dayan's cabinmates: Interview with Aharon Barak.

232   He pursued it with: Bar-On, *Moshe Dayan*, p. 45, pp. 162–63; also see Raz Kletter, "A Very General Archeologist—Moshe Dayan and Israeli Archeology," *Journal of Hebrew Scriptures* 4, article 5 (2003), for a catalog of Dayan's ethical and legal violations.

233   "There is a festive air": Bar-On, *Moshe Dayan*, pp. 142–43.
"The only thing the": Dayan, *Story of My Life*, p. 386.

234   not a single Jew lived: Bar-On, *Moshe Dayan*, p. 145.
"Of course": Rosalynn Carter diary of Camp David.

235   "Sadat is smarter than": Rosalynn Carter diary of Camp David.

236   "You don't understand anything": Kamel, *The Camp David Accords*, pp. 340–41.

238   Sadat told the Jordanian: Ibid., p. 343; Haber, Schiff, and Yaari, *The Year of the Dove*, p. 253.
"We must offer *al-Rayyis*": Boutros-Ghali, *Egypt's Road to Jerusalem*, p. 142.

239   "Mr. Weizman!": Weizman, *The Battle for Peace*, p. 261.

240   Dayan agreed to meet: Rosalynn Carter diary of Camp David.
He also learned that Begin: Interview with Aharon Barak.

DAY EIGHT

246   Unbeknownst to the Americans: Haber, Schiff, and Yaari, *The Year of the Dove*, p. 254.

247   "This is going to end": Weizman, *The Battle for Peace*, p. 367.

"I shall ask for a meeting": Haber, Schiff, and Yaari, *The Year of the Dove*, p. 255.

"There's no sense to": Ibid.

"Moshe," Weizman said: Weizman, *The Battle for Peace*, p. 370.

History would show: Quandt, *Camp David*, p. 232.

248 fifteen feet by twenty-two feet: Hans Mark, personal communication.

"In order to achieve peace": Quandt, *Camp David*, Appendix F.

249 "It's all right": Carter, *Keeping Faith*, p. 385.

"Let me suggest that": Haber, Schiff, and Yaari, *The Year of the Dove*, p. 255.

"I beg your pardon, Mr. President": Ibid., p. 256.

250 "in communication": Boutros-Ghali, *Egypt's Road to Jerusalem*, p. 143.

"It could be really great": Kamel, *The Camp David Accords*, p. 346.

251 An independent authority: Shay Fogelman, "What Israeli and U.S. Leaders of 1977 Hoped Would Be Jerusalem's Fate," *Haaretz*, Nov. 4, 2011.

The Americans and the Israelis: Interview with Elyakim Rubenstein.

Jerusalem was a symbol: Ibn 'Asakir, quoted in Sivan, *Interpretations of Islam*, p. 91.

252 He had always been attracted: Sadat, *Safahat Majhula*, p. 100.

253 as many as one million: Wright, *The Looming Tower*, p. 25.

Some of Sadat's fellow: Sadat, *Revolt on the Nile*, p. 93.

The king himself felt: Heikal, *Autumn of Fury*, p. 25.

254 "This is the most serious talk": Carter, *Keeping Faith*, p. 386.

"Seven hours!": "Behind Camp David," Menachem Begin speech to Conference of Presidents of Major Jewish Organizations, Sept. 20, 1978.

255 "Mr. President, do we ask": Haber, Schiff, and Yaari, *The Year of the Dove*, p. 257.

"the land of our forefathers": "Behind Camp David," Menachem Begin speech to Conference of Presidents of Major Jewish Organizations, Sept. 20, 1978

The Saudis were also: Meir Rosenne, "Legal Aspects of Negotiations in the Peace Treaty with Egypt: Camp David (1978–1979)," in Moshe Fuksman Sha'al, ed., *The Camp David Accords*, p. 35.

256 "Never!" Begin cried: Shilon, *Menachem Begin*, p. 302.

He pointed out that: More than 60 percent of the Israeli public supported return of some of the occupied West Bank if it enabled peace with Egypt. A majority of Israelis did not share Begin's "religious and ideological attachment to the whole of the territory." National Intelligence Cable, Sept. 1, 1978.

257 **Begin responded enigmatically:** Carter, *White House Diary*, p. 235; Carter, *Keeping Faith*, pp. 386–87.

DAY NINE

260 **The West Bank would not:** Eban, *An Autobiography*, p. 436.

The Arab leaders responded: Aburish, *Nasser*, p. 270.

"the first war in history": Quoted in Jack L. Schwartzwald, "Did Golda Meir Cause the 'Yom Kippur War'?" *New Society*, July 9, 2009.

In any case, Israel: Abba Eban made a number of claims that the Israelis had presented such an offer to the Americans, who passed it on to the Arabs, and that the Arabs peremptorily rejected the overture. There seems to be no evidence that the withdrawal proposal, in the form of a cabinet resolution of June 19, 1967, was anything more than a "foreign policy maneuver," or that it was ever intended to go beyond a briefing to the Americans, or that it ever actually got passed to the Arabs. Avi Raz, "The Generous Peace Offer That Was Never Offered: The Israeli Cabinet Resolution of June 19, 1967," *Diplomatic History* 37, no. 1 (2013): 85–108.

Although it is not often: Parker notes that, although the date the War of Attrition began is usually given as March 1969, the opening shots were actually fired the previous autumn. *The Politics of Miscalculation in the Middle East*, p. 130.

War of Attrition: Ibid., p. 125.

Impatient with the state: Parker distinguishes three Israeli-American conceptual errors during this period: "The misjudgment of Egypt's staying power, the misjudgment of Soviet seriousness, and the fascination with the use of force. The fault lay as much with the Americans as with the Israelis." Ibid., p. 163.

261 **"We shall not allow":** Hirst and Beeson, *Sadat*, p. 122.

It was the first time: Kissinger, *White House Years*, p. 569.

262 **That made the White House:** Ibid., p. 585.

"I have decided to dispense": Sadat, *In Search of Identity*, p. 230.

263 **In a single stroke he upended:** Robert Satloff in Alterman, ed., *Sadat and His Legacy*, p. 151.

Moreover, the chastened: Heikal, *Autumn of Fury*, p. 46.

"Why has he done": Hirst and Beeson, *Sadat*, p. 138.

"It was all, as I would": Kissinger, *White House Years*, p. 1299.

264 **"I remember machine guns":** Shavit, *My Promised Land*, p. 143.

This was early in: Goldhagen, *Hitler's Willing Executioners*, pp. 151 and 191–92.

By the end of the war: Holocaust Encyclopedia, http://www.ushmm
.org/wlc/en/article.php?ModuleId=10006124.

265 "useless eaters": Ibid.

"When I took off my": Shavit, *My Promised Land*, p. 145.

266 During cabinet deliberations: Weizman, *The Battle for Peace*, p. 292.

While there, he studied: Interview with Farouk El-Baz.

267 Carter considered Baz: Interviews with Jimmy and Rosalynn
Carter.

He had been head: "The Negotiators for Egypt," *Washington Post*,
Dec. 14, 1977.

Jewish girlfriend: Interview with Meir Rosenne.

Sadat had appointed Baz: Adel Hamouda, "Osama el-Baz: Malaff
Shakhsi Jiddan!" [Osama el-Baz: A Very Personal Portfolio!], *El
Fagr*, Sept. 24, 2013.

As Mubarak's right-hand man: Reedy, *Rihlat al-'umr*, p. 329.

At this signal, Sadat: Interview with Farouk el-Baz.

268 Carter responded by saying: Haber, Schiff, and Yaari, *The Year of
the Dove*, p. 259.

"in all its parts": Carter, *Keeping Faith*, p. 387.

"They have both also stated": Ibid.

269 "My right eye will fall": Temko, *To Win or to Die*, p. 229.

"Reaching agreement with you": Sabry, *Al-Sadat*, p. 454.

"When he gets furious": Haber, Schiff, and Yaari, *The Year of the
Dove*, p. 260.

270 "I won't give up": Weizman, *The Battle for Peace*, p. 369.

"It is out of the question": Haber, Schiff, and Yaari, *The Year of the
Dove*, p. 261.

"You're right," Sadat replied: Sabry, *Al-Sadat*, pp. 454–55.

271 "I don't know exactly why": Carter, *First Lady from Plains*, p. 260.

"Zbig, I am very much": Nelson, *The President Is at Camp David*,
p. 121.

DAY TEN

274 Sadat wondered whether: Jimmy Carter diary of Camp David.

"Come here," he said: Carter, *First Lady from Plains*, p. 260.

Sadat loathed and feared: Interview with Aharon Barak.

275 "for Carter's sake": Boutros-Ghali, *Egypt's Road to Jerusalem*, p. 144.

the Bar-Lev Line: Gamasy, *The October War*, pp. 224–25.

276 "The Egyptian Army today": Reedy, *Rihlat al-'umr*, p. 248.

"There is no more Palestine": "Waiting in the Wings," *Time*, July 30,
1973.

277 Customs officers ripped out: Heikal, *The Road to Ramadan*, p. 247.

Nasser got tapes: Herzog, *The War of Atonement*, p. 13.

Sadat responded a few: Sadat, *In Search of Identity*, p. 219.

278   By that time, Israel: Kipnis, *1973*, pp. 68–69.

She pressured Kissinger: Ibid., pp. 92 and 103.

"the stage of total confrontation": "Arabs v. Israelis in a Suez Showdown," *Time*, Oct. 29, 1973.

"Everything in this country": Arnaud de Borchgrave, "The Battle Is Now Inevitable," *Newsweek*, Apr. 9, 1973.

Menachem Begin warned: Iris Berlatzky interview with Yechiel Kadishai, Menachem Begin Heritage Center.

279   About a third of: Herzog, *The War of Atonement*, p. 12.

"I don't rule out": Kipnis, *1973*, p. 47.

"a new Israel": Ibid., p. 113.

All this confirmed: Ibid., p. 205.

Once the first wave: Herzog, *The War of Atonement*, p. 35.

280   The Russians had told them: Sadat, *A Woman of Egypt*, p. 291.

Replicas of the barricade: Herzog, *The War of Atonement*, pp. 35–36.

"havoc-making" angels: Quran 3:124–25.

281   There was one date: Gamasy, *The October War*, pp. 180–81.

"the lowest of the low": Herzog, *The War of Atonement*, p. 51.

The night before the invasion: Gamasy, *The October War*, p. 210.

That same evening: Kipnis, *1973*, p. 282.

Ashraf Marwan: There is a long and intriguing debate about whether Marwan was actually a double agent. Sadat awarded him a medal after the war, but the head of Mossad at the time defended him as the best agent Israel had ever had. Marwan died after falling off a balcony in London in 2007, in what may have been a homicide. Yigal Kipnis has an informative appendix in his book *1973: The Road to War* about this controversy.

282   It would still take at least: Kipnis, *1973*, p. 273.

And yet, on the day: Blum, *The Eve of Destruction*, p. 157; Dayan, *Story of My Life*, p. 461.

Each of the 750 boats: Blum, *The Eve of Destruction*, p. 159; Gamasy, *The October War*, pp. 207–08.

283   Five infantry divisions: Dayan, *Story of My Life*, p. 474.

"My God," an Israeli: "The War of the Day of Judgment," *Time*, Oct. 22, 1973.

Sadat had to remind: Sadat, *A Woman of Egypt*, p. 293.

The Arabs now had better: Dayan, *Story of My Life*, p. 510.

"In the Golan Heights": Blum, *The Eve of Destruction*, pp. 175–83.

284   Within twenty-four hours: Heikal, *Secret Channels*, p. 181; Dayan, *Story of My Life*, p. 495; Gamasy, *The October War*, pp. 216–17. Heikal

gives a different figure for the loss of Israeli aircraft, which he puts at forty.

The entire population: Dayan, *Story of My Life*, pp. 495–96. Gamasy gives strikingly different figures for Egyptian losses in the first twenty-four hours: 5 planes, 20 tanks, 280 dead. Gamasy, *The October War*, pp. 216–17.

The Syrians sought to take: Gamasy, *The October War*, pp. 138–39. According to Kissinger, Israelis learned from captured Egyptian soldiers that Egypt did not even expect to reach the Sinai passes twenty to thirty miles from the canal. Kissinger, *Years of Upheaval*, p. 459.

On the morning of: Blum, *The Eve of Destruction*, p. 193.

"hold on to the last bullet": Ibid., p. 202.

285 Israeli losses by the end: Kissinger, *Years of Upheaval*, p. 492.

Dayan said he intended: Herzog, *The War of Atonement*, p. 196.

perhaps as many as twenty-five bombs: Hersh, *The Samson Option*, p. 179.

The Israelis may have decided: Ibid., p. 225. Israel has never publicly acknowledged possessing nuclear weapons. Neither Nixon nor Kissinger mentions the Israeli nuclear option in their accounts; however, Zbigniew Brzezinski affirmed it in his discussion with Carter in "Reflections on the Camp David Accords," Hotel Del Coronado, San Diego, CA, March 9, 2012.

he recalls seeing a report: Interview with William Quandt; Elbridge Solby, Avner Cohen, William McCants, Bradley Morris, and William Rosenau, "The Israeli 'Nuclear Alert' of 1973: Deterrence and Signaling in Crisis," CNA report, April 2013, p. 35. The authors conclude, "There was probably a change in the status of Israel's nuclear delivery systems but the Americans did not interpret such activity as an attempt to coerce them" (p. 46).

286 "bleed a bit but not too much": William Quandt, quoted in Elbridge Solby, Avner Cohen, William McCants, Bradley Morris, and William Rosenau, "The Israeli 'Nuclear Alert' of 1973: Deterrence and Signaling in Crisis," CNA report, April 2013, p. 21 fn.

By October 11, Israel: Kissinger, *Years of Upheaval*, p. 504. Dayan himself later claimed, "There was no intention of capturing Damascus or even of bombing it." Dayan, *Story of My Life*, p. 516. Nonetheless, he pressed to get the Syrian capital within artillery range of Israeli forces.

The Egyptians had ventured: Gamasy, *The October War*, p. 277. Heikal, *Secret Channels*, p. 195, claims the losses were 390 tanks.

287 "I am no novice at war": Dayan, *Story of My Life*, p. 532.

He grew pale and gaunt: Sadat, *A Woman of Egypt*, p. 296.

"All those who died for our": Ibid., p. 294.

288   Moreover, they embargoed: Kissinger, *Years of Upheaval*, p. 545.
Kissinger's sympathetic eye: Dayan, *Story of My Life*, p. 537.
Three thousand Israeli: Gordis, *Menachem Begin*, p. 131.

289   "MURDERER": Chafets, *Heroes and Hustlers, Hard Hats and Holy Men*, p. 45.
The Israelis wanted revenge: Kissinger, *Years of Upheaval*, p. 573.
"You won't get any violent": *Foreign Relations of the United States, 1969–1976*, vol. xxv, "Arab-Israeli Crisis and War," pp. 658–60.
Three Soviet airborne divisions: White, *Breach of Faith*, p. 263; Dayan, *Story of My Life*, p. 543.
To block that scenario: Kalb and Kalb, *Kissinger*, pp. 563–64.

290   troops were actually loaded: Interview with Gary Chapman.
"a buffoon, an operatic figure": Gail Sheehy, "The Riddle of Sadat," *Esquire*, Jan. 30, 1979.

291   "It can be called": Kissinger, *Years of Upheaval*, p. 636.

292   "camels and date-palms": Dayan, *Breakthrough*, p. 171.
Dayan's pet project: "A City in Sinai," *Time*, Jan. 22, 1973.
"What did you think": Dayan, *Breakthrough*, p. 172.

293   "If anybody told you that": Hermann Frederick Eilts in Alterman, ed., *Sadat and His Legacy*, p. 40.
"Convey this from me": Carter, *First Lady of Plains*, p. 261; interview with Rosalynn Carter.

294   "Hi, Mohamed": Kamel, *The Camp David Accords*, pp. 352–53.

295   "You're teasing": Interview with Rosalynn Carter.
Carter directed Vice President: Carter, *First Lady of Plains*, p. 261; Rosalynn Carter's Camp David diary.
It was heartbreaking: Carter, *Keeping Faith*, pp. 390–91.

DAY ELEVEN

297   For the last twenty-four: Carter, *First Lady from Plains*, p. 262.
He watched George C. Scott: Interview with Walter Mondale.

298   He had once been so bright and promising: Zev Chafets, personal communication.
The experience had gradually turned: Boutros-Ghali, *Egypt's Road to Jerusalem*, p. 140.
Dayan, on the other hand: Interview with Samuel W. Lewis, Foreign Affairs Oral History Collection of the Association for Diplomatic Studies and Training, http://www.loc.gov/item/mfdipbib000687.

299   Begin, the Polish lawyer: Interview with Zev Chafets.
"my charming naughty boy": "Ezer Weizman," *Telegraph*, Apr. 26, 2005.

300 "FAMILY MAN AND DEMOCRAT": Temko, *To Win or to Die*, p. 195.

"Such withdrawals could only": Gervasi, *The Life and Times of Menahem Begin*, p. 325.

"The West Bank": Shilon, *Menachem Begin*, p. 256.

Before the 1973 Yom Kippur War: Cohen, *Culture and Conflict in Egyptian-Israeli Relations*, p. 38.

"human material": Chafets, *Heroes and Hustlers, Hard Hats and Holy Men*, p. 37.

301 "secure and recognized borders": William Quandt, personal communication.

302 "there has to be a homeland": Gervasi, *The Life and Times of Menahem Begin*, p. 329.

All the other shirts: Shilon, *Menachem Begin*, p. 255.

"Tonight, the history": Ibid., p. 258

303 "The Jews beat": Interview with Zev Chafets.

manoach: Sidney Zion and Uri Dan, "Untold Story of the Mideast Talks," Part II, *New York Times*, Jan. 21, 1979.

304 The first thought that came: Brzezinski, *Power and Principle*, p. 271.

"Sadat is leaving": Carter, *Keeping Faith*, p. 391.

He prayed: Interview with Jimmy Carter.

"I understand you're leaving": Brzezinski, *Power and Principle*, p. 272.

305 "We are wasting our time": Sabry, *Al-Sadat*, p. 453.

"What you could do": Interview with Jimmy Carter.

He promised that if Sadat: Brzezinski, *Power and Principle*, p. 272.

Dayan had convinced him: Interview with Jimmy Carter.

306 "The Egyptians have already agreed to": Carter, *Keeping Faith*, p. 393.

"If you give me this": Ibid., p. 393.

They argued about whether: Interview with Ahmed Abul-Gheit.

Tohamy was furious that: Boutros-Ghali, *Egypt's Road to Jerusalem*, p. 146.

307 "President Carter is a great man": Kamel, *The Camp David Accords*, pp. 352–57.

308 "Sadat agrees to something": Boutros-Ghali, *Egypt's Road to Jerusalem*, p. 146.

"Sherif, you bad boy!": Kamel, *The Camp David Accords*, pp. 357–58.

310 Perhaps he had in mind: Interview with Aharon Barak; Shilon, *Menachem Begin*, p. 276.

Mondale, whom the Israelis: Interview with Walter Mondale.

moreover, Sharon's Polish grandmother: Gordis, *Menachem Begin*, p. 130.

311 **"I see no military objection":** Weizman, *The Battle for Peace,* p. 370.
"Evacuation of the settlements": Ibid. Weizman's chronology is somewhat jumbled; the meeting in which he made this reference seems to be on day nine, which is when Haber et al. place it. Haber, Schiff, and Yaari, *The Year of the Dove,* p. 260.
"President Carter requests": Weizman, *The Battle for Peace,* p. 370.
He made a final plea: Dayan, *Breakthrough,* p. 176.
"You must agree to evacuate": Weizman, *The Battle for Peace,* p. 371.

312 **"We're closer than we've":** Carter, *First Lady from Plains,* p. 262.
Carter would then make: Quandt, *Camp David,* p. 240.

313 **He insisted that they sing songs:** Interview with Elyakim Rubinstein.
Mohamed Kamel went to bed: Kamel, *The Camp David Accords,* pp. 362–63.

DAY TWELVE

315 **He appealed to Carter:** Carter, *Keeping Faith,* p. 394.

316 **"legitimate rights of the Palestinian People":** Temko, *To Win or to Die,* pp. 228–30.
"Palestinian People": Shilon, *Menachem Begin,* p. 311.
"We are colonialists": Rosalynn Carter's personal Camp David diary.

317 **"I want to have a talk":** Kamel, *The Camp David Accords,* pp. 363–69.

319 **"How does the president feel?":** Carter, *First Lady from Plains,* pp. 264–65.
Carter began by reviewing: Jimmy Carter's personal Camp David diary.

320 **Sadat insisted that he:** Rosalynn Carter's personal Camp David diary.
Dayan floated the notion: Dayan, *Breakthrough,* p. 175.
The paragraph would state: Quandt, *Camp David,* p. 244.

321 **"legitimate rights":** Ibid., p. 245.
nonaggression pact: Silver, *Begin,* p. 89.
and they ejected Arab: Neff, *Warriors at Suez,* p. 64.

322 **Jerusalem itself was in the middle:** Montefiore, *Jerusalem,* pp. 490–92.
Haganah, the official Jewish: Silver, *Begin,* p. 91.

323 **"disorganized massacre":** Meir Pa'il, Haganah intelligence officer, quoted in Silver, *Begin,* p. 94.
"We had an agreement": "Deir Yassin: Meir Pail's Eyewitness Account," http://web.archive.org/web/20080419084659/http://www

.ariga.com/peacewatch/dy/dypail.htm. There are contrary reports that people from the neighboring village also took part in the massacre.

Haganah intelligence said: Morris, *Righteous Victims*, p. 208.

About two hundred: Morris, *Righteous Victims*, p. 208; Gervasi, *The Life and Times of Menahem Begin*, p. 234; Benvenisti, *Sacred Landscape*, p. 116.

Others—twenty to twenty-five men: Silver, *Begin*, p. 94. Silver quotes Yehoshua Gorodentchik, an Irgun officer: "We had prisoners, and before the retreat we decided to liquidate them. We also liquidated the wounded, as anyway we could not give them first aid. In one place, about eighty Arab prisoners were killed after some of them had opened fire and killed one of the people who came to give them first aid. Arabs who dressed up as Arab women were also found, and so they started to shoot the women also who did not hurry to the area where the prisoners were concentrated" (p. 91).

Among the attackers: Ibid., p. 207.

each party had an interest: Ibid., p. 209.

324 **Ben-Gurion absolved:** Gervasi, *The Life and Times of Menahem Begin*, p. 235.

"splendid act of conquest": Silver, *Begin*, p. 88.

Later he would defend: Begin, *The Revolt*, p. xxi.

The Palestinians left behind: Benvenisti has many moving and specific accounts in *Sacred Landscape*.

By the end of the war: Montefiore, *Jerusalem*, pp. 493–94.

325 **About four hundred Palestinian:** Morris, *The Birth of the Palestinian Refugee Problem Revisited*, p. 342.

Biblical names: Benvenisti, *Sacred Landscape*, pp. 20–21. The designation of Mount Hor was so egregious that it was eventually renamed Mount Zin.

After sundown, Begin: Haber, Schiff, and Yaari, *The Year of the Dove*, p. 270.

Carter listed the benefits: Jimmy Carter's personal Camp David diary.

326 **"Ultimatum!" Begin cried:** Ibid.

"If agreement is reached": Carter, *Keeping Faith*, p. 396.

"That's what I can do": Haber, Schiff, and Yaari, *The Year of the Dove*, p. 270.

327 **"What is the ultimate importance":** Temko, *To Win or to Die*, pp. 228–29.

"By such verbal acrobatics": Weizman, *The Battle for Peace*, p. 373.

In return for acknowledging: Quandt, *Camp David*, p. 246.

328   **"After the signing":** Ibid., p. 247.

329   **Begin later told the:** Interview with Samuel W. Lewis, Foreign Affairs Oral History Collection of the Association for Diplomatic Studies and Training, http://www.loc.gov/item/mfdipbib000687.

Begin's supposed moratorium: The quarrel about what Begin agreed to that night has never been resolved. Carter's contemporaneous notes of the meeting reflected that Begin had agreed to the open-ended settlement freeze: "On the West Bank settlements, we finally worked out language that was satisfactory, that no new Israeli settlements would be established after the signing of this framework. And that the issue of additional settlements would be resolved by the parties during the negotiations. This would be accomplished with a letter which will be made public from Begin to me." Vance's account echoes Carter's. Vance makes the point in his memoir: "Since we had been discussing only the comprehensive accord and the autonomy negotiations during the Saturday night session, it is difficult to understand how Begin could have so totally misinterpreted what the President was asking." Vance, *Hard Choices*, p. 228. Carter told me, "Begin promised me and Sadat very clearly that he would stop all settlement building. When he got back to civilization, he began to lie. He began to say that he only meant they would stop settlement building during the time of negotiation." At a twenty-fifth anniversary gathering of the principals who were at Camp David, however, Carter was challenged by Justice Elyakim Rubinstein, who said that the disagreement was a misunderstanding, because Begin was a man of honor and would not go back on his word. Carter responded, "I think I agree. It was a misunderstanding. I don't believe that Begin lied to me about it" ("Camp David 25th Anniversary Forum"). Aharon Barak was taking notes at the meeting. He told me, "When the dispute between them came up . . . Begin forgot that I was taking notes. So he was quarrelling with the president, so I called him and said, 'Look, I have notes. And I think you were right.' . . . So I went and took out the notes and read it to him, what he said, and then he asked me to send it to Carter, and I sent it to Carter. [Begin] didn't agree to more than three months. That's it." The cable that Barak sent to Begin containing his notes supports what Begin said to Ambassador Lewis—that he would think about it and give Carter an answer the following day. Harold Saunders, then assistant secretary of state in the Bureau of Near Eastern and South Asian Affairs, testified that the settlement pause was tied to the period of time required for the Palestinians to set up a self-governing authority—three to six months, in his estimation. Future settlements could be discussed after that, but there would be no new settlements unless all parties agreed. "The subject was deliberately left open for that period of negotiations so that the parties involved could discuss this issue further," he said. "Assessment of the 1978 Middle East Camp David Agreements," Hearing before the Subcommittee on Europe and the Middle East of the Committee on International Relations, House of Representatives, Sept. 28, 1978, p. 27. Saunders's view is obviously at odds with Carter's, who believed that settlement building would be halted during the period of negotiations between the Israelis and the Palestinians, which could be as long as five years. William Quandt, in private communication, explained that Begin was concerned that, if the negotiations with the Palestinians never actually began, Israel would be constrained in building new settlements. He remarks, "I think we should have tried to get the freeze for a defined number of months instead of tying it to the beginning of negotiations."

DAY THIRTEEN

331 **"I think we've gotten"**: Carter, *First Lady from Plains*, pp. 265–66.

332 **"Don't smile"**: Interview with Rosalynn Carter.
"I got the settlement freeze": Samuel Lewis, "The Camp David Peace Process," in Sha'al, ed., *The Camp David Accords*, p. 56.
"I have a problem!": Kamel, *The Camp David Accords*, p. 370.

333 **He urged Sadat**: Interview with Nabil el-Arabi.
"I heard you": Interview with Ahmed Abul-Gheit.
"It was not possible": Kamel, *The Camp David Accords*, p. 371.

334 **"How many battalions"**: Weizman, *The Battle for Peace*, p. 374.

335 **The signing would be**: Interview with Gerald Rafshoon.
"does not accept or recognize": United Nations General Assembly, Fifth Emergency Special Session, July 14, 1967.

336 **"regrets and deplores"**: United Nations Security Council, July 1, 1969.
"substantial resettlement": United Nations Security Council, Mar. 23, 1976.
"We can pack our bags": Weizman, *The Battle for Peace*, p. 373.
If the Americans had planned: Dayan, *Breakthrough*, p. 177.

337 **Carter's secretary, Susan Clough**: Interview with Jimmy Carter.

338 **"Mr. Prime Minister, I brought"**: Ibid.
"I wanted to be able": Interview with Gerald Rafshoon.

339 **a Jewish sage**: "Ammon of Mainz" entry, vol. 1, Roth et al., eds., *Encyclopaedia Judaica*.
"I am not like the Rabbi": Shlomo Slonim, "The Issue of Jerusalem

at the Camp David Summit," in Sha'al, ed. *The Camp David Accords,* pp. 65–66; Hasten, *I Shall Not Die!,* p. 212. Hasten has Begin telling Carter the anecdote in Washington, but perhaps he used it more than once. Yechiel Kadishai recalled it being employed at Camp David.

340   **"The position of the United States":** Letter from President Jimmy Carter to Egyptian President Anwar El Sadat, September 22, 1978.

341   **"I will accept":** Carter, *Keeping Faith,* p. 399.
"Should I come back?": Carter, *First Lady from Plains,* p. 266.

342   **"Go back and get the right letter":** Samuel Lewis, "The Camp David Peace Process," in Sha'al, ed., *The Camp David Accords,* p. 56.
"I want you to write": Interview with Meir Rosenne.
He agreed to receive: Quandt, *Camp David,* p. 253.
If Begin had pledged: Alon Ben-Meir, "The Settlements: Israel's Albatross," *Huffington Post,* Nov. 14, 2013.
On the other hand: Interview with Aharon Barak.

343   **Sadat was grim:** Quandt, *Camp David,* p. 253.
"That's it": Brzezinski, *Power and Principle,* p. 270.
For Carter, the thirteen: Jimmy Carter personal Camp David diary.
"We're coming home!": Carter, *First Lady from Plains,* p. 267.
"Children, we've reached": Haber, Schiff, and Yaari, *The Year of the Dove,* p. 274.

344   **"President Sadat told me":** Kamel, *The Camp David Accords,* p. 376.
That Sunday night: I'm grateful for an anonymous audience member from Gaithersburg, MD, who attended a preview of my play, *Camp David,* at the Arena Stage in Washington, DC, for this interesting piece of information.

345   **"Mama, we'll go down":** Carter, *First Lady from Plains,* p. 268.
empty chairs: Kamel, *The Camp David Accords,* p. 378.
Even those who attended: Interview with Samuel W. Lewis, Foreign Affairs Oral History Collection of the Association for Diplomatic Studies and Training, http://www.loc.gov/item/mfdipbib000687.
"When we arrived at Camp David": www.youtube.com/watch?v=QPtMafxVKeA.

346   **"Dear friend":** https://www.youtube.com/watch?v=iy9KIA_lByQ.

347   **"It was the Jimmy Carter conference":** https://www.youtube.com/watch?v=SYkIAnf_bzM.
"I have just signed": Temko, *To Win or to Die,* p. 231.

EPILOGUE

349   **"began to treat":** Weizman, *The Battle for Peace,* p. 384.
"As far as I know": Ibid., p. 382.

350 He told an Israeli: Temko, *To Win or to Die*, p. 233.
"Munich!": "Summit at Camp David: 'Touch and Go,'" http://www
.archives.gov.il/ArchiveGov_Eng/Publications/ElectronicPirsum/
CampDavid/CampDavidIntroductionB2.htm.
"The State of Israel could not": Temko, *To Win or to Die*, p. 234.
351 At four in the morning: Hedrick Smith, "After Camp David Sum-
mit, a Valley of Hard Bargaining," *New York Times*, Nov. 6, 1978.
"Begin wanted to keep": Carter, *Keeping Faith*, p. 405.
"Sadat deserved it": Carter, *White House Diary*, p. 256.
At that point, it had: Quandt, *Camp David*, p. 298.
In the middle of this: Carter, *White House Diary*, p. 268.
The professionals in the State: Interview with Samuel W. Lewis, For-
eign Affairs Oral History Collection of the Association for Diplomatic
Studies and Training, http://www.loc.gov/item/mfdipbib000687.
352 "the largest and most": Carter, *Keeping Faith*, p. 419.
"Perhaps we should move": Sadat, *A Woman of Egypt*, p. 402.
"with apparent relish": Carter, *Keeping Faith*, p. 421.
"the fate of a nation hangs": Haber, Schiff, and Yaari, *The Year of the
Dove*, pp. 297.
353 absence of any sympathy: Carter, *Keeping Faith*, p. 421.
"It was not only the Nazis": Begin, *The Revolt*, p. 36.
he prayed that it would never: Haber, Schiff, and Yaari, *The Year of
the Dove*, pp. 296–97.
354 After the Knesset meeting: Quandt, *Camp David*, p. 309.
Meantime, the press: Haber, Schiff, and Yaari, *The Year of the Dove*,
p. 303.
He urged Carter: William Quandt, personal communication; Louise Fischer, personal communication.
355 "sympathetically": Vance, *Hard Choices*, p. 251.
"with our butts showing": "Reflections on the Camp David
Accords," Carter conversation with Zbigniew Brzezinski, Hotel Del
Coronado, San Diego, CA, March 9, 2012.
"as a gesture for Mrs. Begin": Brzezinski, *Power and Principle*, p.
287.
357 "You look tired": Dayan, *Breakthrough*, p. 281.
358 "*Kach oti eilehem*": "Bygone Days: Oh, for the Embraces of El
Arish," *Jerusalem Post*, May 20, 2008.
359 "Don't be afraid": Ibid.
Then he offered: Interview with Samuel W. Lewis, Foreign Affairs
Oral History Collection of the Association for Diplomatic Studies
and Training.
361 During parliamentary elections: Hirst and Beeson, *Sadat*, pp. 331–32.

he jailed three thousand: Heikal, *Autumn of Fury*, pp. 231–32. Some other sources give the number of arrests as 1,500, but Heikal was among those taken.

"Go, both of you": Quran, 20:43–44.

If Moses, one of the: Ibrahim, *I'adat al-I'tibar lil-Ra'is al-Sadat* [The Vindication of President Sadat], pp. 161–62.

362   Arab nations imposed: Sadat, *A Woman of Egypt*, pp. 416–17.

"cowards and dwarfs": Quandt, *Camp David*, p. 280.

"He was saying things": Interview with Jimmy Carter.

"It was as if": Sadat, *A Woman of Egypt*, p. 441.

Sadat's private secretary: John Bulloch and Nabila Mecalli, "Sadat Killed by Soldiers," *Telegraph*, http://www.telegraph.co.uk/news/*1400131*/Sadat-killed-by-soldiers.html; Sadat, *My Father and I*, p. 175.

363   "I have killed the Pharaoh!": Wright, *The Looming Tower*, p. 50.

Osama el-Baz, who: Interview with Farouk el-Baz.

He had conspired: Wright, *The Looming Tower*, p. 51.

Soldiers in battle dress: Frank J. Prial, "Heavy Security at Funeral Bars Egyptian Public," *New York Times*, Oct. 11, 1981.

364   "I had an interesting life": Shilon, *Menachem Begin*, p. 318.

Ezer Weizman was also: Ibid., p. 328.

"No one here wants peace": Ibid., p. 329.

365   "Do not think of those": Quran 3:169.

"war of choice": "The Lebanon War: Operation Peace for Galilee," Israeli Ministry of Foreign Affairs, http://mfa.gov.il/MFA/About Israel/History/Pages/Operation%20Peace%20for%20Galilee%20 -%201982.aspx.

"forty years of peace": Friedman, *From Beirut to Jerusalem*, p. 145.

The master plan: Yossi Alpher, personal communication.

Begin promised: Gordis, *Menachem Begin*, p. 200.

366   "Two targets in particular": Friedman, *From Beirut to Jerusalem*, p. 159.

When the killers finally left: Fergal Keane, "Syrians Aid 'Butcher of Beirut' to Hide from Justice," *Daily Telegraph* (London), June 17, 2001; Franklin Lamb, "Remembering Janet Lee Stevens, Martyr for the Palestinian Refugees," *Al-Ahram Weekly*, May 6–12, 2010.

The Red Cross estimated: Friedman, *From Beirut to Jerusalem*, p. 163. Carter gives the figure as 1,400 killed. Carter, *The Blood of Abraham*, pp. 2–3.

368   He grew frail: Shilon, *Menachem Begin*, p. 415.

One more thing that: Ibid., p. 419.

"Today I will quit my job": Ibid., pp. 419–20.

"Menachem, why did you do it?": "Begin's Legacy/Yehiel, It Ends Today," *Haaretz*, Nov. 10, 2013.

369 From his window he: Hasten, *I Shall Not Die!*, p. 234.

"Okay, I'll put you": Interview with Yechiel Kadishai.

"How did you succeed": Shilon, *Menachem Begin*, p. 313.

371 "With Carter leading the": Kamel, *The Camp David Accords*, p. 290.

372 His obsession with minutiae: James Fallows, "The Passionless Presidency," *Atlantic*, May 1, 1979.

374 Vance believed that was about: Vance, *Hard Choices*, p. 229.

"Sadat has sold Jerusalem": Jeremy Pressman, "Explaining the Carter Administration's Israeli-Palestinian Solution," *Diplomatic History* 37, no. 5 (2013). Without the leverage that Egypt might have provided, Arafat was unable to achieve a treaty he could accept at the Clinton Camp David conference in 2000, although it's unclear if an Egyptian presence could have made a difference.

Arafat proceeded to boycott: Seth Anziska, personal communication.

Sadat's ambivalence: Interview with Jimmy Carter.

375 Sadat was negotiating mainly: Brzezinski, *Power and Principle*, p. 236.

376 "This will end in Begin's": Kamel, *The Camp David Accords*, p. 283.

No one in the Israeli: Interviews with Ziv Rubinovitz and Louise Fischer; interview with Elyakim Rubinstein.

Begin's main goal: Iris Berlatzky interview with Elyakim Rubinstein, Menachem Begin Archives.

"The Arabs cannot isolate Egypt": Kenneth W. Stein, in Alterman, ed., *Sadat and His Legacy*, p. 36.

Bibliography

Aburish, Saïd K. *Nasser: The Last Arab*. New York: Thomas Dunne, 2004.

Alterman, Jon B., and Eliahu Ben Elissar. *Sadat and His Legacy: Egypt and the World, 1977–1997*. Washington, DC: Washington Institute for Near East Policy, 1998.

Aly, Abdel Monem Said, Shai Feldman, and Khalil Shikaki. *Arabs and Israelis: Conflict and Peacemaking in the Middle East*. UK: Palgrave Macmillan, 2013.

Arabi, Nabil el-. *Taba, Camp David, al-jidar al-'azil* [Taba, Camp David, the Wall]. Cairo: Dar Shorouk, 2012.

Armstrong, Karen. *Jerusalem: One City, Three Faiths*. New York: Knopf, 1996.

Auda, Mohamed Saad el-. *Hasan al-tuhami yaftahu malaffatahu min ihtilal filistin ila kamb difid* [Hassan el-Tohamy Opens His Portfolios from the Occupation of Palestine to Camp David]. Cairo: Dar Diwan, 1998.

Avner, Yehuda. *The Prime Ministers: An Intimate Narrative of Israeli Leadership*. New Milford, CT: Toby Press, 2010.

Bahri, Nasser al-, with George Malbrunot; Susan de Muth, trans. *Guarding Bin Laden: My Life in Al-Qaeda*. UK: Thin Man Press, 2007.

Balmer, Randall. *Redeemer: The Life of Jimmy Carter*. New York: Basic Books, 2014.

Bar-On, Mordechai. *Moshe Dayan: Israel's Controversial Hero*. New Haven, CT: Yale University Press, 2012.

Begin, Menachem. *The Revolt*. New York: Nash Publishing, 1977.

———. *White Nights: The Story of a Prisoner in Russia*. New York: Harper and Row, 1977.

Beinin, Joel. *The Dispersion of Egyptian Jewry: Culture, Politics, and the Formation of a Modern Diaspora*. Cairo: The American University in Cairo, 1998.

Bell, J. Bowyer. *Terror Out of Zion*. New York: St. Martin's Press, 1977.

Ben-Gurion, David. *Israel: A Personal History.* New York: Funk and Wagnalls/Sabra, 1971.

Benvenisti, Meron. *Sacred Landscape: The Buried History of the Holy Land Since 1948.* Berkeley: University of California Press, 2002.

Ben-Zvi, Itzhak. *The Exiled and the Redeemed.* Philadelphia, PA: Jewish Publication Society of America, 1957.

Blum, Howard. *The Eve of Destruction: The Untold Story of the Yom Kippur War.* New York: HarperCollins, 2003.

Bourne, Peter G. *Jimmy Carter: A Comprehensive Biography from Plains to Post-Presidency.* New York: Lisa Drew/Scribner, 1997.

Boutros-Ghali, Boutros. *Egypt's Road to Jerusalem.* New York: Random House, 1997.

Brzezinski, Zbigniew. *Power and Principle.* New York: Farrar, Straus and Giroux, 1983.

"Camp David 25th Anniversary Forum." Washington, DC: Carter Center and Woodrow Wilson International Center for Scholars, September 17, 2003.

Carter, Jimmy. *The Blood of Abraham: Insights into the Middle East.* Fayetteville: University of Arkansas Press, 2007.

———. *An Hour Before Daylight: Memories of a Rural Boyhood.* New York: Simon and Schuster, 2001.

———. *Keeping Faith: Memoirs of a President.* New York: Bantam, 1983.

———. *We Can Have Peace in the Holy Land.* New York: Simon and Schuster, 2009.

———. *White House Diary.* New York: Farrar, Straus and Giroux, 2010.

———. *Why Not the Best?* Nashville: Broadman Press, 1975.

Carter, Rosalynn. *First Lady from Plains.* Boston: Houghton Mifflin, 1984.

Chafets, Ze'ev. *Heroes and Hustlers, Hard Hats and Holy Men: Inside the New Israel.* New York: William Morrow, 1986.

CIA Historical Review Program. *President Carter and the Role of Intelligence in the Camp David Accords.* Jimmy Carter Presidential Library, November 13, 2013.

Cline, Eric H. *From Eden to Exile: Unraveling Mysteries of the Bible.* Washington, DC: National Geographic, 2007.

Cohen, Raymond. *Culture and Conflict in Egyptian-Israeli Relations.* Bloomington: Indiana University Press, 1990.

Dayan, Moshe. *Breakthrough: A Personal Account of the Egypt-Israel Peace Negotiations.* New York: Knopf, 1981.

———. *Living with the Bible.* Jerusalem: Steimatzky's Agency, 1978.

———. *Story of My Life: An Autobiography.* New York: William Morrow, 1976.

Dayan, Yaël. *My Father, His Daughter.* New York: Farrar, Straus and Giroux, 1985.

Eban, Abba. *An Autobiography.* New York: Random House, 1977.

Finkelstein, Israel, and Neil Asher Silberman. *The Bible Unearthed.* New York: Touchstone, 2002.

Friedman, Thomas L. *From Beirut to Jerusalem.* New York: Farrar, Straus, 1989.

Gamasy, Mohamed Abdel Ghani el-. *The October War: Memoirs of Field Marshal el-Gamasy of Egypt.* Cairo: The American University in Cairo, 1993.

Gervasi, Frank. *The Life and Times of Menahem Begin.* New York: Putnam, 1979.

Ghorbal, Ashraf. *Su'ud wa inhiyar: Mudhakkarat Ashraf Ghorbal* [Ascent and Descent: The Memoirs of Ashraf Ghorbal]. Cairo: Markaz al-ahram lil-tarjaa wa-l-nashr, 2004.

Glad, Betty. *Jimmy Carter: In Search of the Great White House.* New York: W. W. Norton, 1980.

———. *An Outsider in the White House: Jimmy Carter, His Advisors, and the Making of American Foreign Policy.* Ithaca, NY: Cornell University Press, 2009.

Godbold, E. Stanly, Jr. *Jimmy & Rosalynn Carter: The Georgia Years, 1924–1974.* New York: Oxford University Press, 2010.

Goldhagen, Daniel Jonah. *Hitler's Willing Executioners: Ordinary Germans and the Holocaust.* New York: Random House, 2007.

Gordis, Daniel. *Menachem Begin: The Battle for Israel's Soul.* New York: Schocken, 2014.

Grief, Howard. *The Legal Foundation and Borders of Israel under International Law.* Jacksonville, FL: Mazo Publishers, 2008.

Gulley, Bill, and Mary Ellen Reese. *Breaking Cover.* New York: Simon and Schuster, 1980.

Gutman, Yechiel. *Ha-Yoetz Ha-Mishpati Neged Ha-Memshalah* [The Attorney-General Versus the Government]. Jerusalem: Edanim Publishers, 1981.

Haber, Eitan. *Menachem Begin: The Legend and the Man.* New York: Delacorte Press, 1978.

Haber, Eitan, Zeev Schiff, and Ehud Yaari. *The Year of the Dove.* New York: Bantam, 1979.

Hasten, Hart N. *I Shall Not Die!* New York: Gefen, 2003.

Heikal, Mohamed. *Autumn of Fury: The Assassination of Sadat.* New York: Random House, 1983.

———. *The Road to Ramadan.* New York: Ballantine Books, 1975.

———. *Secret Channels: The Inside Story of Arab-Israeli Peace Negotiations.* New York: HarperCollins, 1996.

Hersh, Seymour M. *The Samson Option.* New York: Random House, 1991.

Herzog, Chaim. *The War of Atonement.* London: Greenhill Books, 2003.

Hirst, David, and Irene Beeson. *Sadat.* London: Faber and Faber, 1981.

Hoffman, Bruce. *Anonymous Soldiers.* New York: Knopf, 2015 (forthcoming).

————. *Inside Terrorism.* New York: Columbia University, 2006.

Howard, Adam, ed. *Foreign Relations of the United States, 1977–1980,* vol. 8: *Arab-Israeli Dispute, January 1977–August 1978.* Washington, DC: U.S. Government Printing Office, 2013.

Ibrahim, Sa'ad Iddin. *I'adat al-I'tibar lil-Ra'is al-Sadat* [The Vindication of President Sadat]. Cairo: Dar al-Shouk, 1992.

Israeli, Raphael. *Man of Defiance.* Totowa, NJ: Barnes and Noble Books, 1985.

Johnson, Lyndon Baines. *The Vantage Point: Perspectives of the Presidency, 1963–1969.* New York: Holt, Rinehart and Winston, 1971.

Jordan, Hamilton. *Crisis.* New York: G. P. Putnam's Sons, 1982.

Kalb, Bernard, and Marvin Kalb. *Kissinger.* New York: Dell Publishing, 1975.

Kamel, Mohamed Ibrahim. *The Camp David Accords.* London: KPI, 1986.

Kaufman, Scott. *Rosalynn Carter: Equal Partner in the White House.* Lawrence: University Press of Kansas, 2007.

Kays, Doreen. *Frogs and Scorpions: Egypt, Sadat and the Media.* London: Frederick Muller Limited, 1984.

Kipnis, Yigal. *1973: The Road to War.* Charlottesville, VA: Just World Books, 2013.

Kissinger, Henry. *White House Years.* New York: Little, Brown and Company, 1979.

————. *Years of Upheaval.* Boston, MA: Little, Brown and Company, 1982.

Lossin, Yigal. *Pillar of Fire: A Television History of Israel's Rebirth.* Israel Broadcast Authority, Ya'akov Eisenmann, producer, 1981.

Makdisi, Ussama, and Paul A. Silverstein. *Memory and Violence in the Middle East and North Africa.* Bloomington: Indiana University, 2006.

Michelson, Menachem. *Yad Yemino—Ha-Biographia shel Yechiel Kadishai, Mazkiro ve-ish sodo shel Menachem Begini* [His Right Hand: Biography of Yechiel Kadishai, Secretary and Confidant to Menachem Begin]. Jerusalem: Gefen, 2013.

Mitchell, Richard P. *The Society of the Muslim Brothers.* New York: Oxford University Press, 1993.

Montefiore, Simon Sebag. *Jerusalem.* New York: Knopf, 2011.

Morris, Benny. *1948.* New Haven, CT: Yale University Press, 2008.

————. *The Birth of the Palestinian Refugee Problem Revisited.* Cambridge: Cambridge University Press, 2004.

————. *Righteous Victims: A History of the Zionist-Arab Conflict, 1881–2001.* New York: Vintage Books, 2001.

Neff, Donald. *Warriors at Suez.* New York: Linden Press, 1981.

Nelson, W. Dale. *The President Is at Camp David*. Syracuse, NY: Syracuse University Press, 1995.

Nutting, Anthony. *Nasser*. New York: E. P. Dutton, 1972.

Oren, Michael B. *Six Days of War*. New York: Oxford University Press, 2002.

Parker, Richard B. *The Politics of Miscalculation in the Middle East*. Bloomington: Indiana University Press, 1993.

Pedahzur, Ami, and Arie Perliger. *Jewish Terrorism in Israel*. New York: Columbia University Press, 2009.

Quandt, William B. *Camp David: Peacemaking and Politics*. Washington, DC: Brookings Institution, 1986.

Reedy, Abdul Raouf al-. *Rihlat al-'umr* [Journey of a Life]. Cairo: Dar Nahdat Misr lil-Nashr, 2011.

Rogan, Eugene L., and Avi Shlaim. *The War for Palestine*. New York: Cambridge University Press, 2010.

Rosovsky, Nitza. *City of the Great King: Jerusalem from David to the Present*. Cambridge, MA: Harvard University Press, 1996.

Roth, Cecil, and Geoffrey Wigoder. *Encyclopedia Judaica*. Jerusalem: Keter, 1972.

Rubinstein, Elyakim. *Darkey Shalom* [Paths of Peace]. Israel: Ministry of Defense, 1992.

Sabry, Moussa. *Al-Sadat: Al-Haqiqa Wa-l-Ustura* [Sadat: Truth and Myth]. Cairo: Al-Maktab al-Masri al-Hadith, 1985.

Sachar, Howard M. *A History of Israel from the Rise of Zionism to Our Time*. New York: Knopf, 1996.

Sadat, Anwar el-. *In Search of Identity: An Autobiography*. New York: Harper and Row, 1978.

———. *Revolt on the Nile*. New York: John Day Company, 1957.

———. *Safahat Majhula* [Unknown Pages]. Cairo: Dar Tahrir li-l-tab' wa-l-nashr, 1954.

Sadat, Camelia. *My Father and I*. New York: Macmillan, 1985.

Sadat, Jehan. *A Woman of Egypt*. New York: Simon and Schuster, 1987.

Sand, Shlomo. *The Invention of the Land of Israel: From Holy Land to Homeland*. New York: Verso, 2012.

Sha'al, Moshe Fuksman, ed. *The Camp David Accords: A Collection of Articles and Letters*. Jerusalem: Carmel, 2002.

Shavit, Ari. *My Promised Land: The Triumph and Tragedy of Israel*. New York: Spiegel and Grau, 2013.

Shilon, Avi. *Menachem Begin: A Life*. New Haven, CT: Yale University Press, 2012.

Shlaim, Avi. *The Iron Wall: Israel and the Arab World*. New York: W. W. Norton, 2001.

Silver, Eric. *Begin: The Haunted Prophet*. New York: Random House, 1984.

Sivan, Emmanuel. *Interpretations of Islam.* Princeton, NJ: Darwin Press, 1985.

Sofer, Sasson. *Begin: An Anatomy of Leadership.* Oxford: Basil Blackwell, 1988.

Tamir, Avraham, Maj. Gen. *A Soldier in Search of Peace.* New York: Harper and Row, 1988.

Temko, Ned. *To Win or to Die: A Personal Portrait of Menachem Begin.* New York: William Morrow, 1987.

Teveth, Shabtai. *Moshe Dayan: The Soldier, the Man, the Legend.* Boston, MA: Houghton Mifflin, 1973.

Turner, Barry. *Suez 1956.* London: Hodder, 2007.

Vance, Cyrus. *Hard Choices.* New York: Simon and Schuster, 1983.

Varble, Derek. *The Suez Crisis 1956.* Oxford: Osprey Publishing, 2003.

Wagner, Heather Lehr. *Anwar Sadat and Menachem Begin: Negotiating Peace in the Middle East.* New York: Chelsea House, 2007.

Walsh, Kenneth. *From Mount Vernon to Crawford: A History of Presidents and Their Retreats.* New York: Hyperion, 2005.

Weizman, Ezer. *The Battle for Peace.* New York: Bantam, 1981.

———. *On Eagles' Wings.* New York: Macmillan Publishing, 1976.

White, Theodore H. *Breach of Faith: The Fall of Richard Nixon.* New York: Atheneum, 1975.

Wright, Lawrence. *The Looming Tower: Al-Qaeda and the Road to 9/11.* New York: Knopf, 2006.

Index

Note: Page numbers in *italics* refer to illustrations.

Photographic Credits